D0991380

QUEERISTAN

'We're living in a world that is too divided based on who to love, how to love and how to live as a human being. It is time that families, companies and countries wake up to the reality that queer rights are basic human rights. I think that this book is just what India and the world need—a manifesto on what to do and where to go with queer rights now!'

—**Sonam K. Ahuja**, actor

'*Queeristan* is a business book that sparkles! Parmesh Shahani takes us on a vivid tour of queer life in India, showing us how fast things are changing in India's workplaces, films, media, art, families and law. The glitz, glamour and celebrities in Parmesh's account make this an engaging read—and his deep insights and experience in getting workplaces to be more inclusive of LGBTQ people make this book essential for smart strategists working toward a more equal and inclusive world.'

—**Lee Badgett**, professor of economics, University of Massachusetts, Amherst, and author of *The Economic Case for LGBT Equality: Why Fair and Equal Treatment Benefits Us All*

'As I read the book, I was forced to look at LGBTQ and the agenda of inclusion in different ways. Are we creating an inclusive country as visualised by Ambedkar and Gandhi? Are organisations that are quoted in this book the torchbearers to a brighter future? At a personal level, it is about realising your human potential, regardless of your gender identity. You can use this book as a manual to create an inclusive organisational culture; however, the chances are, it will also grip you at a personal level. I loved reading it!'

—**Prasenjit Bhattacharya**, CEO, Great Place to Work Institute, India

'In this trailblazing book, Parmesh Shahani, a brilliant gay man in the corporate world, takes us on a tour de force through the industry, from older established companies like Godrej, Mahindra, Reliance, Tata, VIP and IBM to newer ones like Myntra, and discusses how and why these companies have fiercely included queer Indians in their own commercial success. *Queeristan* is also an important book for a post-September-2018 world, after the Supreme Court decriminalised homosexuality in India. Parmesh rightly recognises that India's private sector, including big and small businesses, will be a major driving force in making the country one in which LGBT Indians will be equal citizens.

—**Menaka Guruswamy**, senior advocate, Supreme Court of India

'*Queeristan*—as colourful and lively as its iconic author—is an inspiring reminder that legal and attitude changes towards LGBT+ people are driven by a coalition of local movements and heroes, including from the corporate world. India did not wait for Obama or Macron to lean on its government on their behalf to make progress on LGBT+ inclusion. Instead, queer people in India made change happen in the living bedroom, the boardroom and, eventually, the courtroom. This book is the story of this journey seen through the eyes of one of its key figures, who sits at the intersection of capitalism, activism and creativity. *Queeristan* is a celebration of being queer in business and outside, a celebration of India and, ultimately, a celebration of a cohesive society. A must-read for anyone who wants to understand the recipe for positive social change.'

—**Fabrice Houdart**, co-author of the United Nations' *Tackling Discrimination Against Lesbian, Gay, Bi, Trans, and Intersex People: Standards of Conduct for Business*, and managing director at Out Leadership

'There is growing evidence which shows that LGBTQ inclusion is good for business. But human stories are the foundation of this evidence—the stories of LGBTQ people who are able to work without fear of discrimination, who are able to bring their unique viewpoints to help companies innovate, who are able to lead with compassion and empathy. In *Queeristan*, Parmesh does a masterful job of seamlessly blending the data with poignant personal and professional anecdotes. He creates a rich picture that presents powerful evidence but maintains a sharp focus on the human component of LGBTQ inclusion.'

—**Drew Keller**, global programme director, Open For Business

'An inspiring and educative narrative that is truly fascinating. A must-read for anyone who wants to create a more inclusive organisation or, for that matter, help create a prejudice-free world.'

—**T. V. Narendran**, CEO and managing director, Tata Steel Ltd

'*Queeristan* is an important book about how certain corporations broke ground in redefining inclusion and of stories from the ground celebrating the move from merely obeying the law to encouraging diversity and celebrating differences.'

—**Zainab Patel**, director of Diversity and Inclusion, KPMG, India

'This book is a must-read for anyone who wants to bring about change in corporate India.'

—**Radhika Piramal**, executive vice chairperson, VIP Industries Ltd

'*Queeristan* is an achievement of a movement's collective effort, and Parmesh, the honorary chief of staff of *Queeristan*, has packed emotions, tears, laughs and love by taking us on a wonderland ride. In this utopia of Queeristan—a happy and respectable homeland of the outcastes—inclusion is the preamble. There are far too many parallels between the Dalit and LGBTIQ+ movements that it is imperative for these two communities to share notes and check on each other. Parmesh has made a newer, sexier and queerer call for social justice in India, and this time the appeal is directed at, but not limited to, the business class of India. Rigorously researched and empirically rich, this book is full of hope and not afraid of the future.'

—**Suraj Yengde**, author of *Caste Matters*

PARMESH SHAHANI

QUEERISTAN

LGBTQ INCLUSION IN THE INDIAN WORKPLACE

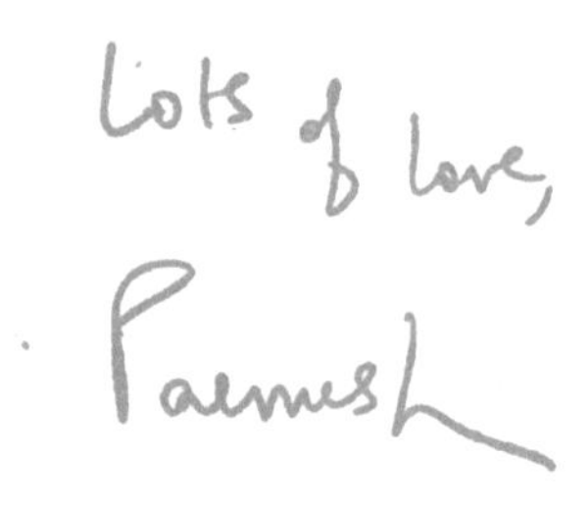

First published by Westland Business, an imprint of Westland Publications Private Limited, in 2020

1st Floor, A Block, East Wing, Plot No. 40, SP Infocity, Dr MGR Salai, Perungudi, Kandanchavadi, Chennai 600096

Westland, the Westland logo, Westland Business and the Westland Business logo are the trademarks of Westland Publications Private Limited, or its affiliates.

Copyright © Parmesh Shahani, 2020

ISBN: 9789389648140

10 9 8 7 6 5 4 3 2 1

The views and opinions expressed in this work are the author's own and the facts are as reported by him, and the publisher is in no way liable for the same.

All rights reserved

Typeset in Adobe Garamond Pro by Jojy Philip, New Delhi
Printed at Thomson Press (India) Ltd

No part of this book may be reproduced, or stored in a retrieval system, or transmitted in any form or by any means, electronic, mechanical, photocopying, recording, or otherwise, without express written permission of the publisher.

For Nisaba Godrej, the wind beneath my wings

Contents

Prologue

If the BBC Says I'm Gay, It Must Be True!

I always knew I was gay. Just as straight people always know they are straight. There was this one moment though, when I was maybe eight years old. I was watching *Naseeb*, a multi-starrer movie featuring Hema Malini, whom I love. Hema is the ultimate queer icon; I don't know why people are obsessed with this Sridevi versus Rekha comparison, and everyone forgets Hema-ji! *Razia Sultan*, anyone? In the *Naseeb* title song, Hema wears a black sequined sheath dress and a pink feather boa, and comes down in a big balloon basket from the ceiling, singing 'Mere Naseeb Mein Tu Hai Ki Nahin'. I mean, how camp was Manmohan Desai? That was it. A light bulb went off in my head. I wanted to be her. I wanted to wear that feather boa and seduce men. I didn't want to be Amitabh. Eek! I wanted to be Hema.

Hello! I am Parmesh Shahani and I am a gay man.

Although this is primarily a business book, it is deeply personal. Memoir meets manifesto is how I described it to Karthika, my publisher, and she was sold. My previous work experience as an entrepreneur has taught me how to make the perfect elevator pitch—I convinced my publisher at the Kitty Su nightclub in Delhi while watching Maya the Drag Queen shake to 'Dreamum Wakeupum', so I think *ki* the atmosphere also helped, *na*? *Thoda sa.*

If you are reading this book, it means that you are somewhat interested in the topic. Maybe the name intrigued you. Maybe you work at a company or maybe you are a student. Maybe you are LGBTQ yourself and are wondering what's next, now that Section 377 is gone. Maybe you are an ally, not lesbian or gay or bi or trans or queer yourself, but have friends who are, or simply care about these issues. Maybe you are a parent or a professor wondering what future your ward is moving towards. Maybe LGBTQ issues don't really interest you, but you care about corporate India, or young India, or ever-changing India. I have written this book hoping it will be eye-opening for all of you.

Through *Queeristan*, I want to share my surreal decade-long journey at my workplace—Godrej—and the path that so many other people have taken across corporate India in their quest for inclusion. The time for LGBTQ inclusion in the Indian workplace is now, and I argue this by using lots of statistics, case studies and general practical gyan. I will also take you on my adventures across India, with some foreign detours as a bonus. (Like those Switzerland songs in old Yash Chopra movies? What to do, we are like that only—bilkul Bollywood-obsessed!) You will also encounter many others like me who are at the vanguard of the LGBTQ inclusion movement in our country.

You can use this book as a roadmap and a compass. Reading about my own experiences as well as other real-life stories will hopefully motivate you to act and help you on your journey. I have complemented these stories with a list of concrete steps you can take and resources that you can use.

If you are LGBTQ yourself, then I hope this book will make you love yourself more and realise that there is a whole world, not just out there, but right here, waiting to welcome you, and we are creating it each day with our actions and our connections. It is rainbow-coloured and beautiful. So let us put on that Hema-inspired black sequined dress and pink feather boa, and sashay towards it, shall we? If you are straight, don't worry. Welcome. Join the party. The category is … inclusion.

This narrative is not in chronological order, nor does it draw a clear separation between memoir and manifesto, but the different chapters and parts still have their own distinct structures and themes.

The first part has more elements of memoir—my roller-coaster career as an entrepreneur, venture capitalist, fashionista, author, culture curator and LGBTQ change-maker. The second part gives a brief overview of different aspects of being LGBTQ in India—including what the acronym stands for, our multiple histories, the legal status and the overwhelming importance of families in our lives. The third part shifts gears towards the manifesto and makes a case for LGBTQ inclusion in Indian companies. The fourth part describes in great detail the exact steps workplaces need to take to make this inclusion happen. The book concludes with the fifth part, an outline of what Queeristan—the dream-like world of equality that so many of us in the LGBTQ movement aspire to and constantly co-create with our daily actions—could look like.

It is going to be an intense read. So grab that bowl of popcorn. Close all those twenty different open windows on your laptop. Stop checking your

Instagram stories. Put your phone down (unless of course, you are reading this book on it!) and dive in.

~

Pehle toh, let me tell you a little more about myself and how I got here. I have a day job at Godrej as vice president and I also have a gay job—being an advocate for change at companies like Goldman Sachs, Tata Steel, KPMG and Visa. In addition to individual companies, I often address corporate collectives too, like the Confederation of Indian Industries (CII) and the American Chamber of Commerce (AMCHAM), about why they should become LGBTQ inclusive, and I am part of the inaugural task force on diversity and inclusion of the Federation of Indian Chambers of Commerce and Industry (FICCI). Wearing one fabulous African-printed suit after another, I cruise from corporate boardrooms to college campuses to global conferences, waving my magic wand and sprinkling rainbow-coloured tinsel over all and sundry.

I use every occasion that I can to talk about LGBTQ issues. The Red Bull Music Academy invites me for a talk? I'll queer it. The Elle Decor India Design ID summit? You bet. A new Columbia Business School batch is visiting India? Time for a gay lecture. The Society for Human Resource Management? Pretty obvious what I'll be speaking about. If I am visiting Yale, Brandeis or Harvard or the Edinburgh International Culture Summit at the Scottish Parliament? The desi rainbow flag flies on foreign soil too.

But it wasn't always like this. Yay! Flashback time. Sepia-toned dissolve.

~

Stranger Things, Bombay edition. Bell-bottoms and sideburns. Campa Cola.

In the early 1980s Bombay, my mother was a clerk in Bank of Baroda and my father was a store manager at Burlington's, the clothes shop at the Taj Mahal Hotel. One of my favourite ways to pass time was going to the Taj and reading magazines in the hotel's Nalanda bookstore. I would admire the glossy pages, close my eyes and smell them—the sweet foreign perfume ads were my escape from middle-class melancholy, much like it was for the protagonist of 'Phoren Soap', a brilliant short story by India's most famous gay artist, Bhupen Khakhar.[1] I couldn't afford these magazines at Nalanda, but I could save up or plead with my mom to let me buy an occasional *Cine Blitz*. ('Yes, I am Sridevi's unknown sister,' declared Anupam Kher, in a late 1980s April Fools' issue, dressed in his drag avatar—Prabhadevi.)

In class nine, a group of classmates humiliated me by pulling my bright neon-green Madonna shorts down—of course, I was a Madonna fan!—in the midst of our annual sports day event. I pulled them back up and ran all the way home, red-faced with anger. Conforming would have been easy. But why fit in, at the cost of squashing your soul? It felt like poetic justice to be wearing the same neon green in a *GQ* photoshoot in 2018—for being part of the country's 100 best-dressed people. But this was way into a future that young, pimply, gay me—an introverted, only child with few friends—couldn't even begin to imagine.

As a kid, Bollywood was the only dream world I could escape into and recreate alternate endings in—where a young Aamir Khan is looking at me and not at Juhi Chawla, as he jogs out of the sunset in his cute sleeveless top, in my very own queer version, *Gayamat Se Gayamat Tak*.

My being gay has been a constant process of articulation. I always knew about my sexuality and was comfortable with it, but while growing up, I didn't have the language or the confidence to express myself. But now, I have both.

My dad's professional break came when he was recruited to work as a supermarket manager in Muscat, Oman. My mom and I went too, and from then on, I was a Gulf kid, growing up between the Middle East and India, shuttling between schools in Muscat and Bahrain as my parents shifted countries. From watching TV in our neighbour's home in Bombay to getting one for ourselves, from wearing hand-me-downs from richer second and third cousins to getting to choose which acid-washed dungarees I would like, my late childhood was a journey out of middle-class frugality to Toblerone heaven. The move also helped my process of self-discovery.

I had my first boyfriend in school in Mumbai—from class eight till we finished our class ten SSC exams in 1991. At the beginning of class ten, a classmate called us 'homo' after seeing us holding hands in class. My boyfriend freaked out. I didn't. I was just glad that there was a word for us. Being effeminate, I was often bullied, and I suppose I was more resilient than he, who managed to pass himself off as straight, and so, was spared. He didn't want to be teased, so he distanced himself. We weren't boyfriends officially, but what else would you call our relationship? There was love. There was intimacy. There was masti.

My second boyfriend came into my life when I was studying for my second bachelor's degree in education in 2002. He was studying to be a doctor. His family knew about us and it was quite wonderful—to be a happy gay couple in an India in which even straight people had to hide their love. He came from a conservative Muslim family, and their acceptance surprised both of us. His dad said to me one day, 'We love our son more than we care about what society thinks.' How simple is that, *na*?

But publicly, I remained closeted. When I first encountered a gay colleague in 2001 while I was working at Sony Entertainment Television, I tried very hard to pretend that I was straight, and when that failed, I swore him to secrecy to not reveal 'the secret' to anyone else. When I was a writer at *Elle* magazine in 1998, my then magazine editor had assigned me, with a smile, to do a feature on covering the changing gay scene in Bombay. This had irked me no end. Why me? Did she suspect something? Perhaps she did suspect and was trying to establish a comfort zone for me, to enable me to come out to her if I chose to? Or perhaps she didn't, and was just assigning me the story because she thought I'd do a good job? It didn't matter at that time. I had a persecution complex and simply denied being gay to whoever managed to ask.

Then, one day in 2002, I went to my first Humsafar Trust event before leaving for my master's programme at the Massachusetts Institute of Technology (MIT). I also stumbled upon Gay Bombay, the incredible internet-based community that had formed in our city during all the years I had been hiding. I spent my time in Boston writing my thesis on this community, which eventually became the book *Gay Bombay: Globalization, Love and (Be)Longing in Contemporary India* that Sage Publications brought out in 2008, with a revised edition in 2020.[2]

~

Spring 2018. A cab ride from Boston's Logan Airport. All these years later, I still love flying over the Atlantic Ocean into this city. The cab emerges on Memorial Drive and crosses the bridge to Cambridge. I see the MIT buildings come up on the right, above the Charles flowing below us, and just like the crystal clear water, the memories come flooding back.

This used to be my home for three years.

I walk down the same old infinite corridor at MIT, past all the community notice boards, including that of the queer association, the Rainbow Lounge. Trident Café hasn't changed at the beginning of Newbury street. I order the same omelette with a side of avocado, but this time I am alone and not with J, my ex. He has dominated my thoughts in the past twelve years. Even now, I carry his brown-and-blue checked Fendi handkerchief in my pocket.

When we broke up and divided our stuff, I took the hanky, and have been using it ever since.

I walk by our former home on Bristol Street. The biotech companies have really taken over, as have the hipster restaurants. But the Kendall Square Cinema still remains, as does Garment District, with its vintage clothes that you take home in bubblegum pink bags, quite popular during Halloween. Emma's Pizza has relocated. We used to go there often. How much of my life was lived on this little block? Between the Frank Gehry–designed, deconstructed Stata Centre in which J had his office, my own more modest office a bit further in Building 14 N, our Kendall Square home, and the Central Square T Station.

MIT made me who I am.

During this visit, I am staying at the Marriot right next to MIT, even though I have to give a lecture at far-away Brandeis. I am here for MIT, for Boston, for friends like Joyce, my loving MIT host parent, who had wanted J and me to adopt. When I show her pictures of my present partner, she asks me with eyes full of love: 'Does he make you happy?'

I am also here for other friends like Arundhati Tuli Banerjee, who runs the MIT Global Initiatives programme, and Michele Oshima, who used to run the MIT arts programmes and used to take me to free plays and at whose home I almost fall asleep one night during this trip, after a meal made by her wonderful partner Jane. Then there are newer friends. DJ Rekha, whom I wrote a recommendation for and who is now finishing her degree at MIT, Anushka Shah, who runs the MIT Media Lab's Civic Entertainment project, Kareem Khubchandani aka LaWhore Vagistan, Tufts professor by day and drag queen by night, and Ulka Anjaria and Jonathan Shapiro, the power couple who run South Asian studies at Brandeis and at whose invitation I am visiting Boston this time around.

We are all gathered around a table at Puritan & Co., an overpriced hipster restaurant at Inman Square. Perfect for my pre-birthday party before my trip to Vancouver to attend a TED conference as a senior fellow. Rekha has driven us to the restaurant after my Brandeis lecture, blasting 'Apna Time Aayega' at full volume in the Zipcar en route.

I pinch myself sometimes during gatherings such as these. How did a boy from Colaba who grew up in a 250-square-foot room and went to a 7-rupees-a-month SSC school—St Joseph's, Colaba—land up with a jet-set business-class lifestyle that involves crossing from Mumbai to Boston to Vancouver in one effing week?

∾

Going to Boston and living freely and openly as a gay person for the first time in my life was a liberating experience. I started my master's programme at MIT in 2003, and witnessed history first-hand as Massachusetts became the first US state to allow gay marriage in 2004. During the three years I was there, being gay became such a non-issue. The matter-of-fact manner in which J and I applied for joint health insurance at MIT or applied to be co-tenants in a rental apartment made me feel like *aayega kya … apna time toh* already *aa gaya*, boss.

I remember my first retreat in 2003 in Provincetown, a queer haven in Cape Cod. Wearing a sleeveless T-shirt with a gold-sequinned Saraswati embroidered on it—bought at Colaba Causeway—over a maroon skirt—which was actually my mom's old sari petticoat repurposed by her tailor with the addition of a gold thread border—I walked down Commercial Street. I had on full make-up, including an exotic little black stick-on bindi. In a drag bar, I sang 'Like a Virgin' off-key to no one in particular.

Some weeks later, at a drag party organised by the Massachusetts Area South Asian LGBTQ Association (MASALA)—the South Asian queer community organisation in Boston—I danced to 'Choli Ke Peechhe Kya Hai' with a group of queens from India, Pakistan and Bangladesh, in synchronised diasporic South Asian harmony.

This feeling of complete heady freedom inspired me to organise a university-funded South Asian LBGTQ film festival in 2004. I wasn't out to my dad yet, when the BBC wrote about my film festival: 'South Asian Gays Find US Voice'.[3] The article was accompanied by my picture, and it appeared on the homepage of the BBC global website. I soon began to get calls from friends all over the world, and figured that I better inform my dad before someone else sent him the link. So I called him and said, 'Dad, as you know, the BBC is well-known for its journalistic accuracy. If the BBC says I'm gay, it must be true!'

~

When I finished my degree at MIT in 2006, I could have stayed back in the US, either at MIT or joined a company. I even interviewed with Microsoft, and their team flew me to Seattle and put me up at a fancy hotel.

I got a chance to recollect this story to Bill Gates on a warm monsoon night in 2009. He was in India to receive the Indira Gandhi Prize for Peace, Disarmament and Development from President Pratibha Patil for his amazing work on HIV prevention and treatment, done through his foundation. He had asked the Microsoft India team to invite a selection of young creative Indians—authors, filmmakers and designers—to meet with him during the trip, and here we were, swimming with him post dinner in a rather large pool on a moonlit night, talking about HIV rates and the future of science education.

I told him that I had turned down the Microsoft offer to return to India. As with most things in my life, Bollywood was to blame, specifically Shah Rukh Khan in *Swades*.

On a cold spring night after the Microsoft interview, I was having dinner with Anand and Anuradha Mahindra in Cambridge. I had known the Mahindras for some years already. I sought Anand's advice on whether I should stay on at MIT—helping run the Convergence Culture Consortium (C3), a think tank I had co-founded as a graduate student with Professor Henry Jenkins the year before—or find a job in the US, or return to India and put my newly minted master's degree to use in the 'real world'. If I returned to India, Anand told me, the Mahindra group would be happy to hire me.

The offer took me by surprise, which is perhaps why, without thinking too much, I responded that I would love the opportunity but was wondering if Mahindra had a diversity policy that included LBGTQ as a category, and, more specifically, if my partner would be offered spousal benefits if he decided to relocate to India. Anand's answer was short and simple. He told me that there wasn't any specific policy that addressed LBGTQ issues, but were I to join the group, I wouldn't be treated any differently from the other employees.

Maybe it was the effect of having seen *Swades* and sobbing through it all of the previous week. Or perhaps I was exhausted and exhilarated from having finished writing my thesis. Whatever the reason, I said yes. Like Mohan Bhargava in the movie, I too wanted to come back to India and light my bulb.

Even though Anand knew I was gay, my immediate boss at Mahindra, Ulhas Yargop, did not. *Gay Bombay* was on the brink of release, and I needed to have this conversation with Ulhas. It was weird. A few months before, I had been an out and proud gay man living in Boston with both my partner's and my name on our apartment lease. I was on my partner's health insurance plan. Suddenly, here I was in Mumbai, feeling awkward to have to come out to my boss? Anyway, the deed was done, and he was very understanding.

There was also humour. Ulhas had the habit of using the term 'bugger' to refer to just about anyone: 'You know what that bugger told me the other day?' and so on. I had to educate him on how 'bugger' might not be a polite term, especially in a gay context. 'So, now I shouldn't call you bugger, is that what you're telling me, bugger?' he replied. I rolled my eyes, and we both laughed.

I was asked to make up my own designation when I joined Mahindra. So I did: Head, Vision and Opportunities. This gave me carte blanche to pursue my interests within the group. Soon, I was helping fund companies, organising innovation challenges and planning senior leadership retreats at the Harvard Business School. After my relationship with J ended rather tragically, to keep me even more busy, Anand and Anuradha asked me to help run *Verve*—the fashion magazine Anuradha had founded some years ago. Luxury magazine publishing was a crowded marketplace by then with the entry of foreign magazines like *Vogue* and *Bazaar*, which were squeezing *Verve* out of its prime position. Given my background in media and journalism and my new MIT-acquired digital chutzpah, I relished the challenge.

~

'Jalwa ... jalwa, fashion ka hai yeh jalwa!'

Alongside venture capital, fashion became another lens through which I could view the change taking place across contemporary India. Soon, I started attending fashion weeks, meeting young designers and understanding the post-liberalisation network of possibilities that fashion offered them.

Consider the designer Jenjum Gadi, who hails from Tirbin, a remote village in Arunachal Pradesh. Electricity came to his village only in the late 1990s. He stumbled upon fashion while going through old issues of *Femina*. Imagine the journey: of transportation (from the Northeast to Delhi, possible because of new post-liberalisation air routes), of education (at Wigan and Leigh College, possible because a post-1990s India needed new kinds of colleges), of internship (with Rohit Bal, the legend who attended Jenjum's graduation at which he won 'Best Designer'), of his debut fashion week presentation (possible because there was now a network of such biannual shows offering visibility to young talent), and of sales (again, this post-liberalisation India had created a new customer base eager to consume fashion).

The fashion industry offered many opportunities to queer people in India to be themselves. It was a relatively safe space for employment, and this is the reason so many queer people are out in this industry. People often have the misconception that there are more queer people here than any other industry. This isn't true. Queer people are everywhere. We might be more closeted in other sectors, but in the fashion field, we feel comfortable enough to come out. Seeing couples like the designer Suneet Varma and his husband Rahul Arora or visiting the late Wendell Rodricks and his husband Jerome Marrel at their beautiful Goa home was tremendously inspiring to me. Even back then, despite the presence of Section 377, they were being who they were, sharing their lives with each other. Seeing so many happy queer couples gave me hope post my break-up that I too could have a happily-ever-after in India.

Being in fashion also gave me the opportunity to dress up. The fashion circuit, complete with sponsors like car manufacturers and alcohol companies that want to bask in its hyper-cool afterglow, meant parties, parties, parties, and dressing up for them. This is how I began my journey as an Indian fashionista—going to fashion weeks and sitting in the front row, being interviewed, wearing big sunglasses and an oversized It bag, sipping champagne, head thrown back, laughing. I began to revel in my flamboyance. *Vogue*'s camp editors André Leon Talley and Hamish Bowles were my costume inspirations. Soon, I started appearing on various Indian 'Best Dressed' lists, and this continues till today. What I love doing the most is bringing my fashion jazz to the stiff corporate environments I float in and out of, inserting my flamboyant queer fashion identity into these drab environments.

In 2008, when I had some editorial control at *Verve*, I started including queerness in the magazine, whether directly through features or indirectly through androgyny in fashion shoots and through events we curated. That year, *Verve* collaborated with Karan Johar's Dharma Productions for the film *Dostana*—a big star-studded absurd Bollywood fantasy in which two straight and super macho heroes, John Abraham and Abhishek Bachchan, pretend to be gay to rent an apartment, but end up falling for and wooing their flatmate played by Priyanka Chopra Jonas. It is a landmark film, despite being problematic, and I'll tell you more about it later.

My first book came out around the same time as *Dostana* in 2008. The people I interviewed for the book were negotiating what it was to be gay in an Indian context, and this negotiation wasn't confined to the courtrooms. Even in the presence of 377, there were gay marriages, commitment ceremonies and anniversary celebrations that took place in the India of the 1990s and early 2000s, and there were several examples, big and small, of society accommodating LBGTQ people. There were struggles, but also happy moments, and I chronicled all of these in my book.

In July 2009, the Delhi High Court decriminalised same-sex relationships between consenting adults, in its landmark Naz verdict.[4] It was finally not illegal to be gay in India. Between 2009 and 2013, I was on a high, and was convinced that I had made the right choice in coming back to India from the US. Nonetheless, I would never have imagined that by 2011, I would be at the Google office in Bengaluru giving a talk to Indian Gayglers, or discussing a diversity policy at my current employer Godrej, or, for that matter, that I would attend a Pride march with Mark Kahn, my straight Godrej colleague, who had brought along his daughter Anushri to show support. Their picture, with her sitting on his shoulders, her face painted in rainbow colours, went viral after *Mid-day* carried it. In 2013, all this exuberance was dashed to the ground with the horrific Koushal verdict in the Supreme Court.

I was also at a career crossroads in 2009. I had changed three different professional avatars already—I had worked in academia as an MIT researcher and author, in business with Mahindra and Sony Entertainment Television, and in the media, with *Times of India*, *Elle* and *Verve*. I had also been an early dotcom pioneer with my web venture *Fresh Lime Soda*—India's first online youth magazine which ran in the late 1990s and early 2000s. What would I do next?

I took two leaps of faith. The first didn't pay off. My plan to do a PhD at the University of Pennsylvania flopped. I hated it. I left UPenn for India again within six months. My next idea was to create a new kind of cultural space in India. The idea found its home at Godrej, and I found my feet, ready to begin a new innings as the founder of the Godrej India Culture Lab—a cultural intervention to enable public conversations on the changing face of contemporary India. You will hear more about this journey throughout the book.

~

While this book is super personal, you will hear not only my voice but also that of so many others in the movement—lawyers like Menaka Guruswamy and Kiruba Munusamy, activists like Abhina Aher, Akkai Padmashali, Pawan Dhall, Sushant Divgikar and Grace Banu, scholars like Dhiren Borisa, and business people like Radhika Piramal, Ramkrishna Sinha, Srini Ramaswamy and Keshav Suri. Feminism has deeply informed this book, and I am grateful to Bishakha Datta and Point of View, Paromita Vohra and Agents of Ishq, Urvashi Butalia and Zubaan Books, Nisha Susan and the *Ladies Finger*, Karla Bookman and the *Swaddle*, among so many others, for collaborating with the Culture Lab over the years—all of these interactions have greatly shaped my own worldview.

More importantly, this book builds on the queer body of written work from the country by Saleem Kidwai and Ruth Vanita, Gautam Bhan and Arvind Narrain, A. Revathi, Maya Sharma, Devdutt Pattanaik, Living Smile Vidya, Akhil Katyal and many others. Some of our country's queer chroniclers are now no more, like Shivananda Khan, visible today only as pixels in *Project Bolo* videos online. Others like Hoshang Merchant continue their fight, but age is catching up with them. Through this book, I honour all our queer heroes—for digging the deep foundations on which my generation is trying to create a strong edifice for the future.

I wish for two outcomes from this book. The first is that many people in the Indian workplace read it and change their company's HR policies and practices, convinced that inclusion makes sense whichever way they look at it. The second is that many of this book's LGBTQ readers find hope and comfort in the micro revolutions of change chronicled here.

This is certainly not the first book about diversity and inclusion. It isn't even the first commercial business book about LGBTQ diversity and inclusion in India. There is, for instance, *Queer at Work* by Sasmita Palo and Kumar Kunal Jha published in 2019.[5] They work just down the road from me in Mumbai at the Tata Institute of Social Sciences (TISS). For their book, they collected stories over a period of five years—mostly from Mumbai and Hyderabad, though the lessons are more or less universal—on queer people and the strategies they use to come out in their workplaces.

Participants in their study were given three pictures. One of a man and a woman, one of two men, and one of two women. Participants were told one of the three pictures was that of a couple, and were asked to guess which one it was. Most of them selected the first option. More exercises like this that betrayed the participants' innate biases, followed by in-depth discussions with them, formed the foundation of their book. Benefiting from being published in 2019, after the 377 and the NALSA Supreme Court decisions, the book also examines the before-after impacts, and gives organisations a handbook on how to create safe spaces within their companies.

The majority of the existing literature on diversity and inclusion that is widely cited in the corporate space comprise reports published on corporate websites or online journals. I am thinking specifically of the seminal *Valuing Diversity: New Tools for a New Reality* edited by Lewis Brown Griggs and Lente-Louise Louw and published in 1995,[6] and also the multiple reports produced by McKinsey, Deloitte, Boston Consulting Group, Community Business and Open for Business, which I will refer to generously in this book.

These books and reports belong to the genre of diversity books that are largely 'guides' for implementing diversity programmes and adapting corporate culture to the changing times. These aren't considered commercial in the way a successful CEO's memoir or a book on how to be more profitable would be. But nowadays, the kind of diversity books that are in demand feels different. There is a strong focus on stories.

Stories help mainstream niche but deeply important topics. In August 2019, *Forbes* had published an article titled '10 Books To Help You Foster a More Diverse and Inclusive Workplace'.[7] I thought, bingo! More guides to read through and assimilate. But the book selection pleasantly surprised me. Almost all of them were personal narratives that told stories, such as *We Are Everywhere: Protest, Power, and Pride in the History of Queer Liberation* that uses photographs with detailed narratives of the Queer Liberation Movement across time.[8] Even in India, if you read the 2018 book *The 99 Day Diversity Challenge: Creating an Inclusive Workplace*,[9] written by award-winning social entrepreneur Dr Saundarya Rajesh, one of India's most prominent diversity strategists, you will understand what I am trying to say. The book is full of stories and other clever tools like crossword puzzles to nudge the readers towards action.

Books like *Blindspot: Hidden Biases of Good People*,[10] *The Loudest Duck: Moving Beyond Diversity While Embracing Differences to Achieve Success at Work*,[11] and *Inclusion Dividend: Why Investing in Diversity & Inclusion Pays Off*[12] follow in this tradition of using strong narratives to provide succinct guides for making workplaces more inclusive. I have also been inspired by corporate memoirs like *Trailblazer: The Power of Business as the Greatest Platform for Change* written by Salesforce CEO Marc Benioff in 2019 as a new corporate manifesto for businesses to serve employees as well as the wider community, rather than just the shareholders.[13]

The premise is simple: only stories that frame existing statistics can sensitise readers. Once sensitised to the lived experience, we then have the drive to actually do something because we now have the conviction. This is why, in this book, there are lots of personal stories, and it also serves as a guide.

~

Before you read the rest of the book, a small note of thanks because it really does take a village. There are people without whom this book would not have happened. My friend, the graphic novelist and designer Vishwajyoti Ghosh for urging me to write it and connecting me to my wonderful Westland team. My brilliant editors V.K. Karthika and Janani Ganesan, who have borne my idiosyncrasies and Bollywood love with patience and kindness. There are three incredibly smart people who helped me with the research for the book: Prathyush Parasuraman, who spent three months assisting on this book project and helped kick-start the interviews and secondary research, and my amazing Culture Lab team members—Saniya Shaikh and Nayanika Nambiar—who have been supporting me on this project from day one right till the end. In fact, the origins of this book lie in a white paper that Nayanika and I wrote for the Culture Lab in 2018. My entire lab team has been super supportive, and this book would not have come about without their contributions—so Dianne Tauro, Mukta Pai, Koninka Roy and Pallavi Khare, thank you!

To my wonderful interviewees—thank you, for all that you do. You inspire me every day. I am grateful to my family and friends, my village, spread out all over the world. But I am most grateful to you, dear reader, for putting your faith in this book. I hope that it entertains and inspires you, but above all, that it spurs you to action.

PART ONE

THIS BOOK IS PERSONAL

Who am I? This opening section tells you about my life, my masaledar journey towards being an inclusion advocate, and the framework and methods I use—jugaad resistance and cultural acupuncture—in making change happen.

1

Jugaad Resistance

I remember the historic morning of 2 July 2009, when the Delhi High Court first decriminalised homosexuality in India in its historic Naz judgement. My cell phone just would not stop buzzing with congratulatory messages. When I entered the Mahindra office, my colleagues clapped.

What a beautifully written verdict it was. Consider this excerpt: 'If there is one constitutional tenet that can be said to be [the] underlying theme of the Indian Constitution, it is that of "inclusiveness". This court believes that Indian Constitution reflects this value deeply ingrained in Indian society, nurtured over several generations. The inclusiveness that Indian society traditionally displayed, literally in every aspect of life, is manifest in recognizing a role in society for everyone.'[1]

Then, four years later, on that fateful day of 11 December 2013, it felt like someone had punched us—the proud queer citizens of this free nation—hard in the gut. I moved from TV studio to studio, along with other queer spokespeople, on the night of the horrific Koushal judgement in the Supreme Court, which effectively overturned the 2009 Naz judgement. How could the country's highest court, which existed largely to protect us, call us a 'miniscule minority'[2] and deny us our constitutional rights?

Four days after the verdict, I joined citizens from eighteen cities, including New York, Boston, London, Sydney and Toronto, in a 'global day of rage' against this verdict. Maheshwari Udyan in Matunga, a historic cruising space, was the site of our Mumbai protest. All around me there was defiant singing and angry sloganeering.

I sat quietly in a corner and began to notice just how many straight supporters there were at the protest. Some had brought their children, others, their parents. 'This is our joint struggle,' said an elderly lady to me. Then, I heard a chorus of voices call out to me: 'Bhaiya.' It was the group of Kranti girls who had performed their play *Kamathipura Ki Zindagi* the previous evening at Vikhroli Skin, a pop-up event at the Godrej India Culture Lab. They were daughters of commercial sex workers, who were collectively challenging their destinies through the awe-inspiring education and life-skills programming provided to them by the NGO Kranti. Most of these young Kranti girls who had come to Maheshwari that evening were not queer. But they were there, for us, for me, in solidarity. Their tight hugs, large smiles, confidence and humour reinvigorated me. We were not alone. I got up from my corner and joined the crowd, shouting out loudly and clearly with everyone: 'We want azadi from 377.'

~

As the morning of 10 July 2018 dawned, millions of Indians, queer and otherwise, held our collective breaths, wondering if the arc of justice,[3] as Martin Luther King had so famously framed it, would bend towards us this time around. The Supreme Court was to commence hearing of the thirty-four pleas grouped together—by transgender individuals like Akkai Padmashali, LGBTQ activists like Arif Jafar and Ashok Row Kavi, business people like Keshav Suri and Ritu Dalmia, groups of individuals representing the alumni of different Indian Institutes of Technology (IIT), collectives like Voices Against 377, parents of LGBTQ individuals, mental health professionals, and more—to review its own 2013 judgement that had overturned the Delhi High Court ruling. So much had happened since 2013. There was a new government in power. Anything could happen.

I would have loved to be present in the court to listen to the arguments and, in fact, I was in Delhi the morning of 6 September, the date the Supreme Court judges announced their final verdict, and read down Section 377. However, I had committed to give a talk to senior leaders at Kohler, the bathroom company, on, guess what—why LGBTQ inclusion was important for them. So I had to forego the chance to witness history being created live and instead experience it vicariously via Twitter updates and daily email briefings by volunteers like Danish Sheikh, who was then working with the advocacy organisation Lawyers Collective. Here is an excerpt from one of Danish's updates:

> Menaka Guruswamy, representing the IIT petitioners, reduced many of us to tears. It wasn't the fact that she was the first female lawyer to speak in a testosterone packed litigation (and courtroom), though that was crucial. It

> wasn't the fact that she made it a point to address the sole female judge on the Bench time and again, though that was significant. No, it was rather the sheer force of her arguments that seemed to rip through the tangles of legal discourse and force the Court to confront the human cost of this case. In 2012 the judges in Koushal would keep asking the lawyers about the existence of LGBT persons. Today, Guruswamy acknowledged the presence of the petitioners who stood in the room, while also invoking the names of those who weren't there. These are the individuals the law affects, and in story after story, she told the judges how many lives were going by living under the shadow of this law. She opened up the space of what it meant to be queer, speaking of the right to love, of the Court's own mandate in protecting individuals, of times when district judges had protected runaway inter-caste lovers from their families. She spoke about the law's specific impact on transgender persons, on how it impeded the promise of full citizenship. … In no uncertain times, she reminded the Court of its duty to not just give a hearing, but to bridge the gap towards emancipation, to fulfil a promise that harks back to the framing of the Constitution.[4]

I get goosebumps every time I think of Menaka in court emphasising to the judges: 'It is not just consensual sex between homosexual partners that this Court should recognize, but their love for each other. How strongly must you love knowing that you are unconvicted felons.'[5]

~

On a balmy Delhi afternoon some weeks later, we sat sipping adrak chai in Menaka's beautifully decorated New Friends Colony apartment, as her partner, Arundhati Katju, asked her which dupatta to wear for a party they were going to later in the evening. They were not publicly out then. They would come out in style a year later in 2019, on CNN with Fareed Zakaria, after receiving the TIME 100 award in New York. Priyanka Chopra Jonas would write their citation in the magazine.[6] Today, there is still no book in the works, no rumour of a movie or mini-series being planned. Just Menaka and Arundhati, two young women in India, who, alongside others, pushed a mountain hard enough, and watched it topple over. 'Just think of how it could have gone, if we hadn't won,' Menaka told me that evening. 'It would have taken us ten more years at the very least.'

I shuddered. Then rage welled up inside me. Why should we be arguing for our own rights in the first place?

~

In court, all the lawyers arguing for us—Anand Grover, Saurabh Kirpal, Menaka Guruswamy and others—emphasised that the presence of the antiquated, colonial Section 377 violated Article 14 (that guarantees all Indians equality before the law), Article 15 (that prohibits discrimination on the grounds of religion, race, caste, sex or place of birth), Article 19 (that guarantees us freedom of speech and expression, and to form associations or unions) and Article 21 (right to life) of the Constitution of India.

I want to pause to acknowledge just how much the queer movement in India is beholden to Dr Babasaheb Ambedkar, something we need to remind ourselves again and again. The scholar Akhil Kang wrote a poignant essay about this debt in *Round Table India*:

> The Naz judgment in 2009 ... goes on to quote Ambedkar who spoke about constitutional morality in the Constituent Assembly Debates in 1948. Ambedkar while speaking of Grote, a Greek historian, spoke of how imperative it is for us, as Indians, to seek constitutional morality because its diffusion is not yet complete in India. He said that democracy in India is only a top-dressing on its soil, which essentially is undemocratic. It is quite telling how the principles on which Ambedkar envisioned the Constitution to thrive on, gave life to legitimate queer spaces. Yet the importance of what was spoken about this diffusion (and *who* spoke about this diffusion, along with everything else that he stood up for) got lost before its actual realization in the queer space.[7]

Thank you, Babasaheb. Your law has protected us. Your law has empowered us. Your law made 2009 possible. The 2018 progressive Supreme Court judgement, commonly referred to as the Navtej judgement, was carefully built on the foundation that you laid for us so many years ago.

I was moved to tears on reading Justice Indu Malhotra's opinion: 'History owes an apology to the members of this community and their families, for the delay in providing redressal for the ignominy and ostracism that they have suffered through the centuries.'[8]

The eminent judges established jurisprudence in 2018 that will be very hard to shake. It protects our country's LGBTQ citizens and also opens the doors to further legal victories. In many countries across the world, LGBTQ equality has led to the eventual legalisation of LGBTQ marriages, clearer laws on inheritance, and equal rights for same-sex couples to adopt children; I see no reason why we would not want to embark on a similar journey in India too.

However, while we have this jurisprudence, we, as civil society, will have to put in a lot of effort to convert the intent of the Supreme Court verdict into action. It is now no longer a crime to be LGBTQ in India, but there are still those who consider it to be a disease, despite very clear statements from organisations like the Indian Psychiatric Society, which says that 'homosexuality is not a psychiatric disorder ... [but] a normal variant of sexuality much like heterosexuality'.[9] Unfortunately, some members of the medical profession in the country consider homosexuality to be a medical condition, ruining the lives of countless queer citizens with their fake methods and claims to 'turn' them straight—everything from yoga to pills to even brutal and harmful shock treatments. And then there is the violence—both physical (petitioner Arif Jafar was thrown in jail, beaten up so violently that he lost most of his teeth, and was denied bail[10]), and psychological.

~

On a flight back home after meeting some of the coolest queer authors and artists at the JCB Prize for Literature in Jaipur in November 2019, I picked up the newspaper. The headline read: 'Won't Tolerate Adultery, Homosexuality: Army'.[11] It had been over a year since the Supreme Court read down 377. The reason cited by the chief of army staff for this statement? 'In the army we never thought this can happen. Anything that was thought of was put in the Army Act. It was something which was unheard of when the Army Act was made. We never thought this is going to happen. We never allow it. Therefore it was not put in the Army Act.' This act governs the conduct of the army personnel, and the 'it' which is being shied away from here is queerness in the armed forces.

I put down the paper, stupefied. All over the world, countries like South Africa, the Philippines and so many more have changed their laws to empower queer people to serve in their armed forces, but in our country, the army wanted to do the opposite, and enshrine in its law a policy against queerness?

I realised once again that while the bigoted views expressed by those opposing decriminalisation in the Supreme Court may have been dismissed by the judges in 2018, many people continue to be biased in our country. Based on what the government counsel argued in court, it is clear that there is ignorance about queer rights and lives among most of our country's elected officials. The additional solicitor general Tushar Mehta openly remarked in court that he was 'worried' that scrapping 377 would open the door to the granting of further rights to India's LGBTQ citizens.[12]

But why shouldn't these doors be opened? Why should we be anything less than equal to other citizens of this country? Why should I not be entitled to every right that other citizens in the country have? I too would like to have a joint bank account with my partner, put our names together on the property deed for our home, and frame a marriage certificate on our living room wall—a certificate which signifies that my country acknowledges and respects our union.

We need to transform the ignorance and bigotry that is still around us, into tolerance, acceptance and inclusion. I have written this book to serve as a small step in this direction.

~

There is already a lot happening on the ground across our country with regard to queer activism—from Pride marches in many cities to film festivals, from support groups to health services, from parent meetings to legal interventions. Because of my own background and experience in corporate India, LGBTQ inclusion in the workplace is the terrain that this book will cover. It is the terrain I know best. It is a terrain I have played an important part in creating. I believe that pushing for inclusion in corporate India can have serious ripple effects in other parts of our society, because, like it or not, we live in an age of neoliberal capitalism. So, please consider this book as a companion piece to all the other brilliant forms of activism prevalent across our country in other spheres.

I must tell you that while writing this, I have fluctuated between hope and despair each day. It is clear that there is a new India forming itself in offices across our country. I have written this book as something that is action-oriented and biased towards the possibility of amplifying and widening the scope of this new India. Some of the initiatives you will read about in this book are simply amazing—progressive companies, queer marriages, sensitive cinema. Many of my friends who are featured in this book—Dhiren Borisa, Zainab Patel, Anubhuti Banerjee, Pawan Dhall, Rafiul Alom Rahman, Gauri Sawant, Neelam Jain and so many others—are awe-inspiring.

At the same time, we need to acknowledge that all of this awesomeness is set against the backdrop of daily violence and persistent homophobia and transphobia. Every day I read of queer people committing suicide because of family pressure to conform, loneliness and more. Even during the course of writing this book, many such incidents came to light. Consider this headline from *Mumbai Mirror* on 24 July 2018 about Aniket Patel, a resident from

Powai, five minutes from my office in Vikhroli: 'Twenty-Five-Year-Old MBA Graduate Ends Life Over "Gay" Jibes, Suicide Note Alleges He Was Taunted at Workplace.'[13]

~

'Not all revolutions take place on the streets. Some take place in boardrooms, behind the scenes, but they are just as important.' This is just one of the things that the legendary English actor Sir Ian McKellen told me in 2016.

'Did he touch you? Do you have Magneto's superpowers now?' a friend's Marvel-obsessed ten-year-old daughter asked me breathlessly. 'Maybe Gandalf's wizardry!' I quipped. Who knows? The encounter was energising in ways that I am still only beginning to fathom.

The common ground between Ian and me is LGBTQ rights. Ian is, of course, one of the world's most lauded Shakespeare actors and a major Hollywood movie star. He was in India, courtesy the British Council and the British Film Institute, to mark Shakespeare's 400th death anniversary. However, as he told me himself, his most important role over the past few years has been that of a global LGBTQ rights champion. Along with some friends, he created Stonewall—an advocacy group for LGBTQ rights, one of the largest in the world today—in 1989. He is one of the most celebrated queer role models, and his outspokenness has made him as much of an icon in the LGBTQ movement as his blockbuster roles in the *Lord of the Rings* or *X-Men* franchises.

We spoke extensively about his activist profile for a video we recorded for the Culture Lab,[14] just before he stepped out to inaugurate Kashish, India's biggest LGBTQ film festival, at Liberty Cinema in Mumbai, which Godrej was co-sponsoring. During our chat, Ian asserted that gay people needed to come out of the closet. Having come out rather late himself, at forty-nine years of age, he told me that he regretted having waited so long. As an out gay person myself, I could relate to his assertion that everything becomes better once you come out.

'I was out to my friends and co-actors for many years,' Ian shared during the video conversation, 'but I wasn't out to my own blood family and to the media. Before I came out publicly in a BBC interview when I was forty-nine, I came out to my stepmother, who was eighty then, and when I did, we got much closer. Coming out was such a relief on all accounts. Everything improved, including my acting. Up until then, my acting was about disguising. After I came out, it became about revelation.'

We discussed the situation in India at length during the time we spent together, and in his video chat with me, he humorously apologised for India's Section 377 on behalf of the UK. 'We are very sorry we gave this to you. It's a British relic, a colonial law, and there's nothing Indian about it. It simply has to go!'

His prophecy would come true within just two years, but at that time, I guess he sensed my enthusiasm was flagging. 'Don't give up; don't be fazed,' he counselled me. 'In the UK, there have been so many changes since 1990 that we never thought possible, but it has happened in our lives. In our time, we had fax machines or letter-writing that we would use to petition for change. Today, you have social media. In fact, the UK government advertises the country as a place where LGBTQ people will be treated well. It is a tourist destination! No politician in the UK can say anything anti-gay today. This has all happened in just the past few years. It will happen in India too. People like you—who can speak the language of activism as well as that of business—will be key in this world. Keep on working for the change you want to see.'

That line really hit home. I am also writing this book because of him. Thank you, Ian.

It was such a joy to see how Ian interacted with the attendees at the Kashish opening. Brushing his aides aside, he rushed into the crowd and happily posed for selfies. On stage, he lifted his candle, Gandalf-like, towards Liberty Cinema's art deco ceiling, as he inaugurated the festival with Sonam Kapoor.

~

Cut to Sonam Kapoor and me in June 2019. I was chilling with Sonam, post-make-up, before we were to go online for a Twitter Blue Room video, which would proceed to break the internet.[15] During the online chat, the paragon of fashion in India asked me who my queer fashion icon was. I gave her the silly look you give someone asking an obvious question, rolled my eyes and proclaimed, 'Me, obviously!'

She was bemused. The half a million people watching us on Twitter live across multiple channels—*Elle* and Sonam's own Twitter account and mine—understood that this was me. There is no place for fake modesty in my life. Call it overconfidence, call it vanity; I call it my truth.

That day, before the show, the skies had been overcast. It had been raining incessantly for twenty hours. The roads were clogged, bridges were shut, traffic was grinding, concrete and the skies merged in sighs and shades of grey, and the driver was forced to look for shortcuts to reach the Bandra Kurla Complex of stone, marble, glass and cement on time. By on time, I mean, before Sonam.

This event was organised at the last moment, and when I was asked if I wanted to be part of the panel, I told them, 'If you're bringing four gay men again, I won't come.' This always happens; while lesbians and trans people are at the vanguard of the movement for LGBTQ liberation, it is mostly gay men who are the visible face of the movement, and this includes me. Get more diversity, *na*, I told them, and also, get Sonam.

They made excuses—she might be busy, travelling, booked, scheduled, on a flight to Delhi or Japan or London or LA. *Yaar, poochne mein kya jata hai*? She has been an ally of monumental importance in getting mainstream visibility by playing the lead role of a lesbian woman in the film *Ek Ladki Ko Dekha Toh Aisa Laga*. Imagine her father Anil Kapoor playing her father on-screen as well, telling Sonam's character that he accepts she is a lesbian. Imagine this film playing on thousands of theatre screens across the country and pulsating through the nerves of Netflix.

Eventually, there she was, dripping beauty, while those around, in a trance, collected whatever remnants they could get of it, as she glided through the halls of the Twitter office.

And then there was Pearl Daruwala, in a crisp white button-down oxford shirt and blue jeans, and with neon-green highlights in her hair—a gender non-confirming lesbian. (Does the term make sense to you? Does it matter if it doesn't? We will get into the details of queer labels in a subsequent chapter.) There was Anjali Lama, one of the most beautiful, tenacious trans models working in India today, dressed in a snappy black blazer over a white polo-neck mini paired with sneakers, who moved comfortably through the linguistics of Hindi and English. *This* was the diversity needed in a panel talking about Pride and inclusion.

I was the first to arrive, and entered a building lobby that approximated nature. There was a vertical garden of fresh and watered verdant leaves, and the real estate company WeWork's logo was bathed in the rainbow of queer corporate liberation. The walls were sky blue, the floor was sand brown, and the paintings were pops of deep green, lipstick red, Nagpur orange and jet black. Psychedelics on a beach. Before I turned to the elevator, I noticed a white board proclaiming, 'Boldly me, proudly we ... Spread the message of inclusion,' with coloured post-its from employees pasted on it.

Be What Ever you want to be

NO JUDGMENT! ONLY LOVE <3

LOVE UNCONDITIONALLY

Not all fish can fly

KISS WHO YOU WANNA [with consent]

LOVE IS LOVE IS LOVE IS LOVE

Love fearlessly

Hey! My Moon, I will find you soon. Be my noon, It's already June

Carpe Diem

Fun fact: The Twitter Blue Room isn't really blue.

As we sat together, waiting for the shoot to start, I told Sonam that nothing gives me more joy than getting up and making my partner's dabba and sending him off to work. She responded by quoting Brecht, then told me that her husband Anand made breakfast for her. 'He pampers me. The younger one should get pampered.' She nodded approvingly when I told her how my younger partner sits at home with his legs propped up on a foot stool every morning, scrolling through YouTube songs on our TV as he slurps up his bowl of granola, while I scurry around, laying out his clothes on the bed, with matching socks and handkerchief.

Ten seconds to go. 5 … 4 … 3 … 2 … 1 and rolling.

Sonam prefaced the discussion saying she doesn't believe in labels (except Prada, Gucci, Anamika Khannna, I said, giggling), but if that simplifies complexity, so be it. I told her I identified as an out and proud gay Indian. I think both these terms are important. I am very proud of being gay, and I am an extremely proud Indian. LGBTQ inclusion and plurality are deeply ingrained in Indian culture.

Anjali spoke of her long and difficult journey from Nepal to India, from a farming community to fashion. Pearl shared how she used to bring her mother along to every LGBTQ event she organised, and how this process of sensitisation took two years, before her mother accepted her fully. The conversation moved around, between Pride and inclusion—not just of the queer community, but within the queer community.

Sonam asked me if I believed in marriage. Seriously? I carry a sindoor box in my man-purse everywhere I go. I really don't see the issue people have with gay marriage, I told her. Even economically, seeing how extravagant some of us queers are, the wedding industry is only going to get a boost with legalising marriage, I added. Sabyasachi Mukherjee and Anita Dongre will be swimming in even more unimaginable profits, and our country's gross domestic product (GDP) would shoot up to the extent that no government could even imagine or take credit for.

After the discussion, all of us went out for dinner, except Sonam, who wanted to go back to her hungry husband. It was still pouring, by then for twenty-eight hours, non-stop. As we walked out of the restaurant in a straight (hmm) line, some people stared at us—a trans woman in a dress, a gender non-confirming lesbian with neon-green hair, and a gay man wearing a kurta with a bow tie. Yes, darlings, I Z-snapped from under my rainbow umbrella. Welcome to Queeristan.

~

Why am I talking about these two specific incidents right at the beginning of the book? Because it illustrates how a global gay icon and a powerful straight Bollywood ally are both using their positions to bring about change in societal mindsets. Influence matters. It doesn't matter whether you are queer or straight. You need to commit to being a part of a changing new India, an inclusive India. Whether you are an employer or employee, a parent or friend, whatever your gender, religion or race, whatever label you put on yourself, I want you to use your unique position to become an advocate for LGBTQ rights. Be like Ian. Be like Sonam.

~

For me, being a change-maker is a simple two-step process. Step one: You have to open your mind and your heart. Step two: You have to do some jugaad resistance and make change happen wherever and however you can.

I use the term 'jugaad resistance' to describe the work I do.

For many years, the word 'jugaad' used to make me slightly queasy. It originally referred to the cobbled-together trucks made from jeep parts that were popular across northern India. The word then came to be appropriated by business school scholars to refer to the Indian knack of low-cost innovation. As I told author Helen Russell when she interviewed me for her book *The Atlas of Happiness: The Global Secrets of How to Be Happy*, 'Indians aren't doing jugaad because it makes them more creative—they are doing it because of lack of opportunity ... we make do with less, we manage, but it is not celebrated as a badge of resourcefulness in India—people have a jugaad mindset to survive.'[16]

After the launch of the 2012 book *Jugaad Innovation: Think Frugal, Be Flexible, Generate Breakthrough Growth* by Simone Ahuja, Jaideep Prabhu and Navi Radjou at our Culture Lab in 2012, I started thinking of jugaad as a framework of possibilities rather than just as business or object innovation.

When 'jugaad' is combined with another word I really like, 'resistance', you get 'jugaad resistance', which to me stands for a resourceful, solution-oriented opposition to established ways of thinking and doing. Jugaad resistance takes place when the revolutionaries locate themselves *within* the establishment they wish to change, so that they can bring about innovative changes to the system from the inside.

The two components of jugaad resistance are infiltration and cultural acupuncture. I will talk more about cultural acupuncture—the method I use in my jugaad resistance at Godrej—in the next chapter, but first, some thoughts on infiltration.

This book is set firmly in corporate India, into which I have infiltrated. I am arguing from my unique inside-out position as a corporate person working on LGBTQ issues, and my outside-in position as an activist and cultural creator using the corporate world to advance my agenda.

There are many friends—activists, artists and others—who are uncomfortable with my location. Likewise, my corporate friends look at my activist and artist friends with unease. To me, the relationship need not be oppositional. Everything in life is not binary. To solve some of our planet's greatest challenges—climate change, gender inequality, you name it—we have to work together across different spheres, including legal entities, NGOs, governments and corporations. None of us can do it by ourselves. There are many points of intersection, and these intersections can be mutually beneficial. What I do in my daily life to make these connections is what I call jugaad resistance.

There are, anyway, so many links, that engagement across these spheres is unavoidable. Corporates provide money to several research initiatives, including universities, research consortia in which they can be directly involved in, and NGOS.

Corporates don't do all of this purely for philanthropic reasons. They all have selfish motives. In order to really engage with their future audiences—the drivers of growth—they need to understand much more than consumption patterns. They need to understand their customers' aspirations. Corporations now seek innovative ideas from their customers on what to make and sell.

They hire expensive 'design-thinking' consultants like Ideo and Frog Design to tell them what to do or how to better do what they do. They seek what management guru Clayton Christenson calls 'discontinuous innovation',[17] and sometimes to do this, they follow the process of what another management guru, C.K. Prahalad, calls 'co-creation'.[18] In this process of co-creation, I believe that it is vital that companies have a meaningful and productive exchange with their stakeholders, which includes LGBTQ employees and customers.

Being inside Godrej, being a part of bodies like the World Economic Forum's Young Global Leader programme and from attending many TED conferences over the years, I have perceived a gradual shift in terms of how businesses think of themselves and their role in the world of today and tomorrow. Post the global financial crisis of the late 2000s, across business schools and in corporate boardrooms, these identity questions are being debated in a way they haven't been before.

None of this means that all corporates or corporate people are *doodh se dhula hua*. There are many companies out there, in India and other parts of the world, that are extractive of the environment, exploitative of their workers and narrow-minded in their dedication to profits at all costs. However, there are many instances when corporate interests and societal development can intersect. I urge the people reading this book to consider the corporate world with hopeful scepticism. We have to criticise them when they get things wrong, of course, but perhaps we can also help them get things right? As part of my jugaad resistance way of functioning, I have chosen to be inside the corporate world to do just that.

Likewise, I urge my friends in the corporate world to not be fearful that academics, scientists, activists and artists will derail their agendas and targets. This is a myopic vision. Look at where we are on climate change, for example. The clock is ticking away. If there is no planet left, what profits and what companies are we talking about? We will all die, *na*? Companies desperately need activists, scientists, scholars and artists to show them society's mirror. Many progressive companies are already engaging meaningfully with these different stakeholders.

I see nothing wrong with all the players acting out of enlightened self-interest; in fact, it can lead to genuinely exciting research work and possibly, change. Corporates spend so much money on research, but sometimes all they need to do is buy a book. Although, how many people in the C-Suite at Walmart have read Mary L. Gray's wonderfully researched *Out in the*

Country: Youth, Media and Queer Visibility in Rural America?[19] This book maps the experiences of young people living in American small towns, and talks about how, in addition to physical spaces like Walmart where they sometimes dress up and have drag parties, rural LGBTQ youth also explore online spaces to shape their queer identities. What will it take for folks at my own company, Godrej, to read Snigdha Poonam's extraordinary 2018 book *Dreamers: How Indians Are Changing the World*,[20] which talks about the thwarted aspirations of young small-town Indians, or Suraj Yengde's searing 2019 book *Caste Matters*?[21] Not very much. These books are life-changing, and can really help impact corporate strategy and hopefully help better the situation on the ground for the people whose stories they tell. I think of my book as a simple nudge. I wrote it with exactly this hope—that it gets read, and leads to change.

~

I am not a business historian. I am not a diversity consultant. I am not an expert. I am writing this from the position of a participant-observer—someone who cares about LGBTQ issues, is queer himself and wants to create a more equal world.

But first, for the straight people reading this book, in case you are worried, reading about LGBTQ issues and trying to make your organisation diverse will not make you LGBTQ. It doesn't happen that way, darlings. If you are straight, you will remain straight. Chill!

Jokes aside, there are some obvious limitations that I want to talk about upfront. I am aware that the changes I write about in this book are taking place in many contradictory Indias. The sociologist Dipankar Gupta uses the term 'mistaken modernity'[22] to refer to India's post-economic reform growth, which has placed a lot of emphasis on technology and consumption, but not on true liberty or pluralistic attitudes. I try and address this where I can, but mostly, it is a given. We are indeed living within a mistaken modernity; all I can do is identify some windows of hope and possibility that can be opened up to let the sunlight in.

The first limitation of this book is the representation of a large number of men. Patriarchy is hegemonic in the corporate world as well. Even in the space of diversity, and LGBTQ diversity in particular, there are more men than women, and mostly cis, not trans. Most people organising conferences are men, most people heading the employee resource groups (ERGs) in corporate India are men, and so on. I have looked and looked and tried to put in the voices of as many women as I could find—and this includes trans women—but it is still not an equal representation.

Secondly, this book is not a comprehensive account—either of the history of the LGBTQ movement or of the actions on the ground. There is simply too much happening to pack it all in. Instead, it offers thin slices, selective fragments, interspersed with my own journey. It is not the definitive workplace LGBTQ book; it is merely one workplace LGBTQ book, which focuses primarily on corporate workplaces and is not representative of all workplaces in the country. Within this selective focus, the book highlights certain parts of the country—cities like Mumbai, Delhi and Bengaluru—where a lot of the action around LGBTQ corporate inclusion is taking place.

Thirdly, this book only focuses on inclusion for LGBTQ people. While I am rooted in intersectionality and firmly believe that inclusion should have a wide range of dimensions—religion, caste, class, geographical location, language, age, disabilities and so on—here, my focus is exclusively on LGBTQ inclusion efforts, and that too, within the corporate world.

Fourthly, this book doesn't meaningfully address or examine the various dissonances within the queer movement. For instance, Akshay Pathak writes in *Round Table India* about how caste supremacy of mainstream Indian society gets replicated within the queer movement too: 'The same caste supremacy gets reflected in the preferred caste names—Iyer, Bhan, Gopalan, Tripathi, Nair, Menon, Bandhopadhay, Row, etc.,—and faces on Brahmanical media—be it TV debates or newspaper columns—on LGBT issues. How does one talk about caste in queer spaces?'[23]

Kiruba Munusamy, an advocate and the founder of Legal Initiative for Equality, echoed Akshay at a Culture Lab discussion during the Mumbai Pride Month—January 2019—around what it means to be dalit and queer in India. 'There is a misconception around the LGBTQ community that they are casteless, i.e., their community is without caste. That's not true.' Kiruba, who, as a distinguished lawyer, has fought cases of various trans people, told us how shocked she was to see caste barriers within the community. 'When a transgender person comes from a dominant caste in a village, they are celebrated, compared to those from the lower caste.'[24]

Grace Banu, activist and India's first trans engineer, added at the same event, 'There are mainstream platforms like the judiciary, education and employment. We are equally skilled and qualified too, but the caste system makes it difficult for us to access these avenues.' Dhiren Borisa, activist, poet and urban sexual geographer, expressed some optimism. 'I see queerness as aspirational, something that can open [up] the possibility of change.' However, the ridiculous audience questions after this panel really deflated my spirits. I couldn't believe some of the casteist rubbish that so many queer audience members thought was okay to spout out loudly, and our panel was frustrated too.

I recognise that the queer movement in India is as deeply fractured as other movements for social justice. Even while I touch upon topics like casteism, patriarchy in the queer movement or transphobia in feminist spaces in subsequent chapters, this book is not an exploration of these fractures in any meaningful way.

My position is very clear: to create an ideal world tomorrow, intersectionality is key. It is in the movement's interest to ensure that all voices are heard and that change is imagined and then actualised for all members of the movement, and not just its privileged elites.

Now, in this ideal world, the human rights paradigm would be enough to bring about change. However, we aren't there yet. So, hybrid people like me, corporate-activists who are pushing for change, have to use other strategies—profitability, innovation and so on—to make a business case for inclusion. How do we translate the language of human rights into these different and largely heterosexual corporate spaces? How do we help mostly straight business people see the range of queer experiences, and help the general public re-imagine what it means to be LGBTQ? This book is one attempt in this direction. I recognise that the relationship between company executives—the intended readers of this book—and the wide range of us LGBTQ citizens—who will be the beneficiaries of their inclusive policies—is structurally unequal. As a translator straddling these worlds, I am consciously engaging with these terms of inequality, in the hope that some good might come out of it.

Do I personally feel I need to make a business case for something that should be pretty damn obvious? Nope. Why have I chosen to argue along these lines, then? Because this is the language that many from the business world understand, and I am happy to speak it if it will mean more jobs and a better life for my LGBTQ brothers and sisters. As of now, I am happy to push corporate India, within which I sit and conduct my jugaad resistance—out of enlightened self-interest—to create windows of opportunity through my 'transactions', such as this book. ('Transactions' are what the queer historian Anjali Arondekar calls the 'necessary narratives traded for one more day of life'.[25] We all engage in them. Yes, you too. Think about it.)

Will I also be part of projects to create new languages and new frameworks? Certainly. But till then, in the here and now, I offer you this book which wants to create an ideal world, but is firmly rooted in the world we live in, with all its flaws and biases. It doesn't have all the answers. It hopes to start a conversation.

2

Cultural Acupuncture
My Godrej Journey

April 2017. I was on stage with the transgender activist Gauri Sawant, who shot to fame for featuring in an advertisement based on her life for Procter & Gamble's Vicks.[1] The ad was first aired during *Kaun Banega Crorepati* hosted by Bollywood superstar Amitabh Bachchan. The video raced to ten million views online and made Gauri a recognisable face. 'Yesterday, I went to the market to get some ginger, a random passer-by recognised me and clicked a selfie,' she said on stage, laughing.

Gauri is a force of nature. She runs the Sakhi Char Chowghi and Sai Sawali foundations for transgender welfare. One of their ambition projects is Aajicha Ghar—a home in which elderly trans people can live together with the girl children of commercial sex workers—and Gauri has been actively fundraising for it to come up in Karjat, a small town on the outskirts of Mumbai. She was one of the key petitioners in the Supreme Court in 2014 for the case that led to the landmark NALSA judgement which affirmed the rights of trans people in India.

'When Gayatri came into my life, she was just five years old,' Gauri said, referring to her adopted daughter. 'Gayatri's mother was HIV positive and passed away after she was born. At age five, her extended family members had taken the decision to sell her. Obviously, I had to intervene and rescue her. What would you have done had you been in my place?'

The Vicks video, part of their #TouchofCare campaign in India, is shot sensitively by Neeraj Ghaywan, the award-winning director of the film *Masaan* and Netflix's *Sacred Games 2* mini-series. In the video, the actor playing Gayatri tells us about how bad she feels that society does not treat her mother well because she is a trans woman. 'When I grow up, I will not be a doctor, but a lawyer, so that I can fight for equal rights for my mother.'

'You can't put anyone in a box,' Gauri told me on stage. 'Love makes you a mother and anyone can be a mother. A lesbian, bisexual, transgender or gay man can also be a mother. Motherhood is a behaviour.'

There wasn't a dry eye in the house.

Welcome to Godrej, the company where interactions such as these are perfectly normal. Gauri was on stage with me at the Godrej Leadership Forum of 2017—the annual meeting of 120 senior leaders from across the world at the Mumbai headquarters of the pedigreed Godrej group, where I work as vice president. The name 'Godrej' itself is synonymous with modern India, and we have made iconic products such as cupboards, locks, typewriters, hair colour, soaps and more over the decades. As one of our recent ads goes, we were 'making in India' before it became a tagline; in fact, we have helped in 'making India'.[2]

But the Godrej of today is not your grandfather's sepia-toned postcard from the past. Our forum is held in the slick, all-white, marble-clad central atrium of Godrej One. Sunlight streams in from skylights that are twelve storeys above us. New Haven–based architect Rafael Pelli designed this building to shock and awe everyone who walks in. You could easily shoot another *Blade Runner* reboot here, with the seemingly endless expanse of stacked glass and suspended bridges soaring over us. The architecture of the building reflects the aspirations of our company—we are super focused on preparing for the future.

I serve as the annual Godrej Leadership Forum's chief curator. I spend pretty much all year bringing together some of the brightest minds from across the world to speak to senior leaders at the gathering. Nobel Prize winners like Kailash Satyarthi, the chairman of HDFC bank Deepak Parekh, and authors like Amitav Ghosh and Mona Eltahawy have spoken at the forum. I make sure I queer up each forum, by inviting friends like Gauri Sawant on stage. Interestingly, there is no resistance from the leaders. Rather, there is anticipation of who I might bring next.

So how did a company that is more than 120 years old become this open to possibilities?

~

In the previous chapter, I introduced the work I do by using the term 'jugaad resistance' and wrote that there were two elements to it—infiltration and cultural acupuncture. I told you briefly about how I had infiltrated the corporate world to bring about change; now let me tell you a little bit about cultural acupuncture.

I am borrowing this term from the Harry Potter Alliance, which is a network of around 100,000 fans of J.K. Rowling's famous book series.[3] The Alliance maps the fictional content of the Harry Potter world on to real-world concerns, such as human rights in Africa, marriage equality, labour rights and net neutrality, and encourages its members to speak out about these contemporary issues. By tapping into the connections fostered in the Harry Potter fandom, they have been able to mobilise their skills towards a new form of youth activism, which inspires all those who have been impacted by the Harry Potter series to participate in it.

Here is how the group's founder, Andrew Slack, describes what cultural acupuncture stands for, in an article in *HuffPost* in 2010:

> Cultural acupuncture is finding where the psychological energy is in the culture, and moving that energy towards creating a healthier world. … We activists may not have the same money as Nike and McDonald's but we have a message that actually means something. … With cultural acupuncture, we will usher in an era of activism that is fun, imaginative, and sexy, yet truly effective.[4]

Let me give you the example of their 2016 campaign, Protego!, to explain the idea of cultural acupuncture more clearly. If you have read the books (and who hasn't!), you will recognise that the wizarding world of Harry Potter tackles a range of issues which we see playing out in our lives—discrimination on the lines of blood into categories of half-blood, pure-blood and muggle; media propaganda as shown through the misreporting in the *Daily Prophet*; incompetency of the increasingly fascist Ministry of Magic—all of which gets challenged by the consolidated power of the students of Hogwarts, who then collectivise into 'Dumbledore's Army' created by Harry.[5]

'Protego' is a shield charm used in the wizarding world to cast an invisible shield that reflects spells and blocks physical entities. Inspired by this, the Harry Potter Alliance started Protego! with the aim of producing resources and creating safe spaces for trans people at the individual, community and policy level. One of the things that the Alliance worked on as part of the campaign was pairing up with the open source project Refuge Restroom for their project Restroom Revelio, encouraging fan activists to plot trans and disability-friendly restrooms, creating a 'Marauder's Map' of safe restrooms.[6]

Performing this kind of civic activism through the infrastructure and skills of fandom is what cultural acupuncture is.

I first heard of this term from my MIT professor Henry Jenkins, now at the University of Southern California, when he visited Mumbai in 2016 on my invitation for a Godrej lecture series. Henry spent the previous decade studying how young activists from around the world were using social media platforms, spreadable videos and memes, and the language of popular culture to bring about civic and political change by 'any media necessary', which incidentally is the title of a recent book of his.[7] I was reminded of Henry's research again when Hong Kong erupted in the summer of 2019. Hong Kong's youth activists appropriated a range of pop culture properties, from *Star Wars* posters to Bruce Lee's karate mantra, 'Be water', to organise and distribute material for their protests.[8]

Within this book, I would like to repurpose the understanding of the term 'cultural acupuncture' to include the smorgasbord of different cultural experiments I have been conducting at Godrej and through Godrej, for which I use whatever resources I can access—corporate funding, physical space, the influence I have, the press attention I can attract, and more—to bring about the attitudinal change I desire.

I conduct two types of cultural acupuncture from my vantage point at Godrej. The first is *within* Godrej, and this includes queering events such as the Godrej Leadership Forum, speaking about queer issues at HR campaigns to recruit students from MBA colleges, helping change Godrej's HR policies and hosting queer events on our campus through the Culture Lab. The second is cultural acupuncture *outside* Godrej, and it comprises ecosystem building, amplification, coalition forming and resource creation. I push Godrej to partner with other companies and organisations like the United Nations, sponsor external LGBTQ cultural events and take part in LGBTQ job fairs and external forums, so that we can collectively form a larger community of change-makers.

Cultural Acupuncture Inside Godrej

While I was working at Mahindra, even though I had just written *Gay Bombay*, I was satisfied with the special treatment I received from my bosses, and didn't think it was important to stand up and ask for organisation-wide inclusion.

Something changed when I moved to Godrej. Maybe I grew in confidence and also became aware of my privilege. I asked myself: What is the point of selfishly demanding special rights when the rest of my community members don't have them? I realised that any benefits I wanted for myself had to be institutionalised at a policy level for all other employees too.

The process of how I joined Godrej is interesting. I had left Mahindra to pursue a PhD in communications at the University of Pennsylvania in 2009. At around the same time, I was selected as a fellow for TED India, and the event took place in the Infosys campus in Mysore. Back then, TED was not the ubiquitous global juggernaut it is now. Attending TED and listening to the mash-up of speakers and performers inspired me to wonder if I might be able to bring together in a more formal way the amazing dialogues going on in India in the creative, not-for-profit and business sectors. To me, these sectors were all addressing common enquiries of what it means to be Indian, but they were doing so in silos. What if we broke down the disciplinary barriers?

This epiphany led me to quit my PhD programme. I just knew that I wanted to create something TED-like, but completely India-focused, and for this, I needed to spread my net wide and not dig deep, and a PhD programme is essentially the latter. So I packed up my saamaan for the second time from the US—my second *Swades* journey back home, if you please—and started talking to different people about my vague idea, which I called the India Culture Lab.

My previous connections were a big help. The venture capitalist Sandeep Murthy, whom I had met while at Mahindra and who now runs Lightbox, one of India's biggest venture funds, connected me to Nisaba Godrej. 'Both of you are slightly nuts,' he told me. 'You might hit it off.'

We sure did! What was meant to be a half-hour coffee meeting turned out to be a full day of hanging out. We ate berry pulao at Britannia, the legendary Iranian cafe at Ballard Estate, and went for a walk on Marine Drive. We talked and talked—about design, our ideas to change the world, my being gay, and more. At the end of the day, Nisa asked, 'I don't know about the Culture Lab idea, but I like you. Do you want to work for Godrej?' I replied that I would, but only if she helped fund the India Culture Lab idea. She agreed, and I joined Godrej on 9 August 2010.

I reported to Nisa after joining. She is now the chairperson of Godrej Consumer Products Limited, but at that time, she was overseeing HR for the entire group. Some months into the job, I went up to her and asked her what the specific HR policies for LGBTQ employees were at Godrej. She said she didn't know. She called Sumit Mitra, the HR head for the group, and when we looked up the Godrej anti-discrimination policy, we realised that there was no mention of sexuality or gender expression in it.

I said that this was not good, that I didn't like this. Nisa and Sumit agreed, and asked me to suggest changes. I immediately called a friend working at a progressive tech company in Bengaluru, to ask if they had a non-discrimination policy pertaining to LGBTQ employees that I could use. They emailed it to me, and using it as a template, we changed our Godrej policy by the end of that working day.

This is how the policy reads now—feel free to copy paste it for your own organisation:

Diversity and Equal Opportunities

> We value diversity within the Godrej Group and are committed to offering equal opportunities in employment. We will not discriminate against any team member or applicant for employment on the basis of nationality, race, colour, religion, caste, gender, gender identity/expression, sexual orientation, disability, social origin and status, indigenous status, political opinion, age, marital status or any other personal characteristic or status.[9]

You see? Sometimes history is made quietly, by simply updating a word document on a corporate server. In the course of just one day, Godrej's journey towards inclusion had begun.

Over the years, we have accomplished a lot on the policy front at Godrej. From starting with this basic statement on non-discrimination to paying for a same-sex partner's health insurance, from replacing the word 'spouse' with 'partner' across communication and documents to having a gender-neutral adoption policy—the changes have happened slowly and steadily. Most of these changes took place in an India in which Section 377 was back in the books, courtesy the Supreme Court decision of 2013.

~

Vivek Gambhir, managing director of Godrej Consumer Products Limited, sent out a long email to all Godrej employees in October 2018:

> On September 6, in a landmark judgment that many of us had long awaited, the Supreme Court of India scrapped Section 377 of the Indian Penal

Code that criminalized homosexuality. 'History owes an apology', as Justice Malhotra so aptly summed it up. People across India celebrated the judgment. However, this is just a start. We still have a very long way to go before we can truly become the inclusive, equal nation that we hope to become. [...]

We have enough catching up to do, so don't wait any longer. Make the change; start now. The real measure of how committed you are, is to take action. Where are the plans and measures, just like for every other business priority? We have a Diversity Council at Godrej, with our senior-most business and HR heads as leads. The Council meets every quarter to define and discuss progress against all our diversity goals. We realize that while we have started, there is a lot that we need to do.

We owe it to our legacy, to lead Godrej into a more inspiring and inclusive tomorrow. We will experiment and make our fair share of mistakes along the way. However, that should not stop us from laying the foundations for tomorrow, making the necessary investments, gearing up and taking the tough calls. We have to ensure that history doesn't repeat itself, so history won't owe an apology again.

I cannot emphasise enough just how important it is for senior leaders to lead inclusion initiatives. When a family member of a family-owned enterprise or a CEO or an MD like Vivek visibly commits to inclusion, the ripple effects are felt throughout the organisation.

At Godrej, all our senior leaders support LGBTQ inclusion. Balram Singh Yadav, the managing director of Godrej Agrovet; Shefali Kohli, the head of Diversity; Sujit Patil, the head of Corporate Communication; and Godrej family members like Nadir Godrej and Pirojsha Godrej have all spoken up for LGBTQ rights over the years, but the number one LGBTQ champion by far has been my boss, Nisa. From the very first policy change, Nisa has explicitly committed herself to inclusion, and demonstrated this commitment through both words and deeds.

Here is an email that she sent to all Godrej employees on 17 May 2015, the International Day Against Homophobia, Transphobia and Biphobia, commonly known as IDAHOBIT, which has been observed since 2014 to draw the attention of policymakers, influencers, social movements, the media and the general public to the discrimination faced by LGBTQ people across the world:[10]

Dear Godrejites,

At Godrej, we strongly believe that each one of us is unique and we can only truly flourish when we can be our 'whole self' at work. As an organisation that deeply values diversity and inclusion, I would be proud of us if we create a culture where our LGBT colleagues can be comfortable being 'out' at work and every single one of us is inclusive and respectful of it.

There is no place for prejudice at Godrej, only space for open minds and hearts. Please feel free to reach out to me personally if you ever need my support in this regard.

Warmly,
Nisa

On 7 September 2018, one day after the Supreme Court read down 377, Nisa posted a powerful message along with a video on Godrej's LinkedIn page. The video featured two gay men and one trans person—all of whom worked at Godrej—talking about how the company's LGBTQ policies were helping them bring their 'whole selves' to work. Here is the message Nisa wrote:

'Where the mind is without fear and the head is held high [...] Into that heaven of freedom, my Father, let my country awake.'

—Rabindranath Tagore

Yesterday was a glorious, rainbow-filled awakening for India, justice and civil rights. I feel so proud and hopeful for my country and grateful to our Honourable Supreme Court for taking the only decision it should take. A shout out of congratulations to all our #LGBTQI brothers and sisters.

Yesterday was a day of rejoicing. Today, we have to roll up our sleeves and march on as there is much work still to be done. Corporate India can play a large role in making sure there is equality and inclusivity in the workplace and be a real role model for other stake holders in the system.

While we at Godrej have same-sex partner benefits, gender neutral adoption leave and an equal opportunity policy, we don't yet offer insurance for gender affirmation surgery and are in the midst of researching Transgender inclusion at the workplace. My hope for Godrej is that we can be a real force for good for our LGBTQI colleagues and community. Not just because it is the right thing to do but because talent is determined by our individual drive, skill and tenacity, not by sexuality, race or gender. And organizations that get the best talent and let them be their 'whole selves' will always win.[11]

A few months later in January 2019, our Corporate HR team sent out a simple email to all the employees announcing the landmark 'Godrej Gender Affirmation Policy'. It stated that employees wanting to undergo gender transition could claim up to ₹500,000 as one-time reimbursement for non-cosmetic surgeries and ₹60,000 per annum for hormone replacement therapy. Within a few minutes, a screenshot of this email went viral on WhatsApp and was shared across other corporate business groups as well as student groups in the country. We were not the first company to have such a policy. But the fact that it was Godrej created a sensation.

A month later, Godrej announced the creation of two all-gender washrooms at our Godrej One headquarters in Mumbai. Later that week, at our annual group HR conclave themed on the future of work, I went on stage with Madhumitha Venkataraman, who used to head Diversity at Coca Cola in India, and Anubhuti Banerjee of Tata Steel, to discuss how Godrej could be more LGBTQ inclusive and to coax all the HR managers present into doing more in this regard.

By June 2019, Godrej's diversity and inclusion (D&I) team, led by Shefali, had kick-started Project Rainbow—to specifically attract LGBTQ talent to the company—by taking part in the two back-to-back LGBTQ job fairs that took place in Bengaluru and Mumbai.

~

My job at Godrej affords me the ability to create a queer ecosystem where the people I work with—right from the chairperson who changes policies at the mere mention of a lacunae, to top-level management and mid-level employees and support staff—have warmed up to the idea of queerness. It is an incredible feeling to be loved and welcomed for who you are at your workplace. I don't know if you have ever felt this kind of acceptance, but I can tell you that it empowered me to be my best, and made me loyal and devoted to the company for life.

Every year, we host an annual Godrej Awards function. The spouses and partners of all senior executives receive a personal handwritten invite from Nisa to attend this grand evening of celebration. How do you think my partner feels when he receives the envelope and sees his name there? How do you think I feel when I see him smile on reading the note inside? The warm afterglow of not only being recognised and respected but also having your same-sex partner be recognised and respected as well is quite indescribable.

Post the Godrej Awards at Mumbai's Sahara Star Hotel in April 2019, singer Daler Mehndi and his troupe made us wish we had packed sunglasses, because there was just too much bling! The strobe lights on stage, the LED lighting all around and the gold on the costumes were a lot. (Just imagine, *hanh*, if a bling lover like me is complaining about too much gold, it must have been really over the top!)

On a giant screen that wrapped around Daler and his back-up singers and dancers on stage were live visuals of the crowd dancing, very much like how the camera zooms in on spectators during an IPL match. Daler was in his element—engaging in call-and-response games with us. He shouted out '*Bolo*!' and we all shouted back loudly, '*Ta ra ra ra*!'

Now imagine my partner and me dancing together wildly alongside senior Godrej leaders like Nisa, her sister Tanya Dubash, their uncle Nadir Godrej and aunt Rati Godrej, as well as CEOs of other companies and their partners. Now imagine this wild dancing scene being beamed on that giant screen. Just think of the 1,000 or so Godrejites in that ballroom, recognising just how casually and comfortably Godrej's senior leaders were including and welcoming a gay couple in their midst. *Tunak tunak tun*? You bet!

Most people in our country haven't even imagined a gay couple, let alone seen one. To see a confident and proud gay couple being made to feel welcome by a company's senior-most leaders is a life-changing experience. This is the kind of Godrej we are creating together, not only in policies and words but also in our actions.

Evenings like these are one of the major reasons for why I haven't left Godrej. I complete a decade in this organisation in 2020. Why would I leave? In 2018, I was offered 2.5 times my salary by one of the biggest tech companies in the world, but what is the premium for respect?

~

Even with the super supportive Nisa and other senior leaders, I don't believe that our success on the LGBTQ front at Godrej would have been possible without the presence of the India Culture Lab.

After I joined Godrej in 2010, I began to develop a structure to enable cross-pollination of ideas. While doing so, I reflected on my own diverse interests and roles in the past, and how they had informed each other in an organic way. The model of the lab emerged from C3, the think tank I managed between 2004 and 2006 at MIT. C3 brought together corporations like Yahoo, Turner, Petrobras, MTV Networks and Fidelity to pool their resources together and fund conferences, workshops, specific kinds of academic research and open-ended conversations at MIT on the theme of media convergence.

However, despite Godrej's involvement and support, and my persistent efforts to court other sponsors over the first year, we could not find willing partners to form a consortium, as we had hoped. We had to take a call—was the Culture Lab a bad idea or was it too far ahead of its time? Thankfully, Nisa took a leap of faith and committed Godrej to funding the lab entirely, and well, the rest is our story!

Freed from the need to constantly fundraise and with a small but decent enough budget for our operations, the lab, set up in 2011, now does many different things—all of which we hope brings about a certain kind of change in the mindset of the people who engage with us. Even though we are funded completely by Godrej, we imagine ourselves as a public resource and not as a private entity, and operate independently within the Godrej set-up.

Our year-round programming focuses on marginality. What conversations are not happening about contemporary India? About identities? About multiple histories? About the environment? About urban-rural circularities? About education alternatives? About dissent frameworks within a democracy? We try and work at the intersection of these issues by curating public events across different formats at the Godrej campus in Vikhroli. Some are talks and lectures while others are performances or even pop-up museums, like the one we built around the issue of migration in June 2019.

When we started the lab, some people expressed doubts: Who would be interested in such serious programming, and that too in Vikhroli, a suburb in Mumbai? We have been happy to prove our naysayers wrong. Nine years since its inception, our lab is constantly courted as the first destination of choice for many cultural interventions in the city. Our Vikhroli location is actually an advantage because we can draw huge crowds to our events—an audience base we have lovingly built over the years. So we are breaking the idea of centre-periphery even with our location, and our programming is, of course, all about marginality and intersectionality.

Parallel to our public events, we run a small two-part educational programme that aims to tap into students at the undergraduate and graduate levels across India and outside. We run a leadership training programme for humanities students in Mumbai and also offer fellowships to humanities students from across India and other countries.

We have gradually become interested in map-making and resource-building for the wider public. We have made a map of 200 cultural institutions across Mumbai, and we often either connect cultural practitioners from across the country to see how we might all be able to collaborate better, or are part of such efforts by others.

Through our programming, map-making and educational outreach, I think we are creating an example of how someone can sit in between different worlds and create value. I firmly believe that hyphenation and translation are going to be key elements of the world of tomorrow—theory and practice and the flow in between, the liminal spaces of what Homi Bhabha called hybridity.[12] Perhaps these are going to be the spaces where solutions to some of our country's most vexing issues will come from. Our lab is one such liminal space and we hope to continue our efforts to impact the intellectual landscape of India, in many small ways, over many more years to come.

Our lab has deeply impacted the mother ship—our sponsor, Godrej. With all the Godrej staff invited to the calendar of events, the HR department involved in the running of the lab, the in-house design teams working in close proximity with us, and my involvement with some of the Godrej group's larger strategies for innovation, we have helped create a certain kind of work atmosphere which encourages new ideas and opportunities.

One of our lab's biggest successes has been in creating a conducive environment for the message of LGBTQ inclusion to spread deep within Godrej. The key driver here has been our sustained LGBTQ programming.

In 2012, we hosted one of the very first performances of *Ek Madhav Baug*—a pioneering one-act play by the late Chetan Datar. The play is performed from the point of view of a mother who discovers that her son is gay, and through his diary, she relives his journey of discovering his sexuality. Originally written in Marathi, it was enacted at our lab by the thespian Mona Ambegaonkar in Hindi, followed by a discussion with the actor and CEO of Humsafar Trust, Vivek Anand. It was the first time that anything queer was happening on the Godrej campus, and almost every person in the audience had tears in their eyes by the end of it. Usha Iyer, my colleague, came to me right after, wiping her eyes. 'I'm going to go home and hug my daughter right away. Whatever she is, straight, lesbian, anything, I just want her to be happy!'

Ek Madhav Baug's success opened the floodgates. Here are just a few highlights of the LGBTQ programming at our lab over the years.

In 2015, we presented the first-ever public performance by the transgender people–led Dancing Queens troupe. We hosted the Queens in a collaborative multimedia performance curated by our lab's very own Fulbright scholar-in-residence that year, Jeff Roy; the performance wove together the troupe's dances and Roy's short films. Jeff did something else that was interesting.

He filmed this historic performance and the making of it, and released the subsequent video as a documentary, in which our lab was listed as a co-producer.[13] Over the years, this documentary has been screened at festivals all over the world.

The same year, we also hosted the winner of the Mr Gay India 2014 title, the brilliant Sushant Divgikar, for his first Culture Lab performance. He has come back many times since. That year, he was fresh off his *Big Boss* reality TV show experience, and was yet to become Rani KoHEnur, India's leading drag star, and was yet to get his second wind of television success with the popular TV show *Sa Re Ga Ma*. Back then, he was just our good old Sushie.

We presented three exciting events for Pride Month in January 2018, which explored youth culture within the Indian LGBTQ movement—how it was pushing beyond the boundaries of activism and configuring new ways of expressing and celebrating queerness through fashion, cinema, theatre and dance. The highlights were *Ehsaas*, a play from Delhi that focused on what it means to be a lesbian living in a heteronormative society, and *Queer Fashion Now*, a special fashion exhibit of garments by some of India's most exciting young designers.

Our Pride programming for the next year—the first Mumbai Pride after the Supreme Court judgement of 2018—focused on queer voices that we felt were being left out of the discourse, such as voices at the intersection of caste and sexuality and queer people from under-represented regions like the Northeast. We framed these under the rubric of 'Queeristan'—yes, that's where the title of this book came from! In 2020, our event 'Queering the Law' examined the future of queer activism in the country in a post-377 world.

Over the years, Godrej employees, along with the general public, have attended all these events and so many others like them at our Mumbai headquarters. Just think about it: being exposed to a wide range of perspectives over a decade expands minds and opens up hearts. Perhaps earlier, people at Godrej might have been conscious of attending something that was LGBTQ themed. Now, it is normal to do so, and we have loads of straight allies who come regularly for our queer programming.

~

Besides these events, which are open to the general public, our lab also intervenes directly to normalise conversations on LGBTQ issues specifically for the Godrej group. In May 2017, our lab marked IDAHOBIT by running a campaign on Workplace, the Facebook-powered social network that connects all Godrej employees. Our campaign was centred on what the word family—the theme of IDAHOBIT 2017—meant to Godrej employees.

Here is what Nyra D'Souza, the first trans employee at Godrej, wrote in that post, which accompanied a picture of her holding a rainbow flag:

> When I count my blessings I count my family twice. The first is where I was born and the second is Godrej where I work. Godrej for me is a place that values my talent above my gender orientation. The kind of space I have here and the friends I have made at work make me feel safe and happy, which is what family is to me.

Think of the impact of such a campaign on every Godrejite who logged on to their Workplace account that morning.

I believe that the secret sauce to my successful cultural acupuncture inside Godrej is a combination of things that have catalysed. If we'd had the policies and a strong leadership backing LGBTQ issues at Godrej but no Culture Lab, it wouldn't have worked. If we'd had the policies and the culture but no thrust from the leadership, it wouldn't have been so good either. It is the combination of these that makes a real and lasting difference.

Cultural Acupuncture Outside Godrej

Our lab does not programme only within Godrej. We often step outside as curatorial partners for festivals like the India Art Fair in Delhi or the Serendipity Festival in Goa. We have queered many of these festivals through our programming. For journalist Barkha Dutt's We the Women conferences in Mumbai and Bengaluru in 2018, we curated a panel on transgender empowerment and also featured the Aravani Art Project, a collective of transgender artists, who made a public installation using saris to spur conversations among attendees about transgender rights in India.

A lot of our lab collaborations take place in the digital domain. On the occasion of the World Human Rights Day on 10 December 2017, we collaborated with the United Nations Development Program (UNDP) for a Facebook Live chat, called 'Trans*forming Asia'.[14] It featured two of my trans friends, Gauri Sawant and Zainab Patel; the latter is now the head of Diversity at KPMG India. We chatted about the struggles and the way forward for trans inclusion in India. The video had 288,000 views at the time of writing this book, and I am sure it will cross 300,000 by the time you are reading this. For something that is a one-hour long serious discussion and not a cat video, this is gold.

Beyond the Culture Lab, my position as vice president at Godrej gives me a pulpit from which I can preach inclusion to other companies. I have done countless such talks over the years.

Along with individual companies, I have also been able to influence industry bodies. In September 2015, I addressed the Society for Human Resource Management about the importance of LGBTQ inclusion for HR managers. This was the first time that such a session was organised at one of their annual conferences. In February 2020, I was invited to speak at the Indian edition of the annual Great Place to Work conclave on the importance of diversity and inclusion for Indian companies. The Great Place to Work Institute assesses and recognises the best workplaces globally. They work with over 10,000 organisations across 58 countries. Their Indian arm works with 900 companies in the country, and many of these companies send their representatives to their annual conference. In December 2019, as a build-up to the conference, I was delighted to see a LinkedIn post by the CEO of the Indian wing of the company, Prasenjit Bhattacharya, in which he wrote about how 'normal' LGBTQ inclusion was for us at Godrej.[15]

At the October 2018 'Queering the Pitch' event in Delhi—organised under the aegis of the Keshav Suri Foundation and FICCI—the joint managing director of Apollo Hospitals, Sangita Reddy, committed to me on stage that she would push her company to hire more LGBTQ people. I have, since then, become a part of FICCI's inaugural advisory group on LGBTQ inclusion, and we help member companies with the resources they need for their own inclusion journeys.

A year later, in November 2019, FICCI opened up its Delhi headquarters to launch a landmark report—prepared by Open For Business, a coalition of leading global companies dedicated to LGBTQ inclusion, and the management consultancy Boston Consulting Group—titled *The New Global Champions.*[16] The report found that thirty-seven of the ninety-six fastest growing companies headquartered in emerging markets have policies specifically prohibiting discrimination against LGBTQ employees. These companies see no negative impact on their revenue or on their EBIT (earnings before interest and taxes) margins, even though many are headquartered in countries in which LGBTQ inclusion is a challenging cause to take on. Furthermore, these companies see a significantly higher proportion of revenue coming from international sources than the companies that do not protect against LGBTQ discrimination. This suggests that support for LGBTQ inclusion is a necessary factor for firms looking to expand globally. I was very proud to write the foreword for this report and even more proud that Godrej was one of the Indian companies they had made a case study of in this report, alongside other respected companies like Wipro.

Alongside FICCI, CII is one of India's most important business establishments—it is a community as well as a lobbying force with the government. In November 2018, I chaired a special session at CII's eighth National HR Conclave in Mumbai. I used the platform to expand on the benefits of diversity and inclusion to an audience comprising board members, CEOs, chief human resources officers (CHROs) and other C-level officers of India's biggest companies. It was the first time that the word 'LGBTQ' was being uttered on the CII platform. From the stage, I could see a sea of men in suits—CII attendees are predominantly male—and many of them had their jaws open at the start, but by the end of it, the session received a standing ovation.

I faced a similar, mostly male, mostly blue-suits audience when I addressed the Organisation of Pharmaceutical Producers of India in September 2019. Not all of these talks are easy to do, and I sometimes find it quite tedious to repeat myself or answer really basic questions. But what to do! Diversity line *mein yeh sab karna padta hai*!

At other times, doing these talks enables me to learn about the wonderful efforts of other companies, or hear about inspiring incidents, like in January 2020, when at a Condé Nast India D&I panel led by their managing director Alex Kuruvilla, my co-panellist Jerry Johnson from Reliance Industries told me that Mukesh Ambani, his company's chairman, had sent him a heartfelt text message of congratulations the day Section 377 was abolished in the country. This simple message had meant so much to Jerry, and it spurred him to work on inclusion efforts at Reliance.

Apart from using my position of influence, I have also facilitated Godrej's sponsoring of external LGBTQ programming. Godrej has consistently served as a co-sponsor of the Kashish Film Festival in Mumbai, and in 2019, we signed up as a sponsor for the Rainbow Literature Festival in Delhi. In 2016, I pushed Godrej Properties to sponsor a unique performance in Bengaluru: the much-decorated Carnatic music singer T.M. Krishna was collaborating with the talented Jogappas—members of a traditional transgender community from North Karnataka, who are associated with Goddess Yellamma—for an unconventional concert. It was a big hit.

Finally, I also use my Godrej position to talk about LGBTQ inclusion in colleges across India.

One of my strategies over the years has been to get as much press as I can for my work, and I use the press coverage as a lever to push for the change I desire. Each time I get invited to conferences like the one hosted by CII or the *Economist* magazine's Pride and Prejudice conference held in Hong Kong in March 2017 or the Bloomberg Equality Summit in Mumbai in October 2019, I make sure that the press knows about it and writes about my participation. I constantly speak up, whether on TV or on podcasts such as the *Canada in India* show, which I recorded with the Consul General of Canada in Mumbai, Annie Dubé.[17] I consider this media outreach a vital part of my outside-in strategy of changing perceptions at Godrej, as well as my inside-out strategy of sharing the work we do with a wider audience. I strongly believe that the media talking about Godrej as an inclusive company has convinced a lot of people within Godrej to act inclusive and has certainly helped in establishing Godrej as one of the early movers on the LGBTQ inclusion scene in India, opening the doors for other companies to follow.

I am sharing all this in the hope that you might be able to unlock your own mind. Pause for a moment. Think. What is *your* particular position? What is your sphere of influence? How can you make a difference, *wherever* you are located? How can *you* do some jugaad resistance?

Then, please, just do it.

I was sitting on a transparent plastic swing right outside our Culture Lab office at Godrej, welcoming the Hollywood star Ellen Page to India in the summer of 2016. She was jetlagged and smiling a lot. *X Men, Juno, Inception* ... and now Vikhroli. It was like the most normal thing in the world to be sitting next to her. Her friend Daniel was kind of cute, and I told him about how Grindr was rocking in Mumbai. There was a *Vice* media crew filming us all the time. This swing-wallah footage eventually opened the *Gaycation* Mumbai episode that Ellen and Daniel had flown to Mumbai to film.[18] Over the week, they played badminton with my lesbian friends from the online zine *Gaysi*, went to a Gay Bombay dance party, hung out with Rajat, a trans man, and his wife, Lakshmi, and also jammed with the 6 Pack Band, India's first transgender band. Towards the end of the episode, they visited Baba Ramdev at his headquarters, where he tried to assure them that homosexuality could be treated, as they looked on sceptically.

My eagerness to speak to the media has meant that we at Godrej are often the first port of call not only for the global media who want to cover LGBTQ issues in India but also for global collaborators and change-makers, like the UN.

I first met the UN team of Charles Radcliffe and Fabrice Houdart in New York in 2014 while I was doing my fellowship at Yale. My classmate Susana Edjang, who was working in the office of the then secretary general Ban Ki-moon, set us up. Charles was then the chief of Equality and Non-Discrimination at the office of the United Nations High Commissioner for Human Rights and also the director of the UN Free and Equal, a global multimedia campaign against homophobia and transphobia. Fabrice was then working alongside Charles, and before joining the UN, he had worked at the World Bank.

In June 2016, Charles and Fabrice, along with the wonderful Salil Tripathi of the London-based Institute for Human Rights and Business, flew down to Mumbai for a consultation with Godrej and other Indian companies. The three of them were deep in the midst of drafting the UN report *Tackling Discrimination Against Lesbian, Gay, Bi, Trans, and Intersex People: Standards of Conduct for Business* (henceforth *Standards of Conduct for Business*) that was to set down guidelines to protect the interests of LGBTQ people in the business world. Godrej proudly hosted the India consultation for this project.

Besides the UN goodwill ambassador and Bollywood star Celina Jaitly, and other prominent voices like Harish Iyer and the late Meera Sanyal from the Aam Aadmi Party, we also invited representatives from about thirty different Indian companies, but only about ten showed up. It was interesting that in 2016, besides Godrej, none of the other companies were even willing to publicly acknowledge that they were present at the consultation.

One year later, the UN team and Salil had concluded their global research, and their report was ready to be released. To our delight, they once again requested that Godrej be the venue for this important launch. These UN standards, very easy to comprehend—respecting rights, eliminating discrimination, supporting colleagues—would go on to have a huge impact worldwide.[19] Launches were planned in many major cities in the world—New York, London, Paris, Hong Kong—and with us in Mumbai.

This event, which took place on 12 October 2017, created history. For the first time in our country, there were about 100 business and HR leaders from leading companies like Hindustan Unilever, Procter & Gamble, Tata Sons, Accenture, SAP, Ikea, Intuit, Mahindra & Mahindra, Aditya Birla

Group, Nomura, Adidas, Deutsche Bank, Marico and many others gathered together in a room, asserting their support for LGBTQ rights. All these leaders unequivocally agreed that LGBTQ rights are human rights and that they would push for change in their respective organisations.

What a difference a year makes, I thought, after seeing the packed auditorium that day. A year ago, we had struggled to fill even half the room, but this time around we couldn't stop the RSVPs from coming in. Furthermore, all the companies in the room were perfectly happy announcing their presence to the media and didn't want us to be secretive about it. Change was definitely in the air, and I was proud that Godrej was at the centre of it. I was most touched that the Bollywood actor and director Farhan Akhtar took the time out to create a special video message in which he spoke about the importance of the UN's *Standards of Conduct for Business.*

~

After seeing the momentum at the launch of the UN report, I felt that it might be a good idea to work on something completely India focused. This is how the idea for writing Godrej's *A Manifesto for Trans Inclusion in the Indian Workplace* was born.[20] I started working on this white paper in June 2018, along with my Culture Lab teammate Nayanika Nambiar, as a guide for Indian companies, and we chose to highlight the transgender community because trans people tend to be neglected in the conversation on LGBTQ issues and also face much more severe discrimination and lack of opportunities than the others.

When the September 2018 Supreme Court verdict was announced, foreseeing a rush of interest among companies to be LGBTQ inclusive, we sped up our research and launched our trans manifesto on 13 December 2018 in the very same Godrej auditorium which saw the UN report's launch the previous year. This time, there were about 300 business leaders in the room from across different companies, and they were all keen to use the manifesto in their own workplaces.

The success and adoption of this manifesto once again made me realise the importance of coalition building and consensus building. I then decided, after taking Nisa's advice, that while I would continue pushing for change within Godrej, I would also use some of my time to help other companies on their inclusion journey. This book is a direct outcome of that decision.

3

Mumbai Meri Jaan

Circulatory Queerness

Does permanence matter, asked my friend Rahul Mehrotra at the TED conference held in April 2019 in Vancouver, which I attended as a senior TED fellow. Rahul, an architect, is the chair of the Harvard Graduate School of Design's Department of Urban Planning and Design. He spoke about the Kumbh Mela, and how he saw within it a clarion call that must inform the future architecture of humanity; the video got half a million views on the day it went up online.[1] Instead of building monumental towers which produce more waste, we must think of loose, light and disposable eco-friendly structures that can go back into the earth. Post Kumbh, the temporary city which would have housed a million people becomes mud and flows with the monsoon floods. Ashes to ashes, dust to dust.

The morning before his talk, we had celebrated my birthday at Scoozi's, a cute Italian breakfast diner, along with his wife and co-conspirator, Nondita. Our future structures, Rahul had posited to me over my breakfast pizza, must be impermanent, much like the impermanent culture that exists within them.

Think about it. Our culture is one that is constantly influenced, constantly contextualised. You can never wipe out anything; you always build on it. And when you build on something, it doesn't mean you should destroy what is below. My MIT guru Henry Jenkins informs this book as much as Rahul. I marry the auto-ethnography, the self-reflexivity that I learnt from Henry with Rahul's broader theories on the kinetic city, porosity and more.

The Urbz think-tank founders Rahul Srivastava and Matias Echanove propose the concept of 'circulatory urbanism', which they have developed over the years.[2] To them, thinking of urban versus rural India, or India versus Bharat, is deeply problematic. In fact, most of us Indians circulate between rurality and urbanity. Rural India is deeply influenced by technologies like the cell phone, and in urban India, we organise ourselves spatially as per village structures. For instance, in my partner's chawl in Mumbai's suburb of Borivali, his family members mimic the living structures in their village in rural Uttar Pradesh—their neighbours in Mumbai are the same as their neighbours from their native place. This ghettoisation is the same across most of the city, whether one lives in a formal settlement, like a building, or an informal one. Meanwhile, in my partner's native village, family members are completely obsessed with TikTok superstars from every corner of the country performing into their cell phones.

Taking off from circulatory urbanism, I would like to present the idea of 'circulatory queerness'. Just as urbanism is circulatory, I propose that the Indian queer identity is not formed due to the tension between global and local influences, but rather due to the constant flow between them. It is an Indian queerness that is here and now, and ever evolving.

In a sense, I build upon my first book, which was both deeply academic and deeply personal. This book too is based on the ideas that informed my first one, its articulated notions of Indianness and the global-local.

In *Gay Bombay*, I explored how this circulatory queerness led to a hybrid identity formation for English-speaking gay men in the city through the late 1990s and mid-2000s.[3] In this book, I find the same identity formation process taking place twenty years later within the corporate world across the country.

Context is everything in architecture, Rahul Mehrotra had told me in August 2018, when he had come to speak at our Culture Lab. I think of how his framework has deeper implications beyond the built landscape. In the rush to eagerly replicate other contexts, we fail to be able to convincingly articulate what our context is. This applies to architecture as much as it does to queerness. What does being an Indian queer person mean, as opposed to just being a queer person? When does Indian stop being an adjective, as opposed to an essential, hyphenated part of the word 'queer'?

In India, everything is inextricably tied to the idea of family and community, and maybe that is where we can locate the hyphenation. This Western post-enlightenment idea of the 'self' that needs to be found, that we need to be the best version of ourselves, that life is a journey of discovering and then polishing ourselves, is not so useful for us in India. Here, we are many selves, there is no one self, and each of our selves is conditional and contextual. And as we spend our lives navigating these multiple selves, it is important for workspaces to become crucibles of identity formation of some kind.

Circulatory queerness is not just about identity formation but also policy formation, and the workplace is an important site for both of these in India.

~

The way we imagine our LGBTQ-inclusive policies needs to be Indian, I told my audience of Franklin Templeton employees in their Mumbai office and the employees from their Gurgaon office being beamed in via video conference, in June 2019. Sanjay Sapre, the president of Franklin Templeton Investments India, had invited me to talk to his employees about what their company could do in terms of LGBTQ-friendly policies. In India, the workplace needs to function in loco parentis, as a custodian, I emphasised to them. This means that the company is the guardian and has to take care of employees in a way that helps them grow.

In most countries, one negotiates their identity at home and not at work. In our country, where the home itself is a space of identity erasure, the negotiation starts at the workplace. Just think, dear HR managers, who I hope are reading this book, who is your employee? Someone who has been writing exams their whole life. Maybe they did well in class ten, and then in class twelve. Pressure from their parents and peers may have forced them to sit for the Joint Entrance Examination (JEE). Whether they got into an IIT or not, they got in somewhere. Completed an engineering degree that they, like most others, would not have used. Then they sat for another set of exams to apply for their MBA. Again, whether they got into an Indian Institute of Management (IIM) or not, they got in somewhere. Finally, at some point in their mid-twenties, the lucky ones are working in corporate India, alongside you.

When these young employees come into your system, I told my Franklin Templeton audience, they are not fully developed. They know how to mug up, write exams and pass tests. They often sacrificed a lot in their quest to emerge from the narrow end of the funnel into your organisation, and this includes sacrificing thinking of things such as their own identity or what makes them happy or gives them purpose in their life. Your workspace needs to welcome them to explore their multiple selves. You need to reassure them that it is okay to be who they are here, that they can engage with the identities which they often tend to suppress at home. As a consequence, an Indian corporate structure, for an Indian LGBTQ person, must be a space for reconciliation.

Your policies need to be about caregiving, because you are supplementing broken infrastructures and an aching lack of information. Most often, you are the only support system available to help them develop their identities. I often see so many employees who are out as gay only at their office, but are closeted everywhere else. So, as an organisation, you have to be nurturing to compensate for the lack of nurture over the years from their families or their educational institutions. And you will have to be prepared.

Let us assume that you do have same-sex partner benefits as a policy. What do you do with an LGBTQ person who is not out at home, but who shares the insurance with their parents as well as their partner whom they are hiding from everyone except their company? Confidentiality becomes key here. You can't tell the parent that their child also has their partner insured. Or, when you hire transgender people and are paying for their gender reassignment surgery, you might also need to provide them a list of safe hospitals, since there are so many quacks out there. If your trans employee is unable to find a house to rent, you must have HR step in and help them. These are things you won't provide your cisgendered employees. Should queer employees in Indian companies be getting special treatment? Yes, we should, because our circumstances are different, the legacy of discrimination and hate is more violent. Sanjay nodded, understandingly. I hope Franklin Templeton will follow up on my talk with concrete action.

It was the month of June, Pride Month in the US, which companies like Franklin Templeton celebrate in India, even though Mumbai celebrates it in January. When I asked the 50 people in the room and the 150-odd people who had dialled in, how many of them identified as queer, there was silence. Sanjay responded that no one in the company was out 'officially'. But does this mean that there is no need for inclusive policies? You don't need people who have come out, to make the policy. You need to make the policy to enable people to come out.

I was told that the staircase at the entrance to their Hyderabad office was painted in the gulaal of the rainbow, and this made me happy because even this performative advocacy contains a seed for real change within. I think of the closeted employees who see this rainbow welcoming them to work, wondering if, finally, their workplace could be a site where they are welcomed, loved and validated.

~

On my way to this talk at the Franklin Templeton office in Lower Parel, my friend Durga had sent me a video on my phone of them getting beaten up. (Some people who are gender fluid or gender nonconforming prefer the pronoun 'they/them' instead of him or her. It's like the Hindi equivalent of 'aap'. Durga is one such person, so I will use 'they' and 'them' to describe their experiences.)

They were riding their bike through Goa when they stopped a man on a bike talking on his phone. The man harassed Durga, pushed them to a corner, flung their keys and touched their crotch. Durga slapped him in retaliation, he hit back violently and a passer-by recorded the incident on his cell phone. Subsequently, an FIR was filed, and the harasser was caught and put behind bars. When he encountered Durga in the police station, he proceeded to rub his genitals even with the policeman in the room, and threatened Durga that whenever he got out of jail, he would find them and rape them.

As I was watching Durga's video on my phone, four hijras swarmed my car at the signal, begging for money, clapping hands, banging doors, being persuasive and endearing by turns, recycling joy and pain. I did not have my wallet with me, so all the money my driver had on him was given, and all the blessings we needed were taken. They laughed loudly as they put their hands on my head through the car window.

Apni behen se paisa legi kya, I teased them and winked. Sisters only in name; we were all conscious of the wide gulf between our realities on either side of the rolled-down car window. How might my visit to a big company like Franklin Templeton change the material condition of their lives?

There are multiple narratives of India. In one, India is a country that is almost a global power. Its financial markets boom, it has rich people who build high towers, its educated workers buzz with energy, and while misery exists, economic progress is bound to ensure a better life for millions, soon enough. Mumbai is the crucible for this narrative. The maximumest city of dreams—come here and make your own destiny. India Shining. *Achhe Din*.

It is a flawed narrative. We residents know this, each time we encounter a builder, a politician, a policeman, a criminal or, worst of all, each other. Each time we spew out pothole-filled road rage or are at the receiving end of it, each time we dangle dangerously from the overworked trains, each time we look out of our windows and see the vast expanse of a garbage dump, or each time we read about a J. Dey or Narendra Dabholkar or Mohammed Akhlaq or Gauri Lankesh killed, only to forget about them. Each time we add a new word to the lexicon of injustice running in our heads, like Unnao or Kathua, we are reminded that this is a harsh country; not a melting pot of unity in diversity, but a cauldron of ferocity—fuelled not by ambition and the brotherhood of citizenry, but by cruelty, hatred and exploitation.

What remains? Pointlessness. Emptiness. A failed attempt at meaning making. Breaking up is really hard, whether with a person, a city or a country. So, finger gets entwined in finger. Stomach pushes against hipbone. Somewhere in this narrative, body parts are strewn across a slick bloodstained floor. But others continue to function. Limb is still attached to limb. It needs to be caressed. Touched. Loved.

On my way back from Lower Parel to Vikhroli, as I waited in the car at the Elphinstone Bridge signal for sixteen minutes without moving, I thought of how often I try to leave this city, and how I just can't. It keeps on drawing me back. Living in aamchi Mumbai is a rush, and the city's culture is my drug of choice.

~

> There is no turning back. You take the blue pill—the story ends, you wake up in your bed and believe whatever you want to believe. You take the red pill—you stay in Wonderland, and I show you how deep the rabbit hole goes. Remember: all I'm offering is the truth. Nothing more.
>
> —Morpheus to Neo, *The Matrix*[4]

I choose the red pill and fly like the pigeons my nani used to feed each evening on the balcony of her Colaba home, right until she died. Fly by leafy Laburnum Road's Mani Bhavan for a Gandhian tableau (For two? Yes please, thank you!), into the red-lit chaos of Falkland Road's old single-screen cinema houses like Alfred, where I salaam old Rahman bhai, the city's last original film hoarding painter. (Hint: He is the uncle crouching over that seven-by-five-foot canvas in the cave-like atelier behind the cinema, painting *Mughal-e-Azam* for me, from memory.)

I fly through the parks and gardens. The Port Trust Garden at Colaba Bus Station, for plant and people lovers of all ages, with its ocean-viewing galleries and cacti houses. The Hanging Gardens in Malabar Hill, where the Old Woman's Shoe evokes aching bouts of nostalgia. Maheshwari Udyan at King's Circle, where our city's famous virtue of accommodation comes alive on Sundays with picnicking families right next to cruising gay men searching for their own private Idaho. The Borivali National Park, the city's lung. My Vikhroli mangroves, now perhaps to have a bullet train slash through them.

'*Pardesi pardesi jaana nahin*
Mujhe chhod ke.'[5]

How can I leave? Where will I go?

Music and mayhem. In this city, beauty is everywhere. So is water. I don't drink it, or swim in it, but fly over it. Over the Chowpatty Beach during the Ganpati festival, where thousands of idols are immersed in the sea by millions of euphoric, chanting, dancing worshippers, and where the sea regularly throws back 1.5 million metric tonnes of garbage during a monsoon high tide. Revenge is the sweetest thing, and Amitav Ghosh will smile wistfully reading this. I fly over the Thane Creek. Over the sacred Banganga Tank. Across the sea to the candle-lit Elephanta Caves to listen to midnight music.

Hello darling, kiss, kiss. Why will you not go to Vakola, rickshaw-wallah? But it's raining! Fine, be like that.

I perch myself on a red BEST bus like a good Bombay crow. Caw caw. Let's start at the very beginning, a very good place to start. So I take Number 1 from the Colaba Bus Station, watch it weave in and out of Mohammed Ali Road, alight at Dadar, walk past the Shiv Sena Bhavan and eat a yummy kothambir vadi at Prakash, washed down with a thick saffrony piyush. Culture is not something to be consumed appointment-based in Mumbai. Every moment here is a cultural experience.

I fly into the flies hovering over the sugarcane juice that I really shouldn't have in the monsoons. Fly into the fly that a cruiser has opened in the corner stall at Churchgate's infamous cruising loo. Yes, there are people and they are watching. Put hand into his fly. Close eyes. Exhale.

'Come away with me, tonight.'[6]

I fly on, from one queer culture scene to another in Mumbai. New ones come up all the time. The QKnit parties. Salvation Star's upper-class soirees with only English music that I try and avoid because I really can't dance to anything other than Bollywood. Gaysi with its LBT parties. Gay Bombay's long-running mostly men-wallah night-outs. Maggi and board games at the queer-managed Guftagu Cafe at Mira Road. Queer kite flying. Queer finance workshops. Queer everything.

I fly into my mobile screen, swiping right on each of the new apps that come calling every few months. Blued. Delta App. Planet Romeo. Grindr. Scruff. Tinder. Private worlds and public cruising, crushed amidst others on trains and during festivals—a pleasurable release, before being enveloped once again by the warm embrace of crowded anonymity.

I wrap the city around me. It is my security blanket. Muse. Nemesis. Home. Mumbai, *meri jaan.*

~

Ashok Row Kavi, in his big black glasses, was next to me in the front row at the Kashish 2019 opening ceremony in Mumbai's Liberty Cinema. 'I used to be your mother, now I'm your sister, darling,' he told me. This is true. Amma never ages! We giggled and bitched about the jury, as the writer Hoshang Merchant was awarded the Rainbow Warrior award. 'Did you know this one is lesbian?' Ashok asked me about a jury member. 'Also, she really shouldn't be wearing that dress. It does nothing for her.'

Housed in a theatre whose architecture is the very embodiment of the performative, this festival served as a ready metaphor for the people present there that day. Influenced by both local and global design, Liberty Cinema is a vanguard for the modern as well as a love letter to the traditional, with its Burma teak, German sound systems and Indian marble—just like how the queer crowd that day oscillated between Beyoncé and Rekha Bhardwaj, RuPaul and Rani KoHEnur.

It was a night without design or structure. People walked in, walked out, performed, elicited euphoria, groans, sighs, impatience and longing, while wearing camp, couture saris, lehengas, dresses, corsages and multiple manifestations of the ubiquitous rainbow.

Being queer is not all about despair. There is also so much joy in our identities as queer persons. It is about holding these contradictions together in the mind, celebrating the flux, mourning the violence, pushing for change and being hopeful for a better tomorrow. I thought of 1861, when Victorian morality informed Section 377 of the Indian Penal Code. The British criminalised what they could not understand, and colonised our minds. Though the law itself did not persecute too many people, it served as what Foucault called the panopticon—the State oversees everything, including our private desires.[7] Homophobia seeped into our consciousness, and we began erasing ourselves and our desires.

But not that night. Not at Kashish.

Kashish is India's Met Gala, only more authentic, more lived in and less pretentious. My outfit that day included a pista-green silk-tissue trench coat, a Swarovski-encrusted headband, my grandmom's vintage art deco earrings, an upcycled white pin-tucked kurti worn over black-and-white shorts, and my trusted Gucci applique clutch. Very Gay Gatsby, *na*?

Sridhar Rangayan, the festival director, chatted with me on oxblood rexine sofas in the cinema's first-floor lobby. 'The main mission of Kashish is the mainstreaming of the LGBTQ community in art and cinema. We decided to make it a celebratory moment for the LGBTQ community, where they can see themselves represented on the big screen. And secondly, we wanted to create awareness among the LGBTQ audience about the community's issues through cinema and art.'

I had hosted Sridhar in Boston in 2006, when I screened his film *Yours Emotionally!*[8] at MIT. This was back when he was still a queer filmmaker and not the celebrated founder of Kashish.

The first Kashish in 2010 had taken place at the PVR Infinity Mall in Andheri, where the lines wound serpentine around the block. 'The idea back then was to place the festival in a mainstream space like a theatre,' recounted Sridhar. 'Earlier, there had been festivals held in colleges, but there was never a festival that had taken place in a mainstream space.'[9] As I look back on my Facebook timeline, I see that my hair back then was all black. Abhina Aher was a shy volunteer then, not the head of Dancing Queens. Zainab Patel was not yet Zainab Patel.

The times were different then. The Delhi High Court had just awarded us legitimacy and the air was hopeful. Over the next ten years, the law kept flip-flopping, but the queer stories kept on coming. In 2019, Kashish screened over 160 films, curated from over 700 submissions.

Kashish was where I met my partner, in 2016. We sat next to each other at an afternoon screening, and our arms touched. It was electrifying. I wondered if I was looking at an apparition or a human being; he was just so gorgeous. I was wearing a shawl, and I asked if he was feeling cold. He wasn't, but of course, he said he was. He knew how to flirt. So we shared the shawl, our hands slowly becoming one under the kantha-silk fabric.

At the 2019 opening, photographers papped us, as the Liberty Cinema dog slept peacefully on the red carpet. We simply circled around the nonchalant canine to get on to the stage. The fabrics kept flowing in and off the stage, the compères shone in their technicolour outfits and spoke with more gusto than was believable, and the white background with the names of sponsors and supporters foregrounded our beautiful faces caked with a mix of foundation, highlighter, glitter and an exclusive concoction of Bombay sweat and drizzle.

'Darling!' Dodo Bhujwala greeted me with plastic flowers enmeshed in his beard. Like Ashok, Dodo is ageless and timeless. We had played Rosencrantz and Guildenstern in Hima Devi's stage version of *Hamlet* that we rehearsed for diligently in 1995, but never performed. I had known then that Dodo was gay, but I had been too shy as a college student to share that I was too. Fabulously out of the closet now, I laughed with Dodo, recollecting those days. Liberty indeed.

~

A few months before the 2019 Kashish opening, Ashok and I had been in another front row, at Utsav—Humsafar Trust's annual talent show, usually held at the police grounds in Santacruz. That day, I walked past some fabulous pink, blue and orange rangoli on an astroturf green carpet, and scanned an array of pull-up vinyl displays, each of which had one initiative of Humsafar printed on it along with its tagline. I saw *Bombay Dost* ('Get your copy now'), Likho ('Awarding excellence in media'), Connect ('Connecting LGBTQ communities worldwide') and Yaariyan ('We don't need taglines'). The Humsafar Trust elders—Ashok, Suhail and Vivek—had just lit a giant brass diya on stage together, a ceremonial welcome to kick-start the four-hour-long event. Behind me was a sea of at least 600 people, screaming, yelling, dancing and catwalking on the sidelines. Everyone was dressed in feathers, saris and skimpy, sequined bikinis.

A Ganesha invocation started the proceedings on stage. In Mumbai, we invoke Ganpati at every instance we can. He is our presiding deity. Of course, what was being performed on stage was a Bollwood version—'Deva Shree Ganesha' from the film *Agneepath*. But instead of the bland, expressionless Hrithik Roshan, there were four exuberant, sinuous, bare-chested men, four gorgeous sari-wearing drag queens, eight saffron flags and sixteen hand-held lit diyas on stage.

One after the other, we were entertained by bodybuilding, fashion and dance performances. There was a Mr and Miss Humsafar beauty pageant done Miss India style, with different Indian and Western rounds, except that the Mr and Miss could be people identifying as any gender. Then the participants came back for the next round in pairs. The peshwa proposed to the begum, the baadshah got on his knees and hands and handed his khanjar to his rani, and a Khilji-and-Bajirao-themed gay couple kissed each other firmly on the lips.

Soon, the Dancing Queens were on stage. My favourite queen, M, was wearing a shiny sequined pink shirt and a neon-green bustier. M and I have our own routine. She looked for me in the audience as always, and when she saw me, she bit her lower lip and winked. M would have been in her early fifties. She has a day job in which she wears a shirt and trousers. She had introduced me to her college-going son after her performance at our Culture Lab. 'Are you proud of your dad?' I had asked the boy. 'Yes,' he had beamed. 'She dances wonderfully.' How many hidden lives we live in this city, I thought to myself as I bit my lip in response. M winked back.

'How do you feel?' I had once asked my partner, about being closeted at work and with his siblings and parents, while being completely out with me, my friends and family, and at my workplace. 'I feel like the superheroes Krrish and Shaktimaan,' he had replied. 'It's like, I put on a mask. But now I forget which is my real avatar and which is my masked avatar.'

The end of the Humsafar Utsav. The bodybuilders were getting the most hoots of the evening. Their coconut-oil-rubbed bodies were clad in the skimpiest of underwear. They were flexing their arms and baring their teeth in faux macho-ness, and we couldn't get enough of it. Each contestant was wearing a cardboard cut-out alphabet dangling from the waistband of his underwear. From A to K, I debated endlessly with the other judges, and we ended up calling three alphabets back on stage for one final round before we decided on the winner.

4

Some Thoughts on Privilege

Late afternoon, on a weekend in June 2019, a posse of people I have mentored—young, dynamic, beautiful, intelligent queers who have worked with me, now with wings flung across the city—were unwinding with me during a chai break. The 'Migration Museum', a pop-up event produced by the Culture Lab and which we were in the midst of, was a resounding success with more foot traffic than cars stuck on a Ghatkopar link road signal at five o'clock on a workday. Over chai, my team cackled in appreciation of my private performance of 'Fevicol Se'.

Who said liberation is only about loud speeches? As activists, we are not just fighting for dignity in the constitutional sense, but the right to be bitchy too. Amira Yahyaoui, my friend from Tunisia with whom I spent five months at the Yale World Fellows programme in 2014, told me something profound when I asked her what she had done first after returning to Tunisia during the political transition and the writing of the new constitution. Out of all the Arab Spring revolutions, the Tunisian Revolution was the only one that succeeded partially. She told me that she went out and bought red high-heeled shoes. They were fighting for many things, but also for the right to wear red stilettos.

In one of the panel discussions at the 'Migration Museum', the mike snaked through the thick, bulging audience of over 500, who were experiencing our Culture Lab–style bhelpuri of academia, art and flux. I chuckled as I decided who the mike would go to next: 'Fastest finger first,' I announced, in my best Bachchan baritone.

What is it about a space that makes you feel comfortable enough to dress, speak, joke, engage and disengage with ease? The right to have fun, to be funny, that too is what we fight for when we ask for safe spaces, and this is what we have tried to create at our Culture Lab.

Pavel Sagolsem, a queer activist, told us their story of being a migrant, escaping violence and living a throttled identity. In the next lecture, Chinmay Tumbe, academic extraordinaire from IIM Ahmedabad, told us that the mikes used by Gandhi to amplify the message of the Swadeshi movement were produced by Sindhi migrants who had formed a company called Chicago Radio—first in Karachi, and then in Bombay. Global-local, urban-rural, Indian-foreign, here-there … I thought to myself how it's the same with queerness and the same with policies that advocate for queer inclusion. There is a global narrative, there is a local context—you keep spinning, round and round. Circulatory queerness.

When Chinmay spoke of amplification, I remembered what trans rights activist Grace Banu had said at our 'Queeristan' event in this very auditorium a few months ago: 'We [marginalised folks] are ready to live a dignified life, but people who have privilege have occupied these spaces. When we get to speak on these platforms, we have to struggle a lot. In fact, we have to fight to access these spaces in the first place.'[1]

So what does one do with one's own privilege, someone in the audience asked. I kept going back to the question and to how Divya Kandukuri, another of our lab speakers from the 2019 'So Many Feminisms!' event, answered it. 'Intersectionality is the key, and solidarities should be built by passing on the mike. Use your social capital to amplify the voices that are not being heard.'[2]

~

Writing this book has been a journey of discovery, of self, of biases, of privilege. Nisa wrote an essay in 2015 on how she felt about winning what she called the ovarian lottery because of her Godrej lineage—'being lucky by birth and opportunity'.[3] Like a good MBA graduate, she pursued this feeling by making a list of questions she could then resolve:

- What is my purpose? What am I passionate about?
- Who are the people I need to learn from?
- What platform do I have to leverage?

She decided to commit to changing 'the educational outcomes for a million Indian girls',[4] and five years later, is well on her way to doing so, alongside running her companies profitably.

Someone who is around Nisa's age and also carries a family legacy, although very different from that of Nisa's, is my World Economic Forum's Young Global Leaders batchmate Sheetal Amte. You have to spend just two minutes with Sheetal to witness her magic. Her positivity and deep commitment to creating a better world are infectious. I got lucky—I spent an entire day with her, her brother Kaustubh Amte and their father Vikas Amte, when they visited us at Godrej in 2017.

Baba Amte—Sheetal and Kaustabh's legendary grandfather—lived many lives in one. The son of a landlord, he was a freedom fighter, sadhu and lawyer, and this was even before he discovered his true calling. One rainy evening, as he walked home after work, he stumbled upon a leprosy patient lying curled up in a gutter. After the initial revulsion, he decided to take care of the patient, but unfortunately the patient died. Baba Amte decided to dedicate the rest of his life to the treatment and rehabilitation of leprosy patients and other social outcasts.

He formed the Maharogi Sewa Samiti in Warora as a not-for-profit organisation in 1949 on barren land in Maharashtra's Chandrapur district, and started operations with six outcast leprosy patients, a lame cow, a capital of just ₹14 and endless optimism. The name chosen for the commune was Anandwan—the Forest of Joy.

Anandwan has touched more than two million lives since its inception. It is very difficult to quantify the success of this institution. The list of awards the institution and Baba Amte have won over the years gives a fair idea of their success—the Templeton Prize, the Gandhi Peace Prize and the Magsaysay Award, for instance—but they reveal very little. Here are some facts that might help understand the institution's impact. Today, the Anandwan campus is spread across 500 acres. There are 4,000 full-time residents. Most of Anandwan is green, all the kitchens are solar-powered, they use battery-operated vehicles and have a net carbon-negative economy. Anandwan includes the world's first therapeutic theatre, a school for the visually challenged, an old-age home, an orphanage, a centre for the hearing impaired, a dairy, a cycle manufacturing unit, a greeting card unit[5]... I could go on and on.

Then, there are the sister campuses. In 1973, Baba Amte set up the 50-acre Lok Biradari Prakalp campus—in Hemalkasa village in Maharashtra's Gadchiroli district—which houses a school, two hostels, a playground, a hospital, living quarters for patients, a dining hall, dormitories for visitors and a zoo. Somnath is another project that Baba Amte set up in 1967 for cured leprosy patients to practise agriculture. Spread over 1,300 acres in the forest of Tadoba, Somnath now grows all the grains and vegetables that are eaten at both Anandwan and Lok Biradari Prakalp.

All these are just data points. The true magic of Baba Amte and his legacy is one of hope and self-belief, of true transformation of the human potential. It is the legacy of how one can create leaders from the most marginalised people in society. Leprosy patients, the visually challenged, the hearing impaired and others help each other at Anandwan. In fact, they have now become trainers, teaching other so-called 'normal' people in society. Anandwan engineers have helped build post-earthquake housing, and have intervened in the drought crisis in the country by conducting employment training and watershed management in two tehsils in Maharashtra.

The Amte family members are all, in their own unique ways, furthering Baba Amte's legacy. As Sheetal told me, each person in her family is so talented that she was anxious while deciding a path for herself. 'How to innovate in such a family?' she said, laughing. She joined Anandwan after studying medicine and acquiring a master's degree in social entrepreneurship, and currently serves as the CEO. Her brother, Kaustubh, who is both a chartered accountant and the company secretary, has led a lot of Anandwan initiatives in the recent past. Their father, Vikas Amte, joined Anandwan in 1971 as a doctor. He drove a lorry across Maharashtra for 300 kilometres and operated on the eyes of tribal leprosy patients, because other doctors refused to touch them.

I asked Sheetal about the family legacy. How is it that three generations of the Amtes have given so selflessly to society? What inspires them to keep building on Baba Amte's work? I will always remember Sheetal's answer: 'Today, people think that we are very rich when, in fact, we have always given all our money to Anandwan. But there are different ways of measuring wealth.' She cited Joseph B. Soloveitchik's book *The Lonely Man of Faith*, in which he proposes that all of us have two warring persons within ourselves.[6] He calls them Adam One and Adam Two. Adam One works on his CV or professional success. Adam Two works on his eulogy speech or on how he wants to be remembered after he is gone—essentially, on his character and his relationships. Adam One works by economic logic that encourages building, innovating and growing. Adam Two works by an internal moral logic of the concept of giving. In the Amte family, Sheetal said, they don't have a good bank balance or CV virtues, but they have built eulogy virtues over the years. 'We have an FD of people's blessings in our bank account that comes handy. Whenever we seek help, we get it in five minutes.'[7]

There are different privileges we all carry with us. Sheetal, like Nisa, is privileged because of her family name, which opens doors for her. I really like what both of them are doing with their privilege—opening doors for others as well.

~

I, too, feel ridiculously privileged. Some of my interlinked privileges include: Privilege of education. Privilege of being relatively affluent. Privilege of having networks to tap into. Privilege of having a supportive family who accepted my sexuality easily. Privilege of caste.

The life I now lead seems so normal to me, although it really isn't—my privileges are now part of my 'habitus', the term that French theorist Pierre Bourdieu used to describe the deep embodied cultural capital we all possess because of our life experiences.[8] The fact that I am able to navigate a corporate boardroom with as much ease as a film festival, Mumbai with as much familiarity as New York, knowledgeable about art or film or *Tales of the City* or the Kashish Film Festival or LGBTQ inclusion or, indeed, Bourdieu himself, has very little to do with me and more with the particular set of conditions and circumstances that have intersected to make this possible.

I have all the three forms of cultural capital that Bourdieu identifies. Embodied—the way I look and sound is a very clear indicator of my privilege. Objectified—my car, phone and clothes, and my penchant for fashion and art. Institutional—be it my education at places like MIT or my affiliation to companies like Godrej. All these give me a certain perceived position in society which is really not linked to anything inherent, and I understand this. I am well aware that this book was written, published and distributed because of these very privileges.

The very fact that I can be out even at Godrej. The fact that I am part of senior management and close to Nisa gives me privileges at Godrej that I wouldn't have possessed had I been lower down in the corporate hierarchy and with no perceived Godrej family connection. Does that affect how flamboyantly I dress and conduct myself at work, and influence my saying 'fastest finger first' to my Culture Lab audience while being extremely camp in my behaviour? For sure!

What do I do with all these privileges? I write. I question. I share. I amplify. I try and create infrastructures of possibility. I learn, constantly.

~

The greatest gift of my life has been the people I have met along the way.

Essam Daod, who is a big fan of India and Bollywood, grew up in a small Arab village in the Galilee, and currently stays in Haifa, Israel. He is a trained child psychiatrist and psychotherapist. He told me at TED 2018 in Vancouver about travelling to Greece to provide psychosocial support to the Syrian refugees landing there by the boatload. This was in November 2015, at the peak of the refugee crisis in Europe. However, a few hours after he reached, he was in the water, unsuccessfully trying to revive a dead Iraqi woman. He told us about how he went through the routine of providing CPR to her, even though he knew she was dead, because her family had been waiting for about four hours for a doctor, and they would not have been able to accept it had he told them right away that she was dead. Essam realised from his experiences early on that mental health needs to be at the forefront of humanitarian aid, next to other basic needs like water, food and shelter. So, three months later, in his small flat in Haifa, he and his wife started their own humanitarian aid organisation, Humanity Crew.

This is one of the very few organisations that provides mental health and psychosocial support to refugees and displaced populations, and in their own language. People who are on refugee boats see so much horror before leaving their homes and also during the difficult journeys they take. And when the boats land, they face an uncertain future. It is not as if the countries they reach on the boats are waiting with open arms to welcome them. In the midst of all the turmoil, folks like Essam are trying their best to ease their suffering.[9]

Ahmed Kathrada or Uncle Kathy, as he is lovingly called by all who know him, has been another of my heroes. One cold June in 2015, I was sitting in a tiny room in a cell block on Robben Island off the coast of Cape Town, listening to him talk to me and my Young Global Leaders classmates about the twenty-six years he had spent as a prisoner alongside his close friend Nelson Mandela, eighteen of those years in the very cell block that we were in. They were seven prisoners together, Uncle Kathy told us, and they had felt they would certainly be given the death penalty in what is famously known as the Rivonia Trial of 1963–1964. Instead, they were sentenced to life imprisonment on this isolated maximum security prison off the coast of Cape Town. Uncle Kathy was the only Indian in the group.

There was segregation everywhere, even in the prison. The black prisoners got less food and had to wear short pants as compared to Indian, mixed race, 'coloured' or white prisoners. But Uncle Kathy's group was united, performed small acts of resistance all the time and continued to struggle peacefully for what they wanted. After fifteen years in prison, they finally won the right to get newspapers, and after twenty years, they got television. Slowly, they were allowed to write and receive more letters, and could have more visits from relatives and friends. After twenty-five years in prison, Uncle Kathy was writing forty letters a year. 'Our spirits never went down. We knew we would definitely win some day.'

As a form of torture, they were made to work with just picks and shovels in the limestone quarry on the island, he recounted, and even though this often gave them blisters on their hands and they bled, they still preferred it to being locked up in their single cells. When I heard about how Mandela couldn't tolerate light for the rest of his life, because his eyes had been damaged due to the constant exposure to sunlight in the quarry, I asked Uncle Kathy: 'Don't you ever feel vengeful? They wronged you all so much ... took away a large part of your life.' 'No,' he replied emphatically. 'Revenge is pointless.' To create an equal country and an equal world, he said, there has to be forgiveness and an absence of hatred. People who harbour negative emotions like anger or bitterness suffer more than the people towards whom these feelings are directed, he cautioned. 'In any case, a lot of work still needs to be done in South Africa and the world. There is no dignity in poverty; there is no dignity in hunger.'

Uncle Kathy used his time in jail to earn bachelor's degrees in history, criminology and bibliography as well as honours degrees in history and African politics from the University of South Africa. After his release from prison, he served in the Mandela government as a minister, but then retired from active politics to focus on his non-profit work. On the boat ride back to Cape Town, he told me about receiving the Pravasi Bharatiya Samman from the Indian government in 2005 and attending the 125th birth anniversary celebrations of Jawaharlal Nehru on the invitation of Sonia Gandhi in 2014. He told me that he would visit India again, but he passed away in 2017 before he could fulfil this promise. I learnt so much about resilience from that one day I spent with him.[10]

~

After Divyanshu Ganatra lost his eyesight at the age of nineteen, he got a lot of unsolicited advice from well-meaning people on what a visually impaired person should and should not do. He paid this no heed, thankfully, and has over the years raked up an impressive list of firsts—India's first blind solo pilot and the first blind tandem cyclist to complete the ride of more than 500 kilometres from Manali to Khardung La—to list just two. Now, he runs the Adventures Beyond Barriers Foundation, a non-profit that promotes inclusivity for people with disabilities through adventure sports.[11] We were honoured to have him at our Culture Lab in 2018.

Another Culture Lab speaker, Bunker Roy, served me a personal jolt of adrenalin when he visited the lab in 2015. Educated at Doon School and at Delhi's St Stephen's College, Bunker would have had a regular privileged career had he not visited Bihar post the 1960s famine and witnessed the abject suffering of the rural poor there. In 1971, Bunker created what is now called the Barefoot College in Tilonia, Rajasthan, as his attempt to find solutions to many rural problems, and since then, the institution has trained more than three million people in acquiring skills they can use to generate income and respect for themselves.[12]

The methodology is radical. They only take illiterate and semi-literate people, often from the lowest castes and from the most inaccessible villages in India, and help them become water and solar engineers, architects, doctors, IT workers, accountants and teachers. These barefoot experts then go on, as catalysts of change, to transform their own village communities. The college is Gandhian in its approach, with everyone eating, sleeping and working on the floor, and it does not grant any paper degrees. Instead, it values traditional and local knowledge more.

Tilonia today has its own telephone exchange, speed-post office and six solar-powered plants—it is the only fully solar-electrified campus in India. They have community radio, their own dentists, acupuncturists, physically challenged pathologists and much more. Bunker's home is a dream world. He was named by *Time* magazine as one of the 100 most influential people in the world in 2010.

My friend and Yale World Fellows senior classmate Chetna Sinha is doing equally inspiring work through her Mann Deshi Foundation in rural Maharashtra. The foundation has already changed the lives of more than 400,000 women who live near the Mann taluka. Mann Deshi's multitude of activities include an all-women-run bank, business schools for rural women, the first chamber of commerce for rural micro entrepreneurs, a community radio service, water conservation programmes and sports programmes ... and they are only just getting started![13]

~

Winner of the Ramon Magsaysay Award, the legendary P. Sainath needs no introduction, but if you haven't heard of him, go get yourself a copy of his classic *Everybody Loves a Good Drought*[14] or, better still, log on to the People's Archive of Rural India (PARI), his volunteer-driven initiative. PARI (ruralindiaonline.org) is already the biggest repository of information and stories about rural India—and like Chetna's Mann Deshi, they too are only just getting started with all their ambitious plans.

When Sainath spoke at the Culture Lab in 2017, he gave us some pretty sobering numbers about the lack of representation of rural India.[15] 'Seventy per cent of our country lives in rural India, but if you study the news coverage from the source-of-origin point of view, rural issues account for 0.76 per cent. If you look at it from the content point of view, this becomes 0.18 per cent ... and even when agriculture is covered, it is about covering what the agricultural ministry does, and not the ground reality of farms and farmers.' When asked why, he spoke about how large media houses had concentrated ownership over the years in our country, and driven purely by the profit motive, they didn't believe that news about rural India would appeal to advertisers. 'This is why there are news outlets that cover golf but not agriculture or labour issues!'

While Sainath's numbers were bleak, his attitude was not. 'Somewhere between cynical pessimism and blind optimism, there exists an island called hope. I live there.' From this island of hope, he and his team have created PARI—which is both an archive and a living journal of the amazing changes taking place in rural India today.[16]

~

I am sure you must have seen Priyanka Chopra Jonas's film *The Sky Is Pink*, based on Aisha Chaudhary and her mom Aditi Chaudhury.[17] In December 2011, I was dancing alongside Aisha and another personal hero, Thermax's chairperson Anu Aga, under a moonlit sky at the City Palace, Jaipur. We were at a grand dinner to celebrate the Ink Conference. Aisha, who was fifteen then, only had a 40 per cent chance of survival at that point, but her incredible spirit had charged the entire conference right from day one. 'My soul would have no rainbow if my eyes would have no tears,' she had told us earlier in the day, and as we danced happily, I thought of how blessed I was to be in this moment.

The feeling of being blessed continues. Where I stand right now in my life, I stand full of gratitude. I think of all the privileges I have as an opportunity to serve.

~

Back to our 'Migration Museum'. People tumbled out of the auditorium after Chinmay's talk, articulating their gratitude in loud sighs and silent gazes; one gave me prasad, another their business card. I listened and meandered between conversations. I am grateful for the work I do. The love that the audience showers on me after every event is humbling.

My queer posse usually stays till the end. Some of them might go get drinks later on, finishing up possible affairs, getting ready for a lazy Sunday. In the 1991 influential book *Families We Choose: Lesbians, Gays, Kinship*, the author Kath Weston writes about how we queer people often assemble our own families from amongst our friends and colleagues, to compensate for the neglect or abuse we may face with our blood families.[18] I feel blessed at having created one such queer family here in Mumbai through our Culture Lab. As I watched my younger mentees—Anish Gawande, Saniya Shaikh, Ojas Kolvankar and so many others—at our 'Migration Museum', I knew that they would be my legacy, more than anything else.

Some months later, I beamed with pride when Saniya conceived, curated and executed India's first ever fandom conference from scratch under the Culture Lab's umbrella. Ojas discovered his love for fashion while working at our lab, and I was happy to network and get him placed in a fashion magazine of his choice. He is now a writer and stylist for the Indian edition of *Grazia*. Rushva Parihar, another queer intern, was instrumental in setting up our lab. He subsequently worked with the UN and is now a sanitation expert, setting up toilets across India as part of a national mission. Anish, who worked at our lab while on a sabbatical from Columbia University, has now started Pink List India, the country's first non-partisan register of queer-friendly politicians, with another of our former lab interns, Devina Buckshee. By the time you read this book, Anish will be at Oxford on a Rhodes scholarship.

I think of all of them and the other youth I have mentored—from Chicago to Jabalpur—as my queer children. This book is also for them and for the future generations of young Indian queers that they will in turn mentor.

Part Two

BEING LGBTQ IN INDIA

AN OVERVIEW

Who are we? What are our multiple identities? What are our diverse histories? Where do we stand in the eyes of the law? What does it mean to be queer in a rapidly transforming Indian society? And most importantly, just how powerful is family acceptance for us?

5

The Queer Alphabet Soup and Why It Matters

I have so far been using the acronym 'LGBTQ' or sometimes the word 'queer', but there are so many other terms that you may have come across like 'LGBTQIA' or 'LGBT+' or 'LGBTQIAHK'. If you are not from the community, you may not know many of these terms. Actually, even if you are from the community, you may not know many of these, because being LGBTQ in India is an ever-changing process.

To start with, let's talk about homosexuals.

I am a **homosexual**; the term refers to a person who is emotionally, physically and sexually attracted to members of the same sex. People who are attracted to members of the opposite sex are called heterosexuals.

You would think there is a clear distinction, but in matters of desire, things often get complicated. Alfred Kinsey, known as the father of the global sexual revolution, along with his associates Wardell Pomeroy and Clyde Martin, both sexologists, came up with the Kinsey scale in 1948, after interviewing thousands of people across the US over a fifteen-year period. The scale went from zero, referring to a person who is exclusively homosexual, to six, referring to a person who is exclusively heterosexual. There was an additional category for those with no sociosexual contact or reaction. The findings of the Kinsey scale showed that 'sexual behavior, thoughts and feelings towards the same or opposite sex were not always consistent across time.'[1] This research created a sensation worldwide. It has been followed by many studies over the years, all of which have stated that between 4 and 10 per cent of any population is homosexual.

According to a report by the not-for-profit LGBT Token, 'Public polls and studies carried out by statistics agencies in advanced economies such as the US and the UK have found that between 3 and 7 per cent of the adult population identify as LGBT. ... When applied on a global scale to the world's adult population (16 years+) of 5.3 billion, the 3–7 percentage range gives an LGBT population estimate of between 160 million and 373 million adults globally.'[2]

A homosexual person could be a **lesbian** woman—who identifies as female and is attracted to other females—or a **gay** man—who identifies as male and is attracted to other males. When actress Sonam Kapoor asked me during our Twitter Blue Room chat to introduce myself and my labels, I told her, I am a proud Indian gay man. Though the word 'gay' is more commonly used to refer to men who are attracted to other men, it can be applied to women as well. In fact, right until the late 1980s, 'gay' was used as the umbrella term.

Siddharth Gautam, who was an advocate in the Delhi High Court and a pioneer of queer activism in the country, published the groundbreaking booklet *Less Than Gay: A Citizens' Report on the Status of Homosexuality in India* in 1991,[3] along with a team that included J.P. Jain, S.A. Lalitha, Shalini SCN, Jagdish Bhardwaje, Arun Bhandari and P.S. Sahni, all of whom were members of the AIDS Bhedbhav Virodhi Andolan (ABVA), a non-profit all-volunteer cadre of social volunteers that worked on social issues like rights of prostitutes and AIDS. Sadly, Siddharth passed away after a long battle with Hodgkin's lymphoma, at the young age of twenty-eight, just a few months after this report was published.

Less Than Gay was the first publication in India to throw light on queer issues in the country with a humane gaze, describing daily life. This is how the document—relevant even today, three decades later—'defines' being gay:

> Gay people, like non-gay people, vary enormously in shape, size, appearance, occupation, viewpoint and self-perception. ... Differences in region (including rural/urban ones), religion and economic class make for widely divergent experiences and attitudes regarding marriage, same sex eroticism and individual identity. There is, therefore, no such thing as 'a gay'. Certainly, also, there are vast differences between gay men and lesbians in the way they experience and think about their sexuality. No consensus exists (as yet) among gay people on issues such as the desirability of marriage, cross-dressing, social roles, sexual roles, necessity of being public about their sexuality, etc.[4]

A **bisexual person** is someone who is attracted to both men and women. Another term, '**pansexual**', describes someone who has the potential for emotional, romantic or sexual attraction to people of any gender, though not necessarily simultaneously or in the same way or to the same degree.[5]

The word '**transgender**' has been defined, mis-defined and debated upon endlessly, both by people within and outside the community. The Vidhi Centre for Legal Policy, in their report *Queering the Law: Making Indian Laws LGBT+ Inclusive* released in 2019, helps track this debate.

> The Supreme Court of India in its landmark judgment National Legal Services Authority of India VS Union of India (NALSA) recognized fundamental rights of transgender persons. … The NALSA struggles with defining who a 'transgender person' is, showcasing the tense relationship between the law and the politics of gender identities. The Supreme Court runs through a range of identities including: individuals whose gender does not conform with the sex assigned at birth, those who identify as neither male or female, the various cultural identities in India such as kothi, arvanis, jogtas etc. At the end … the Supreme Court reduces the transgender identity to the most visible non-normative gender identity in India i.e. the hijra identity. Further, the judgment makes only a passing reference to transgender men, thereby relegating them to the background.[6]

Following the NALSA judgement of 2014, the Transgender Persons (Protection of Rights) Bill, with problematic definitions and provisions, was introduced in the Lok Sabha in 2016. According to this bill:

> Transgender person means a person who is (A) neither wholly female nor wholly male; or (B) a combination of female or male; or (C) neither female nor male; and whose sense of gender does not match the gender assigned to that person at the time of birth and includes transmen and transwomen, persons with intersex variations and gender-queers.[7]

What a ridiculous way to think about transgender people, as half this, half that! The bill got trashed. Another one came up in 2018, which lapsed in the Rajya Sabha.

Finally, after ignoring most of the feedback from queer community organisations, an equally problematic Transgender Persons (Protection of Rights) Bill, 2019, was passed in the Lok Sabha on 5 August. While the bill does not mention anything about reservations in jobs—which was mandated in the progressive NALSA judgement—and makes it compulsory to screen trans people before issuing them ID cards, it does have a more comprehensive definition of a transgender person, as compared to the 2016 version. Moreover, it allows a transgender person to self-identify. I will use the definition from this most recent 2019 bill in this book:

> Transgender person is someone whose gender does not match with the gender assigned to that person at birth, and includes trans-men and trans-women (whether or not they have undergone reassignment surgery or hormone therapy or laser therapy etc.), gender-queers and a number of socio-cultural identities such as kinnars, hijras, aravanis, jogtas etc. [8]

People identify as trans because of gender dysphoria—being transgender is *not* a disorder. Even the American Psychiatric Association, the professional organisation of psychiatrists in the US, has replaced the term 'gender identity disorder' with 'gender dysphoria' to be able to better characterise the experiences of those undergoing it.[9] Gender dysphoria is when the gender assigned at one's birth does not align with the gender one identifies as.

There are two terms here that are important to consider—'gender identity' and 'gender expression'. This is how the US-based Gay and Lesbian Alliance Against Defamation (GLAAD) defines them:

> Gender identity: A person's internal, deeply held sense of their gender. For transgender people, their own internal gender identity does not match the sex they were assigned at birth. Most people have a gender identity of man or woman (or boy or girl). For some people, their gender identity does not fit neatly into one of those two choices. Unlike gender expression (see below) gender identity is not visible to others. [...]
>
> Gender expression: External manifestations of gender, expressed through a person's name, pronouns, clothing, haircut, behaviour, voice, and/or body characteristics. Society identifies these cues as masculine and feminine, although what is considered masculine or feminine changes over time and varies by culture. Typically, transgender people seek to align their gender expression with their gender identity, rather than the sex they were assigned at birth.[10]

'Transgender' is a term that can perhaps be understood better if placed in comparison to the term '**cisgender**'—when the gender matches the gender assigned to a person at birth. If the birth certificate labels a person male, and if he continues to identify as male through his life, he is cisgendered. Here, we are talking about gender, not sexuality. So he could be a cisgendered homosexual or a cisgendered heterosexual. Confused? Don't worry. You'll get the hang of it soon enough.

The letter Q stands for '**queer**'; it is very popular as an umbrella term that encompasses all the other identities and also as a political term that questions heteronormativity and other constructs within which mainstream society operates. But Q could also stand for '**questioning**' and encompasses those who are still exploring their sexualities. Therein lies the beauty of this letter Q—it not only defines but also gives space to the undefined. Thus we come to '**LGBTQ**'—this is the term I have been using in this book throughout, interchangeably with the word queer, as an overarching term.

The tension between queer and LGBT has a history. The poet Akhil Katyal traces it beautifully in his book *The Doubleness of Sexuality* and resolves some of it through the framework of 'doubleness'—using both terms together or interchangeably. He writes, 'Queer, with its emphasis on finding similarities of marginalisation with other social groups, at least rhetorically mobilises a form of politics that reinvents LGBT. It filters LGBT less as types of specific embodied conditions, and uses it—still as the same word LGBT—more as a political viewpoint from where the world looks a little different, where the LGBT movement itself looks more than a single-issue movement. LGBT, inflected thus by queer, tries to operate on a bigger template of alliances, and speak of subjects that it thought the LGBT frame does not allow.'[11]

Soon, **intersex** people too were brought under the umbrella, and then the term became 'LGBTQI'. As defined by the UN High Commissioner for Human Rights in 2015:

> An intersex person is born with sexual anatomy, reproductive organs, and/or chromosome patterns that do not fit the typical definition of male or female. This may be apparent at birth or become so later in life. An intersex person may identify as male or female, or as neither. Intersex status is not about sexual orientation or gender identity.[12]

A lot of people of late have been using 'LGBTQIAA+'. The plus symbol is expansive, referring to any additional aspects, forms and manifestations of sexuality and gender that exist, or might come up in the future. But two A's, you ask? What do they stand for? '**Asexual**'. '**Ally**'.

I take the following two definitions from *Understanding LGBTQ: An Ally's Perspective*, a 2019 report produced by the consultancy Beyond Diversity.

> Asexual: Someone who is not sexually attracted to anyone or doesn't have a sexual orientation.
>
> Ally: A person, regardless of sexual orientation, who has the back of the LGBTQIA community on all fronts. A (typically cisgender) person who supports and respects members of the LGBTQ community.[13]

~

When the dating app Tinder came to India in 2016, they were faced with a burning question—how many gender identities should they have? So they sat down with activists and advocates working in this realm, including me, to come up with their final list of twenty-three gender identities. If and when you are on Tinder next, here are some of the different identities that made the cut, which you can select for yourself or for the person you are swiping right for:

1. **Agender**: Someone who does not identify with any gender. They may also call themselves genderless.
2. **Androgynous**: A person whose gender expression combines aspects of typically masculine as well as feminine characteristics.
3. **Bigender**: Someone who experiences two distinct gender identities either simultaneously or one at a time.
4. **Genderfluid**: A person who rejects the binary of man and woman to describe their gender. They may feel more like a man one day, more like a woman on another, or neither or both on other days.
5. **Gender nonconforming**: A gender identity that does not fit the typical cultural masculine or feminine gender norms.
6. **Gender questioning**: A person who is questioning their gender identity or is in the process of exploring it.
7. **Genderqueer**: Someone who queers gender—for instance, they may express a combination of typical masculine and feminine traits, or neither. It is different from gender fluid in that the person may not experience a change in their identity from day to day.
8. **Non-binary**: A person who rejects the binary of man and woman. Their gender identity expresses a combination of masculinity and femininity or neither.
9. **Female to male**: A person who is assigned female at birth and transitions to male by undergoing masculinisation surgeries.
10. **Male to female**: A person who is assigned male at birth and transitions to female through surgery.
11. **Pangender**: Someone who identifies as having more than one gender or all genders.[14]

~

There are different, rich, non-English 'Indian' categories of desire, dressing and positioning, contained in words like 'kothi' and 'hijra', which the 2019 Transgender Persons Bill called 'socio cultural categories'. These words come from local terms used to describe either gender roles or preferential sexuality or even preference for certain kinds of sexual acts that are performed. It is here that the boundaries between sex, gender, gender expression and sexuality fade.

According to the 2014 NALSA judgement, **hijras** are biological males who reject their masculine identity and identify either as women or 'not-men' or 'in between man and woman' or 'neither man nor woman'. However, intersex people are also part of hijra gharanas—families or lineages. In India, hijras tend to identify as a community with their own initiation rituals and professions, like begging, dancing at weddings or blessing babies. They even have their own secret code language, known as Hijra Farsi, derived from Persian and Hindustani.[15]

If the word '**kothi**' was to be translated, it would probably be 'Queen'. (Yes, with a capital Q, referring to effeminate and flamboyant gay men, like yours truly!) In 'The Kothi Wars: AIDS Cosmopolitanism and the Morality of Classification', the anthropologist Lawrence Cohen writes that the word 'kothi' refers to men who act or identify in some way as a woman, with a desire to be penetrated by those they consider to be the 'real men'—the **panthis**.[16] Kothis could be bisexual, and they could be hijra as well—the word contains within it aspects of both gender and sexuality. Shivananda Khan, founder of Naz Foundation, an NGO that works on sexual health, writes about individuals crossing over these categories—so sometimes a kothi could be dominant, or a panthi could be more submissive. They are then colloquially called 'double decker', or 'do-parathas' in Hindi.[17] (You'll recollect this term the next time you reach for that second paratha during dinner, won't you?)

Here are some more definitions that we collated in the trans manifesto published by the Culture Lab:

> **Kinnar**: The term for hijras in northern India. In other parts of India, such as Maharashtra, the term kinnar is being used more recently by the better-educated hijras to refer to themselves.
>
> **Shiv-shakthis**: Typically referring to a community of transgender people in Andhra Pradesh, Shiv-shakthis are males who consider themselves to be 'possessed by' or 'married to' the gods, particularly Lord Shiva. They have a feminine gender expression and cross-dress as women during religious rituals and festivals. They work typically as astrologers or spiritual healers. The community is guarded by gurus who induct disciples and train them for the work.

Jogtis/Jogtas and **Jogappas**: In Maharashtra and Karnataka, jogtas and jogtis refer to male and female servants who dedicate (or are made to dedicate) their lives to gods in different temples. The terms refer to male-to-female transpeople who devote themselves to the service of a particular god.

Aravani: The term for hijras in Tamil Nadu. The title 'aravani' has mythological significance. Aravan, the son of Arjuna and Nagakanya in the Mahabharata, offers himself to be sacrificed to Goddess Kali to ensure the victory of the Pandavas in the Kurukshetra war. The only condition he makes is that he spends the last night of his life in matrimony. Given no woman would marry someone doomed to be killed, Krishna assumes the form of a beautiful woman called Mohini and marries him. The hijras of Tamil Nadu consider Aravan their progenitor and call themselves aravanis. Many aravanis also prefer to be called thirunangai.[18]

Brian Horton, a dear friend and professor at Brandeis University in Boston—who worked at the Humsafar Trust for some years in India and was also a scholar in residence at the Culture Lab—prefers to use the term 'LGBTKHQ+' including 'hijra (H)' and 'kothi (K)' in an initialism birthed in the West.[19]

Now, you must wonder about how the LGBTQIAHK+ movement can hold all of these intersecting but distinct identities together to forge ahead as one movement. As you can guess, the answer is—not gracefully! Infighting, break-offs, sub-movements are all part of our history.

Brian spoke to me about the historical conflicts among activists in India on using identity-based words like 'gay' or 'kothi-panthi' versus the more behavioural terms like 'MSM' or 'men who have sex with men'. 'It is turf wars. I don't know if it is necessarily the case anymore, but particularly during the height of HIV-AIDS funding [early 2000s], parts of the fight were just fights for resources. After that, there were legitimate fights about queerness and what the framework is. If you look at Lawrence Cohen's "Kothi Wars" which chronicles the debate between Ashok Row Kavi, head of Humsafar, and Shivananda Khan, head of Naz Foundation, part of their debate is this "McDonalds Model of Sexuality" and whether or not we can use these sort of western codified terms like "gay", "lesbian", or whether or not it has to be MSM, kothi, panthi, hijra.'

Turf wars reminded me of TERF Wars: Trans Exclusionary Radical Feminists (TERF). These are feminists who do not think of transgender women as one among them and, as a result, do not feel the need for protecting them or their rights and dignity. From turf to TERF wars, it is complicated, and if you want to understand our community, you need to understand that we are complicated and accept that this is okay.

Brian also noted, 'The other debate, historically, has been about gender, about the lack of space for queer folks, queer women [or assigned female at birth], and to some extent now, the carving off of trans women and hijras and other local-terminologied organisations from the LGBT movement is one of the recent cleavages. Now the kind of cleavages are also more sharply around intersectionality. How do you see the relationship between dalitness and queerness, between Muslims and queerness, the role of Hindutva and patriarchy in shaping queer spaces? How do we think about hegemonic masculinity as shaping spaces? Those are where you see, now, interesting debates happening around identity intersections in queer spaces.'

If the movement is so fractured, how should we speak of it? Does language matter? Do labels matter? Quite simply, yes. The US philosopher and gender theorist Judith Butler in her essay 'On Linguistic Vulnerability' writes about the power of these labels to both be violent by reducing complexity and helpful in being able to articulate complexity.[20] After all, we are linguistic beings. It is also useful to note, as Akhil writes, that 'words do not have inner cores but instead have diverse deployments, they have political implications and that they can be as dynamic as they tend to fatigue, that there is nothing of an essential truth within them outside these many deployments.'[21]

The best thing to do—and in fact the only thing to do—is to just ask someone what they want to be addressed as. It is as simple as that. Don't assume. Just ask: How do you identify and what are your pronouns? And offer to them what your own identity is and what your pronouns are. It may seem strange at first, but it will soon become a habit. So, for example, when I meet someone, I now say, 'Hi, I'm Parmesh, I am gay and my pronouns are "he", "him", "his".' Someone else may prefer the pronoun 'they' if they are gender queer or gender fluid.

~

When a person is not open either to themselves or others about either their gender or sexual identity, they are referred to as '**closeted**'. The process of accepting oneself is called 'coming out of the closet' or '**coming out**'.

I am reproducing here a story I read in *Less Than Gay*. This story might help you understand the promise and heartbreak of queer desire. It has been sourced by the authors of *Less Than Gay* from *Trikone*, the celebrated magazine for South Asian gay men and lesbians brought out by two Indian graduates in California from 1986 onwards.

> Rahul's Story: In my tenth class, I fell hopelessly in love with a boy one year my senior with an incredible body and classic Rajput good looks. We were buddies for a long time and then started flirting and making jokes about how attractive we found each other. The jokes started getting serious. One evening we were at his house and were lying on his bed and talking. The next thing I knew we were hugging madly. We took each other's clothes off and touched for hours. Our affair continued for a year. He always felt guilty after sex and would go to his family mandir to pray. I would feel a little guilty on seeing his guilt, but felt largely happy. Emotionally we were close as any lovers. We wrote love letters, had passionate telephone conversations much to the astonishment of our families. In recent years he got married. When he talked to me about it, what came through was his terror of social disgrace. Right now he is being a good Rajput son with a wife and maybe kids—goes to the mandir for Gita readings—in short, living the classic life of the closet gay. His family will probably never know how scared he is of their rejection.[22]

Coming out of the closet is not simple, and it does not happen just once; one first comes out to oneself, then to one's confidante, siblings, friends, parents, co-workers ... again and again. Office banter always comes down to who is dating whom. Dinner discussions with parents linger around marriage. Conversations with friends, the closest ones especially, always have the element of dating, sex and relationships. How does one handle all of this if they are closeted? It is very difficult. I hope this book, in some small measure, inspires more queer people in our country to accept themselves, and come out, if they feel that they can.

~

'**Homophobia**' is one final word we should talk about right now. What a terrible word to end this chapter with, but it is important because it is prevalent all around us. The US psychotherapist George Weinberg coined this term in the 1960s to explain the discomfort many of his colleagues felt around and expressed about homosexuals.

Weinberg defines homophobia as the dread of being close to homosexuals and self-aversion in the case of homosexuals themselves.[23] Of course, over time it became not just about fear but also disgust and hatred towards people like me. If you believe that homosexuals do not deserve dignity, you are homophobic.

Sometimes, homophobia also gets entangled in notions of masculinity and femininity. Siddharth Dube in his 2015 book *No One Else: A Personal History of Outlawed Love and Sex* writes about how growing up studying in Doon school, the boys who were feminine were always implicated in the witch hunts, and even later, as an adult, he noticed that the police often picked on the feminine men, 'slapping, beating, and terrorising them into emptying their wallets and providing sexual favours. ... Astonishingly, they would let the "top" men—the "penetrator" in homosexual sex—go, treating them as if they were part of the same brotherhood. Just like the abusers at Doon, they believed it was okay for a man to have sex with another man because of a pressing need for release, but that genuinely homosexual males—in their view meaning only those who [were] penetrated or gave oral sex—deserved to be abused because they were despicably unmanly.'[24] The source of homophobia is often seen in these archaic conceptions of masculinity.

One of my mentees, Shubham Singhal, now doing his MBA at IIM Ahmedabad, produced an interesting paper in 2019, when he was a student at IIT Bombay, for the *International Journal of Science and Research*. 'Development of the Acceptance Towards Lesbian, Gay, Bisexual and Transgender Scale' tries to understand Indian homophobia quantitatively.[25]

As his research method, he sent out an email survey to IIT Bombay students to measure LGBTQ acceptance. He ended up with 579 survey responses. Each survey had 18 statements, along with mandatory information on demographics. The respondents had to rate each statement from 1 to 5, 1 being 'Strongly Disagree' to 5 being 'Strongly Agree'.

Below are some of the statements with the average scores. They give a sense of both how open-minded and how homophobic we are as a society. Even though the sample size is extremely skewed, the results are still interesting, given that any IIT has students and faculty from pretty much all across the country.

1. I think the activities of LGBT people are against Indian culture. 1.96
2. I don't mind what LGBT people do in the privacy of their own bedroom. 4.63
3. LGBT people deserve the same rights as everybody else (for example, adoption, marriage etc.) 4.35
4. Love can happen between any two individuals. 4.24
5. LGBT people need support to fight the difficulties associated with being LGBT. 4.09
6. LGBT people can't be blamed for their sexual orientation. 4.28

7. LGBT people can influence a child's sexuality. 2.83
8. People wearing clothes made for the opposite sex make me uncomfortable. 2.80
9. Same-sex parents are capable of being good parents. 3.55
10. I am comfortable with an open LGBT culture. 3.95
11. I would not want my child to be taught by an LGBT teacher. 1.94
12. Allowing same sex marriages will disrupt the functioning of societies. 2.19

Shubham concludes with, 'While there has been a rise in LGBT rights activism, there is still a large section of Indian society which believes that the mainstreaming of homosexuality poses a threat to Indian social and cultural integrity as well as morality.'[26]

He further uses the US psychologist Gregory Herek's 'three levels of homophobia' to theorise on homophobia in India.[27]

> At the first level, homophobic attitudes negatively perceive LGBT people due to their non-heterosexual identity and not due to their individual characteristics. The first level homophobia is evident from the observation that homosexuality is a taboo in India. Second level homophobia manifests itself in the structure of society. In India ... same-sex couples don't have equal rights as opposite-sex couples even in health care and pension schemes. At the third level, individuals internalise their beliefs and reinforce it in an internalised or externalised way. ... In India, homophobia is exhibited at all three levels described by Herek.[28]

How does this translate in the Indian workplace? *In and Out: The Indian LGBT Workplace Climate Survey 2016*, a study by Mission for Indian Gay and Lesbian Empowerment (MINGLE)—a think tank that works towards enabling and empowering LGBTQ youth—reported sobering statistics.[29] About 40 per cent of the people surveyed confided that they sometimes or often faced harassment in the workplace for being LGBTQ. Two-thirds of them reported hearing homophobic slurs from their colleagues or managers and one-fifth had faced discrimination from their HR managers. The report also noted that for 65 per cent of them, inclusive HR policy was a major factor in determining whether they wanted to join an organisation. No one wants to feel marginalised, no one wants to be at the receiving end of homophobic slurs.

There are other variants of homophobia that many people embody, whether they are LGBTQ or not—like biphobia and transphobia. Here is how the glossary of Human Rights Campaign, a civil rights organisation, defines them.

Biphobia: Prejudice, fear or hatred directed toward bisexual people.

Transphobia: The fear and hatred of, or discomfort with, transgender people.[30]

~

I know that I have bombarded you with a lot of terms in this chapter, and the information here might be too much to process. Take your time, keep coming back to this chapter.

I want to end this chapter with two simple requests. If you are a manager in a workplace, I hope this makes you understand just how beautiful and diverse our LGBTQ community is, and that you reconsider your policies and work environment to include all of us. I also hope this chapter makes it easier for you to stand up against homophobia and other forms of phobia against queer people. Also, if you have any LGBTQ friends or colleagues, ask them what they identify as and when they accepted themselves. The range of answers might surprise you. Some of us have lived our entire lives cocooned in the fear that no one will understand us. Start the conversation and become our ally.

If you identify as LGBTQ, I hope this chapter as well as this book give you the courage to ask for what you deserve. Are you perfectly comfortable with yourself? If there is one thing I want you to take away from this book, it is this: You are normal. You are fine. We are going to change the world around us soon to make sure that everyone understands this, but you need to know this right now. You are absolutely fine, however you are and whatever label you want to ascribe or not ascribe to yourself. There is a whole queer alphabet soup you can choose from. Pick one alphabet for yourself, or what the heck, pick a few!

6

Historicising Queer India

In August 2005, the LGBTQ icon Pawan Dhall was going through the archives of Counsel Club (CC) in Kolkata—one of the earliest queer support groups in India—'to look back at some of the "CC birthday parties" through the 1990s and early 2000s' for a series documenting 'the queer movement in Bengal and India'.[1] He was writing for the blog of Varta, a trust that works in the space between sexuality and gender through dialogue and publishing. The introduction to Pawan's piece reads: '... not a chronological narrative of the movement, rather anecdotal histories capturing the little voices that are often lost in general historical accounts—voices from thousands of letters received by Counsel Club, one of India's earliest queer support groups (1993–2002), and from the group's house journal *Naya Pravartak*.'[2]

Pawan was one of the five founding members of CC—two journalists, one engineer, one fashion designer and a student—supported by a lawyer and a businessman. Due to irreconcilable differences, Pawan would leave, CC would subsequently fold, but a decade or so later, he would come back to this gnawing feeling of incompleteness, armed with both the claws of a historian and the beating heart of a survivor who had lived and loved through the 1990s.

'If Counsel Club were functioning today, it might have celebrated its twenty-second birthday party this 15 August,' he writes in his blog post. He weaves a tapestry of time, the warp and weft of events—excessive cakes, birthday celebrations, rainbow walks (the first Pride march in India was in Kolkata in 1999[3]), parties for people to find and be found, and for love, lust and community.

A decade later, in 2016, Pawan and I were dining together at 6 Ballygunge Place, one of my favourite Kolkata restaurants. I told him excitedly about my

LGBTQ inclusion talk at Tata Steel the previous evening, while wolfing down mochchar chops and dab chingri. 'It is the season for nolen gurer mithai; you should take some back with you,' he said, smiling.

People like him are the reason that queer India has a history. Whether it is by painstakingly maintaining personal archives or supporting the movement in whichever way possible, Pawan and his peers have created the foundation on which folks like me are building our arguments. They selflessly mentor us, feed us (quite literally, in this case), and make sure we get up each time we fail or falter.

When I rang him in 2019, months before the publication of his important book *Out of Line and Offline: Queer Mobilizations in '90s Eastern India,*[4] he lamented about how the movement is often seen as synonymous with court cases. Community mobilisation, pioneering conferences and resource books are often omitted, only raising their heads in obscure think pieces in newspapers once in a while. When I asked him what value he holds as an archivist in individual narratives as opposed to large movements, and about the necessity of history itself, he gave me a very moving response: 'It is important for us as we move forward to look at that past. There are lessons in the past we must keep in mind. It is difficult to explain this ... but you can't just move forward in a robotic fashion. You need to have an undefined sense of being whole. You can't be that without knowing what happened in the past.'[5]

Even though Section 377 had by then been read down, Pawan feels that the spirit of 377 still looms. Effeminate men are still told by harassers, 'I will make you a proper man,' before they go on to beat up, taunt and blackmail them. Dating apps are still a minefield, most people are not comfortable telling their parents and families about their sexuality, and public parks and urinals of railways stations continue to be spaces for men to meet other men in secret.

'We need to look at how people were dealing with such issues in the past,' he told me. 'There will be lessons. It will also give a sense of where we started, how did we mobilise, what were the obstacles along the way.'

Pawan's 'Qatha: Queer Kolkata Oral History Project', which he began in December 2013 on the Varta blog, documents five decades of queer life, from the 1960s onwards, and talks about lust, familial abuse, rejections, soaring and seething affairs, cruising in the shadows of the city and much more.[6]

During our phone conversation, he dipped his feet in puddles of nostalgia, taking me back in time to the Calcutta of the 1990s.

'Today, one cannot imagine organising an event without Facebook. There were events happening even then. The audience was small, but there was a certain discipline and diligence. It was [about] making a list of mundane important things—invitees. We would talk to people, look at records, we would think about it. Today, we can send out hundreds of invites within seconds. They go to about 90 per cent who would not be interested, who say they are coming and never turn up.

'In CC, we would have regular meetings. There was a team of letter writers and we would sit together, discuss letters, set out a schedule and what the replies should be. Some of the replies were quite complex. It wasn't just about sharing and sending information. It was about answering the difficult questions and reassuring them they were not alone, connecting them to people in their areas.

'There were people writing about the need for employment, being afraid of coming out at the workplace, there were stories of young people seeking career advice, many of them from smaller towns. Issues around personal aspirations, looking at financial independence—always an important issue, something we often talk about in our community meetings. Being able to stand on your own feet is important to negotiate the challenges you run into because of your sexuality or gender.

'I remember one letter, it is on the Varta website, where there is a young chap from Odisha who wrote about wanting a career in advertising. His issues were, he was not strong in English. Also, he had issues with his personal appearance. He wanted advice on where to go, what courses to do, what kind of openings might be possible for him. Not simply a matter of career advice, but also self-esteem, looking for a freer environment where he could be himself. He was scared about his family coming to know he was gay. To me, it came across as a person looking for liberation, personal liberation, being able to fly unhindered, without any fear. For an outsider, it might feel like here is another person looking for advice, we all do. But career advice for a queer person is always more than just that. It is often about looking for personal freedom.

'Over the years, the movement was growing. In the initial years when things were limited to Delhi ... I shouldn't say Delhi ... Mumbai or Kolkata or Bangalore, there were so many letters from the Northeast and North India where people had no options because these regions did not have support groups in the beginning. When replying to these letters, there was also the letter writers bonding with each other ... a family feeling. We would get together to write letters, but we would also play Scrabble or go to watch a film. Or we would chat about our personal lives, problems at home, lovers, the kinds of sexual encounters we were having. Then the food, the parties we were having. It was such an important part of our lives while we were reaching out to people, we were also building a support system.

'But today … I am fifty-one now. I still keep getting so many calls from people who are isolated and I don't have anywhere to send them to other than saying join so-and-so group on Facebook, which is faceless. They are just not going to get that emotional support there. Imagine yourself standing at a busy street in Mumbai or Kolkata, you feel so lost amidst the immense amount of cars and traffic. There is so much happening, but you don't know where to go for someone to listen to. Those days we had it. I miss it terribly now. I knew twice or thrice a week people would be coming to my place or I would go to theirs. And for a couple of hours we would have our little bubble of happiness where we could share almost everything and anything. Yes, there would be fights and jealousies, but that was our island of happiness. Then, we would go back home and to the workplace to face life again … Everyone needs to put in that personal effort in engaging people—the biggest lesson we can learn from the archives.'[7]

Many of India's early queer communities were postal communities like Counsel Club. Sakhi, one of the first explicitly lesbian support groups in the country, also began as a postbox number, advertised in *Bombay Dost* magazine. Smita Vanniyar writes in the *Swaddle* that 'by mid-1994, there was a large and constant flow of letters to the Sakhi postbox. Many of the letter writers were not women from the big cities. They were often located in smaller towns, with English as their second language if at all.'[8]

Zaid Al Baset, one of the archivists at Counsel Club, writes about some of the letters they had received over the years. Letters about doubt and fear, and some laced with desire.

> The third fold of the inland letter card states 'From a friend to a very close friend'. He calls himself John and makes a sincere request at the end of his letter. He writes:
>
> 'I will ask the person involved to meet me at Cossipur Club Gate, a little away from Dum Dum Junction station at either 10:30 in the morning or 4:30 in the afternoon. There's a cobbler's shop near the gate. Please wait there with a coat in your left and an unlit cigarette in your right hand. My password will be "John".'

> He initially writes the name 'Jay', then strikes it with three fine strokes of the pen. The last two lines on the aging blue paper with paler edges read, 'NB: Please send my partner as quickly as possible, please.' It's a delightful sentence expressing a yearning so urgent, so precisely. The letter was sent through the Quick Mail Service to P.O. Bag No. 10237 (now not functional) and was received on 11 March 1996.
>
> Many such letters speak of such innumerable meetings. They mark the moment of the birth of a community. These collections of letters are a map in themselves—a map of an invisible city; a city that cannot speak its name. They represent a cartography of desire built by anonymous men who walked the city streets to find comfort in each other's company. It's a map, obliterated by official maps, encapsulated inside files of letters. Each letter, an excerpt from a story waiting to be told.[9]

I wonder where these characters are today. For how many days did John wait till he gave up on meeting someone there? Is he alive? Is he in love? Is he married? Is he happy?

~

Sridhar Rangayan created an important archive of queer videos in 2011, called *Project Bolo*.[10] He travelled the length and breadth of the country to interview twenty LGBTQ icons about how they grappled with desire, and about the community and the movement for justice over the decades. I see these videos often on YouTube. Shivananda Khan, Sunil Gupta, Giti Thadani, Ruth Vanita, R. Raj Rao—so many of my queer heroes are recorded for posterity in this online archive. I also see friends like Hoshang Merchant, Saleem Kidwai, Jehangir Jani and Gauri Sawant. Then there are folks like Betu Singh, whom I wish I'd become friends with.

I too am one of the *Project Bolo* interviewees. When I rewatch the video in which I am featured, I notice that I spoke with so much urgency. I read the comments below my video. Someone fawns over my looks; another pronounces suicide and expresses sadness over his own homosexuality. How does one process this—death and desire—one above the other, on a digital timeline?

~

During the Supreme Court hearings for the 377 case in 2013, Siddharth Narrain from the Alternative Law Forum (ALF), an organisation that provides legal services to marginalised groups across the country, used to record transcripts of the court proceedings each day and send them out to a list of activists across the country. Reading these proceedings, it struck Bengaluru-based documentary filmmaker T. Jayashree to interview on camera all the different lawyers fighting the case and also the different petitioners, who included parents and activists.

Jayashree had been documenting the movement since 2001. In 2004, I screened her film *Many People, Many Desires* at the Between the Lines Film Festival that I curated at MIT. Her film documents the daily lives of hijras, kothis, lesbians, transgender and other queer folks in Bengaluru. It masterfully cuts across the different barriers of class, gender, language and caste to tell a moving composite story. Jayashree had continued documenting the queer movement over the years, and she rekindled her efforts post the shocking 2013 Supreme Court judgement. In 2017, after the ten-year anniversary of Bangalore Pride, she finally started looking at all the footage she had gathered over the years, and realised that she had in fact created a huge archive of the movement's contemporary history.

There were other personal archive projects happening all across the country. Photographers Sunil Gupta and Charan Singh had collected oral histories of queer people from across India over the years, and some of their work was showcased at the Kochi Biennale in 2018. Vinay Chandran, the director of the Bengaluru-based Swabhava Trust, had collected mental health narratives of queer people across the country. Many of these queer individuals had been taken by their family members to doctors and mental health professionals against their will. Some of these narratives came out in the 2015 anthology *Nothing to Fix: Medicalisation of Sexual Orientation and Gender*[11]—that Vinay co-edited with Arvind Narrain, advocate and co-founder of ALF, but there are so many others still undocumented.

Meanwhile, the Bengaluru-based NGO Sangama had to move office because of a funding crunch, so Jayshree found herself suddenly entrusted with all their files from 1999 to 2014 for storage. These included press clippings that the Sangama staff used to cull every day from newspapers across the country—all LGBTQ-related news items.

What to do with all of this? Should these different resources be used in the future as 'visual jurisprudence', so that no judge could ever declare, like in 2013, that LGBTQ people are a 'miniscule minority' in our country? So, in 2018, Jayshree, along with Arvind, the advocate Deeptha Rao and other volunteers, began the Queer Archive for Memory Reflection and Activism (QAMRA) as a multimedia archival project 'to chronicle and preserve the stories of communities marginalised on the basis of gender and sexuality in India.'[12] They started collecting more material from other community-run organisations, queer rights activists, lawyers and individuals who had participated in or been allied with dialogues on queer rights.

I visited QAMRA for a day in September 2019. I drove directly from the Bengaluru Airport to their Lewis Road office in Cooke Town, past the Bengaluru East Railway Station, past a blue roadside dhaba with a giant mural of Ambedkar painted on it, alongside his famous quote—'I like the religion that teaches liberty, equality and fraternity'—and past the quaint, winding roads of Fraser Town, into the leafy McPherson Road with its line of elegant bungalows. This is the genteel Bangalore of yesteryears. Garden city.

I walked past the metal gate of a bungalow that housed the Lightroom bookstore on the ground floor. The courtyard was paved with exquisite cement mosaic tiles in a floral pattern. The external wall of the bungalow had peeling paint, and it was covered with posters advertising other Bengaluru events like the Urban Lens Film Festival. The outside garage had been converted into a reading room with the addition of what looked like some gorgeous teak and cane Pierre Jeanneret 'Chandigarh' chairs.

Inside the bookstore, there were paper cut-outs of clouds, umbrellas and raindrops hanging from above. I spotted a book titled *My Brother's Name Is Jessica* right upfront, and I made a mental note to pick up a copy of *The Legend of the Orange Princess*, retold and illustrated by artist Mehlli Gobhai, on my way out. Mehlli, one of my favourite artists, passed away in 2018. I am lucky to have one of his early drawings hanging above me in my bedroom. Some years ago, I had flirted quite scandalously with him over dinner at a common friend's place.

I took the narrow staircase to the left of the bookstore and climbed up to the QAMRA office, operating out of Jayashree's studio on the first floor. So you have the *oopar ka kamra*, I told Jayshree and Arvind, and they laughed. 'I am lucky to have a benefactor, who'd kindly given me this studio space,' Jayashree confided, as we gathered around a long wooden dining table, surrounded by fake Godrej steel cupboards and a mishmash of other furniture.

There were side tables, chairs of different shapes and sizes, and stools. Every surface was covered with papers and books, and every cabinet was overflowing. The tables were groaning under the weight of a three-foot-high stack of legal documents, neatly bound, with yellow post-its peeping out. The cabinets held hard drives, more documents and photo albums. There was a rainbow-coloured feather duster, propped, almost sculpturally, over one of the tables. Sunlight billowed in through the biscuit-coloured curtains. Here was the queer movement of India. All packed into one small room.

Arvind poured us some coffee from a Hatti Kaapi flask that had just arrived. We reminisced about the first time we had met and had dinner together at Koshy's in 2004. I was researching my first book then, and had come to Bengaluru to attend the second International Conference on Sexualities, Masculinities and Cultures in South Asia. I told him how much I loved *Because I Have a Voice: Queer Politics in India*, the anthology he had co-edited with Gautam Bhan in 2005.[13]

Over the years, Arvind co-founded the ALF, left it to go to Geneva to serve as the director of research and practice at the global organisation Arc, and returned to Bengaluru. He now splits his time between research and teaching law. It was so good to meet him in person again. Some of my queer heroes, I realise, are better admired from afar, but with some like Arvind, my respect only grows deeper and deeper with each meeting.

QAMRA's aim is to 'build a resource base for students, educators, artists and scholars working around the history, present and future of the Indian LGBTQ community'. I learnt that the archive already had four categories—video (with more than 1,000 hours of footage), image (more than 1,000 images), audio (more than 500 audio files) and text (personal stories, legal documents and notes). They had also collected personal artefacts and memorabilia from more than two decades of the queer movement in India. The archive is not yet open to the public because, quite honestly, the team is still very busy cataloguing everything they have.

'Privacy and data loss are our two main concerns,' Jayshree told me. Plus, the funds were tight, so the process was taking longer. We sipped our coffee, and excitedly brainstormed about all their challenges and how they might be overcome. What if we had a queer museum attached to the archive, I proposed. I was thinking of New York's Leslie-Lohman Museum as a possible model, while Jayshree told me she was more drawn to what the Schwules Museum had done in Berlin, as the world's first gay and lesbian museum. We planned an event we would do together at the Culture Lab in Mumbai as part of the 2020 Pride programming, along with the Vidhi Centre for Legal Policy in Delhi.

Many of the stories I encounter while going through all these different online and offline archives are not just about despair. There is also an abundance of joy, as portrayed in the work of the historian Anjali Arondekar, for instance. She looks at English, Marathi, Konkani and Portuguese sources to rethink sexuality. It reminds me of how Brian Horton described his Brown University thesis to me: 'What do queer people do when they are not suffering?' Similarly, Arondekar looks at Indian queer history as one of abundance, not loss.[14]

~

Often, I am asked on one of those seizure-inducing newsroom debates if homosexuality, like McDonalds, has been imported to India from the West. My first reaction is, '*Hain*?' I think that most of you reading this book already know this, but let me state it clearly: India has always been open about discussing, accepting and depicting queerness.

Although the term 'homosexuality' is a Western construct and the German term 'homosexualität' was coined around 1868 by the Austro-Hungarian author and journalist Károly Mária Kertbeny,[15] men have always had sex with men, women have always been sexually attracted to other women, and this is across cultures and time. So why think of it as a Western thing just because the word came from there? We have our own words too—lots of them—as you have seen in the previous chapter.

Inclusiveness is very much part of our Indian culture. In fact, it is homophobia that is not Indian! The next time someone brings up the whole 'not in our culture' nonsense, tell them loudly and clearly that to be Indian means to be inclusive, and even the ancient *Rig Veda*, as noted by the mythologist Devdutt Pattanaik, proclaims: '*Vikruti evam prakruti*.' All things queer are also part of nature.[16]

Come with me; let's go on a boat ride. Let us sail away from the concrete charm of the city towards the historic Elephanta Caves perched on the Gharapuri Island. Here, preserved through time, we come across the carving of Ardhanarishwar—half woman, half man, a fully complete god.

So the story goes, as reclaimed and narrated by Devdutt in his book *Shikhandi and Other Tales They Don't Tell You*. Devdutt writes about three stories related to Ardhanarishwar—stories involving Brahma, the sage Bhagiratha and Bhrungi, Shiva's fervent devotee. Bhrungi refuses to pray to Parvati when he visits Mount Kailasa, and only wants to pray to Shiva. To avoid the goddess, who is sitting very close to Shiva, the devotee turns into a bee and tries to fly only around Shiva. Angered, Shiva and Parvati merge to form Ardhanarishwar, teaching the disciple a lesson in equality.[17]

The title story itself, of Shikhandi, is amazing. According to the myth, Shikhandi is a trans warrior who changes the course of the Mahabharata war between the Pandavas and the Kauravas. King Drupada, the father of Draupadi, wants a son for himself. On the birth of his daughter Shikhandi, he decides to raise her as his son, and schools her in statecraft and warcraft. He even forces Shikhandi into marriage with a woman, who is furious when she realises the truth. To satisfy her wife, Shikhandi acquires a male genital organ from Sthuna, a yakshya—a magical forest creature. In battle, Shikhandi is used by Arjuna and the Pandavas to bring down the great Bhishma, who has made a vow never to fight a woman. Bhishma lowers his bow when he sees Shikhandi, who is trans, and thus Arjuna is able to shower him with arrows that bring him down.[18]

The book catalogues many such stories. As Devdutt writes in the introduction: 'Hindu mythology makes constant references to queerness, the idea that questions notions of maleness and femaleness. There are stories of men who become women and women who become men, of men who create children without women and women who create children without men. There are also creatures that are neither this nor that, but a little bit of both, like the makara (a combination of fish and elephant), or the yali (a combination of lion and elephant). There are also many words in Sanskrit, Prakrit and Tamil, such as kliba, napumska, mukhabhaga, sanḍa, panda, pandaka, pedi, that suggest a long familiarity with queer thought and behaviour.'[19]

Each story in the book shows how pervasive gender fluidity is within ancient Indian cultural discourse. It is the erasure of this narrative that is problematic. One example of this erasure is the accusation that has been levelled against the Archaeological Survey of India (ASI) by the Odisha chief minister Naveen Patnaik, that in the name of restoration and conservation, the ASI has used plain stone to replace the sculpted stones of erotic carvings at the Konark Sun Temple.[20]

That it is the state of Odisha standing up against the ASI is telling. It is one of the progressive Indian states that has recognised the rights of transgender people, including employment opportunities for them, and has provided welfare schemes especially for them. It is also a deeply historic site that has produced erotic art and faith together under the same roof.

The temples of Khajuraho—once a cradle of wealth and now falling within present-day Madhya Pradesh, next to economically and socially fraught districts—also often come up in these discussions, with their elaborate, erotic carvings of women embracing and men displaying their genitals to each other.

In India, mythology captures the country's imagination in a way that no other discipline perhaps can. Even the Indian State and our courts refer to mythology extensively in their research and understanding of homosexuality in India. Siddharth Gautam, along with his ABVA teammates, notes in *Less Than Gay* that 'the copy of the original Kamasutra, which has a chapter on homosexuality ... [where] lesbian activity was stated to have been observed in the Anthapura (harem) ... was discovered to be loaned out for the last four years by the Delhi Public Library to none other than the Union Health Ministry.'[21]

Here is another story that Devdutt tells us in *Shikhandi*. One day, Shiva is making love to Parvati in the forest. To make sure she is not embarrassed by a male passer-by, he casts a spell so that anyone who enters the forest is turned into a woman. Prince Sudyumna rides into the forest. Because of this spell, he morphs into a woman, and his horse turns into a mare. Since spells cannot be reversed, on the plea of Prince Sudyumna, Shiva modifies the curse—when the moon waxes, he would be a man, and when the moon wanes, he would be a woman, Ila. The prince goes on to marry Boodh, the lord of the planet Mercury, who is cursed to be neither man nor woman by his father. So when Sudyumna turns into a man, Boodh is his wife. When Sudyumna turns into a woman, Boodh is her husband. Such is their marriage. Heterosexual, yet queer.[22]

Laxmi Narayan Tripathi, a leading hijra icon and activist, channels this deeply rooted mythological context for gender fluidity in her memoir, *Red Lipstick: The Men in My Life*, that came out in 2016.[23] I was on stage at the Title Waves bookstore in Bandra, conducting a Q&A session with her during the book launch. In *Red Lipstick*, she delves into the *Ramayana* and the *Mahabharata*, epics that are entrenched in the collective Indian consciousness, to give context to her identity:

> When Rama was leaving Ayodhya to begin his fourteen-year exile in the forest, such was his popularity, so great the devotion of his people towards him, that the entire kingdom followed him to the outskirts of the city. Touched by their support, Rama turned around and told his subjects, 'I request all the men and women gathered here who truly love me, to please return to their homes. Once the duration of my exile is complete, I shall be back with you.' At the completion of his exile, when Rama returned, he saw that there were several people still waiting at the same spot on the outskirts of Ayodhya where he had bid them farewell all those years ago. There were the hijras, my brethren, who did not return to their homes, since Rama had implored only the men and women to do so and they were neither. Overwhelmed by their dedication, Rama granted them, and future generations of hijras, a

> boon—we would have the power to grant both blessings and curses to men and women which would always come true. When hijras were patronised and indulged by royalty, they were not only visible but respected. It is the history and tradition of the hijra culture—rich, strong, textures—in our country that I found myself most drawn to. A tradition in which even the mighty, macho Arjuna could don the garb and identify as a woman and become Brihannala effortlessly.[24]

Hijras also played a prominent role in the royal courts of the Islamic world, especially in the Ottoman Empire and during the Mughal rule in medieval India. A detailed analysis of this historical background finds a place in the anthropologist Gayatri Reddy's *With Respect to Sex: Negotiating Hijra Identity in South India.*[25] Many travellers have documented the elevated status of trans people in the Mughal empire, specifically in harem management. Hijras also guarded the tomb of the Prophet, according to the British traveller Eldon Rutter's travelogue in 1925.[26]

Another instance of queerness in Islamic literature can be found in the 'Tilism-e-Hoshruba', a section in the Indo-Islamic fantasy epic *Dastan-e-Amir Hamza.* The tradition of reciting texts like *Dastan-e-Amir Hamza* is known as dastangoi, at the centre of which is the storyteller, the dastango. One of India's well-known dastangos Danish Husain writes about the queerness in this story: 'Men impersonate women without any stigma attached to this. The tales transcend gender stereotypes to such an extent that one forgets whether one is experiencing a woman character or a male character dressed as a woman and vice versa. The story runs over 7,000 pages and almost every second episode has a cross-dressing scenario.'[27]

~

In 2014, the Dalai Lama said that gay relationships were acceptable so long as they were consensual.[28] In the 2017 book *I Am Divine. So Are You: How Buddhism, Jainism, Sikhism and Hinduism Affirm the Dignity of Queer Identities and Sexualities,* Devdutt and his co-editor Jerry Johnson write that karmic faiths—Hinduism, Jainism, Sikhism and Buddhism—can be interpreted in ways that 'affirm the dignity of queer individuals.'[29] In the forthcoming book *Behold, I Make All Things New: How Judaism, Christianity and Islam Affirm the Dignity of Queer Identities and Sexualities,* Devdutt, who introduces the book, along with the book's editors, Rev'd Lorraine Tullekan and Rev'd J.P. Mokgethi-Heath, extends the inclusion argument further to the Abrahamic faiths.[30]

'Don't ever forget, queerness is an Indian construct; inclusion is an Indian construct,' Devdutt told me one evening in 2019, as we drove from the Bengaluru Airport to the Lalit, where we were speaking at a conference together. 'In our culture, empathy for the unfamiliar is key, it is the responsibility of the strong to care for the weak, the responsibility of the majority to ensure that the minority feel included.'

A few days later, he forwarded me a brilliant paper, 'Like a City Ablaze: The Third Sex and the Creation of Sexuality in Jain Religious Literature', written by Leonard Zwilling and Michael J. Sweet in 1996. The authors delve deep into the notion of the third sex entrenched in the Jain texts, in addition to the binary of male-female, and conclude that 'what is incontrovertible is that the writers of these [Jain] texts, using the raw materials supplied by Indian culture as well as by their experience, constructed elaborate discourses on the nature of sexuality, sex and gender that offered novel ways of thinking about these crucial and enigmatic facets of human experience.'[31]

~

While historicising queer India, it is vital to punctuate these ancient histories and myths and the scholarship around them with contemporary histories and lived experiences. Along with projects like QAMRA and the Varta Trust, the Culture Lab too works towards contributing to the archiving of the queer movement. Our panel discussion 'So Many Queer Indias' in January 2019 revolved around collectives and individuals who work for LGBTQ rights but don't feature in dominant media narratives. The panellists included Rachana Mudraboyina, the Hyderabad-based founder of TransVision, a YouTube channel that aims to create awareness about the transgender community; Diti, a member of Xukia, an Assam-based queer collective; Yadavendra Singh, the founder of the Awadh Queer Literature Festival; and Maya Sharma, the author of *Loving Women: Being Lesbian in Unprivileged India*.[32]

Diti explained how Assam in the 1990s was a whole different world. 'It was the heyday of the United Liberation Front of Assam (ULFA) and other anti-State movements. The only thing we spoke about was conflict, State and violence. The only reference to gender was in terms of the violence and conflict.' Diti joined Xukia on realising that there was a lack of representation of Assamese queer narratives.

Rachana spoke about her role as an activist and how she organised the first intersectional Pride march in Hyderabad. 'Violence against trans people is a disturbing issue. There's also a lot of chatter about the Pride movement not being our culture. So we wanted to decolonise it and gave it a vernacular name: Queer Swabhimana Yatra. We also changed the rules and didn't allow MNCs to fund it.' She went on to explain why they opted to make it intersectional: 'We wanted to show that transgenders also participated in the sixty-year-old intersectional Telangana struggle, but after the state was formed, our rights have not been acknowledged. So we invited other people's movements—the anti-caste movement, the women's movement and minority movements—to join in, and they came for it.'

Yadavendra discussed his difficult journey from Kanpur, where he was born and brought up, to Hyderabad, where he studied and became pen pals with men whom he began to meet. He also spoke about South Asia's first literature festival dedicated to LGBTQ people that he was organising in Lucknow, and why it was important to have such platforms. 'Literature festivals should not only be about books. We can't separate our movement from political engagement. We have a session with politicians and one with religious leaders as well. We have to engage with stakeholders like political parties and religious leaders to talk about the uncomfortable topics that affect the LGBTQ+ community.'[33]

As Yadavendra spoke, I was reminded of my time in Lucknow, having dinner with another queer icon, historian Saleem Kidwai. Saleem does an Awadhi tehzeeb from a different era. An elegant home. An Afghan hound lying down languorously at the entrance. A library full of old books. I half expected Ghulam Ali's 'Chupke Chupke Raat Din' to start playing from a gramophone somewhere, but instead, Saleem and I filled his study with the reverberating sounds of our cackly gossip.

In *Same-Sex Love in India: Readings from Literature and History*, the editors Saleem and Ruth Vanita, another queer icon and a brilliant teacher, break down time into four parts, while recognising that some leakage and seepage is inevitable:[34]

'Ancient Indian Material', with stories of same-sex love in Sanskrit texts, the *Mahabharata*, the *Kama Sutra*, and even a Pali text, *Manikantha Jataka*.

'Medieval Material in the Sanskritic Tradition', which includes Sanskrit, Odiya and Bengali stories, many of them either local retellings of the *Ramayana* or from the Puranas—stories that mythologise Hindu gods.

'Medieval Material in the Perso-Urdu Tradition', with flavours of Urdu, Persian and Turkish queerness, with writings on *Baburnama* and more, although the stories and poetry overwhelmingly concern men.

'Modern Indian Material'—the part of the book I loved most—talks about artists like Bhupen Khakhar and Amrita Shergill, references queer plays by writers like Vijay Tendulkar and even discusses Gandhi. It has a very interesting chapter on Rekhti poetry, in which male poets used the feminine gaze to write. These poems were considered obscene, once. Now, they are being seriously studied by scholars.[35]

The whirlwind narrations of the book replayed in my head as Saleem and I chatted. We had returned to his home after my session at IIM Lucknow with the first-year MBA batch of 400 students, where I had urged them all to become champions for the LGBTQ community with my over-the-top gayness, all under the guise of recruitment for Godrej's HR department—cultural acupuncture. Saleem had beamed through the entire session, nodding approvingly, and I had performed even more dramatically than I normally would have, knowing that one of my queer gurus was watching.

As I savoured every morsel of the fragrant shami kebabs—a Kidwai family recipe handed down over generations—and tried to lick every grain of biryani off my plate, I was reminded of another friend, the young academic Dhiren Borisa. While Saleem has retired from his teaching, Dhiren is just getting started as an assistant professor at the O.P. Jindal University. When I first met Dhiren, at the Godrej-sponsored MINGLE conference in 2014, he was a PhD student at the Jawaharlal Nehru University (JNU), and we had had a heated public discussion. I am embarrassed to say that I had argued that queer people should subsume all their other identities and convince straight people that we are just like them. Furthermore, even within the movement, I had said, queer people need to rally around 377 and think of other inequalities later. I cringe when I think of myself at that time. Dhiren was kind enough to forgive me for my foolishness, and over the years we have become friends, and bond over, among other things, our love for bow ties.

Dhiren recently came to the lab to speak about caste and queerness, the subject matter of his PhD dissertation, and at the event, he called his intersectional despair a khichdi. When I looked at my plate of biryani in Saleem's home that day, Dhiren's voice spoke back to me.

> There is often silence around caste when you bring it up in queer spaces. There is also hostility. Who desires, whom you desire, who gets to desire, whose desirability counts, is a manifestation of caste, or where you come from is a manifestation of caste.

> When you ask what is a dalit queer, 'dalit' is often mistaken as an additive construct ... as if some khichdi will come out.
>
> Whatever we are, whatever manifestations we are, even in terms of whom I like, whom do I want to sleep with, or my background in terms of bastis, houses, which languages can I speak, what education I could get, what education I could not get, or how I am treated differently by different people at different levels, it all constitutes each other. It is not two separate things that come together.
>
> It is that my queerness is defined by my caste and my caste is defined by my queerness. Neither in the anti-caste spaces will I be fully accepted nor in the queer spaces will I be fully accepted. For me, dalit queerness is then a continuous struggle to recognise what you are, and acknowledge the complexities and histories you come with ... challenging the boundaries.
>
> I see queerness as an aspirational category that can open up possibilities of change, taking you far away from hostilities. But sometimes in queer spaces, hostilities are reproduced, exemplified. Therefore, dalit queerness is this threshold which is always slippery, always soapy, always messy. There is no neat definition or amalgamation of these two entities given the range of possibilities, privileges and burdens we negotiate the world with.[36]

What happens when despair is located at the intersection of identities? What if both the identities, like Dhiren's, are marginalised? Suraj Yengde in his book *Caste Matters* talks about how one movement can support the other, moving both further.

> Historically, the Dalit movement has taken up the cause of the transgender people and prostitutes on par with the Dalit struggle. Firebrand leader of the Dalit Panthers, Namdeo Dhasal, organised Dalits, transgender people and prostitutes under the Samantha Morcha. This coalition advocated for the annihilation of caste-based prejudices by making a clear case against it.[37]

The queer movement as part of the dalit struggle is one thing, and the dalit struggle as part of the queer movement is quite another. The Chennai-based queer activist moulee notes the dissonance in the queer movement, which is largely dominated by gay men from privileged castes. He writes the following in a piece titled '"Safe" Queer Spaces: How Inclusive Is Inclusive?'

> In my experience, the existing oppressive social structure transcends into queer safe spaces as well. I have observed that, invariably, non-Dalit-Bahujan individuals dominate these spaces. And while a small section of cis-gendered queer savarna men acknowledge the importance of intersectionality and

> understand the detrimental role caste plays in these safe spaces; it almost never transforms into action.[38]

This is something to think about, long and hard. Are the histories of the Indian queer movement inclusive? Whose histories have not been told and why? I am conscious that a lot of the different histories I have catalogued in this chapter—whether through the lens of mythology or oral history projects—are male or upper-caste narratives. At the same time, I agree with moulee about the importance of self-representation, when he writes: 'I don't want you to talk about my experiences. Because you have not experienced what it is to be a Dalit-Bahujan. It is my experience and I will share it.'[39]

What I *can* do as a privileged savarna and have tried to do is to amplify the different voices telling our stories. There are so many more intersectional queer histories that need to be acknowledged, recorded, written and disseminated, and some of these projects have already begun. In this book, especially in the last chapter, I will point towards some of these projects that give me hope as we create a more equal Queeristan of the future together.

7

LGBTQ India and the Law

Here is a quick summary of the legal provisions governing LGBTQ folks that the wonderful team at Community Business, a not-for-profit that consults with corporates on inclusion, have put together in their 2019 report *LGBT+ Workplace Inclusion in India: The Definitive Guide.* We have made some progress, but a lot of work is needed for us to go from merely being non-criminals to equal citizens with the same rights as others, as can be seen below.

1. Is consensual gay sex legal in India?
   Yes (since 2018)
2. Is the age of consent the same as for heterosexual sex?
   Yes, eighteen and above
3. Is same-sex marriage recognised?
   No
4. Are same-sex relationships, such as civil partnerships, unions or domestic partnerships legally recognised?
   No
5. Are overseas same-sex marriages, civil partnerships and unions legally recognised in India (for the purpose of immigration, joint tax filing, etc.)?
   No
6. Are there explicit statutory protections to protect LGBT+ individuals from discrimination?
   No, except for trans individuals
7. Can LGBT+ employees be covered by in-house benefits, policy safeguards, grievance redressal mechanisms?
   Yes

8 Are there laws to protect LGBT+ individuals from employment discrimination?
No, except for trans individuals

9. Are transgender or intersex people legally recognised according to their gender identity?
Yes, self-identified gender is recognised

10. Are intersex babies and minors protected from non-consensual conversion surgery?
Only in Tamil Nadu

11. Are LGBT+ individuals able to inherit their same-sex partner's/spouse's property?
No

12. Can LGBT+ individuals make decisions on medical treatments on behalf of their same-sex partner/spouse who is incapacitated?
No

13. Do same-sex couples have adoption rights?
No

14. Are LGBT+ individuals allowed to openly serve in the military?
No

15. Is gay conversion therapy banned?
No[1]

~

In this chapter, I will tell you a story of liberation and hope, but also of pain and rejection. The story is built around the laws and court judgements that so many activists and advocates from our community have relentlessly fought for over the years.

First, there are the various court cases that have been fought around Section 377. There is also the NALSA Supreme Court judgement of 2014 that gave the transgender community an anchor, but it was followed by dejections and rejections, with parliament passing a law that stripped off the progressive nature of the NALSA judgement. Finally, there is the Supreme Court's Right to Privacy judgement of 2017, which we won't discuss in great detail in this chapter, but which is still an important precursor to our 2018 victory. These are the three judgements that directly affect queer people in India today.

~

What came first—the law or the movement?

Section 377 of the Indian Penal Code criminalised sexual acts between same-sex adults, even if they were consensual. It has its origin in the Indian Penal Code of 1860. The Criminal Tribes Act of 1871 that targeted transgender populations by pronouncing them 'criminal' also came from this moment in time.

In 1835, the politician Thomas Babington Macaulay drafted the 'Minute on Education', an essay that sought to create 'a class of persons, Indian in blood and colour, but English in tastes, in opinions, in morals and in intellect'.[2] In the same year, Macaulay wrote the first draft of the Indian Penal Code to create this 'class of people'. Section 377 of this code, passed as law in 1860, reflected this.

> Section 377: Unnatural offences—Whoever voluntarily has carnal intercourse against the order of nature with any man, woman or animal shall be punished with imprisonment for life, or with imprisonment of either description for a term which may extend to ten years, and shall be liable to fine. Explanation—Penetration is sufficient to constitute the carnal intercourse necessary to the offence described in this section.[3]

In brief, if the sex could not lead to babies, then the British considered it 'against the order of nature'. Macaulay and his compatriots and the laws they created moved India away from a rich discourse around queer love and lust.[4]

The Criminal Tribes Act was repealed after Independence in 1952,[5] while the first organised effort to repeal Section 377 of the IPC was taken up by the ABVA in 1994.[6]

It had been eight years since the first case of HIV was detected in India, towards the end of 1985 by Sellappan Nirmala, a microbiology student at a medical college in Chennai. She found her area of research among the sex workers of the city—taking their blood samples, freezing them in her refrigerator at home and getting them tested by travelling to a town 200 kilometres away in an overnight train with her husband. Six of the blood samples returned HIV positive. These samples were flown to the US for confirmation, and the results were the same. By the time this news went from the Indian Council of Medical Research to the then prime minister, Rajiv Gandhi, and the then Tamil Nadu state health minister, H.V. Hande, and finally the state assembly, disbelief had brewed into a storm. The AIDS crisis had arrived in India.[7]

During her research, Nirmala also went to prisons to meet gay men, another at-risk group, to collect their blood. Eight years later, it was from these prisons that the 1994 petition would be born. The team of doctors found that more than 90 per cent of the people in Tihar Jail in Delhi, an overcrowded prison, had engaged in homosexual sex. A public health disaster was looming.

Naisargi N. Dave, an anthropologist and activist, recollected this frenzy during a panel discussion on 'Envisioning Global LGBT Human Rights' at the University of Toronto in 2011, a recorded video of which I saw later:

> The inspector general of Tihar Jail, the well-known Kiran Bedi, came down firmly against the suggestion of WHO to supply condoms in the prison. It instead isolated any and all offenders. A petition was filed with the High Court of Delhi that condom distribution in prisons would be tantamount to anti-national, criminal, immoral and unconstitutional behaviour. The very existence of Section 377 justified this. In response to this writ petition, ABVA challenged the very validity of Section 377. But, predictably, the case languished in the court for years, with no computerised system in place, the ABVA activists had to check the court dockets weekly for years on end. An unfunded group, with pro bono activists, ABVA missed a scheduled appearance. The petition neither decided upon nor disposed, lay buried for eight years under the court.[8]

But all of this had no consequence on the activist space. No collective large-scale movement was being constructed to challenge the law on homosexuality at that time. Arguments were made for first creating a movement before approaching the courts. Siddharth Dube notes in *No One Else*:

> Siddharth [Gautam] and I had often heatedly argued about the possibility of throwing out Section 377. His view was that we needed to build a mass movement in India seeking this goal, akin to the one for African American civil rights. My reaction had always been that something like this was simply not possible in the India of our time. It was too dangerous. There were too few of us who were openly gay, and even fewer with a determined sense of activism ... none of the domestic civil rights groups considered matters of sexuality to be of any relevance to their work. Amnesty International had only just begun to fight for people imprisoned because of their sexual orientation.[9]

ABVA wrote to around 100 activist groups in India seeking support for their petition. However, none came forward, and the ABVA petition was eventually dismissed in 2001, incidentally the same year that the next legal challenge to Section 377 came up.[10] The Naz Foundation, which too had been working actively on the AIDS epidemic of the 1990s, like the ABVA, filed a public interest litigation at the Delhi High Court for reading down Section 377 on the grounds that it was discriminatory to queer people, through their legal counsel, Lawyers Collective. It challenged the constitutionality of the section on the grounds that it violated the right to privacy, dignity and health under Article 21 (it hampered HIV/AIDS intervention and condom distribution programmes), equal protection of law and non-discrimination under Articles 14 and 15, and freedom of expression under Article 19 of the Constitution.[11]

But this too spurred bitter arguments among activists, some of whom believed that the petition had come too soon, without a movement in place, among other objections. Although things had changed since 1994, and pockets of communities had mobilised, it still wasn't enough to fight a case as a unified body. Apart from not consulting with and creating a community, there were a few major problems with the 2001 petition. The first gaping hole was the privacy argument used in it.

Privacy was a privilege in India back then, as it still is today. Many gay men used to cruise for sex in public places like parks and public toilets. There was nothing private about their acts. And these were the people who were mostly affected by the AIDS pandemic. So, if the petition in 2001 was indeed trying to help those at risk of AIDS, which is a public health issue and extends beyond the privacy of bedrooms, why would it opt for the privacy argument—essentially that the government had no business in the privacy of people's bedrooms?

Much later, in August 2017, the Supreme Court would pass the Right to Privacy judgement. For the first time, it would affirm decisively that the right to privacy is a fundamental right, something that had been debated for over four decades. It would conclude that the right to one's sexual orientation is at the core of the fundamental rights outlined in Articles 14, 15 and 21 of the Constitution.[12] In his judgement, Justice Chandrachud, one of the nine judges, would note:

> Dignity cannot exist without privacy. Both reside within the inalienable values of life, liberty and freedom which the Constitution has recognised. Privacy is the ultimate expression of the sanctity of the individual. It is a constitutional value which straddles across the spectrum of fundamental rights and protects for the individual a zone of choice and self-determination. Privacy includes at its core the preservation of personal intimacies, the sanctity of family life,

> marriage, procreation, the home and sexual orientation. Privacy also connotes a right to be left alone.[13]

But there was no such Right to Privacy judgement in 2001.

Furthermore, even within the feminist movement, there were voices that were weary of using an argument for privacy to repeal Section 377. They argued that having the State present in the private sphere actually protects women from domestic violence and toxic patriarchy, which show their ugly heads behind closed doors. They feared that if the courts agreed that the government indeed had no business in people's private lives, violence against women in the private sphere would go unchecked, and so the argument to strike down 377 must not be made by using the right to privacy.

In the Toronto video, Naisargi talks about how the queer movement seeking to make a clear distinction between the private and the public angered the feminists. In the introduction to the 2006 book *Loving Women: Being Lesbian in Unprivileged India*, which has stories from small towns and villages across the country, the author Maya Sharma notes the friction between the two movements.[14]

In the 1990s, lesbian women were categorised under 'single women' at conferences. The mere mention of the word lesbian made people uncomfortable. In *Loving Women*, Maya reminisces with shame about how in 1993 during the Northern Regional Conference of the Women's Movement in Kanpur, they excluded an out lesbian from a session on sexuality because they feared she would not keep a low profile. Maya further writes that in 1997, the Bihar State Coordinating Committee that organised the Ranchi edition of this conference deleted the word 'lesbian' from the invitation letter because they felt that including it would 'alienate many women's groups and individual women' who would 'not want to volunteer at a conference which included a focus on homosexuality'.[15]

The arguments made back then were often the same. 'It is for the greater good of the movement: the presence of lesbians (since they are unacceptable publicly) will fragment whatever collectivity has been established over the years, fewer women will associate with the movement, fewer groups will participate, and mainstream and state support will be seriously compromised … it will raise the issue of lesbian rights at an opportune moment and with the right strategy.'[16]

But what is an opportune moment for intersectionality? What is the right strategy?

Maya writes that 'until 2001 there were no statistics on lesbians in India.' That year, lesbian women were included as research subjects for the first time in a study conducted by TISS on violence against lesbians.[17]

Gautam Bhan, the queer activist and researcher who wrote the foreword to *Loving Women*, was also present at the panel with Naisargi in Toronto in 2011. He wore a white kurta, with most of the buttons undone, chest hair peeking out mischievously. I've had a crush on him for years, and it was difficult to concentrate on what he was saying as I watched the online recording of the discussion. But I somehow managed, for the sake of this book.

In the video, he talks about how important feminists were to the queer movement. 'The largest number of people [in queer politics] came from feminism, the women's movements. Our first meetings were in women's movement offices, because those were the only safe spaces we had. Many of us identified first as feminists before we came to sexuality and queer politics.'[18]

Apart from friction between the feminist and the queer movements, there was also fragmentation within the queer movement itself when Naz filed the petition. One of the arguments made was that the movement should not be associated only with court cases—it must also be about everyday lives; the court petition must be a part of the movement, the movement itself cannot be built around the petition.

Naz too was going through a difficult time. Before the petition was filed, in an unrelated case the same year, the police in Lucknow had arrested outreach workers of the Bharosa Trust, who were doing AIDS awareness work. The office of Naz, which was its affiliate, was also raided, and dildos kept in the office to demonstrate condom use were confiscated. The next day, local newspapers falsely proclaimed, 'Gay Sex Racket Busted'.[19]

There was also a shift in the movement's understanding of what equality meant. One way of fighting injustice was to fight as a minority, vociferously asking the majority for rights to be bestowed and corrections to be made. But the queer movement, or at least a part of it, wanted to do something more radical, as Gautam says in the Toronto discussion video. 'This is not about minority politics—not us and them, the minority asking for rights from the majority. There is a language you get from the West ... is equal rights. We are all the same, we deserve equal rights as you. In India, an equal rights argument meant you had the right to be as fucked up as straight people. No one had sexual freedom. This whole question of compulsory marriage, you have inter-caste couples that were being burnt alive, you had inter-religious couples that were being chased ... What is it? Heterosexual marriage between Mr and Mrs Gupta who came from the same class, the same age, the same income, who had to get married at twenty-six?'[20]

There was a call for queer politics to become broader, more progressive and more demanding, as in Gautam's argument above. Thus, the movement became about class, caste, desire, marriage, freedom—a radical rethinking of how society was structured. As the sociologist Jyoti Puri notes in her 2016 book *Sexual States: Governance and the Struggle over the Antisodomy Law in India*: 'Undoing the social injustices of sexual orientation are contingent on undoing the harms of caste and class inequalities, religious discrimination, nationalisms, racialisms, gender hierarchies and intolerances of gender expression.'[21]

But this impetus towards intersectionality came about over time. In 2001, forget mobilisation and progressive rhetoric, we did not even have the vocabulary to articulate our identities. Gautam says, 'In the early 2000s, there was a palpable sense of excitement in India that for the first time there is going to be this conversation. It was hurtling at us, we had no choice. And the whole thing was, when you have a place to say something, what will you say? What words will you choose? What political identities will you embrace? Will you say "queer"? Will you say "gay"? Will you say "hijra", "kothi", "panthi?"'[22]

These questions would continue to be asked as the movement snowballed. In 2004, when the Delhi High Court dismissed the Naz case, it stated that purely academic issues could not be examined by the court. It is important to note that the 2001 petition was not about people's real-life stories, but merely a common sense perspective on human rights. This need for stories is a very important point to note, as you will soon see.

The Supreme Court reinstated the Naz petition in the Delhi High Court in 2006, after the Naz Foundation filed a special leave petition citing that the case was a matter of public interest. A coalition called Voices Against 377 joined the petition. Following this, two conflicting affidavits were filed: the Ministry of Home Affairs opposed the decriminalisation of Section 377, but the National AIDS Control Organisation, which comes under the Ministry of Health and Family Welfare, provided its support to the movement and the legal case,[23] stating that criminalisation impeded the control of HIV/AIDS.[24] Between 2008 and 2009, the matter remained reserved for judgement.[25]

In 2009, the Delhi High Court read down Section 377. Delivered in the time of social media and the finger-snap spread of information, the historic verdict caused quite a dhamaka. This is how Naisargi describes the moment in the Toronto video:

In the courtroom, activists cried with joy. Outside the court, journalists shouted, photographers craned for a better view and queer people hugged and cheered, taking calls on the phone as the incredible and unimaginable news spread across the country and the world. By nightfall, as celebration turned to reflection, right-wing politicians were already promising to take the case to the Supreme Court, and swamis were reassuring the nation that yoga could be a cure for this sickness of homosexuality. But for a few days, all of this didn't matter. It was all joy, disbelief, euphoria.[26]

But soon after, in 2009 itself, Suresh Kumar Koushal, an astrologer in Delhi, joined hands with a diverse bunch of organisations—such as the All India Muslim Personal Law Board, Trust God Missionaries and Krantikari Manuwadi Morcha—to appeal to the Supreme Court to overrule the Delhi High Court judgement.

In an interview with the *Hindu* in December 2013, Koushal said:

I begged the court to look at some important issues, like, to think about what would happen in the hostels, how rich families will exploit their servants, koi rokne wala nahi hoga (There won't be anybody to stop them.) Un ko kaun control karega? (Who will control them?) It is also directly linked to our national security. Lakhs of jawans and defence personnel stay away from their families to safeguard our borders and important places. If Section 377 is lifted, they would miss their partners and get into consensual relationships with each other. What happens in the long run ... we might lose a battle.[27]

Koushal's appeal, along with that of fourteen others, opposing the Delhi High Court's 2009 verdict were followed by applications to intervene in 2011, the conclusion of final arguments in 2012, and the submission of documents and studies in support of arguments in early 2013. The subsequent Supreme Court judgement in November 2013 overturned the 2009 Delhi High Court judgement.[28]

The observations made in the 2013 judgement still shock me:

While reading down Section 377 IPC, the Division Bench of the High Court overlooked that a miniscule fraction of the country's population constitute lesbians, gays, bisexuals or transgenders and in the last more than 150 years less than 200 persons have been prosecuted (as per the reported orders) for committing offence under Section 377 IPC and this cannot be made sound basis for declaring that section ultra vires the provisions of Articles 14, 15 and 21 of the Constitution. [...]

> Respondent No. 1 attacked Section 377 IPC on the ground that the same has been used to perpetrate harassment, blackmail and torture on certain persons, especially those belonging to the LGBT community. In our opinion, this treatment is neither mandated by the section nor condoned by it and the mere fact that the section is misused by police authorities and others is not a reflection of the vires of the section. It might be a relevant factor for the Legislature to consider while judging the desirability of amending Section 377 IPC.[29]

Essentially, the Supreme Court stated that the LGBTQ community was a 'miniscule' minority in India and therefore not deserving of constitutional protections, and transferred the onus to parliament. We had lost.

~

The lawyer Arundhati Katju appeared for the teachers who were petitioning against 377 during the 2013 courtroom happenings. Six years later, in 2019, during her TEDx Ferhadija talk, she would mention the frustration that the 2013 verdict had brewed and how she and her group of lawyers 'went back to the drawing board'. The biggest gap in the courtroom strategy of 2013 was clear: 'The public and the courts did not know who the LGBTQ people were.'[30]

The lawyers understood that instead of talking about penetrative sex and the right to privacy, a different approach was needed. Stories. Simple stories. Real-life stories about love and loss. Over the next five years, Arundhati and her partner Menaka Guruswamy carefully brought together five prominent members of the LGBTQ community to petition against 377 once again. The classical dancer and yoga instructor Navtej Singh Johar was the lead petitioner. Among the other petitioners were Navtej's partner of twenty-three years, the journalist Sunil Mehra, along with the celebrity chef Ritu Dalmia, hotelier Aman Nath, business executive Ayesha Kapur, and all five of them had stories to tell.

A five-judge bench, comprising Chief Justice Dipak Misra and justices A.K. Sikri, A.M. Khanwilkar, D.Y. Chandrachud and Ashok Bhushan, agreed to review the petition and decided to re-examine the 377 case in January 2018.[31]

There was a deluge of queer people who came out to file supporting petitions. Akkai Padmashali and other transgender people had already filed a writ petition challenging the constitutionality of Section 377 in light of the Supreme Court NALSA verdict of 2014, which spoke of the fundamental rights of trans people. Keshav Suri, the executive director of the Lalit Suri Hospitality Group, filed a separate one. A group of twenty students and alumni from IIT Bombay filed a petition on the mental health issues, harassment and bullying they faced because of 377. And there were many more people who came forward. The age spectrum was varied, and Arundhati in her talk mentioned how this was amplified in the courtroom. 'My co-counsel Menaka Guruswamy compared the stories of Navtej and Sunil, of Aman, Ritu, Ayesha, with the stories of these IIT petitioners. For the older people, in some sense, their lives have gone by. But for our young clients, their lives deserve to be different. And the court responded to these stories.'[32]

On 6 September 2018, the Supreme Court read down Section 377 as a law that violated the dignity and privacy of the LGBTQ community. Victory, at last.

Alongside 377, which deals with homosexuality, it is important to look at the NALSA judgement and why it was important as a pioneering and progressive document, and how its judicial impact relapsed with the Transgender Persons (Protection of Rights) Bill, 2019.

In 2014, the Supreme Court gave a landmark verdict for the transgender community. The National Legal Services Authority vs Union of India judgement, popularly known as the NALSA judgement, recognised the fundamental rights of trans people, and spoke about protection from discrimination, equality of opportunity, freedom of expression and right to dignity.

This progressive judgement recognised the rights of trans people to self-identify with the gender of their choice; it also stated that sex reassignment surgery (SRS), the operation that trans people undergo to make permanent physical changes in their body, was not a prerequisite for identifying as trans.[33] This was huge! Reservation for both education and employment was granted by identifying the transgender community as a socially and economically backward class.[34] The central government and all the state governments were to provide for separate bathrooms and targeted healthcare services in hospitals, and operate HIV serosurveillance centres for trans people. The judgement also mandated social welfare schemes, public awareness and gender sensitisation.[35]

But the NALSA judgement travelled a rocky road to the noisy halls of the Indian Parliament towards becoming a law.

In 2014, a private member's bill on trans people was introduced by Tiruchi Siva, a member of the Dravida Munnetra Kazhagam (DMK) party and member of the Rajya Sabha. It was passed in the Rajya Sabha, but lapsed as the sitting Lok Sabha's term ended and elections took place. The new government's Ministry of Social Justice and Empowerment then drafted another version of the bill in 2015. Many organisations working on trans rights responded to the draft bill and offered strong recommendations.[36]

This 2015 draft bill was a weaker version of the 2014 bill because it was unclear on reservation for the community and mandated that a state-level authority decide whether to give someone a transgender certificate or not. It also contained an unscientific definition of what it means to be a transgender person. The definition didn't account for intersex individuals and their right to self-identify, and it offered a simplistic understanding of how one's gender identity and expression can challenge our existing biomedical framework. For instance, the 2015 definition simply referred to a transgender person as one whose 'gender does not match with the gender assigned to that person at birth', instead of widening the category to include various forms of self-identification.[37]

Despite several activists and collectives responding to this draft bill with recommendations, the government introduced the Transgender Persons (Protection of Rights Bill), 2016, without taking in most of the substantial criticisms, and it was riddled with damaging language. It conflated the categories of trans and intersex, ignored hijra family structures, criminalised begging, made no mention of affirmative action, mandated that a screening committee decide whether a person was trans or not, and also laid down punishment for sexual assault and rape which was not on par with laws for cisgendered people. Many of these omittances were contrary to the provisions of the NALSA judgement.[38]

In 2016 and 2017, trans collectives deposed in front of the Parliamentary Standing Committee on Social Justice about the ways in which the bill was inadequate.

Gee Imaan Semmalar, a trans rights activist, had this to say about the 2016 bill: 'When the issue of self-identification of gender identity as granted by the Supreme Court judgement was raised by the committee, the ministry responded with arguments about physical screenings being necessary to prevent "misuse". It was disappointing to see the committee backtrack on its promises to safeguard our constitutionally granted rights upheld by the Supreme Court and agree with the fallacious arguments made by the Ministry of Social Justice and Empowerment. It is also very disheartening to see that the 2016 version of the same ministry's bill is worse than the earlier version they themselves drafted and released in 2015!'[39]

This bill created a two-tier system within the transgender community, wherein persons who had not had SRS could identify as transgender only after scrutiny and certification by a district screening committee. Moreover, those seeking to identify as male or female needed to have undergone the SRS procedure. Again, like I mentioned earlier, the NALSA verdict recommends self-identification; so, mandating SRS for changing one's declared gender identity was shocking.[40]

Much of the feedback on the 2016 bill, sought by the Lok Sabha in the first place, was ignored. This includes the 2017 Standing Committee report, which was prepared in consultation with NGOs, activists and other concerned individuals. In 2018, an amended bill was introduced and passed in the Lok Sabha. The bill lapsed in the Rajya Sabha when the sitting government's term once again came to an end.[41]

Around the same time, the Trafficking of Persons (Prevention, Protection and Rehabilitation) Bill, 2018, was introduced in parliament. The bill appeared to systematically criminalise hijra homes and trans persons who depended on sex work as a source of livelihood. It made no distinction between coerced labour and the limited choices of employment available to trans people. It endangered those trans persons whose identity documentation might not match what was understood to be their biological sex, by making them liable for fraud. It also criminalised hormone administration as 'aggravated trafficking'. While any coercive act should be criminalised, criminalising *voluntary* hormone administration would endanger trans lives—these nuances were missing from the bill. It should not be shocking then that no trans people or NGO networks were consulted before it was drafted.[42] This bill too lapsed when the sixteenth Lok Sabha dissolved.[43]

Finally, the Transgender Persons (Protection of Rights) Bill, 2019, was introduced and passed in the Lok Sabha. It retained most of its older regressive qualities. While it removed the words 'screening committee' from the bill—it still mandated that the district magistrate and a medical officer be involved in issuing an identity card. In an interview to a news outlet, Grace Banu said, 'What is this if not screening?'[44]

Ironically, another bill was passed the same day, the Surrogacy (Regulation) Bill, 2019, which ensured that same-sex couples, single parents and live-in couples would not be able to pursue the path of surrogacy.[45]

On 26 November 2019, the Transgender Persons (Protection of Rights) Bill was passed in the Rajya Sabha. The motion to send it to a select committee was turned down with seventy noes. It quietly received assent from President Ram Nath Kovind on 5 December, and became law. This disregard of trans voices and concerns about trans livelihoods is a massive setback for trans rights in the country.[46]

However, our struggle still continues. In late 2019, Assam's first transgender judge, Swati Bidhan Baruah, challenged the Trans Act by filing an appeal. She stated that in its current form it does nothing for trans employment and empowerment and is, in fact, 'draconian' and 'humiliating'.[47]

~

It is clear from looking at how things have panned out over the years for the queer community in India, that the law, and by this I mean the courts, mostly put constitutional morality above social acceptance. Our courts have been by and large progressive. The government, on the other hand, has dilly-dallied, its actions all smoke and mirrors.

That is the tricky thing about governments. When there is top-down legal action from the courts, grassroots movement from the activists and corporate acupuncture in terms of political funding and lobbying, the government has the potential to be an important strategic ally, like it has been with bodies like the National Aids Control Organization. But it can also be a deterrent, like it has been with 377 over the years, or the various trans bills.

It is important to mention here that things are quite different at the national and state government level in our country. No matter which government has been in power at the centre, queer rights have never been its priority. But many state governments across the country have chosen to pay attention to the rights of trans citizens.

Tamil Nadu was the first state in India to set up a transgender welfare board in 2008, called the Aravani Welfare Board.[48] It offers loans to incentivise the establishment of businesses, free health insurance and vocational training for transgenders.[49] It was also the first state to ban corrective surgery on intersex babies born with a reproductive system or genital anatomy that does not fit into the binary of male or female. This came on the heels of a Madras High Court judgement in 2019.[50] In April that year, the Madras High Court also recognised the right of trans women to be married under the Hindu Marriage Act, 1955.[51]

Kerala was the first state to formulate a transgender policy in 2015 to protect the community from discrimination.[52] By 2017, both Cochin and Trivandrum in Kerala had transgender welfare boards. Kochi Metro was the first government project in the country to hire transgender people. Kerala also offers pensions for trans people above the age of sixty.[53] The University of Kerala has a trans policy which prohibits and safeguards against ragging and discrimination. It also offers special facilities, awareness programmes and barrier-free access to education.[54] Teachers in more than 2,000 schools in the state have been trained and sensitised about trans rights.[55]

Karnataka, under the Mythri scheme, offers a pension of ₹500 to transgender people aged between eighteen and sixty-four, whose annual income is less than ₹12,000 in rural areas and ₹17,000 in urban areas.[56]

These stories are not unique to the south of India. Chhattisgarh, like Tamil Nadu, offers free SRS in government hospitals. Eleven departments in the state—Health, Higher Education, Women and Child Development, Social Welfare, Technical Education, School Education, Home, Panchayat and Rural Development, Urban Development, Public Relations and General Administration—have announced schemes or activities specifically for the trans community.[57] Odisha is another example of a pioneering state. In 2016, it was the first to give transgender people social welfare benefits such as Below Poverty Line cards, free housing, food grains and pension.[58] The government of Madhya Pradesh appointed its first trans government officer in 2019 and provided kinnars with separate toilets for a grand festival in Ujjain.[59]

As you can see from the above examples, many states in the country are already inclusive. The law too is firmly on our side today. Being LGBTQ is not a crime in India anymore, and there is absolutely nothing in the law that prevents you or your organisation from being inclusive. But the law is only on paper. As citizens, it is our duty to translate the progress made in the courts into something real and tangible. It is also now time for workplaces to participate in this movement.

8

It's All About Loving Your Children

Here is Kusuma Krishna speaking about how her mother accepted her. I had met Kusuma many years ago at the MINGLE summit as a student, then again at the Bengaluru Pride Fair in 2019, which she attended as an out and proud Ola employee, and she now works with Intuit.

'My girlfriend lives in Pune, I live with my mom in Bangalore. I am out to my family. When I got divorced, I tried to tell my mother. When I was growing up, she knew I had this unusual friendship with a girl, and she hated the girl. Even after marriage, when I was alone for the longest time, I told my mom I don't want to be married, I don't like men, I like women. Every time I would tell her that, she would shut me up—she was in denial mode. She wouldn't want to hear me out. For eight long years this kept happening.

'Only a couple of years ago I sat her down and told her I like girls, I am a lesbian, and I don't want to be married to a guy. She cried, and then said, "I will take you to a psychiatrist. If he says you are fine, then it's okay."

'There is a periodical called *Sudha*, a Kannada periodical. My mother has not studied beyond class ten, so she only reads Kannada. In the periodical, there is this doctor, a psychiatrist who gives suggestions for different issues, mostly sex-related but also about family issues. "He is very good," my mother said. He was eighty years old. I was anxious about what this eighty-year-old would tell us, but I still went.

'It was wonderful. I told him the entire story, like I am telling you now, and he got up and hugged me and said, "You are a really strong girl." Then he called my mom inside, explained to her that I was absolutely normal, completely fine, nothing wrong with me, and then told her, "You have two choices—either you want your daughter to marry or you want her to be happy. You can only get one."

'That is when it struck my mother, she wanted her daughter to be happy. She told me that she wanted to understand how all of this works, to get to know me better. I tried to explain it to her theoretically, but she did not understand. There is this beautiful 2016 web series called *The "Other" Love Story*. It is based in Bangalore, about two girls who go to the same college and fall in love. It is set in the same timeframe when I was going to college. So it is very relatable to my own story. We used to have landlines and not mobile phones. We used to give three rings to say, "I love you," and things like that. This series has all of those things. I made her watch the series. It is in Kannada, so she could understand it well. She started watching very intently. She started relating everything from the serial to my own life. "You also used to give missed calls and get missed calls, no? The girls are shown to miss tuitions and then hang out bunking classes—you also used to do it, no?" I was like, "Yeah!"

'Then there came a point in the series when they both were about to get intimate, okay? Obviously, I am an Indian child, and this is my Indian mother, so I asked her, "Should I forward this part?" Mom was like, "No, no, no, *this* is what I wanted to see!" I was like, "You are my mother!" She was like, "No, I want to understand what they are doing!" I was embarrassed and looked here and there, but she watched the whole thing. It wasn't vulgar, it was beautifully done. She saw it, and said, "*Arrey*, this is just like a guy and girl!" I told her, "That is what I told you—we are the same!"

'Then she started asking me really good questions. "What will you do about children?" I told her, "Surrogacy or adoption." "What about security? What if you want to go to a hospital at three in the morning?" I told her, "We have cabs, and I have a brother—don't you think he can help me? Why are you worried?"

'Finally it started settling in. We recently got my younger sister married through the Bharat Matrimony website. My mother told me that if I wanted to marry a girl, I would have to find a Kannada girl only! How do we search for a girl for you, she asked me then. "Do you have some app for that?" I was like, "Yes, we have dating apps," and then she wanted to see those also!

'Eventually I told her about my girlfriend. Now my girlfriend comes home, and my mother gives us a lot of privacy. My girlfriend and I stay in my room. My mom cooks something special for her, asks her about her work and how she is doing. It is nice, it is good.'[1]

~

I sat at Vaango Idli at the central food court of Mumbai's Chhatrapati Shivaji International Airport's T2 terminal, watching the world go by.

I have always loved airports. Ray Oldenburg in his 1989 book *The Great Good Place* famously wrote about 'third places'—not home, not work, but the in-between interstitial public places—like coffee shops or bars or shopping malls in which people congregate, socialise and spend more and more of their time. My 'third place' is T2! Sometimes I think I spend more time there than at home.

I heard a voice I faintly recognised. It was an acquaintance from the Red House in school (I was in the Green House, which was the best, obviously!), whom I hadn't met in years, holding a Starbucks coffee in her hand. There was a time I would meet old friends at the night show at South Mumbai's Sterling Cinema—now I bump into them at the airport. 'Do you know any *real* lesbians,' she asked. The ad agency she worked at was casting for an ad. 'We want a *real-life* lesbian couple.' Everyone wants *real* LGBTQ people suddenly, I thought wryly. In ads, on social media. We are trending. But how about giving us jobs too, instead of just publicity?

On the flight, I reached out for the in-flight magazine and did a double take. The cover had a wild graphic of queer people of all shapes, sizes and colours, wearing saris and shorts, riotously waving rainbow flags as they emerged from an Indigo plane. Many had rainbow accessories in their hair or rainbow-themed sunglasses. Some were captured mid-dance. Firecrackers in the background. Inside, the magazine listed eight things to do if someone came out to you, under the headline, 'Being Pro LGBTQIA+'. I smiled and read along.

When I landed in Chandigarh, Payal Varma, an MBA student, whisked me away in a shiny Land Rover Discovery to the Indian School of Business (ISB) in the neighbouring town of Mohali. More than 1,000 students study each year here at this Perkins Eastman–designed sandstone-and-glass campus.

I was there, in fact, to do some cultural acupuncture for the students, as the guest of honour at ISB Pride. While I was at Yale in 2014, I had met Anjani Jain, the deputy dean of the Yale School of Management. He subsequently brought a batch of his Yale MBA students to visit me at Godrej during their India sojourn. Following this, he connected me to a bunch of students at ISB, where he also flies in to teach every year. One of them was Payal, a straight ally who was keen to kick-start Pride on her campus. So this visit of mine had materialised as a result of my international and domestic wires crossing.

There were further connections. Godrej is a significant donor to ISB Mohali—the college auditorium is named after the company, and when I saw the Godrej plaque, it felt like a homecoming. (Rather, homo coming? Giggle. Okay *bas*, one bad pun per chapter is more than enough!)

I had brought my partner along. The next day, we would take a car up to Shimla. We would stay at the historic Cecil Hotel, where the waiter who brought us room service would recognise that we were a couple and give us complimentary dessert. 'For both of you.' We would go to bed listening to two monkeys mating on the ledge outside our window. Later, we would peep out, and one of the monkeys would leap up and smack the glass pane hard. We would step back in and close the curtain, giving them privacy. They too fiercely guarded their intimacy, like we all must in this country of ours.

But first, a keynote address to the ISB students, followed by a march all around the campus under a big rainbow flag, stopping every two minutes for selfies.

I started by playing a clip from *Satyamev Jayate*'s third episode from season three called 'Accepting Alternative Sexualities,' which first aired on 19 October 2014.[2] Aamir Khan explains to his audience that Gazal Dhaliwal, seated next to him in a gorgeous green salwar kameez, was born a male. He summarises Gazal's gender dysphoria in hobbling, gendered Hindi. '*Gazal uss waqt ladka thi.*' An expression of shock on an old woman's face in the audience.

The gendering of language makes it interesting. When the word 'was' becomes gendered, do you address it as masculine or feminine? What if the 'was' was masculine, but the 'is' is feminine? As I write this book, the *Satyamev Jayate* video on YouTube has 2.5 million views. The reactions of the studio audience cut into the episode mimic what millions around the world may have felt.

Gazal's story is one of both deep pain and great success. Having to live in a boy's body that she did not identify with, she attempted to run away from home, and changed her career and gender, but today, she tells Aamir, she is at peace. Much of it comes from her family's ability to accept her identity. Aamir introduces her parents and brings them on stage, calling them the heroes of the story.

When Gazal first opened up to her parents about how she felt, they did not resist, and they definitely did not chastise or punish her. They simply gave it time. When she ran away from home, they pleaded with her to come back, promising that they wouldn't scold her. When she showed them a film on gender identity that she had made while studying filmmaking in

Mumbai, they asked her when she intended to transition. They recognised that post surgery she could look like a woman, not just feel like one trapped in a different body.

Can you imagine yourself going to each and every house in your neighbourhood, telling your community that the son you have loved is now going to be your daughter, and that you love her still, if not more, and to please accept her for who she is? Well, that is what Gazal's parents did.

'Those who love you, your parents, your friends, they will keep loving you. We love you just as much. Rather, we love you more because we know you are happy now,' one of Gazal's relatives tells her, tearing up on-screen. Aamir then brings it home, proclaiming as much to the show's international audience as to those present in the studio that day, 'When parents accept you, people around you will also start accepting you.'

Gazal would go on to write India's first commercial lesbian love story, *Ek Ladki Ko Dekha Toh Aisa Laga*, starring our very own queer champion Sonam Kapoor.[3] The film is about reconciling a father with his daughter's sexual orientation. It is also very much about family.

The film did not do well commercially on its release in 2019, but like most iconic movies, since its release on Netflix, it has achieved a cult status on the internet, in spaces that exist between keyboards and hearts. Before its release, it wasn't promoted explicitly as a lesbian love story. It cleverly used an iconic heterosexual love song of the 1990s as the title—a song made popular by Sonam's dad, Anil Kapoor. People might have walked in expecting another love story with a generic siyappa.

When Sweety Chaudhary played by Sonam comes out as a lesbian to Sahil Mirza played by Rajkumar Rao, he laughs in a confused haze. So did many in the audience around me at the local multiplex I watched the movie in. Towards the end of the film, when Sweety and Sahil, now her friend and ally, stage a lesbian-themed play in a small-town theatre, some of the audience on-screen walk out in disgust. The director Shelly Chopra Dhar, whose own son is gay and who directed this film as an epistle of solidarity to other parents of queer children, cleverly put in this plot device, anticipating discomfort. In fact, some people did walk out of the theatres in which the film was being screened, even at the multiplex I was in. But most stayed, and how wonderful is that?

As the film's end credits rolled, I was reminded of *Dostana* hitting Indian screens in 2008.[4] And of how the audience had laughed loudly whenever any gayness was insinuated. The film worked for me despite the ridiculous plot.

There is also the preposterous scene of a visa officer who comes to their place to check if they are actually a gay couple, and ends up dancing with them. Only in Bollywood!

On its release, many critics and scholars read *Dostana* as homophobic. Indeed, the film is deeply problematic at a text level, I told the ISB students, who were listening in rapt attention. As business school students, they had rarely got to listen to humanities lectures that involved close readings of texts, and I could see that they were enjoying themselves.

But I am more interested in the subtext of acceptance that lies beneath the main plot, I continued my talk. That is the one thing the filmmakers did get right, apart from casting John Abraham's abs! To me, *Dostana*'s subtext opens up possibilities of re-imagining family acceptance—flawed possibilities, gendered possibilities, but possibilities nonetheless.

The mother, played by Kirron Kher, eventually accepts her son and his sexuality (even if he is only pretending to be gay). She reimagines and repurposes tradition—by welcoming his male partner, with a pot of rice that he has to kick over at the threshold of their house before entering, just as a daughter-in-law would. She offers her son's partner her bangles, just as she would offer a daughter-in-law, and tells him to keep a fast on Karva Chauth for her son's long life. These moments may have elicited laughs from straight audiences, but for us queers, they were revolutionary.

Dostana became a box-office hit in 2008, and beyond the radical subtext of parental acceptance, I was also interested in the paratext that this subtext generated. 'Paratext' is a term that the theorist Gérard Genette coined to define all the conversations that accompany a literary or cinematic text—such as the design of the book or film poster, images, interviews, stills, editorials that appear about the text and so on.[5] *Dostana*'s paratext was simply amazing! It generated global buzz about LGBTQ visibility in Bollywood. In a *Los Angeles Times* piece about *Dostana*, film critic Anupama Chopra quoted me: 'Any mainstream acknowledgment, even if it is tongue-in-cheek, will go a long way. Laughing about it is the first step toward more textured and nuanced characters.'[6]

My position remains the same even today. *Dostana* opened doors, and the key to its enduring appeal is the strong character of the mother who understands, accepts and eventually celebrates her son's sexuality and his choice of life partner. This is the truth: whether cinematically or in real life, the axis of societal change with regard to LGBTQ rights in India is parental acceptance. To invert the tagline of the *Dostana* producer Karan Johar's 2001 *Kabhi Khushi Kabhi Gham*: it is all about loving your children.

Twelve years after *Dostana*'s release, Anupama quoted me again, during an interview on her Film Companion YouTube channel with the cast of *Shubh Mangal Zyaada Saavdhan* and the film's director Hitesh Kewalya. The actors Ayushmann Khurrana and Jitendra Kumar play gay lovers who work to win the hearts of Jitendra's family, *Dilwale Dulhania Le Jayenge* style. Anupama, in fact, read aloud the paragraph above to open her show, including the line 'Its all about loving your children', from an advance copy of this chapter that I had sent her,[7] and it felt surreal to watch Ayushmann, Jitendra and Hitesh nod along excitedly, affirming that this was exactly what they had tried to do with their film, which released in February 2020. It is, as of now, India's biggest queer cinematic hit.

Three years before Gazal and her parents appeared on *Satyamev Jayate* in 2014, Barkha Dutt anchored a beautiful episode on her NDTV show *We The People*, titled 'Being Gay: The Parents' Story'.[8] A salwar-kameez-wearing fun-jabi grandmother, in some ways a mirror image of Kirron's character in *Dostana*, gave a rousing and endearing finger to the homophobic laws that did not let her grandson marry whomever he wanted to: '*Inko jeene ka haq do, agle pal mein kya hota hai kaun jaane?*' Give them the right to live, who knows what's in store?

That force of nature was Rani Sharma—the wonderful septuagenarian grandmother of Delhi's Sambhav Sharma. She remained the symbolic dadi of India's LGBTQ movement until she passed away in 2016. Each time Rani dadi spoke on national TV, India understood, and people's homophobia melted away. Her fierce spirit lives on within so many fabulous parents across India.

~

In December 2018, my partner and I were at the gayest wedding ever in Goa. My friend Keshav Suri was marrying Cyril Feuillebois, the founder of the KronoKare range of cosmetics. Though Keshav and Cyril had officially and legally tied the knot in June 2018 in Paris, they wanted to host a much bigger and fatter Indian wedding, post the reading down of 377.

The location for this extravaganza was the Lalit Goa property that sprawls across ninety acres of a manicured beach-hugging coastline and includes a world-class golf course. The wedding celebrations were surreal. During the day, we jet-skied, got massages at the spa and lazed around the pool sipping champagne. Every night, we headed to the parlour for hair and make-up and then stepped out to witness history being made.

It was the year of some pretty big celeb weddings in our country, but Priyanka-Nick, Deepika-Ranveer, Isha-Anand or any of the other hi-fi couples who had fancy marriages that year were not a patch on Keshav and Cyril.

All the key elements of a big fat Instagram-worthy wedding were there. Beach destination? Check. Extravagant designer clothes on everyone? Check. International performers and DJs flying in from around the world to entertain guests who had also flown in from around the world? Check. Monogrammed bathrobes? Check.

The thing is, Keshav and Cyril took up every element of the traditional wedding template and then queered it. It was subversion at a genius level.

Consider how they entered the venue of their beach ceremony, in decked-up vintage cars. When they got out, they walked towards a white pastel-pink mandap covered with roses, hydrangeas and orchids, accompanied by their sisters, not brothers, and it was Keshav's sister Shraddha Suri Marwah who played the dhol, leading the entourage to the mandap.

Instead of a traditional male pandit, the couple had invited Laxmi Narayan Tripathi, a trans rights activist, author and spiritual leader of the Kinnar Akhara, to officiate. 'By the power invested in me as mahamandaleshwar, I now pronounce you husband and husband,' Laxmi dramatically declared against the setting sun. Keshav's and Cyril's mothers then supervised the exchanging of rings and garlands to the sound of waves lapping up against the beach. I felt two fat teardrops trickle down my cheeks and ruin my mascara. Then, the winner of the reality show *RuPaul's Drag Race* and burlesque performer Violet Chachki did some aerial acrobatics to get us all into a dancing mood, and my smudged eyeliner became part of my look.

Another exciting subversion was the typical sangeet night being converted into a drag ball with global drag stars like Hungry, along with, of course, Kitty Su's desi superstars like Maya the Drag Queen and Rani KoHEnur. The highlight for me was Keshav himself, corseted into a gown—hand-stitched on to him over a period of six hours by the designer Gaurav Gupta, who had flown in from Delhi just to do this—and dancing on stage with his mother Jyotsna to 'Kaisi Paheli Zindagani' from *Parineeta*.

Now, of course, not everyone owns a hotel chain and has the US-based drag queen RuPaul on speed dial, but that mother-son dance continues to give me goosebumps every time I recollect it.

What the Keshav-Cyril wedding did was to create hope for a generation that had never seen a queer Indian wedding. Their public celebration of love was a radical act, and what thrust it right into the mainstream was

Mama Jyotsna Suri. The message she was clearly broadcasting to the world that starlit weekend in Goa was: If I can accept my queer son and dance at his wedding, surely you can too?

~

Some months after this wedding, I was sitting with my friend Sandeep Nair from Community Business and his husband Ruben Boas in their home in Bengaluru. We were eating tamarind rice that Ruben had cooked, as we looked through their wedding pictures, conveniently put up on their living room wall. They had also done it full traditional style. Mandap. Dhotis. Silk-sari-wearing aunties. Only, instead of bride and groom, it was groom and groom.

'I got married legally on 21 May 2016 in Portugal, my husband is Portuguese,' Sandeep told me. 'Then I got illegally married in India on 26 June 2016, in Bengaluru. I wanted a big fat wedding, with a wedding planner. So I walked down the aisle and all in Portugal, and got the big fat wedding with the pandits, prayers, walking around the fire, here!'[9]

They have since relocated to Canada, and are in the process of adopting a child together. I think about Sandeep and Ruben today. There was nothing illegal about their India marriage, *na*? Love is love, and I can't wait for our courts to see this even more clearly in the aftermath of the Section 377 verdict. I would very much like to live in an India where queer marriage is accepted, so that I can marry my partner and, hopefully, adopt a child too. Sandeep and Ruben are doing this in Canada, but why should my partner and I not have the right to be married and create our own family, recognised by law, in India itself?

In September 2019, as I was writing the first draft of this chapter, a sweet post came up on my Facebook timeline: 'Sameer Samudra is feeling lovely with Amit Gokhale.' Sameer relocated from the US to Pune with his husband, Amit, some years ago. Both work at Cummins and are an out and proud gay couple; their companies, in the US as well as in India, have been very accepting of them.

Here is what the post said: '9 years of blessed married life … Columbus, fall wedding, crisp air, wonderful friends helping execute the ceremony, Indian food and rituals, celebration of love, memories for lifetime :-) Happy Anniversary love … here is to many more Amit :-)'

Sameer had put up a bunch of marriage photos from 2010 accompanying this post, but one particular image caught my eye: Amit and Sameer are seated on the floor around a raised silver platform surrounded by marigolds. They are holding their henna-covered hands over a silver bowl that has been placed on the platform. They are decked up in matching silk-brocade sherwanis in different shades of red. Amit is in a dhoti, while Sameer is in a pair of fitted churidars. Pearls adorn traditional headbands. Seated between them is a priest in a sky-blue sherwani, whose eyes are closed mid-chant, while Sameer's mom, in a traditional purple Maharashtrian sari, leans over casually.

The perfect family portrait.

From Rani dadi dreaming of an India in which her grandson *might* get married, to an India in which big fat gay weddings are taking place regularly, how quickly we are changing, and it is the parents who are leading the way, telling their children, just like Mr Tripathi tells his son Aman at the end of *Shubh Mangal Zyaada Saavdhan*: '*Ja, jee le apni zindagi.*'

~

Chitra Palekar, one of the petitioners to the Supreme Court in 2013 who asked that the 2009 Delhi High Court judgement not be overturned, has a lesbian daughter. When her daughter came out to her in 1993, she was initially shocked; there is always an expectation of heterosexuality. But soon, Chitra itched for the world to know that her daughter was in love with another woman and that this love was natural and wonderful. Chitra is not an outlier.

At the Mumbai Pride in January 2019, I was marching alongside Chitra and a group of other parents under the banner of Sweekar: The Rainbow Parents, a Mumbai-based group of parents of LGBTQ children, formed in November 2017. At the time of writing this book, Sweekar, which means acceptance, had sixty members in the city as well as on phone chat groups, which included parents residing in Indian cities like Ahmedabad, Hyderabad, Bengaluru, Indore, and also in countries like Australia, the US, Oman and Thailand. Many more parents interact with the Sweekar group on social media. They hold regular get-togethers, learn new things, understand and accept.

Alongside Chitra, there were other parents like Arundhati Banerjee Sanyal at the march. Some months later, Arundhati was at IIT Bombay, speaking at an acceptance meeting during an annual Humsafar Trust event. She was reading out in Hindi a story of a mother and son: the son comes out to the mother and the acceptance happens immediately. Arundhati had grown in confidence over the course of just one year. Being a part of Sweekar had been good for her. As I scrolled through her timeline on Facebook, her son Deb Sanyal's post came up. It was a picture of the two, under the Kashish rainbow at the film festival in May 2019. Beside it, Deb's post reads, 'When you have your mom beside you, conquering the world seems like a piece of cake! A mother always knows what's best for her child and she has been acing this since forever.'[10]

On Faye D'Souza's Mirror Now prime-time show *The Urban Debate*, on the historic night of 6 September 2018—when the Supreme Court read down 377—it is telling that Faye chose to put the Sweekar parents up front and centre. On the show, the activist Harish Iyer had an emotional message for his mother, Padma Iyer. 'Thank you, for holding my hand when I had no other hand to hold. When I came out and our family didn't support us, you stood with me. Your contribution in this verdict is as important as everyone else's.'[11]

~

At ISB, I told the students about these parents. Padma aunty had famously put out a newspaper ad for Harish in the matrimonial section of a Mumbai newspaper. When she chatted with me on stage at the Culture Lab in October 2015, she told me that she would have done the same if Harish had been heterosexual, so what was the big deal about searching for a groom for her son instead of a bride? Padma's simple assertion that day—he is my child, why should I do anything differently—echoed Kirron's mother character in *Dostana*.

The ISB students smiled. They understood that for all these parents the sexuality of their children was incidental. They just wanted to accept their kids and find happiness for them. Isn't that what good parenting is?

I told the students about my own life. About how when I came out to my mom, she didn't bat an eyelid. She said that it was fine and then proceeded to ask what we should have for dinner.

~

Not everything is hunky dory nor are all Indian parents coming out in droves with artis and kangans to welcome their queer children. Sometimes, acceptance takes time.

In January 2018, the Dancing Queens returned to the Culture Lab after their debut 2015 performance.[12] This time on stage, we had the mother-daughter duo of Mangala and my friend Abhina Aher, dancing together.

It took Mangala, from a middle-class Maharashtrian family, eight years to accept her child, who was born to her as son Abhijeet but gradually transitioned into Abhina. Currently the associate director of the India chapter of HIV/AIDS Alliance, an NGO, Abhina had struggled with her gender identity since childhood. Mangala was a single parent and she blamed everything—from Abhina's pursuit of dance to the absence of a father figure—for Abhina's 'feminine nature'. She even took her to saints and temples in the hope that her child might change. But over the years, as Abhina resolutely transitioned and became her own true self, Mangala stayed by her side, learnt and understood.

Today, Mangala is Abhina's biggest champion and a key member of the Sweekar parents group. A week after their performance at the Culture Lab, she went on to receive the 2018 Queeroes award given by 6 Degrees, an LGBTQ network that honours Indian queer heroes and their allies.

On stage at the Culture Lab, they swayed to the song 'Maa' from the 2007 Bollywood film *Taare Zameen Par*. The thirty-something Abhina and the sixty-something Mangala moved gracefully and in sync to 'Don't send me so far away; That you won't even be able to remember me, mother; Am I so bad, my mother?'[13]

A big fat tear fell on my laptop as I wrote this. If you have some tears too, it's okay. Go on. Let it out.

~

Many think that acceptance is easier for the rich or privileged, but this is not true. Even Manvendra Singh Gohil, the royal prince of Rajpipla in Gujarat, faced a difficult journey. Manvendra is the thirty-ninth direct descendant of the Gohil dynasty, established in 1370. When he came out as gay in 2006, his family disowned him and threw him out of the palace.[14]

'I received death threats and there was even an assassin sent to kill me,' he told the audience in Bengaluru, at an event hosted at the insurance company Swiss Re in November 2019. 'The assassin met me and he couldn't do it, because he saw that I was being honest and living my life honestly.'

Thankfully, Manvendra landed in Oprah's studio, and from there, the fame, attention and his steadfast determination have made him a global superstar and one of India's leading activists. When he realised that 80 per cent of gay men in India were married to women, he started the Lakshya Trust to provide counselling and HIV/AIDS health awareness for both the gay men as well as their wives.[15]

In the winter of 2017, we lazed about in a swimming pool in Powai, not far from my home in Mumbai, where the Impulse Group, which Manvendra advises, had thrown a fun pool party for young queers. There was music, food and dancing. At some point, volunteers elegantly stepped in and did some messaging around safe sex. 'Young people don't listen otherwise,' Manvendra told me as he leaned back in his deck chair, next to his American husband, Duke.

Meanwhile, back in Rajpipla, his family had got over their bias. Manvendra is now back in the palace and building a centre for LGBTQ elders on the palace grounds, between juggling his multiple international commitments. Jetting off to the US to record an episode for the Kardashians is just one of the recent things he has done.

~

Sometimes parents never accept. That too is a reality. Sometimes it is better to not come out—there are enough cases of parents torturing or killing their own children. But I want you to keep in mind that in the India of today, parents are *also* accepting. New paradigms are being created, old ones are being reimagined. This is the lens I want to look at the future through. That is why this is a hopeful chapter, and this is a hopeful book.

In 2018, Sridhar Rangayan, his partner Saagar Gupta and I were at the second birthday of the child of a lesbian couple, our friends. All the kids were siphoned off to one section of the party hall, while parents of all types—single people and couples, lesbian, gay, trans and straight people—mingled. There was laughter as the kids ran all around. Yes, this too is modern India where we queer people are making families of our own and living with them. A year later, Sridhar and Saagar threw a huge party to mark twenty-five years of living and loving together.

It's all about loving your children. Actually, it's all about loving. Period. Love is love is love, as the fabulous lesbian singer Bidisha Mohanta likes to sing out loud whenever she can. Her parents went on national television on the show *India's Got Talent,* in which she was participating in 2018, and they accepted Bidisha for who she was. Millions of other parents across our country saw this, and learnt.[16]

The more I travel and the more people I meet, the more I realise the immense power of parental acceptance to form an exponentially widening circle of inclusion, especially within the corporate world that this book aims to address. At the Reimagining Inclusion for Social Equity (RISE) job fair and conference in Bengaluru in 2019, Pankajam Sridevi, the managing director of ANZ India, said that she was inspired to take her company on an LGBTQ inclusion path after hearing Harish's and his mother Padma's story. At the same conference, Sanket Atal, the managing director of Intuit, shared how it was his father who had opened his eyes to what being trans meant, by telling him about Jan Morris, the celebrated Welsh author of the Pax Britannica series, who was born James Morris before her sex reassignment surgery in 1972.

~

When a parent speaks up for a queer child, it creates magic. I firmly believe that a lot of our work post the 377 verdict has to be about mainstreaming queer lives, and an important way to win the hearts of the general public is to foreground the relationships between LGBTQ children and their accepting parents.

During an explosive 2013 *Frankly Speaking* discussion with the TV anchor Arnab Goswami on Times Now, I lashed out at Rahul Easwar, a controversial right-wing author who has consistently held the position that homosexuality is against Indian 'family values'.

'What do you mean by family values?' I asked him. 'We also have families. We *are* families!'[17]

Part Three

LGBTQ INCLUSION MAKES SENSE, WHICHEVER WAY YOU LOOK AT IT

LGBTQ inclusion is fundamentally a good thing to do. It will also earn you lots of money, make your organisation more innovative, and help you attract and retain talented employees. Plus, you will improve your PR and keep up with the millennials and their changing mindsets. It is a complete win-win scenario.

9

LGBTQ Inclusion Is Fundamentally a Good Thing to Do

Before we talk about money or any of the other arguments for being inclusive, the foremost reason you should do it is because LGBTQ inclusion is fundamentally a good thing to do.

It sounds pretty obvious, but this needs to be said given we often talk about inclusion solely in terms of profits. For starters, there is the famous theory of discrimination that N. Gregory Mankiw, a Harvard economist, writes about in his *Principles of Microeconomics*, which is studied across campuses in the US. The theory states that discrimination is fundamentally unprofitable, as discriminating companies will be driven out of the market.[1]

Imagine a world with only two companies, A and B. If Company A is a sexist jerk that refuses to hire women, Company B, which is less of a jerk, will hire them. But since they are the only company willing to hire them, women will be willing to work for lower wages, so Company B will pay them less and make higher profits. Company A, seeing this, will start hiring women. Company B in turn will raise the salary to attract more women … so on and so forth, till both companies hire women and pay them the same as men, end of story.

A lot of the literature on inclusion, and LGBTQ inclusion specifically, focuses on the business case for being inclusive—the idea is that once people recognise inclusivity as profitable, discriminatory hiring practices would end.

Of course, this classic theory was attacked left, right and centre, especially in the 1980s, as the trend for discriminatory wages kept getting worse—discrimination happens not on the basis of whether the practice is profitable or not profitable, but because of biases and unscientific belief systems. This school of thought argues that inclusion cannot be encouraged by solely proving that it leads to profitability. People refuse to give women the same pay as men because they unfairly believe that women value work less, won't work late hours, will not return after maternity, and so on. The anthropologist Brian Horton explained this to me over Skype.[2]

'A lot of economic theory is based on the rational actor model. However, things like racism challenge the idea that one works rationally in a business or an economic context. So, I imagine, if someone is truly a homophobe, talking to them about pennies and dollars is not going to help because they are already operating with a framework which is not rational, making decisions based on their own biases, which are not for the good of the bottom line of the company.'

Brian felt that people should be inclusive based on their moral compass, not their rupee compass—that to focus on money or utility alone reduces queer people to their profitability. Therefore, if you want to push for the inclusion of queer people in the workplace, you should do it with a larger moral argument: be inclusive because it is the ethical thing to do, not because it can make you money.

'I often feel a lot of the conversation [on inclusion] is not about, ethically, queerness being a thing we should accept because it is part of human diversity. [Instead] it is often the myth of the pink dollar or the pink rupee—queer people are a demographic that have disposable income, or being named as a homophobic organisation would be bad for business, or queer people are creative or innovative which we need to spur growth. Those are the three tracts I see in India, and none of them are ethically robust.'

Oops! These are exactly the three tracts that I am going to be basing my arguments on in the subsequent chapters. Brian cautioned me, with love and concern: 'You don't want to make an argument about a group of people that at the end of the day is contingent upon a trend. Something being good for business is a thing which will change with the direction of the wind. What you are advocating for is a core fundamental framework that is in some ways antithetical to the idea of a trend. Parmesh, in some ways, as the leader of queer activism in the business world in India, you get to set the tone for a conversation. I have never understood why you need to adopt the language of people who, quite frankly, don't care about queerness, in order to be able to make this case. I think you could frame this conversation on its own terms, and do it convincingly enough to bring people to the table.'

Like Brian, Mumbai boy Ali Potia, who is now in Singapore—and who was named in the *Outstanding* list of 'LGBT+ Executive Role Models' for his work at McKinsey in Singapore[3]—is also sceptical about arguing for inclusiveness using the lure of profitability. Ali is a co-founder of Alliance, a global consortium of queer-inclusive companies founded by McKinsey. He told me in June 2018 that he was moving towards a more ethical human rights rhetoric, but for a reason different from Brian's.

'The narrative I use is moving away from the business case only because getting the data is very hard. The moment you brush up against hardcore analytical people, they start probing for facts and figures. The obvious problem with LGBT is that most companies don't track it. And even when they do, a lot of employees choose not to disclose. Therefore it is really hard to have good empirical evidence. There's a lot of anecdotal evidence. But anecdotal evidence only convinces so many people, right? Which is why I love your push around not making this book simply a white paper, and instead making it a proper book. Because in a book, you can use a lot of anecdotal evidence.'[4]

I agree with Ali and Brian that any argument for inclusion has to start with a basic human rights narrative, that queer people are about 4–10 per cent of the potential workforce, and corporates have to treat them with dignity and respect. At the same time, in the process of researching this book, I have also come across enough data that tells me that inclusion *does* make good business sense, and I am going to use all the arsenal available to argue my case. As Fabrice Houdart, the managing director of Global Equality Initiatives at Out Leadership and co-author of the UN's *Standards of Conduct for Business*, wrote in a blog post in January 2020: 'Ultimately, the business case and the moral case are not mutually exclusive; in different contexts, emphasis might be put on one over the other. To remind companies of the (sometimes hidden) costs of LGBTI exclusion or of staying silent in the face of human rights abuses is not to negate the principle that all people deserve to have their dignity and rights respected. The business case needs a foundation of human rights just as human rights arguments can be made more forceful by consideration of the cost of discrimination and lack of protection.'[5]

~

Here is a story about a company that began its inclusive journey simply because it was a decent thing to do, and then discovered that it led to several other benefits for it. Like my own Godrej, it is another really old company—Tata Steel.

On 24 October 2016, I took part in a panel discussion on 'Leveraging the Power of Diversity' at the Tata Centre in Kolkata, on the invitation of Tata

Steel, under their D&I programme, Mosaic. The discussion was broadcast at all the Tata Steel manufacturing plants in Jamshedpur and their marketing and sales locations across India. My co-panellists were from other Tata companies like Tata Consultancy Sevices and Titan. I was the sole non-Tata person on stage and perhaps in the room, and I was the only one who spoke about LGBTQ inclusion.

During the course of my presentation, I had a heated interaction with one of Tata Steel's senior HR leaders. He asked if they could structure their inclusion journey in a linear fashion, to first focus on gender and then on sexuality. He mentioned that all of Tata Steel's activities since 2014 were geared towards the inclusion of women, and also spoke of some policies they were coming up with for people with disabilities. He asked if inclusion of LGBTQ people could be something that the company might take up after one or two years.

I retorted by telling the audience, 'Everyone who belongs to the LGBTQ community, even if as allies, please raise your hand. If you believe Tata Steel should have inclusive LGBTQ policies now and not later, then raise your hand.' Almost everyone raised their hand.

'Don't you want to work for a company that considers all kinds of inclusion the same? For how long will we LGBTQ people have to wait in line for our turn to come?' I asked the senior manager who had raised this query. He nodded in acknowledgement.

Among the young employees present in the audience that day was Anubhuti Banerjee, a trans woman who was out of the closet to only a few people in the company. Two years later, she was my guest at the We the Women conference hosted by Barkha Dutt in Mumbai, at which I had curated a panel on transgender visibility.

Before we went on stage in Mumbai, Anubhuti, resplendent in an elegant black-and-gold kurta and dupatta, offset by a rebellious Billie Eilish green streak in her hair, reminisced about the Kolkata event where our paths had first crossed: 'Back then, I was talking only about trans inclusion. The priority then, the company said, was to bring in trans inclusion policies, and that they would think about the rest later, since 377 was still there. Listening to you speak so unabashedly was a huge boost to my confidence. Your visit there caused a lot of kneejerk reactions; within months, things were happening. We started having more discussions about having LGBT policies, and also around a few months after that, this catalysed into the idea for creating an employee resource group for LGBT people. It was something of a dream come true. I had mentioned [setting up an ERG] much earlier in my first interaction with the diversity and inclusion people. But after your visit, this quest seemed to take wings.'

Anubhuti took the lead in pushing for change at Tata Steel. Less than two years after my visit, in May 2018, Tata Steel launched Wings—their queer support ERG—and also announced LGBTQ-inclusive policies. Close to 100 senior executives of Tata Steel and its associated companies were present for the launch, which was also webcast to various locations. Here is what Peeyush Gupta, the vice president of Steel, Sales and Marketing, said in his address to all of them that day: 'Today is probably the right time. We cannot be remorseful of the fact that we have not done it in the past, but we also do not want to repent many months or years later that we did not do it today. As a pioneering company, we have done a number of pioneering things in the past, this is one such pioneering thing we can do for the steel industry.'[6]

The launch of Wings was a validation of Anubhuti's hard work, and on Tata Steel's part, their recognition of a valuable employee. But increasingly, in her personal life too, Anubhuti began moving steadfastly towards her goal of transitioning completely. She spoke to me about this journey in July 2019.[7]

'I started having a lot more confidence in the person that I was becoming. Earlier, I did not connect to a lot of people and was rather timid. That completely changed. I suddenly discovered parts of my identity through which I was able to find artistic expression and connect with society and, most importantly, with my parents. I hardly spoke to them before transitioning. But after I transitioned, the whole dynamic of the relationship changed. I have become super confident, super comfortable, okay to speak on and express a lot of things and relish such opportunities, and have closer person-to-person relations with other people. I have also created friendships I could live for, found the real meaning of love, and a loving queer family, which I never had earlier. This is something I realised, that I was finally a person who could be themselves.'

I asked her about the expense of transitioning. 'All those initial costs were out of pocket, not covered by any of the company policies. I was quite unsure of what the policies of the workplace were, even for something like psychiatric counselling, hormonal replacement treatment and therapy. I could not have approached them. I was in Jamshedpur when I was doing this, I was not confident enough to go to the company hospital to get medical advice. There was always this fear that it might not be allowed, and since this medical facility is directly linked to the company, I feared it might actually have a negative impact on my career, or my position.

'Later on, after I was done with my transition, I started talking about the entire process—which includes psychiatric, hormonal and, later, surgical interventions—to the management. Tata Steel reimbursed the costs for the surgical intervention. This wasn't part of the traditional medical insurance plan then, but since there was an intent of bringing it in as part of our policies, Tata Steel was able to reimburse the cost for the surgery, and this also brought about a policy change. The company now pledges to cover the cost of the surgery as well as give a month's leave for it. It is public knowledge.'

See, this is what I mean by 'good' or 'ethical'. Tata Steel stood by Anubhuti not out of any corporate greed but because they valued her as an employee, and so they helped her affirm her identity. Of course, once this becomes policy, as it did at Tata Steel, it also acts as a form of signalling that you are a progressive company, and pulls in talent from all corners of the country. The more Anubhuti told me about Tata Steel's multiple interventions on her behalf, the more impressed I was.

'Coming out is one thing. Then comes the difficult part of living through it. In a small industrial town like Jamshedpur, it seemed like the entire city knew that I was transitioning, and that got a lot of people questioning, not necessarily to my face, but quite often they questioned my friends, about what exactly I was going through, followed by a lot of judgement. The society had woken up to the fact that an officer, a manager at Tata Steel, was doing this. The city always knew about the existence of LGBT people, but it had never had the opportunity of hearing someone talk about it, of someone who was proud of it, proud of being themselves.

'Tata Steel took the whole department for a set of sessions, for which the only person who wasn't invited was me. That was when they spoke of what I was going through. At the session, they spoke about how they were supposed to refer to me as "her", that my chosen name was not my old legal name anymore, that people should call me by my new name, that I would be using the women's washroom, that I was someone they should treat with respect.'

I had a lump in my throat when she told me about just how special her company had made her feel. 'When the new Bombay House was being renovated and launched on J.R.D. Tata's birth anniversary, they created something called Tata Experiential Centre (TXC), a state-of-the-art audio-visual interactive and immersive "Experience Zone" showcasing the impact Tata has had over the years—on people, society, sports, technology and all the other things. Here, you can see the first steel bar created by Tata Steel. Under the "People" section, one of the first stories is of me. If you look up, there is

J.R.D. Tata, but look a little to the right, and you see me and my story, which is unbelievable. The most incredible kind of appreciation someone can get! I still have issues accepting that I do deserve that kind of recognition, but getting it makes me extremely happy and empowered, and it empowers other people also. An initiative you take for yourself for bringing about what you think of as a small change ends up bringing about a humongous change.'

~

It was the day after RISE, India's first LGBTQ job fair. I was at the Lalit in Bengaluru. It was two o'clock in the afternoon, and Keshav Suri had just come down from his suite, in bright red pyjamas, an electric-blue Issey Miyake pleated trench, and oversized rainbow-framed dark glasses. 'Honey, you don't want to see me in the morning without my make-up, trust me!' It felt weird interviewing him formally, after having known him for all these years. 'Come on, focus!' he scolded me. 'This book is important.' So now, listen to Keshav, in his own words.

'We have fifteen hotels inside and outside India. My journey towards inclusion began with my own family being very supportive of me as a gay person. Over the years, I realised that I should use my position to do something more for the community. There were two triggers. The first reason is actually you, Parmesh! When you called me to Godrej for the UN's *Standards of Conduct for Business* launch, I was very motivated that if one of India's oldest business groups can do something like this, what is stopping the rest of us?

'The second reason was one of my own employees Hamza, who transitioned to Mahi. Witnessing this, I became aware of how important representation is for our community. Mahi wanted to be seen, and I realised that I also wanted people from the LGBTQ community to be seen and represented at all Lalit properties.

'Over the years, we have rapidly hired more and more LGBTQ people as Lalit staff. As of June 2019, we have thirty-five trans people working with us out of sixty-six LGBTQ employees overall. [When I checked with Keshav again in March 2020, just before submitting the final draft of this book, I was happy to hear that their LGBTQ employee count has gone up to a hundred.] We are also working at intersectional inclusion, so we have a trans acid attack survivor for instance, or a queer DJ who happens to be disabled. We have also created an ecosystem for queer performers through Kitty Su. Right from our very own Lalit Bangalore employee Alex—who becomes Maya the

Drag Queen when he performs on the Kitty Su stage, a performance space under the Lalit label—to so many others, we have empowered more than forty queer artists to perform on the Kitty Su stage. We have launched a scholarship worth ₹1.5 lakh each for five trans students to cover all the costs for a diploma in food production and bakery at the Lalit Suri Hospitality School. We're just getting started, by the way. There's a lot more we are going to do!'

~

I am glad that my being from Godrej, a really old Indian company, has helped Tata, another really old and large Indian company, and Lalit, a relatively young and small Indian company, gain confidence in starting their own inclusion journeys. When it comes to inclusion, size doesn't matter. Age doesn't matter. What matters is decency, and a willingness to do the right thing. All three—Godrej, Tata and Lalit—are deeply linked to the idea of India itself. Secular. Plural. Inclusive. If we can do it, surely other companies can too?

Nisa told me, as we were discussing this book before I wrapped it up, 'It is very clear to me that LGBT inclusion is the right thing to do for us at Godrej from both a moral and business point of view. There is a lot of data coming out that links inclusion to profitability worldwide. I know that you are drawing on a lot of these global studies in your book, Parmesh, and while there isn't enough data in India to make this case, I think it is only a matter of time. I know that you have bought your own house through Godrej Properties not because there was any employee discount but because you felt that you wanted to support a company that's queer friendly.'

She is right. The spirit of the ethical arguments made in this chapter underlies all the other reasons covered in the rest of the book—money, innovation, talent and reputation—for why inclusion is important. I have never been a minimalist in any case. As one of my favourite Madonna songs goes: 'Something's better than nothing, but nothing's better than more.'[8] So why have one reason to be inclusive when you can have many?

10

LGBTQ Inclusion Can Make You Money

Let me tell you a secret. Being inclusive can make you money. Lots and lots of it! I'll give you some numbers.

To start with—US $5 trillion. As of 2018, the global spending power of LGBTQ consumers was estimated to be between US $3.6 trillion and US $4.6 trillion per annum according to LGBT Capital, an advisory firm with a focus on LGBT consumers and corporate investment.[1] This is not inclusive of those who identify as allies of the community. According to another 2018 report by PricewaterhouseCoopers, the global spending power of LGBTQ consumers is estimated to be more than US $5 trillion a year.[2] In a white paper published in April 2018, the non-profit LGBT Foundation in Hong Kong calculated that if the LGBTQ community worldwide were a country, it would be the fourth largest economy in terms of GDP.[3]

Here's another number for you: US $200 billion. This is the size of India's queer economy. Out Now Consulting, a lesbian and gay marketing specialist, estimated India's LGBTQ population to be 6 per cent. This would suggest that 'just under US $200 billion (6 per cent of GDP) can be assumed to be earned income from India's estimated 45 million gay and lesbian adults,' said Ian Johnson, the firm's chief executive, who did a global report with *Forbes* in 2009.[4] This was a long time ago, so the number would be higher now.

So, who wants a piece of this pie worth at least US $200 billion?

Just listen to what McKinsey, Deloitte and Boston Consulting Group, three of the most prestigious consulting firms in the world, have to say about the link between inclusivity and profitability.

In 2019, McKinsey produced a report, *Delivering Through Diversity*, based on a data set of over 1,000 companies in 12 countries, and which looked at profitability measured as average EBIT margin.[5] Companies in the top quartile for gender diversity on their executive teams were 21 per cent more likely to have above-average profitability than companies in the fourth quartile. And it is not just gender. Companies in the top quartile for ethnic/cultural diversity on executive teams were 33 per cent more likely to have industry-leading profitability than companies in the fourth quartile. That this trend continues to be strong suggests that inclusion of diverse individuals—not only LGBTQ but also age, international experience and other diversity categories—can be a key differentiator among companies.

Deloitte Australia produced a report in 2018, *The Diversity and Inclusion Revolution*, in which it cited one of its partners Juliet Bourke's 2016 research which showed that organisations with inclusive cultures are:

2 × more likely to meet or exceed financial targets
3 × more likely to be high performing
6 × more likely to be agile and innovative
8 × more likely to achieve better business outcomes[6]

A study by the Boston Consulting Group in 2018 found that companies that had above-average diversity in their management teams reported innovation revenue—the percentage of total revenue from new products and services launched over the past three years—to be 45 per cent, versus an innovation revenue of 26 per cent for companies with below-average leadership diversity—a difference of 19 percentage points.[7]

A 2019 report by AMCHAM in Singapore, where again the link between diversity/inclusion and corporate profits is pretty clear, states, 'The researchers argue that diversity and inclusion together—i.e., diverse collaboration—delivers more creative thinking and the innovation necessary to thrive in highly uncertain and competitive markets.'[8]

Now that you know that being inclusive is profitable, let me tell you that the reverse is also true. Discriminating against LGBTQ people costs a lot of money as well.

Lee Badgett, an economist and the author of the landmark 2014 World Bank report on the economic cost of homophobia—with whom I hung out in Hong Kong at the *Economist* magazine's Pride and Prejudice conference in 2017—estimated that homophobia could have cost India up to US $30.8 billion in 2012.[9] This was equivalent to 1.7 per cent of the country's potential GDP that year. In fact, Badgett believes that India's loss in GDP to be far more than the reported numbers. 'Other kinds of costs that are not in the study include the brain drain cost—people leaving India because of the stigma of being a LGBT person. [...] So there are lots of things I cannot take into account. If I could, it would simply add to my estimate and make it larger; that's why I believe my numbers are conservative.'[10]

If any politician is reading this, I want you to remember this number. Set our country on an LGBTQ inclusion trajectory and you can get a GDP bump of at least 1.7 per cent.

In July 2019, I was in Radhika Piramal's apartment in Worli's Pochkhanawala Road, a discreet leafy part of the city where many of our billionaires stay. Radhika had an intimate wedding in 2011 with 120 family members and friends in London, and now she and her American wife, Amanda, live between their London home and this Worli apartment in Mumbai.

At the entrance of the apartment, there was a gorgeous wall-sized charcoal portrait of the vintage Bollywood star Leela Chitnis—one of the earliest works by the New York–based queer artist Chitra Ganesh, whom I adore, and who is best friends with my dear friend DJ Rekha. Yes, we are all interconnected in this global queer world, and this is how the pink economy churns.

As an art lover myself, I revelled in the queer energy in the room. Radhika and Amanda have been building up their collection of strong feminist women artists over the years. A Minam Apang mountain peak hung over the marble backlit bar to my right. Radhika was in the kitchen, heating up some palak paneer and kali dal, along with gobi aloo and a nice Rajasthani gatte ki kadhi that her mother had sent them.

As we settled down to eat, we reminisced about how many years we had known each other. Radhika was doing her MBA at Harvard when I was at MIT, and she even attended the big party with the community group MASALA as part of the South Asian LGBTQ film festival I had organised in 2004. She was closeted then, so she hadn't come up to me, and had exited the party quietly.

Now, of course, Radhika is far from closeted. As the first out and proud lesbian vice chairperson of a major Indian company, VIP Industries, she is the most powerful queer person in Indian business. In fact, her own public coming out happened at the Culture Lab stage in 2015 at the event 'Breaking Free—Life Gets Better Together'. LGBT, get it? She leapt right from there to the front page. Since then, she has been forthcoming in talking about her sexuality in public—be it while delivering the keynote at the Chief Marketing Officer Summit of India in 2017 on 'Authenticity as the Key to Winning in the Marketplace and in Life' or at a panel discussion on the road ahead for LGBTQ inclusion at the Ananta Aspen Summit in 2019.

Just like with my boss, Nisa, when Radhika talks, people listen. Godrej, Piramal, these dynastic Indian family business names go a long way in our country and help overcome acceptance barriers. This is not so different from other countries, such as the US where company CEOs carry enormous clout. So when people like the Apple CEO Tim Cook declares publicly in a 2014 opinion piece in *Bloomberg Businessweek*, 'I'm proud to be gay, and I consider being gay among the greatest gifts God has given me,' it really shifts the needle of acceptance.[11]

At the launch of our Godrej trans manifesto in 2018, Radhika was in the front row when I presented a case study on how VIP's profits jumped from ₹660 million to ₹880 million after she came out as a lesbian.[12] I have a theory, I told my audience that day. We queers saw that Radhika was one of us, and we went out and bought more suitcases and backpacks! Then I showed some slides of VIP's share price going up, and speculated about us queers huddled and muddled, calling brokers to buy more of the company's shares.

I tell this story at every talk I give, and it always gets me lots of laughs. 'Come out!' I nudge the CEOs of companies I visit. 'Be like Radhika. Your profits will increase and your share price will go up!'

Back in her apartment, Radhika laughed, totally dissing my theory. 'Please don't write this in the book. It's simply not true! You really can't make a correlation between my coming out and the success of VIP.'

Of course it's a stretch, and I know it. But I am *still* talking about it in this book because my theory is very much in line with what research suggests. The New York–based Center for Talent Innovation found in its research of US companies in 2013 that consciously talking about diversity and inclusion makes an organisation 45 per cent more likely to increase its market share.[13]

Secondly, as one of the senior-most people in her company, once she came out, Radhika did not have the additional baggage of trying to hide who she was. The 2019 report from Community Business, *LGBT+ Workplace Inclusion in India*, cites Stonewall, Sir Ian McKellen's organisation: '… concealing sexual orientation at work reduces productivity by up to 30 per cent'.[14] Coming out frees up your mental bandwidth to be productive, without worrying about the consequences of hiding your sexuality. This too has a premium. When I pointed this out to Radhika, she simply did a cute little Indian head wiggle and smiled. 'Some more palak paneer?'

This is why, dear Radhika, sorry, but I am going to continue using your story as a case study in all my presentations, and yes, in fact, I would love some more palak paneer, thank you!

~

My friends at Open for Business recognise the importance of inclusion-linked profits all too well. The framework they use has twenty-three propositions under three broad categories. It is more detailed on their website, but here is a quick snapshot.

> Economic Performance: Evidence shows that open, inclusive and diverse societies are better for economic growth and that discrimination on the basis of sexual orientation or gender identity can damage long-term economic prospects. [...]
>
> Business Performance: Stronger financial performance flows from the increased ability of LGBT+ inclusive companies to attract and retain talent, to innovate and to build customer loyalty and brand strength. [...]
>
> Individual Performance: Individuals working in open, diverse and inclusive environments tend to perform better. A culture of inclusion and diversity can boost individual performance—for everyone, not just LGBT+ individuals.[15]

~

In September 2019, I received a lovely email invitation from McKinsey to attend their next GLAM masterclass cohort, a networking and learning retreat for senior leaders working on LGBTQ inclusion all around the world. (GLAM—Grow Lead Advance Mobilize—is a network of their LGBTQ employees.) This retreat was going to be held in late October in Johannesburg, South Africa.

I couldn't make it, but from the email I could see how McKinsey, with its history of progressive LGBTQ policies and practices, was leveraging its expertise into community outreach and leadership training. It is a good cause to start with, and who knows, perhaps programmes such as these might also translate into client engagements in the future? I am all for these win-win scenarios. If you are doing the kind of good work that McKinsey has been doing, why shouldn't it also translate into money?

~

When I saw Ritesh Rajani dancing vigorously in his slinky T-shirt at a post-Pride party in Mumbai in January 2017, I chuckled to myself. When did this good Sindhi boy become such a flaming diva? We were at Verbena, a rooftop bar in Lower Parel's Kamala Mills, the venue of just one of four post-Pride parties happening simultaneously across the city.

Over the years, I have become Ritesh's friend and fan. We have attended drag parties together during Namma Pride in Bengaluru and have shared countless dosas over early-morning hotel breakfasts in different cities across India while attending various diversity conferences. I have teased him mischievously from the Kashish stage—where his company, IBM, and my company, Godrej, were co-sponsors—that Godrej was better than his US-origin company because we were swadeshi. To pay for my snarkiness, I have enviously watched IBM go on to pick up an award for its LGBTQ inclusion strategies at the first Community Business diversity awards. 'What was that you said again from the Kashish stage, Parmesh?' Touché.

This then is the story of Ritesh Rajani, whose family has, for four generations, acclimated to the coastal heat of Chennai.

'I used to be very paranoid, that if I went online and chatted with someone on a gay forum, my IP address would be tracked, and someone would come to my home and out me to my family. My paranoia came from that—it was stupid, of course. In hindsight, I would live my life totally differently,' he told me over the phone in 2019.[16] This is something I often hear from queer folks who have spent a lot of their early twenties in the closet. There is this pressing sense of time lost, sex not had, relationships not experienced, heartbreaks not mourned over.

Amidst the burning legacies of the Tamil poet Thiruvalluvar's acerbic philosophy and St Thomas's martyrdom, lived Ritesh. He was with a Silicon Valley–based start-up in Chennai. He worked there for eight and a half years, burning the midnight oil, running away from confronting his sexuality, pushing himself headlong into assignments which he loved doing. But there must be a point where your work ends and your life begins. For Ritesh, they were one and the same. 'I built those walls around myself. I thought work was everything, and when you're having a great time at work and you love doing things, you do it for twelve to sixteen hours a day. While I was doing it because I liked it, I was also doing it to fill a void.'

Since he had studied, lived and worked in the same city, he was afraid of running into someone—friends from school or relatives. This fear of being recognised—while going on dates, holding hands, locking eyes for longer than a few seconds—convinced him to stay in the closet. 'Till about when I was twenty-six or twenty-seven, I was so closeted, I hadn't met or chatted with a single person from the community. You can imagine how much that bottling up affected me.'

Ritesh waited for his sister to be married, then came out to his boss, took a break and shifted to a start-up in Bengaluru, just to live his life a little more unapologetically. His boss, also the co-founder of the start-up, was a woman he considered his second mother. She was an Indian-American who understood him. Remember what I told you earlier? Indian workplaces need to be in loco parentis of their employees. Ritesh joined IBM after they acquired the start-up, and began his journey as one of corporate India's inclusion stars.

IBM has always been considered a global first-mover, especially for LGBTQ inclusion. The company included sexual orientation as part of its global non-discrimination policy in 1984. Since then, they have been the gold standard, globally as well as in India. 'I still waited for six to eight months. My first priority was to be independent. Initially, there was an event for Pride Month in 2013, around the time of the 377 judgement. IBM was one of the companies that always had a support system, and that did not reduce because of the 377 ruling. In fact, it got louder after the 2013 judgement.'

But for Ritesh to get to a point when he could take part in IBM's inclusion activities, he had to first address his anxiety and fear. He told me how he used to take time off to secretly go to Pride events that IBM organised because he didn't want his immediate manager to know he was attending them. This was how he found a few people at IBM who were out and proud.

'They became my mentors. Slowly, there was a rapport. You won't believe this, but there was a Pride T-shirt given for this group. I would not wear that T-shirt at work. I would change into the Pride T-shirt in the washroom in a different office, or a different building, and then go for the event. If you ask me what I was afraid of ... I was probably afraid of my colleagues and managers suddenly treating me differently. They saw me as a qualified person who knew his job, who was good at his job. I didn't want that equilibrium to change.'

This is something I repeatedly heard among the people I interviewed for this book. They didn't want to be seen as queer first, they wanted to be viewed as qualified professionals who just happened to be queer. Even in a company as progressive as IBM, Ritesh had the same concern. 'I wasn't afraid of losing my job or being treated badly. I was prepared to show my middle finger and walk out if that happened. I was confident enough to find something else. The problem was more about dealing with a situation where you are suddenly looked upon differently.'

But how long could he stay away from an enticing scene of out and proud Bengaluru queers? Eventually, he started contributing in the background—doing mailers, designing flyers—all the while making sure he wasn't the face of anything.

Then things changed. This was around the time he had started dating and had come out to his parents, which he thought had gone 'okay-okay'. 'One of the people who was leading the IBM LGBTQ group had to leave the company, and he asked if I could lead the group. HR came in and asked me the same thing. I thought, "Oh my god, I am not ready for this," though I was past the point where I was completely closeted.'

He recognised that this was about more than just him and took the plunge. 'It was about the void in the leadership of the group. If the void was there, someone would have lost out. I realised that just being there for someone else is important. Finally, I said, "Let me lead this group and see what happens." That would mean a mailer going out to 100,000 people with my name on it, saying, "This is the Pride charter," or something like that. It means 100,000 people will know or suspect you are gay because people associate you being in the group to your status. And the fact that there are 100,000 people at IBM means you will have friends, extended family and relatives there! And I did have someone from my sister's marital family in IBM.'

That is where the journey, from being in the shadows as a beneficiary to being in the forefront, started for Ritesh. His climb was rapid. From leading the Pride group, Ritesh eventually became part of the official D&I team at IBM in 2015–16.

Soon, Ritesh began giving talks at other companies. There were a lot of companies tiptoeing around inclusion, afraid of doing something 'illegal', even though there is no law stopping a company from creating an inclusive environment for their employees. 'Corporate India', felt Ritesh, 'was not being honest.'

Ritesh shifted gears. Along with friends, he formed the group Diversity Dialogues. They produced content—videos, papers, slides—that would help corporates understand what to do and how to go about doing it. They even produced an *Employers' Guide to Making Indian Workplaces LGBTIQ+*.[17] The book you are reading now is built on the foundation of efforts such as these.

There you have it—the coming out story of Ritesh Rajani, the good Sindhi boy from Chennai, who was once anxious and closeted but transformed into the person who danced wildly with me in a slinky T-shirt at a Mumbai bar in 2017, carefree, confident, out and proud. One of the main reasons for his transformation was that he had a supportive company, IBM, to nurture him.

Achha, so why am I telling you Ritesh's story in a chapter about how LGBTQ inclusion can make you money? The thing is, over the years, many other companies all over the world looked up to IBM and their inclusive policies, and reached out to them for help. So IBM, having the foresight and business sense, decided to make their LGBTQ inclusion practices into a service they could monetise, as part of their consulting. Yes, you got it right! They decided to make money out of showing others how to be inclusive.

Ritesh told me about this. 'In the early 2000s, there was a team formed. It was called LGBT Consulting team, which was a sales and business development team. It was not an HR team. Of course, it consisted of a lot of members from the community, but it was part of the business development team. So where IBM was selling software and services, they would go to those clients, the client would also ask us if we could help them make changes on LGBT inclusion. There were also some customers who asked us to help them design products for the community.'

The US Chamber of Commerce Foundation noted the rousing success of this team for its 'reputation for being an effective competitive differentiator in its ability to share best practices with customers, leverage its longstanding partnerships with NGOs to access decision makers, and offer diversity and inclusion workshops and commercialised assets. The chair of the team reports directly to the company CEO to make certain that leadership hears about LGBT issues at the company.'[18]

When I asked Ritesh about what IBM offered their clients, he mentioned there was both a product and a service. 'This is a service that includes workshops—it includes sensitisation, leadership, policy recommendations. When I say product, I am specifically talking about the learning material that we have. We had created resources to assist managers when an employee is transitioning. We created resources on being an ally. A little bit about educating people about the LGBT community. Because it was created with a lot of stories of members from the community, it was a good learning module that was also a product that IBM was selling a few years ago, and still sells.'[19]

Todd Sears, the founder of Out Leadership—a global strategic advisory firm that connects leaders across the world's most influential industries to create business opportunities and cultivate talent—also benefited greatly from focusing on the LGBTQ community while he was at the investment management company Merrill Lynch. He chose to address the obstacles that queer people face while managing their wealth or bequeathing it to partners or family members, so as to ensure the firm's presence in these matters. This was the early 2000s. His marketing team of 10 financial advisors across 6 major cities in the US, educated more than 250 financial advisors to better serve Merrill Lynch's LGBTQ clients around the globe. The initial target was to bring in US $24 million in 2 years. However, his team brought in US $1.4 billion in 4 years![20]

You see how LGBTQ people are a big market? If you are from a company looking at growing rapidly, you should really be paying attention.

The IBM team Ritesh spoke about, which consists of people focusing on diversity and inclusion full-time, has grown to work on other aspects of inclusion even as it remains firmly rooted in LGBTQ inclusion. This is the beauty of the queer movement. It might start off as a fight for the dignity of queer folks, but it only takes a while before the umbrella opens out to include others. The movement broadens, the mandate widens, and justice can eventually become an intersectional wonderland. Another testimonial of this intersectional journey: Ritesh and Madhumitha Venkataraman met at IBM's LGBTQ conference in 2016, bonded over their shared passion for inclusion and went on to become best friends. In late 2019, they formalised their collective, Diversity Dialogues, into a company that helps organisations on their inclusion journey.

11

LGBTQ Inclusion Can Make Your Company More Innovative, and Help Attract and Retain Talent

Below is a message that Nisa got on LinkedIn in June 2019. She proudly forwarded it to Sumit Mitra, Shefali Kohli and me.

Hi Nisaba

I am writing this message to let you know that Godrej for me is a trailblazer and will always be. To know the reason, please read on and no I am not seeking a job.

Since the last few months I have seen posts of diversity and inclusion on your LinkedIn pages, which is great. It is sad that even today most of the top companies (even mine, which is one of the largest conglomerates in India) thinks that diversity is just about 'women'. When I was in college, for the very reason GCPL was my dream company, it was of most of our batchmates but for 'other reasons'. Today I am earning what Godrej offers to its best talent, but still Godrej holds a very special place in my heart and always will.

I have decided once I come out (planning in a few years) I'll surely look for an opportunity in Godrej and if I am lucky take my retirement from there, alas! Long dream! I am only 25 now.

I was scared of my life ahead in Indian corporate ecosystem but your organization has given me lot of courage. Hence congratulations of having touched so many hearts, but many might not come and thank you (it's a harsh world out there) perhaps that's why I wanted to do it. I respect you and congratulate you for this big feat.

Do let me know if you read this, I'd feel my job is done :)

Cheers!

This was not a one-off message. In 2017, I presented the work of the Culture Lab as well as our efforts to make Godrej LGBTQ inclusive to a small group of international investors in our company. I didn't know at that time that one of these global visitors happened to be lesbian. She wrote a beautiful email to Nisa after going back to her base in Singapore, about how she and her wife were looking to raise their daughter in a prejudice-free world and how they would now look towards Godrej for inspiration. Can you imagine the pride Nisa would have felt after reading this email?

Nisa is obsessed with innovation. At our very first meeting in 2010, we spent half the day talking about design thinking, about the innovation consultancy IDEO and the different books we had read around innovation. One of her favourite words is 'antevasin'—a Sanskrit word that refers to someone who lives on the edge of the forest, no longer of the town but not yet an ascetic. More loosely, it describes embracing both the old and the new; it means staying within the parameters while crossing the boundaries. Nisa is committed to making Godrej an antevasin company—and being innovative is central to the transformation process.

A central pillar of Nisa's innovation quest is making Godrej an inclusive place to work in. What does it mean to create an organisation that talented people want to join, an organisation that investors value because of its inclusive policies and work culture? When she gets emails like the ones above, she knows that she is on the right track.

Here is what Nisa said to the audience at our Culture Lab event 'Breaking Free: Life Gets Better Together (LGBT)' in October 2015. 'Inclusivity means innovation. The more inclusive you are, the more debates you can have, the less hierarchy you have, the faster it is to recover from failure. If you say, "Everyone should talk like me, look like me, be like me, have the same background as me," I don't think that would work well for companies.'[1]

Nisa is not alone in thinking along these lines. According to a 2011 Deloitte report, *Diversity as the Engine of Innovation*, the top 50 of the Fortune 500 companies believe that they benefit from a diverse workplace for this very reason—the quality of ideas.[2] The more diverse your team is, the more points of view and better ideas you will get. Diverse teams perform better as well. The 2010 study *Better Decisions Through Diversity* from *Kellogg Insight*, the Kellogg School of Management's magazine, shows that mixed groups do better than homogenous groups due to alternative perspectives and 'more careful processing of information'.[3]

A 2015 Open for Business report tells us that employees who perceive that their organisation is committed to diversity and feel included are 83 per cent more likely to see their company as one that 'develop[s] innovative solutions'.[4]

C. Lakshmi, managing director at Accenture Solutions, spoke at the RISE job fair in Bengaluru about how an inclusive work environment can unleash the innovation potential of LGBTQ employees. 'We have found that inclusivity fosters and guides creativity, and a culture of equality is an innovation multiplier. Studies have shown that LGBTQ individuals are seven times more likely to innovate in a more equal work culture.'[5]

To put it simply, more innovation at your workplace means:

- More money to be made from these innovations
- More employees who feel like they are part of an innovative firm, which increases employee satisfaction and retention
- More potential employees with incredible skill sets flocking to your company to be hired

While the business case is strong, I also urge you to look beyond the numbers, at the people who inhabit these statistics. Here is one—my friend Anubhuti Banerjee from Tata Steel, who you know well by now.

'I was able to take up quite a few projects which fostered the idea of innovation. One of the things I got to do was host something with the CII called Digital Jharkhand, which looked at how digital technology and innovation were progressing. It was attended by the chief minister of Jharkhand, along with many organisations based in the state and in eastern India. I was the person who got to lead this initiative, anchored it and created quite a few of the modules.

'One effect that doing this had was that I was sent to a Tata Steel project in Canada. As far as I know, I was one of the first people who got to go this young in their career to a foreign project location, which was something almost everyone wanted. In Tata Steel's culture, which was in place till a few years ago, you didn't go anywhere unless you created a certain image and had quite a few years of experience behind you. Because of all these factors, at least in my department and also in the company, I was someone very visible. Knowing that, and the position I had, and knowing I was considered a good, valuable, talented employee, with a penchant of championing new ideas, I then had to think that this [the gender-affirming process] was something I could take up.'[6]

It is amazing to see the circle of trust between a company and an employee. Tata Steel empowers Anubhuti, she innovates, Tata Steel rewards her, she gets the confidence to transition at Tata Steel. What a wonderful story this is!

If you are heading HR in a company, think of the innovators you could have on your team, and think of the innovator you could be in your company. Also, think of what stories like Anubhuti's do to attract talent to you.

Today, all companies are fighting for the same talent, chasing the elusive millennials graduating from universities with incredibly progressive values. You need to know, first and foremost, that being inclusive will help you attract the best LGBTQ talent. According to a survey commissioned by Vodafone in 2018 from Out Now Consulting, 83 per cent of more than the 3,000 LGBTQ people surveyed preferred to work with visible LGBTQ leaders.[7] MINGLE's 2016 survey of Indian companies states that 65 per cent of LGBTQ employees look at HR policies as a major factor before joining a company.[8]

Secondly, if you are inclusive as a company, you are more likely to attract a larger and better talent pool not only from the LGBTQ community but also straight allies. A study on LGBTQ rights in the marketplace by the non-profit think tank Center for Talent Innovation found that 72 per cent of allies are more likely to accept a job at a company that is supportive of LGBTQ employees, and 82 per cent of allies are more likely to consume goods and services from a company that supports LGBTQ equality.[9]

According to the 2015 report by Open for Business on the economic and business case for LGBTQ inclusion, companies like Ford Motor Company, Alcoa, British Petroleum and Goldman Sachs have already seen the benefits of LGBTQ-inclusive policies, which make the companies come across as forward-thinking and meritocratic to millennials considering them as potential employers.[10]

Let me tell you about Godrej LOUD, a programme that I am extremely proud of helping co-create, which enables us to showcase our forward-thinking values to potential employees and encourages them to join us. LOUD's origin story dates back to 2007. While I was still at Mahindra, my friend from my MIT days Sidharth Jaggi, now a professor in Hong Kong, invited me to serve as an advisor for an initiative he had started, called Life Unlimited. He had set up a scholarship the previous year with a bunch of friends, and their aim was to give college students in Mumbai funds as well as mentorship to help them convert their non-academic dreams into reality. I readily agreed, and was eventually matched to Pallavi, Harshad and Partho, three students from St Xavier's College, who wanted to create a graphic novel about life under the Westside Overbridge of Mumbai's Dadar Station. I had a blast! I think I enjoyed the mentoring much more than the students did.

In 2011, soon after joining Godrej, when Nisa and Sumit asked me to think of innovative ideas to recruit MBA students as interns for Godrej every summer, I came up with a plan that was pretty much a spin-off of Life Unlimited. I called the project 'Godrej LOUD—Live Out Ur Dream'. I know, wrong spelling, but the acronym had to work for the millennials, *na*? LOUD sounded kind of cool, and plus, it describes my fashion sense perfectly.

What if, I proposed to Godrej, instead of looking at the grades of prospective students or making them do the same old group discussions or case studies, we ask them to tell us their dreams? What if we tell them that these ideas and how creatively the students present them will be their application to Godrej? Then, what if we fund the dreams of those we select, with one condition—the students must fulfil their dreams *before* they join us the following summer?

We would be helping the students by allowing them to spend time doing things that mattered to them at a visceral level, I argued. We would also be reversing Maslow's hierarchy of needs pyramid, and indicating to the students that self-actualisation is possible alongside meeting the other needs of life, like food, clothing, shelter and a job. But most of all, we would gain access to some great talent by seeing the creative and passionate side of our student applicants, something that companies rarely come across in hiring processes. Finally, I argued, think of how loyal these students would be, given that they had joined Godrej *after* we fulfilled their personal dreams.

After sitting on it for about a year, the management suddenly approved LOUD. Nisa and Sumit assigned the project to my colleague Vandana Lisa Scolt, who was at that time part of the Corporate HR Campus Recruitment team. Vandana was on a pretty atypical Godrej career path herself, with her unique combination of an undergraduate degree in literature from St Stephen's College in Delhi and an MBA from the Xavier's Institute of Management in Bhubaneshwar. Thus, the Godrej LOUD journey began, with Vandana and me as the parents of LOUD.

This programme has been extremely successful over the years. Every assumption that we started LOUD with has proven itself to be true. LOUD has won awards for innovative campus recruitment. It has featured in a mini-series on CNBC India in 2014.[11] We have so far funded more than fifty dreams over eight years—including a painting holiday in Spain, a bike ride through Thailand, the creation of a pan-India network of blood and organ banks, and an affordable wheelchair for Indian children.

Eight years down the line, I still continue to travel from campus to campus with the LOUD team. I tell the students about my own journey as an out and proud gay Godrej employee and my dreams for the future. You know what? The fact that Godrej is so committed to LGBTQ inclusion deeply connects with the students, and they swarm to me after every talk, hungry to learn more about us.

For queer students, my presence and my openness on campus is often transformational. I think I have a parallel profession as an honorary founder of many LGBTQ clubs in MBA college campuses across the country. In August 2015, I helped launch Ally—the LGBTQ students' association of IIM Ahmedabad. Two years later, in August 2017, I was hanging out with the students of Ummeed—the LGBTQ association at IIM Kozhikode—on their verdant campus. They told me that they were inspired to start Ummeed after my Godrej LOUD talk to them in 2016.

A student at that 2016 talk had just stood in a corner and stared at me, without saying a word. During my 2017 visit, she mustered up the courage to come up to me, and told me that over the past year she had come out as a lesbian and was now confident of herself.

In August 2019, I was at IIM Trichy, helping kick-start Prism, their LGBTQ students' association, in the midst of my Godrej LOUD visit. All IIM campuses are blessed with loads of land, but the Trichy one, the newest, felt like it was from another planet altogether because of its central attraction—the futuristic spaceship-like Learning Resource Centre, a library building with a finance lab, a behavioural science lab and a day-care centre for kids. The newly formed Prism club members met me at the entrance of the campus, and as they walked me to the auditorium, they excitedly told me about their plans for the year.

As far as LOUD presentations go, what I witnessed next was special. Even before I entered the auditorium, an installation of hundreds of paper cranes greeted me. About forty students burst into a nukkad natak that ended with them shouting in unison, 'LOUD, LOUD, LOUD!' As I opened the door of the auditorium, twenty students exploded into a Bollywood song-and-dance routine on stage (the 'Aankh Maare' remix, if you please!), and they were then joined by twenty more from among the students who were seated. Soon, we were all dancing. Then there was a classical music performance, followed by a fusion dance and rock music performance. By the time I finally got to speak, we were one hour into the session, but who cares when you're having so much fun.

LOUD for these students was a chance to unleash the talent they had kept bottled up for pretty much all their lives. Some version of this grand welcome happens at every college; the students do this for Godrej each year and for no other company. There is only one word for this—'love'. We show the students that we care about them, and they in turn respond with so much love that we can't help but burst into song-and-dance on campus with them.

At each campus I go to, I make it a point to ask: How many LGBTQ students and professors are there in the audience, please raise your hands. Do you know how many hands went up in Trichy in 2019? Nine. This was the highest number I had ever seen. Nine confident students, willing to share their identity with their peers in a second-tier city in southern Tamil Nadu. Then I ask: How many people in the audience support LGBTQ equality, raise your hands. In Trichy, all hands were up in the air.

After we finish our campus tours every year, we receive hundreds of applications from these students. We invite the best applicants to our headquarters in Mumbai for a reality-TV-style face-off. Think TED Talk meets *Shark Tank*. It is heart-warming that many of the applications we receive from the students are about LGBTQ inclusion.

Let me tell you a story about one of the dreams that made it to the grand finale of LOUD 2019. Gokul Chhabra from the Management Development Institute in Gurgaon pitched us his dream of opening beauty salons run by LGBTQ people. He had already helped set up VIBGYOR, the first Indian beauty parlour solely run by transgender people, in Delhi's Saket. Inspired by the success of VIBGYOR, he wanted to partner with community-run NGOs to set up open-to-all salons. At the LOUD finale, Gokul made a compelling pitch for his dream with a well thought-out presentation of budget requirements and revenue models. But what was most special about Gokul's application was the video he played towards the end—his friends from the trans community sharing their aspiration of becoming beauticians and speaking about Gokul as a sincere ally.

On the one hand, Gokul's LOUD dream matched our vision of empowering LGBTQ-inclusive workplaces, on the other, it spoke to the work done by Godrej's Salon-i initiative which trains women in beauty and hair care, soft skills and entrepreneurship. What a clever idea—combining community outreach with Godrej's CSR efforts. Obviously the dream won. Welcome to Godrej, Gokul.

~

Attracting talent is one thing. Retaining it is another. Millennials are notorious for their transient loyalty. How do you as a company get them to stay on? I would say, by being so inclusive that they never want to leave.

You should create an environment that enables employees to bring their whole self to work, and you will see how that impacts their happiness, productivity and willingness to stay and grow within the organisation. When talking to Sandeep Nair at Community Business, I could hear the contentment he felt with the company, especially given the really bad experiences he had been through before.

'My CB experience has been fantastic. I have never had to hide my true self at work. I got married four months after joining. When I was joining itself, I told them I would need some days off because I was getting married. The whole team was supportive.

'Even in terms of benefits, we do not have any issues with same-sex partner benefits. There was this incident with me. They had hired this lady who wasn't aware of the LGBTQ context, and she assumed I was straight. When I said I was married, she asked me what my wife did. When I told her I was gay, she retorted by asking me, "Are you number nine?" I had not heard this term for the longest time in my life! I was just laughing. I am not transgender, I am gay, I had to explain. Finally, I narrated this incident to my manager. My manager didn't say anything immediately, but soon after that, I received an email from the CEO apologising to me. Later, they asked the concerned person to learn what the LGBTQ context in India is.'[12] Why would Sandeep leave such a progressive company?

These stories aggregate into numbers too. Look at what the *The Indian LGBT Workplace Climate Survey 2016* conducted by MINGLE has to say: 'Overall, we found that LGBT employees who are out and supported in the workplace have greater trust in their employers, are more satisfied with their rate of promotions, feel that their performance is judged more fairly, and are generally more comfortable in their interactions with their managers and colleagues. More importantly, their stress levels are lower and are more likely to continue with the same organisation in the future.'[13]

If you work in HR, you should be thinking of this in terms of the real cost of losing an employee. Studies from the Society for Human Resource Management in 2008 show that replacing a salaried employee costs six to nine months of their salary on average.[14] And here is the thing. This is just a low-end approximation. It could go as high as twice their annual salary. HR heads, who have come face-to-face with the attrition monster, need to think about the cost of advertising, hiring, interviewing, selecting, on-boarding, transitioning, training and then, the loss of morale when the employee quits.

~

I was driving along the Mumbai–Pune expressway, en route to meet my friend Sameer Samudra, the director of Customer Support Excellence at Cummins India. I love this drive and always stop at McDonalds on the way to Pune, for a loo break and a Filet-o-Fish, and at Shree Datta Snacks on the way back for their legendary vada pav.

It felt strange to be doing Pune as a day trip. Pune used to be an adventure in my childhood. Train rides on the Deccan Queen or Indrayani Express, with fried cheese toast and horrible ketchup, and buying chikki from the vendors at Lonavala Station. Now it is a day trip, and with the housing complexes lining both sides of the expressway all through, it feels like wherever I go, it is a suburb of either Mumbai or Pune. (The Harvard professor Sai Balakrishnan calls these connecting urban corridors 'shareholder cities', and has a brilliant book by the same name.[15])

Pune is Sameer's hometown. Having been raised in a traditional, lower middle-class Maharashtrian background and studied in a Marathi-medium school, he took an adventurous journey to the other side of the world, to the University of Cincinnati in the US, to fully embrace his sexuality. He came back home to where it had all begun, with his husband Amit Gokhale, who also works at Cummins.

Sameer and Amit are examples of reverse brain drain—when talent return to be innovative on home soil. Sameer gave me two reasons for why they had come back. 'First, we wanted to be closer to our families. Our parents live here in India, we wanted to be close to them, especially as they are ageing. Second, we were always scared India wouldn't accept us, but we started realising, just because of that fear we might be losing out on some things; both of us are very much Indian at heart—we missed our festivals, our food, our culture. I lived in the US for twenty years, Amit lived there for fifteen years, we enjoyed the US life, but we wanted to at least try and see how the experience would be here.

'We also realised that actually this is, right now, a good opportunity to make an impact not just in the organisation but in the community too, by living as an openly gay couple—Hey, this life can be a reality. I believe I can be a change agent. I told Amit, we might be able to do something more, not just for the organisation, but for the community, just by showcasing our true life.

'I moved in July 2017, and in 2018 launched an ERG here in Pune. Now we have a very active LGBTQ resource group with almost thirty-two members, which is big for a manufacturing company in Pune. We participated in Pune Pride even when Section 377 was still there. We have the Pride flag being hoisted in our campuses the whole month of June. We are changing a lot of policies to be LGBT inclusive.

'It has been two years since we began working here. We have been out from day one, even Amit is. There are a couple of individuals who are out to us, but are not out to the organisation. The organisation's climate is still something people are not comfortable with. I am working to change that. It is a manufacturing setting, traditional mindset and culture. It is going to take some time. This is one of my goals.'[16]

One way of looking at Sameer and Amit and their position in Pune is: lucky them, they got to work at Cummins, a company that is sensitive to their needs. But another way to look at it is: lucky Cummins, they got such talent and have retained them, simply because they are inclusive.

~

By the way, it is not just companies that are realising that the more inclusive they are, the more talent they can attract and retain, and the better it will be for them economically. This realisation has occurred at the city and national level as well.

The Gallup World Poll in 2012 conducted a survey in 160 nations to find out whether or not a defined geography—a country, state or city—was 'a good place for gays and lesbians'. The economists Richard Florida and Charlotta Mellander correlated this data with GDP per capita in 2014. They found a significant positive correlation between the two—0.72.[17] This means that places that are friendlier to queer people have better economies.

Florida writes about the rise of the 'creative class'.[18] The creative class include scientists, lawyers, designers, as well as people involved in education, technology and the arts, because they innovate, create technologies and new ideas, and are also skilled at problem-solving. They usually come from a background of formal education and draw from a knowledge base to perform their creative economic role. He concludes that to be a creative hub, a place needs talent, technology and tolerance, the '3 T's' that will attract the creative class—talent being a highly educated population, technology being the infrastructure necessary to facilitate their work, and tolerance being a diverse community with a culture of tolerance and acceptance. The creative class is drawn to cities and countries that are liberal and tolerant, and the presence of a strong, involved LGBTQ community signals just that.

Diverse populations foster innovation, lateral thinking and the development of fertile ground for new ideas to take root. Corporate values that reflect tolerance, acceptance and inclusion attract an international workforce as well as international investment because they indicate the presence of 'quality of life' factors. An increase in foreign direct investment is also seen as a positive outcome of these initiatives, according to the 2014 Deloitte report *Foreign Direct Investment and Inclusive Growth: The Impacts on Social Progress.*[19]

There was an exciting white paper produced in 2019 by the Singapore AMCHAM's Government and Regional Affairs Committee and Human Capital Committee. *Companion Paper—Increasing Innovation and Productivity in Singapore: The Role of Diversity and Inclusion*[20] cites a 2016 study by the professors Huasheng Gao from the Nanyang Technology University and Wei Zhang from the Shanghai University of Economics and Finance on this topic. Their research, published in *Harvard Business Review*, studied the impact of non-discrimination employment laws in different states in the US. Gao and Zhang surveyed the patent filings of thousands of firms between 1976 and 2008, controlling for variations in company and state characteristics.

They found that firms in the states that implemented laws prohibiting discrimination against LGBTQ employees received 8 per cent more patents and 11 per cent more patent citations than comparable firms in the states without such laws. The results typically showed up about two years after the laws went into effect. In addition, they found that 'pro-LGBT employees' and inventors who moved into the states with anti-discrimination laws tended to produce 30 per cent more patents than employees who moved away from such states.

The 2015 Open for Business report claims that work-related migration, globally, has seen an increase by one-third since 2000. A part of this migration is because of discrimination. The reports says that significant emigration specifically as a result of anti-LGBTQ laws and culture has taken place in India, Jamaica, Nigeria, Russia and Uganda.[21] According to a 2016 study by Waverly Deutsch and others on LGBT entrepreneurship in the US, there is a clear migration away from intolerant locales towards pro-diversity states and cities.[22]

Until Section 377 was read down in September 2018, India was facing a similar backlash due to the discriminatory colonial-era law. The IIT petition filed in 2018 had several alumni citing Section 377 as the reason for brain drain among the IIT alumni. The petitioners were all part of Pravritti, an informal pan-IIT LGBTQ group with more than 350 members.[23] Tony Christopher, a senior technology lead at Infosys, writes in an article for *NDTV* that many of his queer friends considered applying to Canada for permanent residency due to the anti-discrimination laws there.[24]

This is a larger question for our country's politicians. Why should Canada get our queer talent? Dialling it back to the companies, the question you should all be asking yourselves is, why should some other company attract the brightest queer people out there, or straight allies who support queer inclusion, instead of your own company?

12

LGBTQ-Inclusive Messaging Helps You Improve Your PR and Keep Up with the Millennials

In 2018, when Section 377 was unequivocally struck down by the Supreme Court of India, I did a lot of press that included newspaper interviews and radio, and of course, I mentioned Godrej in each of these. Godrej's PR agency, Adfactors, measured the coverage we received in the verdicts week after week using a method called AVE or Advertising Value Equivalent. Guess what? For just one week of talking about something I care about and that Godrej believes in, we received ₹117 million in positive publicity! I have been doing this for the past eight years—can you add up the millions of goodwill generated for Godrej?

The Humsafar Trust in their catalogue, 'List of Brands Supporting the LGBTQ', estimated that there were seventy-nine Indian and international companies who produced ads supporting the queer community in the immediate aftermath of the verdict.[1] Google, Facebook and YouTube introduced rainbow Pride colours on their homepages, profile pictures and logos, and tweeted about the judgement. Some of the other brands included IndiGo, Starbucks, HBO, Nykaa, L'Oreal, Café Coffee Day, Discovery Networks, Swiggy, Ola, KFC, Star TV, Zee TV, Colors, GoAir and Titan Eyeplus. Hashtags such as '#LoveIsLove' and '#Section377' were trending on Twitter and used by many companies to advance their messages.[2]

Tata Group's tweet read, 'We welcome the landmark judgement by the Supreme Court on #Section377. We have always provided equal opportunities for employment at Tata, irrespective of race, caste, gender, religion or sexual orientation. #PrideIndia,' while Rekha M. Menon, the chairman of Accenture India tweeted, '#Inclusion is the bedrock of innovation and growth. And it gives me immense pride to be part of @Accenture, where Inclusion and diversity are fundamental to our culture and core values. A welcome change! #Section377 @AccentureIndia.'[3]

The e-commerce giant Flipkart posted an advertisement about how Section 377 is the only 'cancellation' they look forward to. L'Oreal tweaked their popular tagline, 'Because you're worth it' to 'Because we're ALL worth it'.[4] This PR blitz has continued ever since, throughout 2019 and early 2020, throughout the course of my writing this book, on the first Valentine's Day after the reading down of 377, the first Pride Month and so on. Why? Because it makes sense. Companies and the brands attached to them have realised that young India, the India full of millennials that organisations are dying to attract and sell to, really cares about how companies communicate their inclusivity.

~

On 9 December 2018, at four o'clock in the afternoon, I pull up to the House of Party, or HOP, an uber-cool bar in Andheri. It is usually buzzing post nine o'clock at night, but I am here for an afternoon play. I am greeted at the entrance with wonderful pastel pink cupcakes sponsored by Tinder. I enter the bar, which is tastefully done up Prohibition style, with plush sofas, dimly lit lamps on side tables, and an art deco console serving free vodka cocktails, courtesy the second sponsor, Stoli. On stage, I see the Gaysi logo right next to that of their third sponsor, the Canadian Consulate. Just two months after the reading down of Section 377, we are already in queer sponsorship heaven. Smart organisations are lining up to swipe right for the pink rupee.

Gaysi is one of my favourite LGBTQ media networks. Maybe because ten years ago, when they first started as a simple blog, I was featured in it as their favourite fashionista, wearing big red sunglasses and my signature pout. Over the years, the Gaysi team have started their own paper zine and branched out into live events, like the wildly popular 'Dirty Talk' open mic bar nights, across the city. My favourite RJ Rohini has hosted many of these over the years. Then Gaysi got more ambitious and started supporting queer-themed plays; their first was *The Gentlemen's Club a.k.a. Tape*, written and directed by the theatre stalwart Vikram Phukan, and produced as a joint effort with the Patchworks Ensemble theatre group.

I remember sitting in the audience at another bar called Tilt, this time in Lower Parel, in September 2015, for the first ever show of *Tape*. '*Kis ko pyaar karoon, kaise pyaar karoon, tu bhi hai, yeh bhi hai, woh bhi hai …*' A gold-sequined Shammi Kapoor lookalike burst on to the stage with a bang and thus began India's first drag king show. *Tape* was funny, poignant, cool, fierce and unapologetic theatre. Structured as a play within a play and set in a fantasy Mumbai where drag king performances are the norm, *Tape* had Shammi Kapoor's character hanging out with a Justin Timberlake impersonator, and a supporting cast of other fantastic characters like the raunchy Mr 55.

It was exciting because all the drag I had seen in India at that time had men dressed up as women, but not the other way around. Women performing masculinity—overtly and flamboyantly—had been rather invisible, except in occasional Bollywood film songs like in the 1994 film *Hum Aapke Hain Koun*. *Tape* was an attempt to address this imbalance. The title refers to something that many, but not all, drag kings do before they get on stage—tape their breasts to flatten them. The play dealt with this act of personal politics, as it did with many other aspects of gender, societal expectations, conformity and performativity, and it did so with such a light and fabulous touch that it never felt heavy or preachy. I just couldn't stop smiling.

I smile non-stop again at HOP as *Pinky Promise*, the latest Gaysi–Patchworks Ensemble collaboration, unfolds via six short vignettes, crowdsourced from the queer community. As a gay man who has travelled by local trains regularly, I can relate to 'Two by Two', which is about a flirtatious encounter in a local Mumbai train. *Kya* chemistry! Another vignette, 'Trans in Transit', takes the audience inside a trans person's confusion about which queue to stand in at an airport. My favourite vignette is 'Paying Guest', which mashes up the real-life challenge of being gay and looking for a housemate, with the zombie genre.

~

Ghun-ghun-ghun, the ghunghroos pulsate on the feet like a beating heart. The ring in the hand of a man on his knees. Whoosh-whoosh, an old woman skipping in the park. Salwar kameez and confidence on a woman riding a bike. This is an e-Bay ad. 'Things don't judge' is the tagline. The man is proposing to his lover, also a man. The dancer too is a man, flexing, reaching into the camera with mudras as soft and gentle as the wind itself.

Ritesh Rajani analyses this ad, among others, in his 2016 research paper 'LGBTQ+ Inclusion at Indian Workspaces'.[5] The ad became the most watched video on the eBay YouTube channel, a feat that took a month to achieve, garnering likes and comments both positive and product-oriented. Commercial success and LGBTQ inclusion are increasingly becoming intertwined in today's India.

A beautiful trans woman with brown highlights, in a yellow salwar kameez and a red dupatta, with her lunchbox and handbag in hand, is waiting at the bus stop with a crowd of others. Children are going to school, and there are men and women in corporate clothes. The bus arrives, and the crowd surges to grab a seat. She isn't sure whether to enter from the front door of the bus near where the women sit, or through the back door to where the men sit. A habit from years bygone makes her venture to the back door of the bus first, but her identity has changed, and so she walks back to the front. A woman in the crowd shoos her to the back door but the conductor has already banged the tin wall, thrum-thrum-thrum, and the bus departs. She is at the bus stop alone, and late for work. When she asks a taxi driver to drop her off, he gives her money, assuming she is asking for alms. She is despondent and sweating. Then a man comes on a bike and offers to give her a ride. A voice-over says, '*Badlaav ke pahiye sirf pannon par hi nahin, raaston par bhi chalne chahiye, na?*' as the translation appears on-screen: 'The wheels of change shouldn't just remain on paper, they should ride the streets too.'

This was the Ralco Tyres ad for Independence Day 2019. I was in tears when I first saw it. The company partnered with Humsafar Trust's TRANScend initiative 'to support, empower and provide employment to the transgender community across our country. Because when we free our roads from bias, each one of us becomes free! #FreeTheRoads.'[6] As I typed out my concluding thoughts in this chapter in March 2020, the ad already had 1.2 million views on YouTube.[7]

This isn't unusual. Remember Gauri Sawant's 'Touch of Care' video for Vicks? With a viewership of 37.21 million, it also received national as well as international press coverage.[8] The company's 2016–17 annual report states that the previous year's 'growth was driven by a strong focus on brand fundamentals and equity building campaigns like #TouchOfCare.'[9]

In fact, even in 2013, when the Supreme Court reversed the 2009 Delhi High Court decision and recriminalised homosexuality, a few brands stood up to support the community and criticise the judgement. Fastrack used the critical moment of public outrage by running an ad that asked their viewers to 'come out of the closet' and 'move on'. It was aired during the IPL tournament in 2013.[10] The 2012–13 Titan annual report states, 'Fastrack ran impactful marketing campaigns for each of its product categories and had successful activations. ... Its edgy style of communication resonates with the youth across the length and breadth of India.'[11]

Back in 2015, *Business Standard* had this headline: 'Almost Half Indian Millennials Favour Marriage Equality'.[12] The writer Debra Donston-Miller wrote in 2016 that by 2025 millennials would make up 75 per cent of the global workforce.[13] In this age of the personal being political, India's new generation is slowly developing into an ethical consumer base. They make choices based on causes they identify with and support. A Boston Consulting Group report in 2014, titled *How Millennials Are Changing the Face of Marketing Forever*, says that millennials want their purchases and the brands they endorse to reflect their politics—which is inseparable from their identity.[14]

This new India sees brands going for advertising approaches that are centred around social causes rather than product-driven approaches. Not just millennials, a representative sample of India's population in the World Values Survey indicates that the number of Indians who believe that 'homosexuality is never justifiable' fell from 89 per cent to 24 per cent between 1990 and 2014.[15] Savvy companies are riding this attitudinal shift with their communication strategies.

K.V. Sridhar, a former chief creative officer of the advertising agency Leo Burnett and now the founder of the marketing agency Hyper Collective, says, '[The youth] don't want to be left out of social decisions, such as politics, that impact them directly [...] they want purpose, and to feel like they are part of something big and important, even when shopping for tea or timepieces.'[16]

Seema Chawla, the chief marketing officer of the online fashion portal Ajio, which ran a successful Instagram campaign #PrideNotPrejudice in 2017, is pretty clear that in today's India, 'Brands must embrace the LBGTQ community. Neutrality will not inspire the deep relationships they want with their consumers.'[17] I couldn't agree more with Seema. To connect to young people today, you need to wear your inclusive values on your sleeves, and you need to speak up about what you stand for in all your communication. Quite frankly, what is the difference between your product or service versus that of your competitors? In a world where products and services and even experiences are becoming increasingly standardised, what will differentiate you from the rest are the ideals you stand for and how authentically you communicate these to your savvy millennial audience.

~

Sunlight streaming in, a sunset-kissed breeze flowing through a cross-ventilated room. White curtains, feather light, like Sridevi's chiffon sari. A lesbian couple hold hands, the dying embers of the sun lighting up their silhouettes. One of the lovers' parents are to arrive at their home shortly. 'I really want them to like me,' the other lover declares.

This is a 2015 ad for Myntra's private label apparel brand Anouk.[18] It made sense. Myntra, like eBay, works mostly through online purchases. Research that looks into the LGBTQ consumer base's purchasing power and characteristics indicate that the average queer consumer is college educated, shops online and is interested in purchasing the latest technology. LGBTQ-friendly brands inculcate a sense of loyalty among queer consumers because these brands reflect their values. A 2011 Deloitte study found that 78 per cent of online gay consumers prefer to buy from companies that have targeted advertising for the gay community.[19]

The Myntra ad online got ten million views in ten days.

Ritesh does a sentiment analysis of this ad in his research. At the time he wrote his paper, this video was the second in number of views and first in number of likes on Myntra's YouTube channel, way above the fray with ten times more views and likes than any other video on their page.

He cautions, however, that 'successful advertising is about not just standing up for the right thing, but also finding an elegant way to tie it to one's organisation's products and brands. If the mapping is not done elegantly, it may come across as a shoddy attempt to just piggyback on the LGBTQ community, just to get a sales leverage.'[20]

He gives examples of those that got it right, like Tanishq earrings. 'When Section 377 was reinforced in 2013, they released an ad that said, "Two of a kind make a pair". It was a great message against the Supreme Court and at the same time they branded their product, and it was not looking like they were making money out of the community. It was very clear that they were taking a stand with their own product branding involved. I think Red Label also did that well. They can't make a product for us, right? But what they did was that they sponsored a music band which comprised transpeople. And then they got Sonu Nigam to endorse the band. I mean, is it having too much impact? No. But they did something beyond just looking at us as a customer.'[21]

Globally, too, being authentic is something brands supporting LGBTQ issues are cognizant of. The carmaker Subaru is a popular case study in this regard. In the 1990s, they decided to move away from the standard target population in the US of white male aged between eighteen and thirty-five. Their search for niche groups to connect to led them to their lesbian market. Remember, this was a time when the queer movement in the US wasn't as strong as it is today, and public discussion was sparse and violently polarising. To make a statement in this atmosphere needed grit and conviction. An article in the *Atlantic*, 'How Subaru Came to Be Seen As a Car for Lesbians', speaks of how they crashed into this context head on.

'For its first Subaru ads, Mulryan/Nash hired women to portray lesbian couples. But the ads didn't get good reactions from lesbian audiences. What worked were winks and nudges. One campaign showed Subaru cars that had license plates that said "Xena LVR" (a reference to *Xena: Warrior Princess,* a TV show whose female protagonists seemed to be lovers) or "P-TOWN" (a moniker for Provincetown, Massachusetts, a popular LGBTQ vacation spot). Many ads had taglines with double meanings. "Get Out. And Stay Out" could refer to exploring the outdoors in a Subaru—or coming out as gay. "It's Not a Choice. It's the Way We're Built" could refer to all Subarus coming with all-wheel-drive—or LGBT identity. "Each year we've done this, we've learned more about our target audience," John Nash, the creative director of the ad agency told the website *AdRespect*. "We've found that playful coding is really, really appreciated by our consumers. They like deciphering it."'[22]

Lesbians were four times more likely than the average consumer to buy a Subaru. Therefore, Subaru cultivated a brand campaign that catered especially to this market. They sponsored Pride parades and also partnered with the Rainbow Card, a credit card that used the cashback mechanism to donate to gay and lesbian causes. They hired the tennis legend Martina Navratilova, an out and proud lesbian, as their brand ambassador. This new brand image resulted in tangible financial success.[23]

~

In June 2019, I was giving a talk at the Mumbai headquarters of Visa, the credit card company. I should really charge for my consulting advice, *na*? (A credit card will do!) My great idea was for them to launch a Pride or rainbow card for India. 'Do it soon or your rival will,' I told them. 'We don't have any rivals,' one of their employees told me, cattily. 'Cash is our rival.' 'Ooh,' I retorted. So smart you are. I'll go talk to the cash then, honey!

Two weeks after my visit to Visa, I got a call from the agency Interactive Avenues. They were making a queer national anthem video and were also wooing potential clients with LGBTQ-themed ideas. They had already pitched the idea of a rainbow card to a major Indian bank, they told me. Wow. News travels fast. A few weeks later, I got another call that the Lalit was considering introducing a rainbow loyalty card soon.

At the launch of the 2019 *New Global Champions* report at FICCI in Delhi with Boston Consulting Group and Open for Business, I met a representative from American Express, to whom I narrated the above incidents. His eyes lit up. 'This is a great idea,' he told me, smiling. 'Let me take it back to the team.'

Who knows, by the time you read this book, the Indian rainbow card may already be a reality. Maybe you have bought this book using one such card?

~

Millennials are not just customers. They are also employees.

When companies are committed to diversity, the 2011 Deloitte report finds, their employees are 31 per cent more likely to perceive their company as one that responds to the changing needs of their customers and clients. Their customer service is perceived to be better due to their ability to adapt to diverse and changing needs.[24]

Many of the millennials I meet during my campus-and-conference-hopping trips across India tell me that they value benchmarks. Whether they are potential employees or not, they like to look up where companies stand on inclusivity. The presence of benchmarking surveys and the reputational boost they give companies has urged businesses to speed up their inclusion efforts.

In the US, the Human Rights Campaign Foundation's seventeenth edition of the Corporate Equality Index (CEI) in 2019 gave 572 businesses a score of 100 per cent on all criteria, and these were given the title of 'Best Place to Work for LGBTQ Equality'. Of the Fortune 500, 193 businesses achieved a 100 per cent rating in 2019.[25] The number of companies rated 100 per cent has increased exponentially since 2002, the year of the first CEI, when only 13 companies received a 100 per cent rating.[26]

On the other side of the world, in Australia and New Zealand, there is the Rainbow Tick, a benchmark for LGBTQ-inclusive practices in organisations. To achieve this tick, organisations are required to undergo accreditation against six standards, which are assessed independently by experts working in Australian health, community and human services sectors. These standards are: 1. Organisational capability 2. Workforce development 3. Consumer participation 4. A welcoming and accessible organisation 5. Disclosure and documentation 6. Culturally safe and acceptable services. On receiving a Rainbow Tick, the organisation is added to a national register of Rainbow Tick–accredited organisations, which helps consumers identify them.[27]

I love the idea behind Rainbow Tick. As someone who was very competitive in school (I used to love getting gold stars in my books for good work), I would love a rainbow tick against my organisation's name. Wouldn't you?

This benchmarking practice has now made its way to India too. Community Business has developed an online assessment designed to help companies in India create inclusive workplaces for their LGBTQ employees—a benchmark exercise that will enable Indian companies to understand D&I best practices. This is what Jiby Joyce, a programme manager with Community Business, told me about the company's plans when I spoke to him:

'We've been working with the corporate sector to address LGBT+ inclusion in the workplace in Asia for over a decade—compiling research, providing training, and introducing the region's first LGBT+ inclusion index and awards to publicly recognise companies' performances. Through this work, we've seen a huge shift—the index in particular, has been a complete game-changer in prioritising LGBT+ inclusion on the corporate agenda. With the change on Section 377, we now want to bring this model to India—and in fact, we have already developed a robust framework for our India LGBT+ inclusion index. But we recognise that many companies may not feel comfortable participating in an external exercise where their performance is publicly ranked. So we've developed an online assessment tool that's designed to be the precursor to the index and help companies get ready. By reviewing a set of best practice indicators in nine categories, companies can assess their current performance and get advice from us on how to improve moving forward—on a one-to-one basis. As a tool, it's not only a great way to drive the adoption of best practice, but also to engage key stakeholders internally, which is critically important.' [28]

Community Business is hoping to launch their full-fledged India index in 2021. As a build-up, they launched the D&I in India Best Practice Benchmark and Awards in 2018 which featured titles such as Employee Network Award and LGBT+ Inclusion Award. As I mentioned earlier, I was in the audience, feeling rather jealous, when Ritesh Rajani and his IBM team walked away with the honours. From fifteen in 2018, the entries went up to twenty-two in 2019[29]—clearly, more and more companies are doing good work and want to be recognised for it. The winner for 2019? The Lalit Suri Hospitality Group.

One more point. As an organisation, you need to be inclusive across company policies, in your products, campaigns and even in the supply chains that make and distribute the product. Savvy millennials will call you out if you are not. The Open for Business 2015 report too notes that companies across the globe are now trying to ensure that their supply chains are inclusive and that there are a mix of suppliers owned by minority groups, especially LGBTQ people. Companies such as Apple, Ernst & Young, HTC, Sony and IBM require their clients to be non-discriminatory on the basis of gender identity and sexual orientation, and they have included it in their global supplier codes of conduct.[30]

The reputation of a company is fragile. Slip-ups will be amplified. As I have shown in the case studies described above, if things are done right, there will be loads of appreciation. But in our hyper-mediated world, where even the smallest blunder is retweeted, shared, shredded across FB walls and Instagram timelines with hashtags and mentions, the repercussions will be bad in case of a bungle.

Remember what a complete disaster the Dolce & Gabbana founder's racist rant on Instagram was? In the aftermath of that rant, the runway show in China was cancelled, and the brand was boycotted by celebrities and consumers in China, one of Dolce & Gabbana's main markets. L2, a digital intelligence company, found that in the first quarter of 2019, Dolce & Gabbana's Chinese social-media engagement—measured as a mix of likes, comments and shares—was down 98 per cent from the same period the previous year.[31]

When during our Twitter Blue Room chat, Sonam Kapoor told me she doesn't believe in labels, I prodded her. 'Except Prada, Dolce, Anamika?' She laughed and emphasised, 'No, *not* Dolce!'

I'll leave you with a cautionary tale of how another company's reputation took a beating because of negative publicity, even though they responded quickly to limit the damage.

When I spoke to Gaurav Pramanik about nine months after the Section 377 judgement in 2018, he sounded content. A freelance writer who teaches Indian literature part-time at a college in Siliguri and occasionally delivers lectures at youth summits in Sikkim, he goes to Delhi now and then to address employees of tech start-ups on LGBTQ inclusivity. He too was part of the corporate system at one point.

In 2018, the Supreme Court had just passed its Section 377 verdict. Gaurav had been waiting for this moment. He could finally send out an important email that he had promised himself he would the day Section 377 was to be read down. He sent the mail, but did not receive a response. So he posted the text of that email on his Twitter handle.[32] Here is an edited excerpt:

Dear XX,

I hope this email finds you in the best of health and progress.

This might come to you as a surprise, I'd be surprised too had I been in your place. But, let me start by telling you that I had promised to write to you the day IPC Section 377 was scrapped and being a homosexual in a country as great as India was legal. Mind you, it's the same country where Kamasutra came from, the same great nation where tales of transsexuals in scriptures play a prominent role. However, over the past couple of decades, even centuries, the archaic law imposed on us by the British was still valued and held high over our treasure troves of history and cultural precipice.

You might be wondering why I speak of all of this. Let me put things in perspective for you here: Remember a time in 2015 when one of your managers left after much drama. You huddled everyone in a room, every single member of the extended training team was nervously waiting in a training room to be addressed by you. Address, you did, and that was historic, never in my life had I heard a leader, albeit a Global Head of a department of a global company like Tech Mahindra speak so callously and in such a bigoted way and the most insulting way ever. Let me remind you of your words (I remember every word of it, because it has stayed with me ever since), you said and I quote: When I asked him the reason, he started crying and I told him are you a gay that you are crying like this?

My rebuttal here: Why XXX, do only gay men cry, and even if he was gay how would that be of any problem to you, until he let it affect his work? Why the sweeping generalization and stereotyping of someone's sexuality. Let me educate you a little, being gay is not a crime anymore (as of 6 September 2018, the Honourable Supreme Court of India has scrapped a part of the law).

I know, I know, you being the Chief Diversity and Inclusivity Officer at Tech Mahindra almost feels like a sick joke on us by the top management. Why, you might ask, but look deeper, you know you have the answer.

There were times you made mocking judgments on me about how you thought I was effeminate and that it affected my work, pardon me but what affected my work was how I was treated by my leaders and how it was almost bullying and jeering that I had to undergo each day in the organization. The last I checked with Mr. Anand Mahindra, the Mahindra Group takes inclusivity and diversity very importantly in all its companies, I wonder when it would trickle down to Tech Mahindra and then further down to BSG.

This email is not meant to change your opinions about the above mentioned things but is to rather call you out for who you are. You, Mrs.

> XXX, are a bigot, you are vile, vitriolic and hateful. You are everything that communals and extremists are made of and luckily enough for us, space for the likes of you is diminishing and it will soon disappear. I hope this email still finds you in the best of health.
>
> If your blood is boiling right now, sit down and have a glass of water.
>
> Thank you for these experiences which made me take a greater resolve to call out bigots and racists at higher level.

Gaurav's post blew up on Twitter, and the response was equally swift. The chairperson, Anand Mahindra, himself tweeted out his support for an investigation to take place as soon as possible. C.P. Gurnani, the CEO at Tech Mahindra, also wrote: 'Gaurav, you have my personal assurance that this will be thoroughly investigated. We remain committed to supporting and promoting a diverse workforce at TechM.'[33]

As part of the internal investigation, twelve other people came forward. Gaurav had never met any of these people. They had worked with his former manager years before he had come in. 'They went through the same harassment, discrimination. They contacted me that they would speak to the investigative team and put their story forward. Their statements were taken and that's how they came to the conclusion that she was wrong and was fired. The justice was timely, and quick. I was hoping it would take weeks, but it took three days,' Gaurav told me.

Now, from a PR perspective, Tech Mahindra's swift action meant that all the press stories that ensued became about the values Tech Mahindra stood for as opposed to the values that had been disregarded. Most of the pieces were about how quickly the company had responded in firing the perpetrator of abuse. The story ended there, at least from a press perspective. Even the Open for Business 2019 report praised Tech Mahindra's rapid response. It says, 'Mahindra Group, a multinational conglomerate headquartered in Mumbai, made a clear statement by firing an employee that made homophobic comments. Mahindra Group chairman, Anand Mahindra, tweeted, "I can categorically assure you that we celebrate diversity in our workplace. Our Code of Conduct is explicit on this subject. Fairness & dignity of the individual is enshrined in our core values."'[34]

But there has been no closure for Gaurav, personally. 'It was for five years that I suffered, I was deeply humiliated, bullied, jeered. It was quite a long time. I don't think that feeling will ever go away. I tried to get closure, I thought I would get it, but I didn't.'[35]

As Gaurav relived his nightmare with me, I was unable to reconcile his experience with my own time at Mahindra. When I had broken up with my ex, Anand Mahindra had personally comforted me. My boss Ulhas and my colleague Shubha had been very supportive. How differently does the inclusion story play out at different levels? Maybe I wasn't discriminated against at Mahindra because I was close to the leaders? Would it have been different otherwise? Is it the same at Godrej now? Does my proximity to Nisa Godrej save me from possible harassment of this kind? I am afraid that the answer to all of these questions might be: yes.

Part Four

A FIVE-STEP GUIDE FOR MAKING YOUR WORKPLACE LGBTQ INCLUSIVE

This action-oriented section of the book has five steps arranged in sequential order. If you want to be really basic, follow step number one. If you want to be relatively comprehensive, follow steps two, three and four as well. And if you want to be a superstar company, then please follow steps one to five and become a champion. To make it easy for you, I have summarised all the steps on the next page, in bullet points. Tear this page out and stick it over your desk, and tick off each step as you accomplish it.

Step One: Set in Place Strong Policies and Specific Benefits for LGBTQ Employees

a) Policies
   i. Equal Opportunity and Anti-Discrimination Policy
   ii. Gender-Neutral Prevention of Sexual Harassment (POSH) Policy
   iii. Gender-Neutral Dress-Code Policy
   iv. LGBTQ-Friendly Relocation Policy
   v. LGBTQ-Friendly Leave Policy

b) Benefits
   i. Health Insurance for Partners of Employees
   ii. Gender Affirmation Support
   iii. Adoption and Parental Leave

Step Two: Actively Recruit LGBTQ Employees

a) Participate in LGBTQ Job Fairs
b) Tap into Your Existing LGBTQ Employee Networks
c) Work with LGBTQ Community Organisations
d) Make Sure That Every Step of Your Recruitment Process Is LGBTQ Friendly

Step Three: Create an LGBTQ-Friendly Work Culture Within the Company

a) LGBTQ Sensitisation Workshops
b) Roundtables with Senior Leaders
c) An LGBTQ Employee Resource Group

Step Four: Address the Specific Circumstances of Trans Employees

a) Provide Gender-Neutral Restroom Infrastructure
b) Help with Housing
c) Provide Commute Alternatives If Needed
d) Be Flexible with Documents and Qualifications, and Help with Opening Bank Accounts
e) Set Up a Support System for Employees Who Wish to Transition

Step Five: Become an Advocate for LGBTQ Inclusion Outside Your Company

a) Participate in External Forums, Pride Marches and Events as a Champion of LGBTQ Issues
b) Support LGBTQ Grassroots Organising Efforts and NGOs
c) Sponsor LGBTQ Events, Film Festivals, Literature Festivals and Pride Marches

13

Step One: Set in Place Strong Policies and Specific Benefits for LGBTQ Employees

Every so often I get a call from someone saying, 'Fine, I believe that diversity makes complete sense; now please tell me what I can do to make my organisation more LGBTQ inclusive?' There are five simple steps I recommend to them. We are going to start with the most basic step in this chapter—policies and benefits.

Here are the policies you should consider implementing immediately at your workplace.

i. Equal Opportunity and Anti-Discrimination Policy

> We value diversity within the Godrej Group and are committed to offering equal opportunities in employment. We will not discriminate against any team member or applicant for employment on the basis of nationality, race, colour, religion, caste, gender, gender identity/expression, sexual orientation, disability, social origin and status, indigenous status, political opinion, age, marital status or any other personal characteristic or status.[1]

Just copy paste this excerpt from Godrej's policy and make things easy for yourself. If you are crafting your own policy, make sure that it explicitly states that discrimination based on sexual orientation, gender identity and gender expression is strictly prohibited. The 2018 *Humsafar Trust Manual for Corporates* advises that a policy should also provide examples of what LGBTQ discrimination looks like, and be reviewed at least every three to five years to make sure the policy language is not dated and that it is in accordance with human rights requirements as well as corporate values.[2]

Some companies like IBM and Intel have separate policies for equal opportunity and anti-discrimination. This is different from what we have at Godrej, as laid out above. Here is IBM's equal opportunity policy:

> The employees of IBM represent a talented and diverse workforce. Achieving the full potential of this diversity is a business priority that is fundamental to our competitive success. A key element in our workforce diversity programs is IBM's long-standing commitment to equal opportunity. Business activities such as hiring, promotion, and compensation of employees, are conducted without regard to race, color, religion, gender, gender identity or expression, sexual orientation, national origin, genetics, disability, or age. These business activities and the design and administration of IBM benefit plans comply with all applicable laws, including those dealing with equal opportunity. For qualified people with disabilities, IBM makes workplace accommodations that comply with applicable laws, and which IBM determines are reasonable and needed for effective job performance. In respecting and valuing the diversity among our employees, and all those with whom we do business, managers are expected to ensure a working environment that is free of all forms of harassment. This policy is based on sound business judgment and anchored in our IBM Values. Every manager in IBM is expected to abide by our policy, and all applicable laws on this subject, and to uphold IBM's commitment to workforce diversity.[3]

And this is how IBM's anti-discrimination policy reads:

> IBM will not discriminate in hiring, promotion, training, compensation of employees and employment practices on grounds of race, color, religion, age, nationality, social or ethnic origin, sexual orientation, gender, gender identity and expression, marital status, pregnancy, political affiliation, union membership, protected genetic information or disability, or covered veteran status. IBM will create a work environment free of discrimination or harassment based on the noted categories. Workers shall be provided with reasonable accommodation for religious practices. In addition, workers or potential workers should not be subjected to medical tests or physical exams that could be used in a discriminatory way.[4]

Of course, 'discrimination' is an expansive word, encompassing many kinds of behaviours. But for the purpose of this book, I am focusing specifically on discrimination against LGBTQ people. In 2018, UN Globe, a staff group from the UN fighting for the equality and non-discrimination of LGBTQ employees within the organisation, outlined what qualifies as discriminatory behaviour, towards trans people in particular, but this could be easily extrapolated to

LGBTQ people at large. You could use these points below to specifically outline what constitutes discrimination in your own company.

1. Refusing to issue ground passes and conference badges to staff and other stakeholders that reflect a person's gender identity and expression, including their preferred name and pronoun
2. Non-consenting disclosure of details of an employee's trans history
3. Denying staff members and other stakeholders access to locker rooms and/or restrooms that correspond to their self-identified gender identity
4. Prohibiting staff members and other stakeholders from dressing or otherwise expressing themselves according to their gender identity or expression
5. Refusing to respect staff members and other stakeholders' gender identity or expression
6. Intentionally and/or persistently referring to a staff member or other stakeholder by a name or pronoun that either does not correspond to their self-identified gender identity or expression, or is not in accordance with their expressed wishes
7. Comments that denigrate or mock the gender identity or expression of a staff member or other stakeholder, based on individually held gender expectations. These comments can be directed to a staff member, be in reference to a staff member, or be directed towards a category of people in general
8. Physical, verbal, or sexual harassment
9. Failure to hire, to promote, or to terminate a staff member's contract of employment because of the staff member's actual or perceived gender identity or expression[5]

ii. Gender-Neutral Prevention of Sexual Harassment (POSH) Policy

According to the Sexual Harassment of Women at Workplace (Prevention, Prohibition and Redressal) Act, 2013, or the POSH Act, sexual harassment is considered a violation of the right to practise any profession or carry out any business, trade or occupation. The act requires every employer to constitute an internal committee to attend to the complaints made by any aggrieved woman at the workplace.[6]

This act replaced the Vishaka guidelines, the fountainhead of the act. The POSH Act defines the term sexual harassment to include any unwelcome acts or behaviour—whether directly or by implication—such as physical contact and advances, demands or requests for sexual favours, making sexually coloured remarks, showing pornography, any other unwelcome physical, verbal or non-verbal sexual conduct, creating an intimidating work environment or engaging in humiliating treatment which could possibly affect women's health and safety.[7] The key difference between the Vishaka guidelines and the POSH Act is the definition of the term 'workplace', which was missing in the earlier guidelines, and now includes government bodies, private and public sector organisations, non-governmental organisations, organisations carrying out commercial, vocational, educational, entertainment, industrial and financial activities, hospitals and nursing homes, educational institutions, sports institutions and stadiums used for training individuals, and even dwelling places or houses.[8]

Although the aim of the POSH Act is to specifically prevent the harassment of women, progressive companies have started implementing gender-neutral POSH policies, and this is what I recommend that every company do. Feel free to tweak and use Godrej's gender-neutral POSH policy below at your own workplace:

> We are committed to creating and maintaining an atmosphere in which our team members can work together, without fear of sexual harassment, exploitation or intimidation ('Sexual Harassment' is defined as unwelcome sexual advances, requests for sexual favours and other verbal, non-verbal or physical conduct of a sexual nature). Every team member should be aware that the Godrej Group is strongly opposed to sexual harassment and that such behaviour is prohibited both by law and the Group policy. We will take all necessary action(s) required to prevent, correct and if necessary, discipline behaviour which violates this policy.[9]

Madhumitha Venkataraman told me that what is an 'absolute non-negotiable is the prevention of sexual harassment. By not making this gender neutral, LGBT inclusion will not fly; you can keep doing rainbow cakes! If people don't have the space to report sexual harassment, if men cannot report it, if you are only looking at it from a legal angle with women as victims and men as the perpetrators, it is problematic. You have to make it gender neutral, and make sure the team which is managing this knows the space of gender expression and sexual identity, and knows how to handle these cases.'[10]

iii. Gender-Neutral Dress-Code Policy

Some might consider dress-code policies a trivial matter, but it can be a cause of anxiety for many of us LGBTQ people. If your company does have a dress-code policy, please check if it contains language such as, 'Women must wear skirts and men must wear ties.' Should an employee who is trans dress according to their preferred gender identity or the gender listed on their official documents that legalese binds them to? The correct answer is the former. You should empower your employees to dress in accordance with their preferred gender identity or gender expression.

Ritesh Rajani put it eloquently to me, 'If you have a dress code, define the dress code, not the person wearing it.'[11] This will make it easier for people transitioning, and also for non-binary, intersex and genderqueer folks. Madhumitha added, 'What if a man wants to wear a sari, is that okay? No one talks about that. You have to realise that there is going to be a section of the audience that would want to cross-dress. That is what being inclusive means.'[12]

Richa Singh who heads Learning, Development and Diversity at the Lalit told me about how their HR gives people like Alex Mathew, who works at their Bengaluru property, the freedom to come to work as they please. 'As a hotel, we have strict grooming guidelines, but it is Alex who decides to dress as Alex or as Maya while still adhering to the grooming standards, and they have also represented the group at various public platforms.'[13]

Needless to say, all the HR heads reading this: please do not apply dress codes to your employees' off-duty presentation. What people do and wear in private is completely their business. (Speaking of which, you should see what I wear at home. On second thoughts, maybe not.)

iv. LGBTQ-Friendly Relocation Policy

Sameer Samudra at Cummins, who had moved back to India from the US with his husband and faced his share of hurdles in acclimatising to the Indian workplace, insisted on the importance of a queer-friendly relocation policy. 'We [Cummins] are looking into the whole relocation policy. If a gay or lesbian couple is relocating, how are we making sure we are being sensitive? The HR here had never handled a gay couple finding a home; it took us seven months to rent a home in Pune. The realtors weren't sensitive to the needs of a gay couple. How to sensitise not just the company but our suppliers as well, who are part of the relocation process? The principle that should be followed is that LGBT employees should have the same benefits as those of other employees. In some cases like in India, where LGBT marriages are not legal, the company should show consideration and treat LGBT spouses as the equivalent of legally married spouses of their heterosexual employees.'[14]

Bindumadhav Khire, an activist and the president of the Samapathik Trust in Pune, highlights Cummins when giving examples of companies that provide spousal benefits for same-sex couples, the credit for which goes to Sameer and his partner Amit Gokhale. In his 2018 report *Considerations in Framing LGBTI Inclusive Policies for Corporates*, Bindu writes about the financial benefits provided by Cummins for the relocation of same-sex partners and also other miscellaneous benefits such as discounts for spouses for joining a gym or providing financial assistance to the spouse for advanced studies.[15]

In June 2019, the *Economic Times* reported that Citigroup, which had around 17,000 employees in India then, was extending health benefits, including relocation benefits, to all 'domestic partners' in India. Padmaja Chakravarty, the business sponsor of the Citi India Pride Network, was quoted in the article as having said, 'We are extending medical insurance benefits to domestic partners of our employees. This includes partners, of the same sex or otherwise, who live together. … We are also extending domestic relocation benefits that usually apply to spouses, parents or dependent children of employees to such domestic partners of employees.'[16]

v. LGBTQ-Friendly Leave Policy

Companies should accommodate single parents and non-married or same-sex couples in their official leave policy. Jiby Joyce told me, 'Few companies like Goldman Sachs have a marriage leave policy that is inclusive of same-sex couples. There is no onus of legally registering your wedding. If you are getting married, you get leave.'[17] So cool! I want to join Goldman Sachs after hearing this, but I don't think my boss would like that very much. Let me just petition her to change our leave policies at Godrej instead. (Nisa, are you listening? Ahem.)

Now that I have told you about the policies, let me tell you about three broad types of benefits you need to offer your LGBTQ employees.

i. Health Insurance Benefits for Partners of Employees

Apekshit Khare, my colleague at Godrej Properties, was born in Bhopal and completed his MBA from IIM Kozhikode. He joined Godrej directly out of B-school. Apekshit started living with his partner Manoj and his family in 2012. When I visited them one weekend at their Thane apartment in 2017, I was greeted enthusiastically by their dog, Vichy, with the most licks any dog has ever given me. It was the most natural thing in the world to see these two gay men, their parents and pet dog living together. Total *Hum Aapke Hain Koun*–wallah feeling.

Apekshit was the first Godrej employee to claim health insurance for his partner, so his name has gone down in our company history. We made a video of him in 2016, in which he says: 'The diversity policy at Godrej is something which helps us bring our whole selves to work. I reached out to HR and they came back with same-sex partner benefits for me, and I was one of the first people in the company to register my partner for those policies. I don't have to live two lives, one which is personal and one which is professional. So that is something which is a great burden off oneself. I am sure it helps in being productive because I am not diverting my energies pretending to be somebody I am not.'[18]

I show Apekshit's video to every new batch of incoming employees, and they almost always applaud at the end. I tell them that my own partner is registered at Godrej as one of the three beneficiaries of my health insurance plan, alongside my parents. The process was simple. One email to HR and that was it.

The principle is simple and clear: LGBTQ workers' spouses, domestic partners, children and step-children should be offered the same benefits as family members of non-LGBTQ workers. Community Business, in its 2019 report *LGBT+ Workplace Inclusion in India* details the work carried out by the Royal Bank of Scotland (RBS) in this regard:

> RBS made the headlines in April 2018 when it announced that it was extending medical hospitalization benefits to same-sex partners, making it one of the first companies in India to do so. This was just part of its programme to review all its employee policies to ensure that they protected the rights and provided benefits to all its employees irrespective of their gender, sexual orientation and family composition. In so doing, the bank sought to remove all exclusionary language like traditional definitions of the term 'family' to include not just husbands and wives, but partners, parents of partners, etc. As a result its benefits such as accident cover, life insurance, leave cover for adoption, surrogacy, bereavement, compassionate, paternity, maternity and domestic relocation now apply equally to LGBT+ employees. It has also expanded the scope of policies such as prevention of sexual harassment (POSH) to include harassment of non-female staff, namely men, transgender people, gender non-binary folks and any others.[19]

Similarly, in December 2019, Tata Consultancy Services (TCS), India's largest private sector employer with more than 400,000 people on its payroll, tweaked its health insurance policy to cover partners of employees in same-sex relationships, irrespective of their marital status, and these partners became entitled to the same benefits that partners of heterosexual TCS employees were entitled to.[20]

ii. Gender Affirmation Support and Benefits

August 2019 brought in a heartwarming headline from the *Economic Times*. In Bengaluru, Intuit India had rolled out gender affirmation–related benefits. The company was to reimburse trans employees for gender affirmation surgery of up to ₹500,000 through its insurance vendor. This was to be supplemented by reimbursements for hormone replacement therapy of up to ₹60,000 a year, also to be made part of the insurance coverage. Sanket Atal, the managing director of Intuit India's Product Development Centre, was quoted in the article as saying, 'Our benefits philosophy is aimed to make employees feel valued and supported in both their professional and personal lives.'[21]

As I already mentioned, a similar gender affirmation benefits policy is in place at Godrej as well. Richa Singh from the Lalit told me that the hotel group also offers its employees a 'one-month post-operative fully paid leave after [their] gender affirmation surgery. The employee has the flexibility to break these leaves into parts depending on their need and complications.'[22]

While drafting gender affirmation benefits, it is vital to talk to existing insurance providers to ensure that they do not categorise gender affirmation surgery and hormone therapy as cosmetic procedures. Ideally, the insurance company should include these in their coverage, or if you can't manage to swing that, then you should just pay for it yourself. Whichever route you opt for—having the insurer pay for it or choosing to pay for it out of the company's pocket—you should recognise that providing for transition procedures is one of the best things you could do for your trans employees.

There will always be at least one irritating person at a diversity meeting who will express silly objections like, 'Oh, all these benefits are going to cost so much money.' This person will usually preface their comments by saying something innocuous like, 'Let me play devil's advocate for a moment.' My strategy is to shut up the naysayer immediately by saying, 'Please don't! The devil doesn't need any more advocates, thank you!' But in case you aren't as mooh-phat as me, here is a more level-headed argument from Amita Karadkhedkar, who transitioned while at Barclays: 'It boils down to employee care. If you are rolling out tens of thousands of policies and coverages for your cis employees, then why not at least one for the trans community? Gay men are covered under the normal insurance coverage, as are lesbian women. But when it comes to somebody who is going through gender transition, there is often nothing. So that employee is bound to be discriminated against when it comes to corporate insurance. If you really care for each and every employee, your policies should be inclusive, even if only one person is going through gender transition.'[23]

Anubhuti Banerjee further added, 'It is not going to be that everyone is going to come up for an operation. It comes with the premise that it is only a small number of people who want to medically transition. It doesn't even affect the bottom line of the company, that small percentage. A pay-out you might have to do once or twice in ten years at best.'[24]

While designing these benefits, one of the questions that will come up is: What are necessary procedures and what are aesthetic procedures? Many insurers will also try and push back on this—they obviously want to pay for as little as they can. Madhumitha told me her secret of how to get insurance companies to agree to do more: 'Insurance companies are always looking at how they can avoid paying for something. That's their major goal. If they have to pay for it, it becomes a problem. So, in order to push them to be inclusive—I feel bad revealing this—I tell them, "I will pull you off as my insurance provider if you don't cover gender affirmation procedures and hormone therapy!" That's what you do. That works. Coke is not a small company. I used to be with GE and Snapdeal earlier, and those weren't small either. In terms of the number of employees, none of them are chitku-putku—7k, 8k, 10k, 15k, 20k employees! Your insurance company will definitely not want to lose this. Therefore, my job has been to eat my CEO's and HR's heads, convincing them to arm-twist the insurer, saying we will not give them the business if they don't cover. It is also important to find out which are the insurance companies that do cover these procedures. You can use their examples against your insurance provider to convince them. It is a hard negotiation.'[25]

The medical criteria for undergoing these procedures can be referred to in the *Standards of Care for the Health of Transsexual, Transgender and Gender Nonconforming People* published in 2011 by the World Professional Association for Transgender Health (WPATH). It outlines the many referrals required for a procedure and the medical protocol to be followed. On reconstructive versus aesthetic procedures, the WPATH's *Standards of*

Care has this to say: 'While most professionals agree that genital surgery and mastectomy cannot be considered purely cosmetic, opinions diverge as to what degree other surgical procedures (e.g., breast augmentation, facial feminization surgery) can be considered purely reconstructive. Although it may be much easier to see a phalloplasty or a vaginoplasty as an intervention to end lifelong suffering, for certain patients an intervention like a reduction rhinoplasty can have a radical and permanent effect on their quality of life, and therefore is much more medically necessary than for somebody without Gender Dysphoria.'[26]

In addition to this, the HR team must be sensitised to trans healthcare issues, along with instituting policies on how to implement them. For most trans people, physical examinations and a review of their previous health records would disclose their gender identity—this is not something they might be comfortable doing, and it might also make them vulnerable to discrimination and violence. If the medical professional interacting with them is prejudiced, patient confidentiality might be breached.

Nyra D'Souza, Godrej's first out trans employee who worked in Corporate HR until late 2019, told my colleague Nayanika Nambiar and me when we interviewed her for our white paper in 2018 that there was a dire need for trustworthy medical professionals for the trans community. Undergoing transition and other medical procedures is difficult without counselling or guidance. To help, you could compile a resource/referral list of trained doctors and psychiatrists, counsellors and psychologists who have experience in the field of gender dysphoria and are well versed with the process of transition.[27]

iii. Adoption and Parental Leave Benefits

Your adoption and parental leave benefits should apply to mothers and fathers as well as co-mothers and co-fathers, and the language must reflect that. Ritesh insisted, 'We need adoption policies, parental leave policies, where you are not looking at maternity and paternity as a binary. Again, this is an evolving thing. In the US, they have a maternity policy that can cover trans men, or trans masculine persons, since they can go through pregnancy.'[28] Ritesh is also aware of the context in India, where people are not quite ready to accept trans men as 'fathers who can give birth'. I asked him how the language could be made inclusive. How can a company be gender neutral about pregnancy, which is inherently about the biological sex? His solution: 'Remove the word woman, replace it with "person going through pregnancy".

Pregnancy is a biological term. Remove gender from policies and, at the same time, make it inclusive for any person.' Ramkrishna Sinha from Pride Circle, a D&I consultancy, put it rather simply to me. 'Generally, all benefits which are gendered, we need to look at un-gendering them.'[29]

In December 2019, the IT major Tech Mahindra announced that same-sex couples would be able to take twelve weeks of paid adoption leave as per their new policies, with the aim of encouraging new parents of all genders to spend more time with their newborns and families.[30]

Like Tech Mahindra, many other companies in India, including Godrej, have already made their adoption policies gender neutral, even if adoption by LGBTQ couples in India is a far-away reality. Doing so indicates that your commitment to equality precedes legal sanction, and goes a long way in earning the trust of your LGBTQ employees.

This is the adoption policy at Godrej:

> In case the employee is the primary caregiver and if the child is less than one year of age:
>
> - The company provides an initial 3 months of leave with full pay and benefits
> - On rejoining work the employee could opt for Flexible Work Arrangements applicable for a maximum of six months from the date of resuming work
>
> In case the employee is the primary caregiver and the child is more than one year of age:
>
> - The employee is entitled to 3 months of leave with full pay and benefits
>
> In case the employee is not the primary caregiver
>
> - Employee is entitled to 7 working days of leave with full pay and benefits[31]

Do you see how we have used the words 'primary caregiver' instead of identifying them by their sex or gender? It is as simple as that, really.

Before we move on to the next steps in the subsequent chapters, two quick points. First, you don't need to wait for LGBTQ people to come out in your company in order to put policies and benefits in place. A lot of misguided HR heads tell me, '*Arrey,* we *toh* don't have any queer employees, so why should we do all of this?' I calmly tell them that it is only when you create progressive policies that your queer employees will be empowered to come out and avail of them. Progressive policies need to precede employees coming out, not the other way around.

Second, please don't be hush-hush about any steps that you do take. Support your inclusive policies and benefits with strong information campaigns that inform all employees about what it means to be inclusive and about the course of action LGBTQ employees should take if they face discriminatory behaviour. These resources should be made easily available to everyone and be simple to locate on the company's website.

14

Step Two: Actively Recruit LGBTQ Employees

a) Participate in LGBTQ Job Fairs

I arrive early for the RISE job fair in Bengaluru. It's July 2019. Right outside the venue, the Lalit, I am greeted by a gigantic rainbow hoarding sponsored by Uber that declares, 'All roads lead to equal opportunity.' Uber has programmed its app for a rainbow route to pop up on the map for anyone who books a cab to the location today.

As I enter the hotel's convention centre, I am greeted by a huge banner listing the different sponsors of the fair. In the 'gold' category are companies like American Express, Nielson and Salesforce. The 'silver' sponsors include GE, Mastercard and my own Godrej, while the 'bronze' sponsors include, among others, Deutsche Bank, Paypal and Capgemini. HSBC has sponsored the check-in experience, Unilever's toothpaste brand Close-up has sponsored the online job site, and a roster of different brands, including McKinsey, have sponsored the breakout sessions. This feels surreal. I am reminded of the LGBTQ mixer that the management consulting firm Bain and Company had hosted during my graduation year at MIT more than a decade ago. I had felt so proud then that such a big company had reached out to me for my talent and had wanted me. I feel the same in Bengaluru today.

The job fair is spread across four conference rooms. There are stalls set up by the companies mentioned above, as well as others by Cummins, Goldman Sachs, VIP Industries and PayPal in the Kalinga room. Amidst day-long sessions and talks in the conference room Siddhartha, are stalls selling artisanal products in the conference rooms Lalit One and Two—everything from pickles to cupcakes to bowties—made by queer entrepreneurs. The line-up at Siddhartha includes fifty speakers and the talks are interspersed with screenings and workshops.

I enter Kalinga, the main fair site, and scan the room. There are forty-five companies present and hundreds of job seekers flitting from stall to stall. A father has come to scout the fair with his queer son, who is in the final year of his college education, to see which company might be the best for him. This is what queer utopia looks like.

The Godrej rainbow pen drives are a hit, our stall-wallahs tell me. Phew! I am relieved because our stall is rather modest, compared to other companies who have decorated their stalls much more creatively. Every company here is competing to tell the queer job-seeking community why they are the best. Outside the Royal Bank of Scotland's stall, a rainbow banner asks, 'Why choose us?' with a list of benefits the company offers its LGBTQ employees, such as health insurance for same-sex partners.

At the Intuit stall, there are little rainbow slats at the entrance, and the message 'Pride and no Prejudice—inclusion benefits all' is printed across the wall. J.P. Morgan's stall has a wall covered with pictures of their out and proud employees. Ford's stall proudly declares that Ford Globe—their LGBTQ employee resource group—is celebrating its twenty-fifth anniversary this year.

The financial solutions company Refinitiv's stall has the word 'love' written in nine different Indian languages against a rainbow background with the slogan 'Everyone has a right to it' below. I take a selfie and send it to my partner. (Do you also disturb your partner in the middle of the day with random WhatsApp messages? It's fun, *na*?)

My favourite stall is by Accenture. They too have used rainbows to decorate their space dramatically, but they have also added three really clever public engagement tricks. The first is a selfie booth with the tagline 'Equality is non-negotiable' set against a rainbowed Accenture logo. I pick up one of the many props they have stacked up on a table—a handheld sign that reads 'Dream alchemist'—and pose. Two minutes later, I am given a Polaroid that has been neatly fitted inside a rainbowed Accenture photo frame, with a note to check out their careers page online. Next to the photo booth is a giant heart-shaped wall with hundreds of post-its. I am encouraged to 'Heart it out'—write a message of support on a post-it and stick it back on the wall. I go through some of the messages already up. 'Think about intersectionality, about people from the working class, about transmen and about dalits,' urges a yellow note. 'If you are happy with what you are, the world will be happy,' professes its purple neighbour. Their third engagement tool is an LGBTQ inclusion quiz on an iPad. I swipe through the questions, which deal with gender, appropriate office behaviour, biases and more, and as I answer them,

I learn more about Accenture's own progressive policies and benefits. What a smart way of selling your company. I am maha impressed.

At one in the afternoon, famished and *thoda sa* exhausted from all the mingling, I go to the speakers' lounge for lunch and hang out with my old friend Somak Ghoshal, whom I had gently nudged into covering the conference for a piece in *Mint* (cultural acupuncture!). Many of the people you are reading about in this book are in that room with me. CNN is doing a sound bite with Keshav Suri. Devdutt Pattanaik is holding court with Ali Potia on the corner sofa. Kusuma Krishna and I chat a bit about life, and she seems happy.

I get a plate of fish curry and rice, and sit with Ramkrishna Sinha and Srini Ramaswamy, the founders of Pride Circle and under whose aegis this fair has been organised, to talk about what we are witnessing around us and why it is historic. Ram tells me, 'Today, there are companies who are rolling out the red carpet, literally! These recruiters would have come across two to three LGBT people in their life. In this room, for once, they are the minority. That is the change we want to bring. Times are changing, there is a growing list of inclusive companies that want to do the right thing, and it is an opportunity for the community to make the most of it. Being LGBT and different need not necessarily be negative. It is not something you need to hide or change. Wear it like a badge and be proud of it, and have the career which you deserve.'

'You know, a lot of LGBT people are unemployed, or underemployed,' Srini adds. 'For the same skill set or performance, they are paid far less than their cisgendered counterparts. For example, there was this transgender nurse, at her previous job she was paid a third of what a cisgendered person was paid. That is the sad reality we live in. Another person said she went through seventy-five interviews because she was trans. It's not that she is unskilled, but she isn't getting a job because of transphobia.'

~

A few months later, in October 2019, Srini was sitting with me in my Godrej office while Ram was at the other end of the phone line in Bengaluru. We had just finished a marathon meeting with different Godrej HR heads about how Godrej could participate in future editions of RISE in Mumbai and Delhi.

Srini called out some heartwarming numbers. The RISE Bengaluru fair had attracted 320 job seekers, of which 152 had been shortlisted for final interviews, and 35 job offers had been made and accepted. Some of the diverse roles that companies hired for included: document review specialist, full stack developer, software engineer, technical programme manager, tenant acquisition champion, content writer and graphic designer. They also hired for departments like commercial banking operations, HR operations and investment banking. The parallelly held RISE conference had seen 415 attendees. The entire event had witnessed more than 1,000 attendees. After the meeting ended, we kicked back and reminisced about the past few years.

I first met Ram when he was at Intel and a part of the organising team of MINGLE. I have quite a few connections with the organisation—I had recruited their founder, Udayan Dhar, into Godrej; I used to serve as an informal advisor to them; and we hosted the first few MINGLE summits at the Godrej campus. These summits were full-day events, at which queer youth leaders from across the country came together to learn from veteran activists and pioneers of the queer movement, and to network with each other. In 2016, MINGLE also released a pioneering report on the state of inclusion at the Indian workplace, which I have quoted from extensively throughout this book.

I first chatted with Ram at MINGLE in Mumbai in 2015. By 2017, he was running the show, and the UK-based *Financial Times* had mentioned him in their 'OUTStanding' list of top fifty LGBTQ leaders in the world.[1]

Now, about Srini. It was August 2015, and I was attending one of the early Community Business's D&I forums hosted at the Hindustan Unilever headquarters in Mumbai. Srini was then working at Intuit, and he had come for the conference with his boss, Vijay Anand. Srini had mostly kept to himself. I met him again at the Open for Business networking breakfast in September 2016 at the Google office. Once again, he came across as shy and unassuming.

By 2017, Srini had begun to hit his stride. He had left Intuit for Cisco and headed their D&I team for the Asia-Pacific region. I heard him speak for the first time at the MINGLE conference in Bengaluru in December 2017. He spoke about what it meant to be a straight man working on LGBTQ inclusion, and I was blown away. Just like Ram, what a transformation!

In my Godrej office, Srini was advising my colleague Ruhie Pande, the head of the newly launched venture Godrej Housing Finance Limited. She was looking to hire salespersons from the LGBTQ community for their Mumbai office, and was seeking Pride Circle's help for it.

Srini shared with us his experience of being 'othered' as a South Indian and Mumbai-born person growing up in Jaipur. 'Madrasi, idli-dosa ...' He spoke about the taunts from his childhood, when kids made fun of his skin colour, his non-conventional Hindi and his economic status. As he grew up, the jokes turned into name-calling and bullying. Srini retreated into himself and became introverted, and his grades dropped steadily. Who could he talk to about what he was going through? His parents were struggling to make ends meet.

The spark was lit. 'First year of graduation, I decided I needed to do something about this. I had to fight by myself, I had no support. I said I need to do something in this space, because I don't really like how people treat one another. The closest I could do was a master's in HR. That way, I thought I can work with people, organisations, and can look at culture and transformation.'

By 2009, Srini had entered the space of corporate D&I, and was working with people with disabilities and LGBTQ persons. When he grew close to those still closeted, he was brought back to the time he had felt unhappy as a child in an unfamiliar city. He decided that he would dedicate his time and energy to stand up and speak up for equal rights for LGBTQ people.

I have constantly been reminding you, dear readers, about how to be a good ally to us, right? Be like Srini, who is straight as an arrow but has realised that the queer struggle is not ours alone. He made the link between his own victimisation and ours. We need this solidarity if we are to create a new world together.

Srini and Ram met each other at many of these diversity events they were attending, and at some point in 2017, decided to co-found Pride Circle. Today, they are the Jai and Veeru of LGBTQ inclusion in corporate India. From July 2017 till December 2018, Pride Circle continued with their monthly meetups, networking, and the sharing of best practices online. The next logical step was to sensitise and mentor organisations, and help them with policies.

This informal, decentralised network has grown rapidly to include representatives from more than 100 companies across 10 cities. Each city has its own WhatsApp group, its own Pride Circle chapter. Mumbai, Pune, Hyderabad and Delhi are up and running, with new places being added each month. From coffee shops, where they used to hold their meetings in the early days, to large corporate host organisations, including Godrej, they have expanded fast.

All along, Ram and Srini had also been having a parallel conversation on the skilling of semi-skilled and unskilled folks from the queer community, to facilitate their entry into the corporate world. The idea of RISE was born in 2019—of getting people from corporate India and queer job-seekers on a common platform across India. The July 2019 RISE job fair in Bengaluru was the proof of concept, and it was followed by RISE Delhi in February 2020. The success of both these fairs means that they are going to scale RISE to ten cities across India by 2021.

~

RISE is not the only LGBTQ job fair that took place in the country in 2019.

Two weeks after the RISE fair in Bengaluru, I make my way to the appropriately named Hall of Vision at the Nehru Centre in Mumbai, for Vividh, India's second queer job fair. Obviously, Godrej is also a part of this. When I enter the fair hall, my Godrej team rushes to me excitedly. We have received 200 resumes just four hours into the fair.

I explore the fair with the same sense of incredulity I had felt in Bengaluru two weeks ago. Everywhere, there are queer couples walking around, holding hands, going from stall to stall. I join one of them, and together, we check out the different pitches from different companies who want to hire them. There is Ernst & Young, promising to 'Build a better working world'. There is Standard Chartered, 'Celebrating our diversity'. There is Barclays, proclaiming how each day working with them is about 'Being more valued'.

Praful Baweja, the fair organiser, is running around. His parents are standing in a corner with a tiffin dabba and unsuccessfully trying to get him to grab a bite. Rajat, a trans man, tells Harish Iyer and me over chai that this is the best day of his life. 'A job is everything. With a job you can have a life. One IBM person liked me, I hope I get hired!' We wish him the best. Rajat tells us a horrible story about the time he had gone for an interview in another company, all had gone well until the interviewer came to know he was trans, and things changed. 'While saying bye, he just touched my fingers quickly and did not even shake my full hand properly. He was so uncomfortable.'

But not today, Harish tells Rajat, after giving him a warm hug, and Rajat agrees, beaming back at us. Not here. Not now.

b) Tap into Your Existing LGBTQ Employee Networks

Job fairs are just one way of actively recruiting queer people. There are many others. An easy way is to simply use existing LGBTQ employees as ambassadors. If companies treat us well and champion our issues, obviously we will bring in the talent we know. This is what I did at Godrej when we recruited MINGLE founder Udayan to the Godrej D&I team, right out of his MBA programme, or when I recruited Koninika Roy from Humsafar Trust to the Culture Lab or we recruited Nyra D'Souza to Godrej's Corporate HR team.

This is also what Swiggy, the food-tech start-up, is doing. In April 2019, they recruited former Amazon techie Samyuktha Vijayan as their first trans employee. Samyuktha had moved back to India from the US in 2017 with the desire to do something more for the trans community here, and when Swiggy came calling, she decided to take it up. Now she balances two roles there—a tech role to launch innovative delivery ideas and a D&I role, as a member of the company's D&I council. Samyuktha previously helped launch the India chapter of Glamazon, Amazon's LGBTQ employee group. She is working hard to get more LGBTQ talent into Swiggy, and the company is fully behind her.[2]

In November 2019, Swiggy announced the 'Swiggy Pride Network', an affinity group for LGBTQ people, with the aim of engaging with the community members to take forward the inclusivity agenda in their company.[3] Swiggy collaborated with Pride Circle for this initiative, and Samyuktha was at the forefront, leading the charge.

c) Work with LGBTQ Community Organisations

While white-collar professionals can be recruited from job fairs, reaching out to LGBTQ community organisations would be especially useful to find candidates for jobs that might not need a higher level of education or previous work experience. For example, in September 2018, the Transgender Welfare Equity and Empowerment Trust (TWEET) and Samjhota Foundation worked alongside Sodexo to place Paras Thakur, a trans woman, in an administrative job at the Bank of America. It is common for trans people like Paras and Rajat to go through several rounds of interviews and get rejected in the last round with no feedback or any explanation given. If corporates and facilities management companies form an alliance with community-based organisations, like how Sodexo has with TWEET, then the process of hiring queer people at scale would be better facilitated.

I am enthused by Project Vayati in this regard. It is a collaborative project between two organisations—Interweave Consulting and the Solidarity Foundation in Bengaluru—which works towards helping transgender people find jobs in the formal sector. The areas of employment involve skills such as data entry, mailroom administration and security or facilities management. Companies can collaborate with such organisations to assist with skilling efforts and then see which of the trainees can be recruited.[4]

Neelam Jain's PeriFerry conducts excellent skilling workshops for trans people.[5] Her own story is very interesting. In June 2016, Neelam, a cisgendered straight woman working up the corporate ladder, suddenly left her Goldman Sachs job to dedicate her time to the cause of transgender employment. In May 2017, she founded PerriFerry to work on transgender inclusion by training transgender candidates and matching them with corporates looking to be more trans inclusive in the composition of their selection pool.

Here is an Instagram post from PeriFerry dated 4 October 2019 that announced one of their exciting projects, which ANZ Australia is supporting:

> Our FIRST COHORT is here! After months of preparation, we are super excited to kickstart our first residential training program, Revive. Over 25 transgender people from Karnataka, Kerala, Andhra Pradesh, West Bengal, Delhi, Tamil Nadu, Rajasthan have come together for this program.
>
> Over the next 20 days they'll be introduced to various subjects and taught the essence of being a part of the modern day workplace. At the end of training, our trainees will also be interviewed by selected companies to be placed in meaningful jobs.
>
> This historic initiative would not have been possible without our corporate partner and sponsor, @anz_au. We know that is only the beginning and that this bold initiative will only encourage more organisations to take the leap and support the community. We also thank @solidarityfoundation for being our advisor in this initiative.[6]

Here is another Instagram post from them, exactly one month later.

> 100% JOB PLACEMENT. Can you believe it? We can't either. Each of our 25 candidates have been shortlisted by at least 2 companies or more. All we wait for now is for them to start working in these companies.
>
> After a month of sheer hard work and rigour, we are unimaginably proud of our community and the value they have brought in.
>
> A huge thank you to all our employers from today. Society Generale | ANZ | The Lalit Ashok | Max | Deutsche Bank | Vodafone | Walmart. For truly proving that 'Talent has No Gender'.[7]

Ritesh Rajani told me about a similar project that IBM had done with the Solidarity Foundation in 2016. 'It was a programme where we looked at a few months of skilling and vocational jobs. Remember, you can't just do skilling, and invite people and train them. They are living hand-to-mouth in a lot of cases, earning a daily wage which could be through begging or sex work. If you are telling them to come to your training programme, they are losing out on their daily wage by coming to your programme. If they are going to do that for two to three months, they can't feed themselves for that long. So you need to give a stipend, food, rehabilitation, similar to what government schools do with children—incentivise them. However you do it, it is not a free task you can just provide, being benevolent, expecting people to come. The fact that there is hate, violence, prejudice towards the community, they will look at you with a bit of paranoia, they won't look at you as a benefactor: Why are you suddenly giving me a job? Will I be a token trans person? Are you doing charity? Are you going to give me 10–15k per month and treat me badly? Any such affirmative action needs to be done sensitively. It is a two-way street—them adjusting to the mainstream and the mainstream adjusting to them.'[8]

Understand the spirit of Ritesh's comments and then reach out to Pride Circle, TWEET Foundation, Solidarity Foundation, PeriFerry or any of the other organisations that work with LGBTQ community recruitment, and get started!

d) Make Sure That Every Step of Your Recruitment Process Is LGBTQ Friendly

However you recruit us, whether through fairs or through community organisations, you need to make sure that all stages of the hiring process are inclusive. Here are some tips:

- Organsations like Out and Equal and Community Business recommend advertising yourself as an equal opportunity employer, to encourage gender and sexual minorities to apply for *all* job postings. Non-discrimination policies and gender or diversity strategies should be given on your company website and in job announcements.[9] Ali Potia too told me that companies should communicate their inclusiveness to candidates. 'If you signal to LGBT people, their antennas are finely tuned to watch. If you are recruiting at colleges and if one slide addresses the topic, 80 per cent of the LGBT candidates will notice it. All you are doing is that you are signalling to this section of the population that they are welcome, because often times this section of the population will censor itself and not apply.'[10]

- The job application process itself must be inclusive. The initial job application filled out by the applicant could contain the following gender categories: 'male', 'female', 'trans' and 'prefer to self-identify as'. The job applicant should be able to specify their gender identity on an optional basis. Community Business's 2012 report *Creating Inclusive Workplaces for LGBT Employees in India: The Definitive Guide* gives the examples of Infosys and Goldman Sachs as companies that have gender as a non-mandatory category.[11]

  In addition, the job application could ask the applicant for their preferred self-identified name and pronoun. During the application process as well as for the announcement upon selection and all future communications, the job applicant should be referred to by their self-identified name and pronoun. For trans employees, Sandeep Nair told me, 'If a company believes in inclusivity, the person can be employed based on a notarised affidavit declaring their name and gender, and then the company can further assist them in applying for the Central Gazette notification.'[12]
- You need to protect the anonymity and privacy of LGBTQ employees during and after the hiring process—the candidate alone can decide whether to disclose their LGBTQ status or not, and their decision should be treated as sacrosanct. UN Globe's 2018 report *Recommendations for an Inclusive Workplace for Trans and Gender Nonconforming Staff Members, Dependents, and Other Stakeholders of the UN System* states that disclosure or non-disclosure should not be grounds for dismissal under any circumstances. Background checks should also be conducted with utmost respect to the rights and dignity of the applicant, and in full confidentiality. The report further recommends that an applicant's previous name or gender not be disclosed against their wishes under any circumstances—even if these changes occurred in between employment.[13]
- Finally, you need to monitor the exits of LGBTQ employees. Amita Karadkhedkar told me that companies should find out the exact reason for queer employees leaving the organisation, and take strict action if it has to do with discrimination. This will ensure that discriminatory acts do not go under the radar and that processes are further improved for incoming LGBTQ candidates.[14]

I want to end this chapter with some cautionary thoughts from Zainab Patel. I have known her from much before she transitioned into the gorgeous diva whose status updates and pout pictures I wait for eagerly and watched with pride as she worked with Humsafar Trust, then joined the UN and blazed a trail of success with the UNDP in Bangkok. When she wanted to leave Bangkok and return to India, she interviewed with us at Godrej for a D&I role. She was liked by all who interviewed her, but it was ultimately decided that since she came from the development sphere, she might not have the corporate chops needed.

She was understandably frustrated. 'With corporations the problem is that they say that they don't mind hiring trans people and LGBTQ folks if they match a particular competency. What is there for them to mind? It is not like trans people are alien. Just a set of marginalised people who need to come to the mainstream. You make changes in policy to accommodate people from socioeconomically marginalised communities even if they are not as technically competent because you wanted to see certain kinds of people in certain positions.

'I did D&I all my life. It is just that the way they articulated D&I in the development sector is different from the way the corporate sector sees it. If you have to have trans inclusion, women's empowerment, dalit empowerment, you will have to get us into positions of power. Even in a forward-thinking institution, they will have to take a chance, get people in, to bring in a different class of individuals who would add value to the institutional arrangement and help it become more organic. How are you going to add elements of diversity if you stick to rigid rules that are archaic? This is the question corporate India should ask itself: In order to recruit a diverse set of individuals, should you stick to rigid rules, or should you do business beyond the usual?'[15]

I share Zainab's position on positive discrimination. As she told me, 'Positive discrimination has to happen; there is no other way. We have been positively discriminating for women of late, because for about every waking year of mankind, there was positive discrimination for men. Even with all the right policies and language, workplace equality for women [is] still not a practice. Thirty-three per cent reservation in parliament is still a distant dream. Thirty per cent hiring is still a distant dream for just about every corporate. Imagine an LGBT population which is 5 per cent of the population; how much more time will it take to bring in that workplace equality? Till the time we have legislation backing this, you will have to have policies which explicitly, positively discriminate for the marginalised.'

Some months after this chat, Zainab told me that she had joined KPMG as their head of Diversity. *Chalo*, not Godrej, but at least someone else took that leap of faith. I felt happy for her, but was regretful that it wasn't us. She told me that the next five years would be the litmus test, and I want all of you reading this, including my own colleagues at Godrej, to pay attention to the next few lines from Zainab.

'Are companies recruiting, providing these benefits, are people's lives changing, are we able to change societal norms? You could have the most inclusive policy and do nothing about it. You could have a Parmesh actively recruiting and also match that by having at least a few positions in your senior management for which you indicate that you are looking for LGBTQI leadership because that will then send a certain message across. Only then will you be able to say that these policy recommendations have been successful. Otherwise, it is just talk.'

I couldn't agree more with Zainab. It's time to walk the talk, dear HR managers, and hire more of us, across all levels of your organisations.

15

Step Three: Create an LGBTQ-Friendly Work Culture Within the Company

June 2019, in the bubbling heat of humid Bengaluru. The centre court of the Wipro campus in Electronic City is transformed. More than 1,000 Wiproites have gathered to take part in various fun activities celebrating Pride. This is a carnival organised by Neelam Jain's PeriFerry and staffed entirely by representatives from the queer community. An event open to all.

A photo booth with Pride props punctuates the space. There is even a Genderbread Mascot. One of the stalls is called 'In a Situation'. People walk into the stall and encounter LGBTQ community members standing on the other side, throwing situations at them. 'How did school or college feel? Safe, unsafe, unsure?' A line is drawn in front of the stall, and the participants have to take a step forward if they agree with the statement. If not, they have to remain standing in the same place. Then there is 'Ring-a-Thing'. A bunch of objects are placed on the ground, including a miniature house and an office, and the participant has to throw a ring at them. If the ring falls on the house, the participant is asked, 'How inclusive does your house feel to you?' The participant then shares their story, and the community members staffing the booth share their stories in turn.

There is also a game called 'Guess Who?' In this, stories of famous LGBTQ people from India and around the world are shared without revealing whose story it is, and participants are asked to guess. Angelina Jolie identifies as bisexual, the game organiser discloses. The crowd collectively gasps.[1]

~

This chapter is all about creating an inclusive culture within the workplace. Just having policies is not enough, obviously; much like merely having laws in a country is not enough. How are laws enforced? Similarly, what kind of corporate environment are the policies embedded in?

MINGLE's 2016 *Indian LGBT Workplace Climate Survey* tells us, 'Most [employees] are not comfortable coming out yet—an indication that policies and workplace culture may not necessarily be aligned.'[2] The same study found that only 25 per cent of queer people were out to their colleagues and 28 per cent were out to their managers.

What does being out at the workplace mean? Putting photos of loved ones on the desk or being part of the lunchroom talks on dating and social life—these are the bedrock questions on the basis of which corporate working relationships blossom into friendships, and 75 per cent of those closeted at the workplace cannot partake in these conversations and experiences.[3]

The question arises, what is an inclusive workplace? How can incoming employees and existing employees across the board—from the security guard to the CEO—be sensitised? Throwing a big carnival like Wipro did is one cool idea. This chapter presents three specific tools that can be used to create an inclusive workplace culture.

a) LGBTQ Sensitisation Workshops

Sandeep Nair is an expert at walking into corporate spaces to conduct LGBTQ sensitisation workshops. I asked him what a typical workshop for queer inclusivity looks like. Not surprisingly, it involves a lot of storytelling, much like what PeriFerry does. They invite an LGBTQ person to share their life story from their childhood onwards, along with challenges they have faced and issues that have come up at their workplace. This is followed by a group discussion.

These workshops are often a space for employees to ask questions they wouldn't ask otherwise, and the workshop facilitator can then provide the correct answers. Sandeep recalled, 'One time, this lady told me, "I think my son is gay." I asked her, "What makes you think that?" She said, "He is a teenager without facial hair." I said, "That does not make him gay. He is probably a late bloomer. Even if he is gay, I am sure he will be a wonderful son and you should be proud of him." Another time, someone else told me, "I think somebody in my office is gay because [they are] very effeminate." I had to say, "That does not necessarily make them gay!"'[4]

I strongly recommend that you have LGBTQ community professionals conduct your sensitisation workshops. Shubha Chacko from the Solidarity

Foundation told me that if these training sessions are held by people from within the company, then employees might feel obliged to answer in ways that they feel the company would approve of, hence constraining them.[5]

Personal stories are important within these workshops, as opposed to cold facts and steely PowerPoint presentations. What PeriFerry did by staffing the Wipro carnival with queer folks was to highlight our existence as stories that go beyond mere statistics. Most Wipro employees would never have interacted with someone who was queer and out. Intel India too sensitises its employees by sharing with them the stories of LGBTQ Intel employees from their other offices across the world or by getting its employees to interact with local LGBTQ people in Bengaluru.[6]

Neelam told me that theatre is a powerful workshop tool. Crea-Shakthi, one of the leading theatre companies in South India, served as an advisor to a twenty-five-minute play created by the S.S.N. Engineering College play team to be used for advocacy by PerriFerry. 'It speaks about regional characters like, say, a Ramu Kaka and about him being gay. Then, there's a college girl who comes out to her parents. We also have another method called "the monologue" which is fairly small and intimate because it involves two people. Both are trans women. They share their journey, of what it means to be in society, to come out to family and at the workplace. Most of it is about what it means to have a supportive workplace.'[7]

Godrej's PR agency, Adfactors, also used theatre effectively to conduct workshops on LGBTQ inclusion for their Mumbai, Delhi and Bengaluru employees in August 2019. Swagato Mallick, a senior accounts manager in the Mumbai office, told me about how he proposed these D&I workshops to the Adfactors managing director, Madan Bahl, at the end of December 2018, and got an approval immediately. He then spent the next few months developing a twenty-five-minute skit with the Delhi-based theatre professionals Kaustav Sinha, Dheer Hira, Dhiraj Wadhwani and Biswajit Maity.

'The session involves everything from mentioning gender identities to sexual orientations to sensitivity towards those who are in live-in relationships or have undergone divorce or, for that matter, those with a different opinion or an unconventional way of life—every facet that comes under the ambit of diversity and inclusion.'[8] Each skit performance is followed by a thirty-five-minute facilitated discussion, and at each session they conduct, 'employees galore come forward, share experiences, speak up on doubts and confusions, myths get busted,' revealed Swagato.

The success of these internal office sessions has inspired Adfactors to think of this inclusion module as a product they can offer their clients. 'We have around 400 clients at Adfactors, and to start with, we are targeting a small number—of about 10 clients—to take up this module in 2020,' Swagato informed me in March 2020, as they were gearing up for their product rollout.[9]

Rashmi Vikram, who now works with D&I at Microsoft, spoke to me about her time at Community Business. She strongly feels that the sensitisation workshops should be conducted for everyone, not just the senior management. She and her team had spent a year travelling to Pune, Mumbai, Delhi and Hyderabad, conducting workshops at all the divisions of one company. They witnessed the lack of awareness up close:

'One of the places that I covered was Delhi. You know, Delhi is quite different when it comes to mindsets and how people behave when compared to the rest of India. That was the only place where a person was not allowed to come inside the office building because the security person did not feel that she was dressed appropriately for office. She was wearing a sari with heavy make-up and jewellery. That was a really good example for me to highlight to the team that came for the training. I refused to do the training until that person came to the room. I apologised to her in front of everyone that she had to go through that. And she said, "*Didi, hamare saath ye hota hai.*"' Sister, this keeps happening with us. 'And I was like, "*Tumhare saath nahi hona chahiye ye.*"' This shouldn't happen to you. 'I told the group that we are doing sessions for you as leaders but your security and housekeeping staff are still not aware of inclusion. What if this individual was a client of yours? Would you have treated her the same way?'[10]

b) Roundtables with Senior Leaders

Roundtables are high-level interactions and they are specifically designed to be useful for senior leaders to discuss the steps being taken towards LGBTQ inclusion in their respective companies. These roundtables can also be held within a company, with different departments coming together to discuss the progress and the road ahead.

IBM's Global LGBTQ Council holds LGBTQ roundtables, which are diversity training programmes for IBM representatives from all around the world.[11] The formal launch of the Indian chapter of the AMCHAM's LGBTQ initiative in 2019 was organised as a roundtable, and I was one of the panellists. We were seated in a square formation around a centrepiece of flowers. Okay, so maybe a roundtable may not always happen at round tables, but everyone, at any given point, needs to be facing everyone else, and that's the point!

Roundtables are not sensitisation workshops. Senior leaders come in with relatively informed ideas, to discuss, share and learn best practices. Sandeep told me about a roundtable that the Royal Bank of Scotland had organised. 'When RBS had one of their senior leaders come to India, he wore a rainbow lanyard. That was something they wanted Indian employees to understand, that one of the senior leaders of the company is someone who is pro-LGBT. It is a simple gesture. For them to see the leader wearing the lanyard and talk about the work they do, and actually invite the other senior leaders in India to attend a sensitisation talk which he kick-started ... it makes a difference.'[12]

c) An LGBTQ Employee Resource Group

'Today is a little different. *Aaj*, we are not having Radio Friday. Instead we are having Radio Pride Day!' Aritra Kanjilal's voice produced a little static over the radio as it segued into Queen's 'I Want to Break Free'. This was at Nielson's office in Kolkata. It was March 2019 and Nielson South Asia had just launched PRIDE, Promoting Respect in Diverse Environments, its employee resource group.

Nielson had had this global ERG since 2007. Around June 2018, Aritra, who is gay and out and proud, had asked the global D&I team about starting a Pride ERG for South Asia. They agreed and asked him to lead it. He had no experience leading an ERG, but why not, he thought. An idea struck him. Radio Friday had been active for a while across the company. Every Friday evening, many of the Indian offices could tune in to an hour of radio, with one of the employees as the RJ. Some of these employee RJs talked in between, others just played music. Aritra thought, what about giving it a queer twist? Introducing, Radio Pride Day!

'The idea is really simple. We play songs by LGBT+ artists and composers and talk about movies with LGBT+ protagonists, side characters or movies by LGBT+ directors. That's how we got started. In between songs, we introduce the movie, say for example, *My Brother Nikhil* or *Memories in March*. Irrespective of the popularity of the movie or song, we introduce it, and give its background. For example, if we have Freddie Mercury, we could give some background about his journey of orientation and his journey of expression. At the same time, we ask open questions like: Why do we need to tag something as macho, masculine or feminine? One session takes about fifteen songs. We encourage our RJs to include some regional movies or artists. So, when I did it for Kolkata, I included Bengali movies and artists, and even pieces by Tagore. It makes it easier for people in that office to relate to.'

Beginning with two sessions at their Kolkata office, Radio Pride Day was eventually replicated in Gurgaon and Mumbai. Nielson has sixteen offices of varying sizes across India. Soon, more and more of their office Fridays are going to turn into Pride melas, galvanised by the voices of those who love queer music.[13] This is the power of ERGs.

A staple in most large organisations, ERGs are of different kinds—there are groups for parents, for women and for many other communities. Global queer ERGs like GLEAM (Global LGBTQI+ Employees and Allies at Microsoft), GLAM at McKinsey or Gayglers at Google have inspired other companies to get started on theirs too, and there are already many successful queer ERGs in Indian companies such as Wipro Pride and IGLU (Infosys Gays Lesbians and You) at Infosys.

I asked Ram, who has worked at Intel and pioneered their LGBTQ ERG, about what an ideal ERG looks like. The points I have highlighted below are culled from our conversation.[14]

- You don't need an LGBTQ person in your office to have an ERG. As an employee, do you feel strongly about the issue, but identify as straight or cisgender? Start an ERG!
- An ERG should have specific goals. There is a huge amount of misinformation and stigma. How can that be tackled? A movie screening? Plays? Sensitisation workshops? The ideal would be to show colleagues or employees the lived reality of a queer person; everything straight cisgender people take for granted. It could be restrooms, it could be health insurance. For many, the only visible LGBTQ people are the trans people on the streets. They are not seen as people who would fit at the workplace. There is an urgent need to break that stereotyping. It is important to show successful queer role models and 'out' champions. The 2018 *Humsafar Trust Manual for Corporates* states that reverse mentoring—LGBTQ junior employees interacting with senior employees and sensitising them—and volunteering with community organisations can go a long way in showing employees the realities on the ground for the LGBTQ community in India.[15]
- An ERG should have visible and constant leadership participation and a leadership structure. If it is voluntary, it may fizzle out. For Intel,

Ram told me, the larger D&I team used to have representatives from various ERGs, and each ERG had its own sub-team that took care of its functioning. At the beginning of the year, they would form the charter for the whole year, and each ERG team would break down their deliverables for the month or quarter, location-wise.

Ally support is really key in the formation of ERGs. Many of the leaders of queer inclusion in our country are allies. Rashmi, Srini, Madhumitha, Shubha and Nisa are all straight and extremely supportive allies.

Shubha told me about how she became an ally of the LGBTQ movement —one of her friends came out to her when she was in her thirties. 'At that point, I thought I had never met any gay person before in my life. Of course, later I realised that, obviously, I had met many people from the community. They just hadn't come out. The fact that I was so completely ignorant and not even thinking about it was one thing that shook me. It also had to do with this idea of feeling like an outsider, of feeling that you don't belong. I relate to that. I am not exactly an academic, not entirely an activist, somewhere in between. My languages—I am Tamil-speaking but I grew up in Karnataka. This thing of where do you come from, where do you belong—the fact that people from the community are considered outsiders, it struck a chord.

'The other thing is, as a feminist, issues around sexuality had been used to keep women in their place, give them a sense of shame, which I had experienced. So, this idea of seeing sexuality as empowering, liberating, affirming, was a factor for me. The community is so much fun, so why would I not want to stay engaged?'[16]

Many of you who are straight and reading this book as allies may have a story similar to Shubha's. You feel a connection with us, and want to work alongside us in the LGBTQ community to create a better society. Here are some thoughts on how you can be a good ally. The points below are culled from the global think tank Beyond Diversity's 2018 report *Understanding LGBTQ: An Ally's Perspective*. According to this report, as a good ally, you need to:

- Not assume that all your peers and co-workers are straight
- Be an empathetic listener
- Confront unconscious and implicit biases against alternative sexual orientations
- Reassure peers from the LGBT+ community of your acceptance through public support like Pride marches and by saying no to homophobic jokes

- Stand up against LGBT+ discrimination, whether domestic, public or professional
- Learn the queer vocabulary, and be mindful of what terminology you use while addressing a particular person
- Use gender sensitive language, especially pronouns[17]

Doesn't sound too hard, does it?

16

Step Four: Address the Specific Circumstances of Trans Employees

Why is there a separate chapter focusing exclusively on trans employees when 'T' is already a part of the LGBTQ alphabet soup? To answer this, I go back to Godrej's *A Manifesto for Trans Inclusion in the Indian Workplace*, in which my colleague Nayanika Nambiar and I note:

> Trans employees face a distinctly different set of challenges in the workplace that are not a part of the lesbian, gay or bi experience. According to the National Human Rights Commission report in 2018 on the living conditions of transgender people, 92% of India's 4.9 lakh trans persons (according to the 2011 census—a significantly under-reported number, activists believe) are unable to participate in any economic activity. Less than half of them have access to education, and 62% of those that do, face abuse and discrimination. Moreover, only 2% live with their families. [...]
>
> One of the biggest perpetrators of violence against the community are the police and law-enforcing authorities. The 2011 census revealed that 52% of trans people surveyed face violence from the police. [...]
>
> The Indian government publishes annual statistics about crimes against men and women, but it doesn't do the same for trans people. A survey conducted by the Swasti Health Resource Centre, a Bengaluru-based non-profit group, interviewed 2169 trans people from Maharashtra, Tamil Nadu and Karnataka. It revealed that 40% of trans people have experienced sexual abuse in India before turning 18. It begins as early as age 5, and continues even after childhood.[1]

We argue in the manifesto that trans people need special attention because they are the most vulnerable and most victimised amongst the wider

LGBTQ population. We also state that even though we are in the midst of a skilling revolution in India right now, it is perplexing that there aren't any consolidated, large-scale efforts to reach the trans community. While there were 249 national and state government schemes as of December 2018 that could potentially be accessed by trans people, only the Deen Dayal Upadhyaya Grameen Kaushalya Yojana, a youth employment scheme under the central government, mentioned transgender persons as beneficiaries.

Nayanika and I had concluded that if corporate entities focused on trans employment and attached it to the larger tapestry of skilling, it would turn out to be a good thing for all parties concerned. Trans people would get jobs, private companies would get talent, and state governments across the country would have programmes that address a gap in unemployment policies.

It is clear that there is a big gap in trans employment, which corporate India can help fill. But if you are serious about bringing trans people into the workplace, you should first take a comprehensive look at your work culture, infrastructure and policies beforehand, and ask, are all of these trans friendly and will they help attract trans talent? This chapter is a guide for answering this question with a resounding yes.

⁂

Here is Amita Karadkhedkar talking about her transition and workplace acceptance.[2] 'I transitioned while working for Barclays. When it comes to Barclays or my transition, Barclays globally may have had policies on transition, but in India, something like this had never happened. In fact, they didn't even have visible role models. Again, it is not completely about organisation culture. It is also the milieu, the cultural condition we come from.

'My transition within Barclays led to policy changes. Nothing like that had happened before. So the organisation also grew in the space of inclusion with me. My legal documents were not changed initially, but I wanted my correct name to be reflected everywhere. They did not have any policy on how to go with it; now the policy is that the display name can be changed without legal documents, but the legal name with HR can only be changed once the employee furnishes the legal documents. Then, the washroom policy. There was no mention or discussion around a gender-neutral washroom. During my transition, I wasn't comfortable using the men's washroom, and entering the women's washroom wasn't the correct option ethically. That's how the discussion around gender-neutral washrooms started. They had never even considered financial assistance for transition, or transition guidelines, and that was the discussion I initiated.

'Just having a visible role model plays a very important role in driving inclusion forward. Otherwise, people think it is some alien concept which cannot happen around us. But when you have a visible role model who is sitting next to you, delivering the task which you are also doing, walking shoulder to shoulder, at par, then you realise this is not alien, it is very much real, and happening. That is how it was with Barclays.

'Through Barclays, I also led an ERG to drive inclusion forward. I led various sensitisation workshops and organised events. I also went to external platforms and bodies, getting opportunities to drive inclusion forward with various organisations. It could be IBM, Infosys, KPMG, Northern Trust, Dow Chemicals, Godrej ... so many. Then, I was a speaker for NASSCOM. On all these platforms, the main agenda was to be there as a visible role model, share my journey, and help the audience understand the marginalised community and what they can do to be a proud ally and help drive inclusion forward.'

Barclays, like many other companies, went on its trans inclusion journey only after their first trans employee, Amita, joined them. But others don't need to wait. This chapter is founded on the work of our country's leading trans activists and organisations working for trans inclusion, whom I spoke to for this book. So here is a simple five-step guide to create a welcoming workplace for existing and potential trans employees.

a) Provide for Gender-Neutral Restroom Infrastructure

Trans or gender-nonconforming people are frequently denied access to washrooms or are made to feel uncomfortable in the washroom of their choice. I strongly urge that workplaces construct gender-neutral restrooms. My take on this echoes Sandeep Nair's: labelling washrooms 'gender neutral' is better than labelling them 'third gender' or 'transgender', as these would create an obvious divide. Trans employees who aren't out might not want to use a restroom labelled 'third gender', whereas gender-neutral washrooms are open to everyone.

However, Anubhuti Banerjee pointed out that gender-neutral restrooms may function as de facto male spaces, and make both ciswomen and trans women uncomfortable because it is not a safe space away from the male gaze. She said that an organisation should have gender-neutral restrooms with single cubicles, wherever possible, as well as gender-specific restrooms—with the premise that people are allowed to use the washrooms congruent to their gender identity or expression.[3] Ritesh Rajani suggested that if the restrooms are already gender segregated in a company, one restroom in the building can be designated as gender-neutral. If a company already has a PWD (persons with disability) cubicle/washroom, that can be made a gender-neutral restroom as well.

Shubha Chacko said that the term 'gender neutral' does not convey inclusivity in the way that the term 'gender inclusive' might, so companies could consider using 'gender inclusive' instead.[4]

Madhumitha Venkataraman had another take. No matter what you call it, it is important to have the infrastructure, she emphasised. 'It is not rocket science to have a gender-neutral washroom which is accessible to all. It is the most basic thing; most of our homes have gender-neutral washrooms. I know of a case of a trans person in a company—they had a gender-neutral washroom but it was only permitted to employees of a certain level and above. I don't understand how companies do this. They discriminate based on washrooms? If you don't have that, and you say that you are going to recruit 100 transgender people and change the world for the LGBT community, what are you dreaming of?'[5]

b) Help with Housing

In 2017, Kochi Metro made the news with an exciting announcement. Twenty-three trans people had been hired from the self-help group Kudumbashree in housekeeping and ticketing.[6] The move earned Kerala national as well as international attention. In terms of publicity, it also functioned as a 'significant symbol of the modernity of Kerala's outlook as a state with the visible third sex presence in the public utility sending an important message to society at large', according to Kerala's finance minister, T.M. Thomas Isaac.[7] As mentioned earlier, Kerala was the first state to formulate a transgender policy to protect the community from discrimination in 2015.[8]

However, within a week of the metro's launch, eight of the trans hires quit.[9] Many of them had difficulties with paying rent or even finding a place to rent. 'Though there are many vacant houses for rent, the owners refuse to lease them out to us. We're forced to stay in lodges coughing up over ₹600 per day. The problem of finding a shelter turned out to be an unexpected issue,' said Sheetal Shyam, a ticketing officer.[10]

My friend Urmi Jadhav from the Humsafar Trust had to vacate her rented apartment in Mumbai because the neighbours and the landlord felt that a transgender person should not live in their society. Several trans individuals we spoke to for Godrej's trans manifesto, too, brought up the issue of not being able to pay their rent because hormone therapy was costing them a lot.[11]

It is imperative that you help your trans employees find secure housing. For instance, at Godrej, our HR team actively helped Nyra D'Souza get a home in the Godrej housing colony, and it made a world of difference to her. This is not to be seen as something extra you do, as a favour, but rather as something that needs to be done to counter the marginalisation that trans employees have been facing their entire lives.

c) Provide Commute Alternatives If Needed

You may go to great lengths to further inclusion, and yet it will only succeed partially, because it doesn't counter the discrimination that happens outside of your company. Shubha cited the buses in Bengaluru as an example. Women sit on one side and men on the other. In such a situation, a trans person might face judgement, discrimination or harassment. Shuttle services or a carpooling policy, like the one offered by the software consultancy firm ThoughtWorks, could be helpful for trans employees, and it will be one more way of showing them that you really value them and care for their safety and well-being.[12]

d) Be Flexible with Documents and Qualifications, and Help with Opening Bank Accounts

Shubha explained to me that educational qualifications are hard to come by because trans people often have to drop out of schools and colleges due to violence or discrimination.[13] You have to be lenient in these circumstances. I agree with Urmi that most companies have very high expectations from their trans candidates. You should relax your criteria and instead evaluate skills such as communication if you want to further inclusion in the company. Nirmala Menon from Interweave Consulting too emphasised the need to measure skills and not qualifications.[14]

Both Nirmala and Shubha suggested that if a company is serious, it should collaborate with other organisations such as Project Vayati to assist with skilling efforts.[15] In late 2019, Solidarity Foundation partnered with the global company Altran India and the Bengaluru-based NGO Best Practices Foundation, for their upcoming Project Arise, which would work towards supporting working-class sexual minorities and sex workers through grants, fellowships, building links to resources and community involvement.[16]

Many of the people I talked to suggested internships as a way of easing trans people into a company. This functions as a good testing period for the candidate as well as the company. The candidate can check whether they like the environment or not, and the manager need not be worried about the company's image being affected should the trans person choose to leave the organisation. The internship period is also a good way to assess the skills the employee brings to the job and the training they need, as well as to get feedback on how inclusive the company is and what can be improved.

Amit Kekre, the head of National Strategy of the DDB Mudra group, told me in January 2020 about DDB Transit—their pilot internship programme for the trans community. 'Interns under the programme have been sourced from community talent pools, and selected keeping in mind their skill set compatibility. We have designed the programme as a two-step phased module that eases the interns into the organisation—an offline induction followed by on-floor integration. Throughout their programme, they will have mentors and "coaching buddies" to guide them on their journey and to aid them in the process. We hope that by the end of the programme, the interns have a memorable experience, and successful interns are able to secure a longer engagement within the organisation and/or they are able to use the experience of the internship as a foundation for their career anywhere in the advertising and communications industry.'[17]

Zainab Patel added that a company should help its trans employees open bank accounts, arrange for necessary documents such as a PAN card, and provide legal help when it comes to procuring these documents.[18]

e) Set Up a Support System for Employees Who Wish to Transition

Up until now, we have discussed best practices that a company should follow for trans employees who have already transitioned. But what if an employee wishes to transition during the course of their employment? Are you equipped to deal with this? If not, you need to be, and set up the appropriate support systems.

Remember that when an individual chooses to transition, the organisation will also transition with them. Understanding the three key aspects of transitioning, as outlined by the Human Rights Campaign Foundation's 2016 *Transgender Inclusion in the Workplace: A Toolkit for Employers*[19] and the 2018 *Humsafar Trust Manual for Corporates*[20], is the first step towards putting appropriate policies in place.

- Expression
  This would involve a change in name, pronoun choice and appearance (dress and/or cosmetic modifications) and also change in vocal tone.
- Medical
  There are medical procedures that align one's physical body with one's gender identity. This would include hormone replacement therapy for secondary sexual characteristics—testosterone for transmen, and oestrogen and testosterone blockers for transwomen. It also includes female-to-male (FtM) and male-to-female (MtF) gender affirmation surgical procedures. To understand therapies, procedures and hormone treatments, refer to the WPATH's 2011 *Standards of Care*.[21]
- Legal
  Legal changes would include changes to company documentation and records, and identification documents such as passports, Aadhar, PAN card and driver's license. This is often not easy, in terms of time and effort involved.

The following are the steps you should take within your company when an employee chooses to transition:

i. Having the Conversation

Having a point of contact for the employee to speak to about their intention to transition is essential. According to the Out and Equal Workplace Advocates' 2015 *Workplace Gender Identity and Transition Guidelines*, persons to include in a support team are:

- The employee's manager
- Their HR representative
- An employee assistance programme resource person
- A member of the company's LGBTQ employee resource group
- A representative from the office of D&I
- Someone in the company who has already transitioned[22]

Ideally, all the above people should go through a sensitisation module about the transition process and be aware of medical professionals to point the employee towards. Neelam Jain noted that it is absolutely necessary to make sure the employee in question is offered psychiatric help so as to ensure they are ready for medical transition. They may have gender dysphoria, but sometimes they may not be prepared for the procedure.[23]

ii. Charting a Timeline

A rigid timeline is not recommended, as each person transitions differently, and it should be decided on a case-by-case basis. However, charting a tentative timeline with the support team helps put HR practices in motion, as some milestones can be planned to ensure that the process is smooth. These include:

- What the period of medical leave will be, when it will begin and who will act as backup for the employee
- When particular medical procedures will take place
- Whether the employee would like to relocate to a different office after their transition and when this change should be effected
- When the employee will begin to present themselves in their new gender identity
- When/whether the work team will be informed about the transition, and the manner in which they will be informed
- When the change of name and photographs in documentation and ID will occur
- How long these changes will take in terms of HR processes (changing company directories, online references, etc.)

iii. Telling the Co-workers

The Out and Equal 2015 report talks about a meeting with co-workers who are in close contact with the transitioning employee. This should ideally occur before the individual begins to present themselves in their new gender role. The co-workers must be acquainted with the organisation's policies. They should be advised to respect the fact that the transitioning individual will be presenting themselves differently. They must also be told about the importance of using the individual's new name and pronoun in all communication—be it written, oral or informal. A workshop should also be conducted, preferably by an organisation that works with transgender individuals and is familiar with how to sensitise individuals to the transition process.[24] The 2016 Human Rights Campaign Foundation report states that senior management should also express solidarity and be supportive of the employee—you could do this via a letter or a memo too.

This report also notes that conversations among co-workers that do not relate to work often revolve around gender and sexuality—especially childhood, relationships, partners, family and sex. Discussing these things in casual, informal conversations is inevitable. However, transgender employees may feel uncomfortable about participating in these because even casual conversations mean they have to 'come out' to people in some way. Using inclusive language and avoiding assumptions about how people identify would help a trans person feel comfortable enough to talk freely. It would encourage them to participate in conversations without the fear of backlash or judgement. Relationships at work affect an employee's productivity. So, fostering this culture in the workplace is of great importance.[25]

iv. Sensitising External Stakeholders

External individuals, such as customers, should also be sensitised to the company's policies. Anti-discrimination should be embedded in the messaging of your company, so outside parties interacting with trans employees are aware of the company's stance on discriminatory behaviour. The 2015 Out and Equal report notes that customer preference should not be a reason to deny an employee the right to dress in accordance to their gender identity.[26] The 2018 Humsafar Trust report notes that companies often don't make this sensitisation compulsory for their suppliers and vendors—places from where the organisation orders office supplies or employs caterers and hires for cleaning, or any other company from which it outsources services. If vendors take a transphobic or homophobic stance, you must be willing and ready to re-evaluate your company's relationship with them.[27]

Many companies are already on their way to becoming trans inclusive, by putting in place policies based on the five steps outlined above. I hope these steps help you along the right path as well.

17

Step Five: Become an Advocate for LGBTQ Issues Outside the Company

On a crisp fall morning in October 2014, I was tucking into scrambled eggs and a croissant at a cute Greenwich village cafe in New York, with Kenji Yoshino, the Chief Justice Earl Warren Professor of Constitutional Law at the New York University School of Law and also the director of the Center for Diversity, Inclusion and Belonging. Isn't that a beautiful name for the centre? 'Belonging' is such an evocative word.

I took the day off from Yale, woke up at four o'clock and rode on the six o'clock train from New Haven into New York just for this meeting. Kenji had a schedule that was absolutely nuts, plus a husband and two children, so half past eight was the only time he could meet me. We have many common friends including Menaka Guruswamy, and I was honoured that Kenji had, in fact, read my first book while researching for a paper on LGBTQ globalisation.

As he sipped his orange juice, I gushed over his award-winning book *Covering: The Hidden Assault on Our Civil Rights*, in which he argues that it is not just queer people who hide their whole selves from others.[1] All of us 'cover', in some way or the other, aspects of ourselves that we feel others might not appreciate. What if we all stopped covering? Might we not have better professional and personal lives? It is a powerful intersectional argument for queer inclusion.

Two years after our meeting, Kenji wrote a research paper with his colleague Sylvia Ann Hewlett, titled *Out in the World: Securing LGBT Rights in the Global Marketplace*.[2] It outlines three approaches that a company might take towards their LGBTQ employees, and it is now considered the gospel for all global companies that are working on formulating their own inclusion strategies. Anyone and everyone who works on diversity and inclusion anywhere in the world has read this paper. Here are the three approaches that they talk about, in brief:

- As the name indicates, the 'When in Rome' model proposes that you adhere to the norms and local laws of the jurisdiction you are operating in, and don't rock the boat in any way.
- The 'Embassy' model proposes that you enforce pro-LGBTQ policies within your company's walls, but don't push for change in the wider community.
- The 'Advocate' model proposes that you actively seek to effect change in the wider society at large.

I am partial to the advocacy model. We simply can't afford to be passive any more. We *all* need to be advocates.

~

All through 2019, I was rummaging through reports, scrolling frantically, looking for narratives and studies that I could source for this book. While I was greedy for reports written about India, I sometimes strayed and found myself looking at what was happening in other parts of the world.

On one such day, I was reading a 2019 report by the US Chamber of Commerce Foundation, titled *Business Success and Growth Through LGBT Inclusive Culture*.[3] If only for a moment, I was transported to North Carolina in 2016.

House Bill No. 2 had been passed in the state. This meant that:

- Anti-discrimination policies that protected LGBTQ people were to be eliminated.
- In all government buildings, people could only use restrooms and changing facilities according to the sex mentioned in their birth certificate.

Public outrage was sparked.

Companies like United, IBM and DSM lobbied to repeal House Bill No. 2. Dan Schulman, the PayPal CEO, decided not to expand their activities into Charlotte in North Carolina as a form of protest, and said that the bill violated the principles and values integral to the functioning of PayPal. He ended his statement with, 'It is the right thing to do for our employees, our customers, and our communities.'[4]

The Republican governor Patrick McCrory who signed this bill into law, lost his bid for re-election in 2016 to the Democrat attorney general Roy

Cooper, a vocal critic of the bill. A *New York Times* article in 2017 cited a study showing a potential loss of US $3.7 billion to North Carolina if the bill was not repealed.[5]

The outrage worked. The portion of the law regarding bathroom use was nullified on 30 March 2017.[6]

Coming back to our own desh, this is not North Carolina for sure, and I don't expect you to put out ads in newspapers supporting LGBTQ rights. Well, at least, not yet. But if you have implemented all the steps detailed above, it is now essential for you to look at what you can do *outside* your organisation—support LGBTQ grassroots efforts and be a sponsor for LGBTQ culture in our country.

In short, I want you to come out as an inclusive company.

a) Participate in External Forums, Pride Marches and Events as a Champion of LGBTQ Issues

To start with, consider how you might be able to insert yourself into the process of justice in the country. Look at the legal landscape here, and use corporate lobbying efforts to change the narrative. There are already so many community efforts happening within organisations like FICCI, for instance, that you, as a company, could participate in.

In November 2019, I was proud to be part of the launch of a landmark report at the FICCI headquarters in Delhi. The report, *New Global Champions: Why Fast-Growing Companies from Emerging Markets Are Embracing LGBT+ Inclusion*, by Open for Business, catalogues the LGBTQ inclusion strategies of companies in countries like India, and makes a clear connection between LGBTQ inclusion, growth and brand favourability.[7]

It was a rare, sunny, smog-free day in the capital. Drew Keller, the global programme director of Open for Business, had come in from New York. Elliot Vaughn, the managing director of Boston Consulting Group, who had funded and supported the report, had flown in from London just for this evening, to be alongside Seema Bansal from their India office. Mellissa Ferrier, the global LGBTQ leader from Wipro, had come up from Bengaluru. In the audience were representatives of other companies, journalists and heads of different LGBTQ organisations. This was a historic day as it was the first time that the FICCI headquarters was hosting something queer.

I was deeply moved by the remarks that Dilip Chenoy, the FICCI secretary general, made on stage. He shared that when FICCI started their LGBTQ inclusion efforts in 2018, many of the member companies asked him why he was doing this. They even wondered if he was gay. But he continued to be a tireless advocate, and the FICCI member companies finally started coming around. The Supreme Court's 2018 verdict was a tremendous catalysing force.

This is the power of coalition building and collective advocacy. If you care about inclusion, reach out to FICCI and help amplify the excellent work. If you are a part of another organisation, like CII, then push your institution to constantly put LGBTQ inclusion on their agenda. If you are a part of senior management in a company, you have the power and the financial and cultural capital that can really shift gears on inclusion in the country, and like Dilip, who is doing cultural acupuncture using his position at FICCI, do something about it, wherever and however you can.

When I say organisations should come out, I mean that everyone and their nani should know that a company proudly supports inclusion. No being hush-hush. The time for that has passed. An organisation could declare their support by participating in Pride marches, like Intel and Symantec in Pune;[8] or take part in diversity conventions, like Bajaj Allianz and Eureka Forbes at the 2019 RISE job fair[9] or like Cisco and UrbanClap at the Out and Equal Workplace Advocates India Forum 2018.[10] Or like Godrej, which has associated itself with organisations such as the Society for Human Resource Management and Aon Hewitt, and events like the CII HR Conclave.

Aditya Ghosh, a board member of Oyo Hotels and a former head of Indigo Airlines, flew in to Mumbai from Delhi to launch Godrej's trans manifesto in December 2018. It was his first public event after taking up the Oyo job, and he wanted to send a clear message to the world about his support for LGBTQ rights. Like Aditya, you too need to show up for the LGBTQ community and speak up for us.

Once you decide to have LGBTQ-inclusive policies in your company, it is important that you make a loud noise about launching them—perhaps through a big event or publications like the company newsletter and by empowering different ERGs to spread awareness about these initiatives within the organisation. For the launch of our trans manifesto, we invited members from the activist circuit, the corporate world and the academia. Inviting clients to these events may prove to be beneficial from a business point of view.

Nirmala Menon told me another important thing. If your company can send out LGBTQ employees to be the face of the company and its inclusive policies at many of these external forums, it will not only empower them but also send out a strong message about what your company stands for. This is what Keshav Suri does so well at the Lalit by choosing different employees each time to represent the company at public events.

At a talk at the insurance company Swiss Re in November 2019, I was impressed with Mohul Sharma, a smiling twenty-two-year-old Food-and-Beverage associate at the Lalit in Delhi, who had recently transitioned into Mohul after having lived as Megha for two decades.

Mohul's parents had separated when he was ten, and he moved in with his father and newly born younger brother. As he grew up, he struggled to come to terms with his sexuality and with the feeling of being trapped inside the wrong body. 'I used to lock myself in a room and cry all day because I didn't like what was happening in my body at puberty. Society doesn't know, and for a lot of trans men, too, growing up, we have to educate ourselves.'

Mohul's eureka moment came when he saw the *Satyamev Jayate* episode that dealt with sexualities.[11] This led him to reach out to the queer people featured on that episode, like the counsellor Deepak Kashyap and the trans activist Abhina Aher. Interacting with them over email and further research on the internet about transition armed him to bring up his gender dysphoria with his father. He shared the story of Aryan Pasha—the first trans body builder in India—with his father, but it was not easy to convince him. 'It took me one and a half years of patiently waiting for him to understand.'

Unfortunately, in July 2017, just six months into his transition, Mohul's father died in an accident, leaving Mohul to look after his ten-year-old brother. Having studied only till class ten, Mohul tried hard to find a job, but his lack of higher formal education and husky voice—he was in the midst of hormone therapy—acted as obstacles. 'BPOs would reject me and say that your voice doesn't match your resume. It says you are Megha, but you don't sound like a Megha.'

Finally, Mohul approached the Lalit, where he was accepted and trained under the guidance of Keshav, who personally funded his operation. 'The best part of working at the Lalit is that I'm treated as who I am. I use the male washroom. Everyone addresses me as Mohul. If I do well, I am praised. If I make a mistake, I am scolded. There is no difference. I used to be in the in the Room-Dining department, but now I have got a promotion, and I'm on the executive floor interacting with CEOs and MDs. It is so exciting! I have got my pehchaan at the Lalit.'

Mohul is now trying to finish his education through open schooling, and has big ambitions for his twelve-year-old brother. 'I want him to have all the things that I didn't while growing up, and it is my goal to give him a better life.'

A month before I'd met Mohul, this inspiring post from Suresh Ramdas came up in my social media feed. Suresh is the reigning Mr Gay World India, who I, as a member of the jury, was happy to have helped select for the title some months ago. Do you see how grateful he is to his organisation, HP, for constantly pushing him to be the best version of himself? This is what he posted on his Instagram page:

> Thrilled to be in the list of Top 50 OUTstanding LGBT+ Future Leaders of the world, 2019 presented by OUTstanding. This is a great moment of pride for me to be in this list, representing HP HQ Palo Alto, HP India & India.
>
> I have to thank my organization HP, which has shown me what authentic efforts on Inclusion and Diversity mean. HP has allowed me to be my authentic self and our leaders have always been very supportive. I thank my manager Nazia Syed Mujeeb and my colleagues who have supported and encouraged me, contributing to my success. The HP India D&I team has also played a vital role in shaping me for who I am.
>
> I also owe to India's first Inter-company alliance on Inclusive collaborations and LGBTQI advocacy, Working with Pride team, which has significantly contributed in shaping me and my perspectives. It has helped me immensely to learn more about fostering inclusion, have a well-rounded view of organization culture and gave me opportunities to lead efforts on LGBTQI advocacy.
>
> Thank you to the MGWI Official (Mr. Gay World India) Team for the platform and the enormous learning experiences. This platform gave me a huge leverage to bring awareness around LGBTQ+ people in India.
>
> None of this would be possible without the love and support of my parents Ramadhas Muthuswamy, my partner, सोहम सेनगुप्ता & my dear friends who stood by me and cheered for me throughout! This meant a lot when I was navigating challenges and amplified my happiness when recognition came. I truly feel grateful to them.
>
> Last but not the least, thank you to Fern Ngai, CEO of Community Business to nominate me for this award. It goes to show that I am in the right path and guided towards more—Miles to go before I can rest for sure! This award is a representation of the path i am on and the initiatives that I plan to lead going ahead.[12]

b) Support LGBTQ Grassroots Organising Efforts and NGOs

There are some wonderful LGBTQ NGOs and community organisations in the country, and most of them have a severe funding crunch. Contributions to them will go a long way.

When I give talks at companies, I make it a point to request them to make a financial contribution to a queer NGO in their city. Franklin Templeton contributed to the TWEET Foundation after my talk there. Similarly, Swiss Re donated to the Solidarity Foundation after I spoke to them in Bengaluru.

At the launch of AMCHAM India's LGBTQ chapter in June 2019, during a panel discussion, Sudhir Jain, managing director and chief risk officer at Bank of America, told Neelam Jain that visiting some of the transgender people whom Neelam's PeriFerry had placed in Chennai had given his company the impetus to work harder and stronger on the mandate of LGBTQ inclusiveness.

Giving money to the LGBTQ community is not the only way to show your support. Often, other things can be as valuable. For example, inviting LGBTQ collectives like the Aravani Art Project to office campuses as artists in residence, like Goldman Sachs did. The Aravani Art Project is an artistic collective of people who identify as transgender and use public art as a form of social intervention. In May 2019, they painted the entire entrance wall at the Goldman Sachs Bengaluru headquarters.[13] Having queer art like this present in office buildings would be a wonderful place to start a conversation about inclusion. A label introducing the work and the artists and explaining why a company is supporting the project can go a long way in changing the mindsets of employees.

LGBTQ organisations can be invited to host community events on campus, and given whatever support they need in this regard. Godrej did this with the MINGLE summit—we hosted it on our campus in Mumbai between 2014 and 2016. When Udayan Dhar left MINGLE in 2016 to pursue his PhD in the US, the organisation relocated to Bengaluru under the guidance of Ramkrishna Sinha. Now the annual summit is held at the ThoughtWorks office in Koramangala.

If something big like hosting a summit is not possible, start at a smaller level, like many other companies across the country that are offering their office spaces for Pride Circle meetups in different cities.

c) Sponsor LGBTQ Cultural Events Like Film Festivals, Literature Festivals and Pride Marches

There are now many queer events that you can sponsor. Each city has its own film festival, from the Rainbow Literature Festival in Delhi to the RISE job fair in Bengaluru and other cities across India. Take your pick and be creative with sponsorship.

Mona Thangaraj, the recruitment lead at Uber India and South Asia, explained to me that Uber's involvement in the Bengaluru RISE fair had been inspired by similar Pride initiatives taken up by their US team: 'Our diversity and inclusivity agenda is an organisational priority at Uber. The RISE fair was a very good fit with our vision to open doors to talented and creative individuals from the LGBTQ+ community. In today's work environment, we understand the need to focus on not just supporting the community, but actively driving awareness around the challenges they face. In addition to participating in the job fair, we changed all in-app Uber routes in Bengaluru with rainbow colours for the entire day, mobilising the city to come out in support of the LGBTQ+ community and pave a path for equal opportunities in the workplace.'[14]

This is clever, this is cool. Like Uber, other sponsors today are competing to be more and more innovative to attract the maximum attention for their efforts.

Here are four pointers to keep in mind while considering sponsorship strategies:

- Sponsorship money need not only come from budgets for corporate social responsibility or diversity. It could come from one of the brands or from innovation or even HR. At Godrej, the sponsorship for Kashish comes from our Corporate Communication department, and the Kashish platform is used by us to promote a range of Godrej products like the BBlunt haircare range.
- A sponsor must create a win-win situation for the company and brand, but without being too pushy—like splashing the brand name all over the festival (especially if the amount is not high enough) or trying to influence the programming in any way.
- Instead, you should think of how you can use the LGBTQ platform you are riding on to promote your brand in innovative ways. LGBTQ audiences don't want to be patronised, but we are happy to be marketed to in creative ways. VIP Industries with their Skybags range and the Lalit with their Kitty Su nightclub do this well. Richa Singh told me that the '#PureLove Nights' at their Kitty Su chain of nightclubs are frequently sponsored by brands like Bacardi, Stolichnaya, Moet Hennessy and Audible by Amazon. Levi's even sponsored a complete three-city tour with the international drag artist Peppermint in 2019.[15]

Sridhar Rangayan told me, 'We believe there is a strong case for brands to use the Kashish platform to market their products to the upper-middle-class audience segment of the film festival—they are brand loyal and have good spending power.'[16]

You could also see how you could use your brand to empower the community at the event you are supporting. For instance, at Kashish, Godrej provides free passes for students who want to attend—all they have to do is show the festival organisers their college ID card. Godrej picks up the tab for their passes. This is a great way of building brand awareness and also doing something good. Think along these lines.

- Finally, you should make sure you have a long-term commitment from the top management. By commitment, I mean money for sponsorship as well as the presence of the top management at these cultural events to indicate that the company really cares. Pallav Patankar, the director of Marketing for Kashish told me, 'From a Kashish point of view, things have worked and associations have been long term only when there has been a push from top management.'[17] I agree with him. Be it Pirojsha Godrej lighting the lamp to inaugurate Kashish or Nadir Godrej reading out a poem he wrote for the festival or Nisa inaugurating the event as the first public engagement she takes up after becoming the chairperson of Godrej Consumer Products Limited, this kind of signalling and participation from senior leadership is key, both from a PR perspective and also to make an impact within the company itself.

18

But No Token Rainbows, Please. We Want Jobs, Not Your Instagram Filters!

In Chapter Six, when I wrote about the queer alphabet soup, I purposely left out a word. Pinkwashing. No, baba, this is not when you accidently put your whites with your reds in the washing machine. Pinkwashing is a term that is used to describe companies that promote themselves as queer friendly in an attempt to tap into the LGBTQ consumer market without authentically championing the rights of the community.[1]

Post the 377 judgement, when there was a barrage of corporates supporting us, putting up photos in rainbow shades and filters with tinsel and glitter, I wasn't irked at first. The thing is, often, when one hasn't had attention for years, one is happy with even a little bit. So my initial reaction on seeing all the branded posts was that of joy. But this soon changed to irritation, especially after I spoke to one of my gurus, the feminist author and queer rights advocate Mona Eltahawy. There is a whole cake to be shared, she reminded me, bringing the same argument she makes with feminism into the queer space. Why should we be happy with crumbs? We want a large piece. In fact, we want to bake a bigger cake.

This is where I stand right now. If you care for LGBTQ issues, you need to show us that you are genuine. Are your HR policies inclusive? Do you have a non-discrimination policy and partner benefits? Are you creating an internal culture of inclusion? Are you valuing your LGBTQ customers? If yes, then please, by all means, go out and blow your trumpet. If not, then all the rainbow-themed 'memes' that companies hope would 'go viral' are inauthentic; the queer community sees it as that, and we will call out the hypocrisy.

For example, post the 2018 judgement, Yatra.com had advertised honeymoon packages for same-sex couples starting from ₹377 onwards.[2]

Ritesh Rajani had a huge problem with this, and rightfully so. He reminded me of a transphobic advertisement Yatra.com had made years ago, in which an NRI woman in jeans and a red top comes home to a semi-rural set-up, to tie a rakhi to her brother. She finds out he has now transitioned into a woman, who shows up on-screen, backlit. '*Kaisi ho behen*?' the sister who has transitioned asks her foreign-returned sister. The last shot of the advertisement is the NRI sister's disgusted expression. Cut to white screen, with sea-green text: 'Visit home more often.'[3]

The Yatra.com ad was clearly transphobic, and it was playing on televisions across the country. But the moment Section 377 was read down, rainbow filters were out for the company? 'How do you move from one to the other without understanding the community?' Ritesh questioned. 'Inclusion requires a lot of effort. It is a journey of many years before you start tom-tomming yourself. Unfortunately, it has become a game of show! How many likes on social media? It's happening all around. It's sad because it is going to be counterproductive. The two token trans employees are soon going to find out this is just a show. It will blow up at some point. Have you hired people from the community? Have you done affirmative action? Have you sponsored some initiative which makes sense? If you can't make your product inclusive, then can you do something beyond looking at us as a customer?'[4]

I urge companies to consider each of Ritesh's questions carefully before promoting themselves as inclusive.

~

In July 2019, my partner and I were in Pondicherry. After visiting the Matrimandir in Auroville and picking up our stash of Om and Earth eau de colognes from Laboratoires Senteurs, we went to the bar at the Promenade Hotel on the seafront in the picturesque White Town. The hotel is owned by the Hidesign group, and I had heard great things about their new Storyteller's Bar, which is supposed to be covered with book pages all over.

When we tried to enter the bar, we were stopped by two bouncers. One of them looked us over, and told us, 'Couples entry only.' We smiled, and told him that we were indeed a couple. He laughed out loud and nudged the other bouncer; both of them smirked and refused us entry. How can two men be a couple, they asked. I tapped into my privilege and contacts, and called my friend Srimoyi Bhattacharya who heads Peepul PR, which manages the Hidesign account, who in turn called Dipen Desai, the director of Marketing at Hidesign.

We had left the hotel and were tucking into the 'Posh'n Pink' tagliatelle at the much more welcoming Coromandel Cafe, when Dipen came over, apologised profusely and asked if he could take us back to the Promenade. I didn't want to spend my pink rupees at a business unfriendly to LGBTQ people, I told him point blank. He assured me that Hidesign was LGBTQ inclusive. 'Do you have any formal non-discrimination policies?' my partner asked him. 'Does your company pay for the health insurance of same-sex partners?' Dipen confessed that he didn't know.

I was surprised. In 2013, after the horrible Supreme Court verdict, Hidesign had posted a wonderful image on Facebook of their bags in the colours of the rainbow—one for each of the seven colours. The post read: 'Every Color, Every Shape, Every Size is BEAUTIFUL. In a world full of diversities we are EQUAL. #Sec377.'[5]

I went to the Hidesign Facebook page after we got back to our hotel, and, ironically, below is what I found their latest post to be. Dated 6 July 2019, it was a personal message from the Hidesign founder Dilip Kapur: '"#StorytellingSaturdays Castro Street's Favourite. On my first visit to Castro Street, San Francisco, in 1984, I was thrilled to find eight stores carrying Hidesign bags. This was when Castro Street was at the height of its political and artistic activism, at the centre of the fight for human rights and equality, led by the LGBT community. It was the heart of an exciting and incredibly creative community, and Hidesign was its preferred bag."—Dilip Kapur #storytellingsaturdays #hidesign #castrostreet #sanfrancisco #bags #leatherbags #leather #handcrafted #handmade #craftsmanship #ecology #sustainability #consiousdesign'.[6]

Now, I have no bone to pick with Hidesign in particular. Indeed, on a previous Pondicherry trip in 2009, I had had a wonderful visit to their factory and hung out with Dilip and Dipen. They had even gifted me a lovely custom-made bag that I continue to use, even after a decade, and even after the incident. Also, to repeat, I also have no problems with rainbow filters and rah-rah posts. I have been telling you throughout this book that I want you to be an advocate for inclusion, right? But, darlings, and this is important, all of this should come *after* doing a lot of work on the ground. If you haven't sensitised your employees and they have no clarity on whether you have inclusive policies and benefits, then what is the point, seriously?

~

Things are not always black and white. Sometimes there's the grey-wallah shade.

In November 2019, I came across a TV ad with the Bollywood filmmaker Karan Johar playing himself. Before I tell you about the actual ad, some context. Karan's public persona—whether as a participant in the *All India Bakchod Knockout* or as a host or judge of different reality TV shows and award functions—is delightfully camp. He is always flamboyantly dressed, and winks at us about his sexuality by dropping risque one-liners and double entendres, even if he doesn't address his sexuality directly. As a director, he has often showcased queer themes in films like *Student of the Year* and *Bombay Talkies*, and he has also done this as a producer in films like *Kal Ho Na Ho*, *Kapoor & Sons* and *Dostana*.

In his 2017 autobiography, *An Unsuitable Boy*, Karan firmly declared that his sexuality was his business alone and he would never say 'those three words' publicly.[7] I may not agree with him on this, but I empathise with his choice. I think that what Karan has done by his sheer presence on mainstream media is commendable; he has widened the scope of popular television in the country through his persona, and through all that he has chosen to produce and direct. He has also stood up for queer rights and queer people as a reality TV host, whether on his musical shows like *India's Got Talent*, or *What the Love!* on Netflix. The parts of his personal life that he has chosen to share publicly, like him raising twins as a single parent, are deeply inspiring. We even did a cute little 'Paani with Parmesh' event together, as an ode to his *Koffee With Karan* show, when he visited Godrej in April 2018 to speak at our Godrej Leadership Forum.

But then I came across this ad for Knorr soup that irked the hell out of me.

As the ad begins, we see Karan, in pyjamas and a silk dressing gown, welcoming his muscular, alpha male, suited-booted, rain-soaked neighbour into his house. The neighbour has lost his home keys in the wee hours. When Karan offers him a blanket, the neighbour, portrayed as flirtatious, playful and confident, refuses it, telling Karan that there is something else that might make him warm. This seems to enthuse Karan, who inches towards the neighbour, only to be told that he wants some soup. Karan then quickly whips up some Knorr soup and serves it to him. Towards the end, after the soup has been praised, the neighbour calls out to Karan suggestively and says there is something else he needs. I am excited by this point. Wow. Where could this lead? Alas, the neighbour clarifies that all he wants is more soup! The ad ends with a close-up of Karan's frustrated expression.[8]

The first time I saw it, I found the ad to be a chalu mainstreaming of queer possibilities using humour. Is it a big thing to show queer desire on mainstream TV? Sure. Then, I saw the ad a second time. This time round, I decided that I didn't like how Karan had been portrayed, as a self-sacrificing friend who will continue to smile and serve despite having his desires thwarted. The supposedly straight neighbour is happy to flirt with the queer person to get what he wants, soup in this case.

As I saw the ad a third time, I was reminded of the line in Hansda Sowvendra Shekhar's searing 2018 novel *My Father's Garden*: 'I had made a lifeboat of just two kind words from Samir.'[9] In the book, the protagonist is queer and desperately seeks love and affection. He is callously used by his male medical college crushes—for sex, for money, for everything—without any reciprocity, and is simply chucked aside as college ends. I can see the same power dynamic play out in this ad too. And it angers me. I also see shades of Kaizad Khambatta, the 'villain' character Karan portrayed in Anurag Kashyap's 2015 film *Bombay Velvet*,[10] who yearns unsuccessfully for the affection of the 'straight' protagonist Johnny, played by Ranbir Kapoor.

I dislike this trope of the eternally simpering queer devotee, waiting hopefully with a towel or some soup in return for … nothing! Perhaps to show a queer romantic relationship being consummated is too much for Indian advertising at this point. But why end the possibility definitively for all of us queer viewers? Why not have an ambiguous ending that helps us imagine something else? They could have just cut the ad after the neighbour says, 'Karan …?' and looks at Karan suggestively. How delicious that would have been!

I wonder who the ad is directed towards. Queer people? I am certainly *not* going to buy any Knorr soup after seeing this. Straight people? If so, is featuring a queer character for mere comic relief the only way to advertise to them? A queer character whose desires are thwarted in the end? How is this progressive?

Twitter *ka zamana hai, toh*, I tweeted about my discomfort and watched the comments flow back and forth. There were two comments from media friends that I particularly mulled over. Anindita Ghose, the editor of *Mint Lounge*, tweeted to me: 'Quite like the ad. Radical in the sense that Karan is in it today and wouldn't have been in it even five years ago. And actually the "unhappy" ending builds empathy and helps audiences identify with a queer protagonist I think. It's less Othering.'[11] Anuradha Sengupta, the consulting editor for CNBC-TV18, tweeted that the ad was simply 'piggybacking on changed social realities. It's not a PSA. The ad is not aiming to mainstream queer folk it's using them like it would straight people to sell. In this case: soup.'[12]

I showed the ad to my partner when he came home from office. He laughed and said he found it cute. When I told him about my discomfort, he replied, 'At least it is there.' But how much of 'at least it is there' will our community take, I retorted and tweeted back to Anindita and Anuradha. I was reminded of Mona's 'crumbs' analogy. I don't want crumbs, yaar! Still, both Anuradha and Anindita are liberal, LGBTQ-friendly feminists and staunch allies, and my partner is, well, my partner, so I wondered. Was I overreacting, and like the three of them, should I also interpret the Knorr ad as progress?

Take a look at this exchange on Instagram between Ritesh Rajani and Harish Iyer, both LGBTQ activists and personal friends. They were discussing a video posted by Bajaj Allianz on Instagram for Independence Day 2019 that featured different queer people saluting the national flag as the score soared to Vande Mataram, with the slogan '*Desh Ki Azadi, Pyaar Ki Azadi*'. This was one among the several queer-themed campaigns from different brands that were rolled out around 15 August 2019, the first Independence Day since the reading down of Section 377.

> Ritesh: Great video. Can you please share the links to the policies with inclusive coverage where same-gender partners are covered, and where gender affirmation surgeries are covered?

> Bajaj: Glad you liked our video. Our policies are inclusive in nature, irrespective of gender or orientation. Anyone can buy our policies and avail the coverage offered.

> Ritesh: I understand that anyone can buy your policies. But unless your coverage actively accounts for the actual needs of the community, it can't be inclusive. For example your family floater plan says "For the purpose of Family Floater—includes the insured: his/her lawfully wedded spouse and dependent children' meaning it doesn't cover same gender partners. All your health plans including the "extra care plus" lists the following as a general exclusion. "Cosmetic or aesthetic treatments of any description, treatment, or surgery for change of life/gender" meaning it does nothing for transgender healthcare. Please send me any plans that are actually inclusive. Else this remains a marketing gimmick.

> Harish: Achaa Ritesh. This brand has taken the first step towards sensitization. Internally, Bajaj Allianz has non discrimination policies that include discrimination on the basis of gender identity or sexual orientation. So that's a brilliant first step. You are right, there are many more steps to be taken. And they are on that path ... I'm certain they will be able to do more once they review and monitor the legal system in India ... And of course, become more inclusive. This could be catalyzed once the legal framework of the nation becomes more inclusive to same-sex partners/gender identity. The brand is in touch with me and they are working on it. And while it will take time, they have their heart in the right place and are heading in that direction. Also, thank you for writing and sharing your views. It is much needed that brands have a longer commitment, something that extends beyond a queer positive video as much as we need to encourage them and partner with them patiently in their path towards inclusivity.[13]

Grey-wallah shade again, no? I am not arguing that Bajaj Allianz isn't doing enough. But in this era of dense and abundant information, it is hard to believe that brands are truly trying to be inclusive as opposed to doing the minimum to get the maximum exposure and goodwill. Ritesh's doubts are not unfounded. And neither is Harish's optimism. Somewhere between these two shores, the boat of queer inclusion rocks.

~

Bajaj Allianz was not the only queer national anthem campaign that ran in August 2019. There were others, and I was part of one such campaign. Let me tell you about it.

In June 2019, I received an email from the ad agency Interactive Avenues. Over a subsequent call, their representative told me about a video they wanted to make, featuring queer people looking into the distance as the national anthem plays, and wondered what I thought of it. I asked them point blank if this video would help queer people in any way or were they making it to submit it for some international award? I urged them to work with a local community organisation like the Humsafar Trust and to financially contribute to one of the queer welfare programmes.

There was radio silence for a month. Then on 30 July, I got an email from Vivek Anand, the CEO of Humsafar Trust and a dear friend. He told me that the trust was helping out with the making of the video. Would I like to feature in it? Given that it was Humsafar, I said yes, assuming that perhaps the ad agency had paid heed to my suggestions.

There was little contact from the agency till the evening before the shoot. A young assistant called to tell me that I was expected to be on site throughout the night on 3 August, but was unable to give me details of the director or even the exact address or the clothes I would need to wear. She told me that she didn't know much and had just been hired to help coordinate the shoot. I didn't have a good feeling about this by now, so I finally called Suhail Abbasi of Humsafar Trust and was told that the location was Golden Tobacco, a rundown factory in Vile Parle that is now used for commercial shoots.

On the evening of the scheduled shoot, it took me about two hours to reach the spot in pouring rain at seven in the evening, the time they had asked me to come. My apprehension was not unfounded. Nothing was ready! There were a few vanity vans in which some of the participants who had been called for the shoot were sitting, including Simran Shaikh from the India HIV/AIDS Alliance, Arif Jafar from Bharosa Trust, who was one of the petitioners for the reading down of Section 377 in 2018, Anjali Gopalan of Naz Foundation, Ashok Row Kavi from Humsafar, some Sweekar parents like Chitra Palekar and the director Onir. It was nice to meet them all, of course, but what about the video for which we had assembled? Everyone was as clueless as I.

Outside, there was a dimly lit set with smoke machines on and multi-coloured lights piercing through the smoke. A few trippy set-ups were being assembled. In one, there was a vintage car in the background, in another, there was an umbrella suspended from the ceiling, and in a third, the words 'Love wins' were projected on to the dilapidated brick wall of the factory. The floor was mucky and slippery, and there were puddles of water everywhere. I was scared of tripping or falling and hitting my head on something. How would senior people like Ashok and Anjali manage, I wondered.

I tiptoed around a giant puddle to reach A. Sajeed, the director of the video, for a quick chat. Did he know any of the queer people he was going to shoot today? He didn't. Was he queer himself? He wasn't. Did he have any experience in working on queer issues? No, his experience was in making music videos and he had, in fact, got this project just a week ago. That explains the completely random set, I thought to myself. My final question: Was he being paid? Of course. Was his unit being paid? Of course.

You know who wasn't being paid? All of us queer people who were being featured in the video, who were contributing our free labour just so some agency could claim to be LGBTQ friendly. Some of the people featured in the video told me that they weren't offered transportation and had taken an Uber to the venue.

You know who else wasn't being paid? Humsafar Trust. I asked Vivek and Suhail, *thoda* angrily, why had they agreed to facilitate this production? None of us would have come had Humsafar not made the calls, right? At the very least, did the agency make a donation to Humsafar, I asked. No. Why then did Humsafar agree to be a part of this, I asked them again. The visibility, they told me. I was exasperated. I thought of Mona and her crumbs analogy, and begged the Humsafar team to not do things just for visibility any more.

I was persuaded to give my shot. I left immediately after, but I heard that the shoot wrapped up at around four in the morning. I don't think anyone who participated in it was happy with their experience.

When I saw the final product online on 15 August, I felt that the video would have been much nicer had some more thought gone into it and had the people the video was claiming to serve been valued in the making of it.

~

I was posing wearing a Levi's jacket for *Elle* magazine's June 2019 Pride Month special. Harish was beside me, and we wrapped up the shoot in ten minutes. We are such old hands at this. Here is how the magazine article introduced the Levi's sponsorship: 'In order to capture the zeitgeist and its accompanying optimism, we teamed up with Levi's, a brand that has long been associated with the importance of unleashing authentic self-expression, while speaking truth to power in a quest for absolute freedom—because nothing other than total equality is acceptable. June is International Pride month, so we wanted to celebrate and further drive home the message that we *all* belong, and that we are all proud, together.'[14]

When I saw the final article, I was not happy. Where was the 'all'? They had chosen six queer heroes of which five were gay men and one was a lesbian woman. Everyone else in the feature was a friend, so I have nothing against any of them—but couldn't the magazine have found at least one trans person? Someone who might be dalit and queer or Muslim and queer? The next time I got called for a media feature, I told the magazine honestly that I would not be doing this unless they got a wide range of queer people on board.

Levi's seemed to have gotten the memo. In November 2019, they released a much more inclusive campaign featuring Onir, Sushant Divgikar, Jyothi and Purushi from the Aravani Art Project, and the artist-poet Priyanka Paul.

Titled #ProudToBeMore, the campaign showcased evocative videos narrated by LGBTQ persons, telling their stories in their own words.[15]

When I spoke to Pride Circle's Ramkrishna Sinha, he brought up the food delivery app Zomato. In April 2019, one of the Zomato Gold restaurants had refused to serve a gay couple on a date.[16] The couple tweeted their outrage, and the tweet went viral. This was especially egregious, for in the flutter of ecstasy post the 377 judgement in 2018, Zomato had advertised, 'Let's get one thing straight, love is love,' with a rainbow-coloured burger graphic.[17] Internet outrage, activist tweets and a petition later, Zomato now marks LGBTQ-friendly restaurants with tags, for us queer folks to know where we can house our love and our purring hungry bellies (or six pack abs).[18]

~

Tokenism can come in many forms. It is not just restricted to the queer community. The writer Rachelle Bharathi Chandran wrote about tokenism and caste issues for *Round Table India* in 2018:

> Why it matters who tells our stories. It matters who has access to our stories and experiences. In the rush to be able to share our pain and experience, larger platforms which have a history of casteism either use money or fame to bait the marginalized to share their stories. But we need to ask ourselves, would having just one token Dalit, Adivasi, OBC person endorse a publication make it okay for these organizations to share our stories. Who benefits from it? ... Is it enough that they can engage in one-off conversations? Why are we still pushing for reservations in private sector? Isn't it because of this rigid refusal of publications in media who do nothing to reveal the caste of the people in their organizations but feel comfortable fronting a certain image of progressiveness. Allyship requires sacrifice, as the saying goes. The sacrifice required is to give up their caste positions of power. The sacrifice required is to transparently show how young 20-year old upper castes can run organizations that have immense following on social media and who want to do work on Dalit persons but don't reveal who funds it or don't reveal how they started because it will betray the social capital, connections and network they benefit from which DBA people so often lack. The sacrifice required is for upper caste *savarnas* to leave their comfort zones of caste bubble and privilege.[19]

Another form of tokenism is feigning intent and what I call 'panellitis'—talking a lot on panels but not converting it into anything concrete. Devdutt Pattanaik said from the stage in his cutting talk at RISE in Bengaluru,

'In India, *Natyashastra* is more popular than the Dharmashastra—talking is much easier than doing.'

Madhumitha Venkataraman echoed Devdutt when she spoke to me for this book. 'I am very clear when I am walking into an organisation that I am not keen on eating rainbow cakes or on fancy events. It is good to have fun, but I go to a workplace to do a good job and get a salary home, to live my life and to be promoted. I am saying this with so much confidence because it rings true with most people I have been an HR business partner to. The questions I hear from employees are along the lines of—why is my rating low this year, why am I not being sent on this training programme, why is my compensation not increasing, why am I not getting opportunities? Nobody comes and asks me—why haven't you had a panel discussion on this topic?

'It's good to have conversations at the top-management level, but it needs to go to other spaces that also matter. If you hire a transgender person, you need to understand their needs. What might matter to them is whether there's a washroom in the office, if they will have access to basic amenities, if they choose to opt for gender affirmation surgery, will it be a smooth process, will they be able to use email IDs with names of their choice? The main complaint I have heard, and the complaint continues to stay in the space of diversity and inclusion panels I have done, is that it becomes all about rainbows and flags, but when will it translate to on-ground change?'[20]

Dear companies, do remember that our LGBTQ community is watching you carefully as you woo us, either as customers or employees. We will celebrate you and put you on a wonderful rainbow pedestal when you do good, and make sure you course correct when you falter.

Part Five

QUEERISTAN

A CALL TO ACTION

Field notes from the frontlines of change. The concluding section of this book imagines a new world of possibilities and inclusion within India. It shows you how we are creating this world and are already living in it. It invites you to join in.

19

Queeristan

Other Worlds Are Possible

Every morning, I wake up to a new India. A country where you can open the *Times of India* on the morning of 17 May 2019 and see a gay couple on the front page, advertising the paper's 'Out and Proud' classified section. Inside, an announcement reads, '"As we approach our 15th year together, we want to thank our families and friends, straight and gay, for being by our side and making us feel like a normal couple."—Dr Prasad Dandekar, oncologist, and Shripad Ranade, leadership coach.'[1]

An India in which you can be browsing through *Vogue*'s November 2019 issue at the dentist's and see Dutee Chand, India's first out lesbian athlete, featured on the cover.[2] An India in which the constable Lalita Salve can rejoin the police force in Maharashtra as Lalit Salve, after completing his sex reassignment surgery, with the support of the state's chief minister.[3] An India in which Swati Bidhan Baruah is appointed Assam's first transgender Lokpal judge.[4] An India in which Sathyasri Sharmila becomes the first transgender lawyer to register with the Bar Council of Tamil Nadu and Puducherry.[5] An Indian in which M. Monisha becomes the first trans person to be appointed to a state secretariat, in Karnataka.[6] An India in which the state of West Bengal constitutes a trans development board with Manobi Bandyopadhyay, the first transgender principal of a college, as the vice chairperson.[7]

This is an India in which, at nationwide, student-led protests against the Citizenship Amendment Act, there is heart-warming solidarity across the anti-caste, feminist, queer and environmental protection movements. At one such spontaneous gathering at the Gateway of India the day after the horrific attack on JNU students on 5 January 2020, I was with a group of friends who were holding a 'Queers Against Discrimination' banner, and together we watched a bunch of young parents with their children on their shoulders dancing to the call of 'Jai Bhim', while two hijab-clad young women nearby handed out biscuits and water. Above us, a college student in a hoodie climbed a street lamp and waved the Indian flag. I took out my cell phone and clicked a picture that captured the sea beyond, the soft-lit arch of the Gateway and the ocean of love flowing beneath. There was a gentle breeze. It was hard to hold back the tears.

I am affectionately calling this new, inclusive, intersectional India 'Queeristan'. I am offering this idea of Queeristan as a redemptive force, as a unifying force, as a way of breaking through the binaries that are all around us and as an invitation to imagine alternative worlds. Other worlds are indeed possible. But before we live in a utopia, we have to first imagine it.

We are already living in the beginnings of Queeristan, as I have shown you in this book through the countless examples of people and organisations I have encountered in my work and through the story of my own professional life.

> Habitus is neither a result of free will, nor determined by structures, but created by a kind of interplay between the two over time: dispositions that are both shaped by past events and structures, and that shape current practices and structures and also, importantly, that condition our very perceptions of these. In this sense, habitus is created and reproduced unconsciously, without any deliberate pursuit of coherence ... without any conscious concentration.[8]

As Pierre Bourdieu says, we create more powerful representations of our ideal selves through the interplay of structure and agency. If structure is the world around us as it is, we can push for change by using our agency. The ensuing structural changes in turn will influence our agency. This cycle will lead to a new kind of normal. Queeristan encompasses this reimagination of the Indian society that is taking place all around us.

Is Queeristan a perfect space? As it comes up around us, will it replicate existing structures of inequality or find ways to dismantle them? I don't know. I certainly hope for the latter.

~

Let me quickly revise some key themes that you have encountered in the book. (Baba, last-minute revision is vital! Didn't you learn that from *Competition Success Review*?) First is the idea of Indian queerness as a polyphonous queerness, a circulatory queerness, an ever-evolving queerness due to the constant flow between its deep-rooted history and the many global influences. To me, what it means to be Indian and queer is to first realise that we are part of a long tradition of queerness and that throughout history, and even in our mythology, there was always space for queer ideas and identities. To be Indian is to be inclusive of queer people.

The second part of being Indian and queer, to me, is the deep connection with the idea of family. Queer children seek acceptance from their families, and many parents, including my own, have embraced their queer children. Being an inclusive parent is a very desi thing to do.

Actually, being an inclusive company is also a very desi thing to do. We often spend more time with our workplace families these days, and I have already made the case for why all of us in corporate India need to act in loco parentis—as guardians and custodians of our queer employees. Unlike in other parts of the world, Indian workspaces are vital crucibles of identity formation, spaces that should support queer employees to safely explore their selves. LGBTQ-inclusive workplace policies need to be about purposeful caregiving, because most often, workplaces are the only support systems queer employees have. So we have to go beyond being just good colleagues. We have to be good workplace family members.

I have done the math in this book, and it is very simple. Take both the above points—the deep-rootedness of queer inclusion in our culture and our family-orientedness, whether at home or at work. Add to it the extremely strong business case for LGBTQ inclusion—money, talent, innovation and reputation. What is the sum total? Correct answer! Being inclusive is a win-win proposition, whichever way you look at it.

I have shown you how you can do jugaad resistance through cultural acupuncture—from your location inside the system—and bring about a micro revolution both within and outside your organisation. What happens when you perform this cultural acupuncture? You create a new kind of space—Queeristan. By understanding the logic of Part Three of this book and following the steps in Part Four to make your company inclusive, you are becoming a co-creator of Queeristan.

~

Here are some of the components of the inclusive, intersectional Queeristan that I see coming up around me at this moment, giving me hope for the future.

In Queeristan, the Government Honours and Empowers Its LGBTQ Citizens

On 26 January 2019, India's seventieth Republic Day, fifty-four-year-old Narthaki Natraj created history. She became the first trans person in the country to receive the Padma Shri from the hands of the country's President. This is India's third-highest civilian honour, which she received for her accomplishments as a bharatanatyam dancer.[9]

While the national government acknowledged and honoured one of India's LGBTQ champions, many state governments have been doing more to not only acknowledge but also support queer people and the queer movement in various ways.

The Raipur Pride, held on 29 September 2019 amidst torrential rains in the state of Chhattisgarh, created a world record for the longest Pride flag—2.5 kilometres long. Sushant Divgikar, aka Rani KoHEnur, the guest of honour at the march, wrote this on his Facebook wall the next day: 'The youngest person attending was 4 and the oldest 86. Several schools and colleges sent volunteers to help ... If anyone had any preconceived notions about "smaller" cities not being inclusive, let me tell you Raipur is one of the safest cities for LGBTQIA+ people in India with huge support from the government as well as police officials.'[10]

The formation of the LGBTQ Chhattisgarh group in 2018 was an important catalyst for Raipur Pride, but equally important was the support of the state's progressive chief minister, Bhupesh Baghel.[11] In March 2019, he attended a mass wedding of fifteen transgender women in Raipur, arranged by trans activists. The prominent media coverage and government support for this event buoyed the organisers of LGBTQ Chhattisgarh, and they went ahead with Raipur Pride a few months later.[12]

Vidhya Rajput, a transgender activist in Raipur, helped the state's officials conduct a regional census of transgender Indians. She also persuaded the government to include sections about LGBTQ people in high-school textbooks, to donate 190 apartments to transgender people and to spend around US $22,000 on a project to recruit transgender police officers in 2017.[13] What's more, the progressive state government empowered her to lead sensitivity training for state employees, and officials in Chhattisgarh even supported transgender beauty contests and sporting events that Vidhya had organised.[14]

Just two weeks after Raipur Pride, on 16 and 17 November 2019, Kochi marked the tenth anniversary of Queer Pride Keralam, with a two-day celebration of dance, music and film, which preceded the Pride march.[15] Kerala is one of India's most progressive states in terms of LGBTQ rights, and the state government has been consistent in its efforts to create a better future for its queer citizens. In 2017, Adam Harry from Kerala became the first trans pilot in the country to get a private pilot license, and in October 2019, the state's Social Justice department sanctioned ₹2.3 million in scholarship for him to train as a commercial pilot at the Rajiv Gandhi Academy for Aviation Technology in Thiruvananthapuram.[16]

In the same month, in the neighbouring state of Karnataka, sixty-two-year-old Jogati Manjamma became the first trans woman to be appointed the chairperson of the Karnataka Janapada Academy, which is part of the state's Department of Kannada and Culture that works for the protection and conservation of folklore and the welfare of the state's folk artistes.[17]

In July 2019, yet another southern state, Tamil Nadu, laid the foundation for a hostel for transgender students in a school in the town of Trichy, which once completed could house forty gender nonconforming students thrown out of their homes by their families.[18] In December 2019, twenty-five-year-old Anbu Ruby became the first trans nurse to be hired by the state's Health and Family Welfare department. Anbu received her appointment order from the state's chief minister, Edappadi K. Palaniswami, and the health minister, C. Vijayabaskar. The latter told ANI news service that it was 'a very proud moment for the state'.[19]

In February 2019, the state government of Maharashtra announced that it was setting up a transgender welfare board. In an article in *Business Standard*, the Maharashtra social justice minister Rajkumar Badole was quoted as saying, 'The state government has accepted guardianship of this community and we will protect their rights.'[20]

Tamil Nadu, Kerala, Karnataka, Chhattisgarh, Maharashtra. The progressive moves by these states have to, and will, percolate horizontally to other states as well as vertically upwards to the centre.

~

When I ask the many young people I encounter to imagine Queeristan, they express it in terms of dreams and hopes they have for their particular states. In *Letters from Queeristan*, an oral history project from the Culture Lab in January 2019, young LGBTQ individuals from across India wrote about what it was like to grow up LGBTQ in their home state and their hopes for the future.[21]

Can you feel the hope that shines through in these excerpts from their letters below?

> *Sree, West Bengal*
> I dream of my beloved Paschim Banga (West Bengal) to be more open and more accepting so that no one feels uncomfortable about being who they are. I feel gender-neutral washrooms are the need of the hour. We know queer people face embarrassment in public restrooms when their gender is questioned. To avoid the embarrassment, they often avoid using the facilities, even at the cost of their health. I hope better healthcare is made accessible to queer people, especially in rural areas. May we all live with dignity.
>
> *Saniya Sood, model and MissTransQueen India 2018, Himachal Pradesh*
> Although simple and loving, people in Himachal are not very exposed to the outside world, and like everyone else they fear the unknown. My message to my home state is to accept and love every child, even if he or she may be different in their likes, choices, looks or opinions or have different dreams. I hope and dream for my state to be known not just for its natural beauty and loving people, but as a diverse and progressive state that accepts, loves and lets every child be who they wish to be. And when they grow up, no one should ever have to say that they had a rough childhood. Love is the answer to all your questions. Oh, my Himachal, my heart beats for you …
>
> *Sadam Sharma Hanjabam, founder, Ya-All Manipur*
> Born and raised in the border-conflicted state of Manipur, there was negligible focus given on queer issues. The state had bigger issues to deal with like insurgency, substance abuse, outbreak of HIV/AIDS and youth unemployment. There was neither an inclusive support system for queers who openly guided queer youths on their understanding of sexualities, nor did the government or society show any interest in discussing it. … In the coming years, we hope that agencies who work for inclusive growth and providing equal opportunities acknowledge the hidden and under-represented population (of Manipur) amidst the larger queer movement in the country.
>
> We respect the larger organizations outside the region that have worked hard to decriminalise homosexuality, but there is so much of work that needs to be done in Manipur and North East India. We need support and guidance. We would like to see our state as a safe space for queers where we don't have to migrate in search of acceptance, love, peace and dignity.

In Queeristan, different state governments as well as the national government will listen to the young voices of Sadam, Saniya, Sree and countless others.

In Queeristan, the Law Evolves to Safeguard the Interests of the LGBTQ Community

Okay, 377 is gone. Now what? In Queeristan, we move ahead from decriminalisation to the actual realisation of equality in every aspect of our lives. There is already some amazing work going on in this regard at places like the Centre for Law and Policy Research in Bengaluru and the Vidhi Centre for Legal Policy in Delhi.

Vidhi's new report *Queering the Law: Making Indian Laws LGBT+ Inclusive* analyses India's legal regime across the broad themes of 'identity', 'violence', 'family' and 'employment', post the Supreme Court's landmark decisions, to identify laws that either continue to operate in the male-female binary or discriminate against LGBTQ persons.[22] At the time I was writing this book, the Vidhi team was consulting lawyers and activists across the country to further add to the report, and I was delighted to conduct one such roundtable in January 2020 at the Culture Lab.

The report, a work in progress, suggests making changes to existing identity documents which either operate in the male-female binary and exclude transgender persons or violate the directives of the NALSA judgement. It also engages with existing debates around victim neutrality, the legal complexities post decriminalisation and neutrality in workplace harassment laws, and highlights the need for enacting a comprehensive anti-discrimination law that accounts for discrimination on the basis of both gender identity and sexual orientation. Finally, it also grapples with questions like whether inclusion should take place by facilitating LGBTQ persons' access to social institutions such as marriage or by other strategies such as spreading awareness on the value of caregiving and dependency outside of conventional relationships.

The International Commission of Jurists (ICJ), established in 1952, is a unique organisation made up of sixty eminent judges and lawyers from all over the world. Their aim is to develop and strengthen both national and international justice systems. In June 2019, ICJ came out with an extraordinary report, titled *Living with Dignity: Sexual Orientation and Gender Identity–Based Human Rights Violations in Housing, Work, and Public Spaces in India*, written by Maitreyi Gupta, the head of ICJ's India team, along with many other contributors.[23] The report makes some wonderful recommendations, and I urge you to read it in its entirety on the ICJ website.

To summarise some of these recommendations very briefly, the report urges the Parliament of India to enact a comprehensive anti-discrimination law in line with international law and standards and also amend the provisions in the Indian Penal Code on sexual assault, sexual harassment, disrobing, voyeurism, stalking, rape and gang rape to introduce gender neutrality for victims. It urges the central government of India to develop a uniform, accessible and understandable process for identity documentation for changing gender markers. It also urges both the state and central governments to ensure that all administrative bodies set up under them provide critical documents including birth certificates, graduation certificates, marksheets, passports, among others, in the applicant's preferred name and gender, without the need for proof of medical intervention, through a simple and accessible process. It further recommends that state and central governments conduct training programmes for all public services officers, including the police, in consultation with LGBTQ community organisations.

In Queeristan, all these vital recommendations from ICJ and reports such as the one from Vidhi would be implemented and become a reality. Given the problematic Transgender Persons (Protection of Rights) Bill, 2019, is now an act, this dream may seem like too much of a fantasy. But the struggle for our rights will continue. At the time of finishing this book, Swati Bidhan Baruah, Assam's first transgender judge, has challenged the Trans Act on the grounds that it is 'draconian' and 'humiliating',[24] and a gay couple from Kerala have moved the Kerala High Court, seeking to amend the Special Marriage Act, 1954, to include homosexual marriages in its ambit.[25]

Judgements like that of the Madras High Court from mid-2019 that recognised transgender people's right to marry allow us the space for hope. On 22 April 2019, the marriage between a cisgender man and a transgender woman was recognised by the Madras High Court. At the Madurai bench of the high court, Justice G.R. Swaminathan observed: 'A marriage solemnized between a male and a transwoman, both professing Hindu religion, is a valid marriage in terms of Section 5 of the Hindu Marriage Act, 1955, and the Registrar of Marriages is bound to register the same.'[26] He also added that in recognising this marriage the court was not breaking any new ground but merely stating the obvious. 'Sometimes to see the obvious, one needs not only physical vision in the eye but also love in the heart.'[27] What a beautiful sentiment! Thank you, Justice Swaminathan. Love in the heart is indeed the need of the hour. Let's hope for the 'love in the heart' of so many more judges in our country to come pouring out in Queeristan and express itself in the form of progressive verdicts in favour of the LGBTQ community.

In Queeristan, Politicians Across Party Lines Stand Up for Queer Rights

'Pink List India' is a list of candidates who contested the 2019 Lok Sabha elections and explicitly supported LGBTQ rights.[28] It was compiled by two former Culture Lab interns, Anish Gawande and Devina Buckshee, along with the designer Smriti Deora, and gives us much hope for the road ahead.

Anish, Devina and Smriti classified the candidates into different categories: The 'Trailblazers' category comprised LGBTQ people who have plunged into politics as Lok Sabha election candidates. These include M. Radha, Tamil Nadu's only transgender candidate, who contested from Chennai South as an independent, and Chirpi Bhawani, the Aam Aadmi Party's first transgender candidate, who contested from Prayagraj in Uttar Pradesh.[29] The 'Changemakers' and 'Outspoken Allies' categories included straight politicians who have spoken up for LGBTQ issues over the years. Here are the 'Pink List' citations for some of these supportive politicians:

Shashi Tharoor, Thiruvananthapuram, Kerala, Indian National Congress
One of India's LGBTQ+ ally superstars, and one of the most vocal supporters of queer rights on a national and international level, Tharoor has made the most audacious attempts at making LGBTQ+ rights a part of his national agenda. From writing articles to speaking at panels, from introducing not one but two bills for repealing Section 377 in the Lok Sabha to supporting the Transgender Persons Bill, he's been at the forefront of queer political activism in India.

HD Deve Gowda, Tumakuru, Karnataka, Janata Dal (Secular)
'Constitutional guarantees can't be denied to a section of the population just because they are a "minuscule minority" ... We will extend our support to repeal this outdated and draconian provision, brought to India more than 150 years ago by the colonial British rulers.' The former Prime Minister of India, in a letter after Section 377 was put back on the books by the Supreme Court, came out vocally in support of the LGBTQ+ community. He is the first Prime Minister of India to take a stand on queer rights!

Supriya Sule, Baramati, Maharashtra, Nationalist Congress Party
Has vocally supported the transgender community and worked towards making the NCP trans-inclusive. Moved amendments to the regressive Transgender Persons (Protection of Rights) Bill, 2016 in the Lok Sabha. 'Transgender Rights are Human Rights and Human Rights are Transgender Rights. Remembering all those who have lost their lives to Transgender Hate

and violence. Remember, gender identity is not a choice, Trans hate is!' she tweeted in 2018.

Gautam Gambhir, East Delhi, Bharatiya Janata Party
After Section 377 was decriminalised, Gautam Gambhir inaugurated the Hijra Habba in New Delhi. 'It's not about being a man or a woman. It's about being a HUMAN,' he tweeted after a Raksha Bandhan ceremony with transgender community members and activists in New Delhi in August 2018.

Kanimozhi, Thoothukudi, Tamil Nadu, Dravida Munnetra Kazhagam
First in her party to come out in support of the LGBT community. 'Personal choices we make in our lives should not be dictated by law—well done SC for this historic verdict,' she tweeted after Section 377 was decriminalised. 'The rights of #LGBTQ community are finally recognised and India has taken an important step towards fulfilling its universal human rights obligations. Hope we move towards a more liberal, tolerant and inclusive society,' she added.[30]

For all those who think that Indian politicians are not concerned about queer citizens, please read the comments above once again. Since the publication of the 'Pink List', there have been two significant queer political appointees. In January 2019, the Indian National Congress appointed a trans woman, Apsara Reddy, as the national general secretary of its women's wing, the All India Mahila Congress. In February 2019, Prakash Ambedkar–led Vanchit Bahujan Aghadi appointed the trans writer and poet Disha Pinky Shaikh as its spokesperson for Maharashtra.

As I told the president of the Mumbai Regional Congress Committee and former minister of state Milind Deora, at the launch of the Keshav Suri Foundation in Delhi in October 2018, we queer citizens are also voters, and given that we make up 4 to 10 per cent of the population, our votes are valuable. It's time to flip the equation, I added. Instead of us beseeching them to think of us favourably, it is in the interest of the country's politicians to reach out to us, understand our issues, serve us better as our elected representatives and then seek our valuable votes. More and more of our country's politicians, across party lines, would come to realise this in Queeristan.

In Queeristan, Parental Acceptance Is the New Normal

Samyuktha Vijayan joined Swiggy after working at Amazon for over nine years in different parts of the world—Chennai, Bengaluru, Luxembourg and Seattle. When I met her at the Out and Equal LGBTQ India Forum in Bengaluru in July 2018, she told me about the days of moving back and forth between these cities and recalled one particular incident that moved me to tears.

In May 2017, Samyuktha had come back to India to attend her younger brother's wedding. 'It was the first time when I got introduced to all my relatives as a woman,' she said. 'Because, until then, they had known me as a man. At the wedding, my mother proudly took me around telling everyone, "Hey, this is my daughter! Have you met my daughter?" It was such a wonderful feeling!'

That year, Samyuktha relinquished her US citizenship to return to India, with the aim of doing something for the betterment of the transgender community. She told me about the incident that triggered this decision to return. 'I was flying back to the US after a visit, and a sales lady at Sri Krishna Sweets at the Bengaluru Airport complimented me on my beauty. Then she told me that my voice was very rough and that I should have hot water with honey to open up my throat. When I told her that I was trans, she couldn't believe it. She confided in me that she had always thought that trans people could not have respectable lives or professional careers and would never have imagined encountering a trans person at an airport.

'This is when I realised how important it was for people to see beyond the stereotypes associated with transgender women in India. I felt that it didn't make sense for me to sit comfortably back in the US. Things were too easy there. On Friday, I could go to work at Amazon as Santhosh, my older self, and on Monday I could return as Samyuktha, and there was no problem. I decided to come back and make a difference in India.'

'What did you parents say about you giving up your Green Card?' I asked in shock, my own decision of returning to India years ago lingering at the back of my mind. 'My mother was just so happy,' Samyuktha said. 'You see, for my parents, Bangalore and the US are all the same. It just means that your child is away from you. Now that I am in India, they can come and live with me whenever. She was just so happy about that.'[31]

My twenty-one-year-old friend Aditya Tiwari has a similar story. He is out to his family, lives with them happily in Jabalpur in Madhya Pradesh and has just published his first book of poems *April Is Lush*.[32] In December 2019, he visited Mumbai for the first time as part of a youth delegation for the Humsafar Trust's Likho programme, and he told me over dinner about how his parents' acceptance had empowered him to create his own queer-friendly universe in Jabalpur. He had come to dinner wearing full make-up, and when

I complimented him on his appearance, he nonchalantly revealed that his father had got him the mascara he was wearing, and that, in fact, his parents often bought his make-up for him.

In Queeristan, we will hear more and more stories like Samyukta's and Aditya's. Their families, without making a big deal of the sexuality or gender of their children, are focusing on love and inclusion. Yes, parental acceptance is the new normal in Queeristan.

In Queeristan, Inclusion Starts Early, in Schools and Colleges

Delhi's Tagore International School has a landmark campaign called Breaking Barriers—on LGBTQ rights, awareness and sensitisation—that was launched in 2013. Vedica Saxena, the current project director at Tagore International, told me in December 2019 that they've so far reached out to over 3,500 students and more than 30 schools in 7 years through their sensitisation workshops. 'Every year, we have students from class nine to class twelve joining Breaking Barriers as volunteers. Currently, we have about 30 dedicated and passionate volunteers who work on all the campaigns. None of the work is teacher-driven. Through intensive training, our students are very well aware of what it means to be LGBTQ, the history, the legal aspects. We conduct hour-long sessions on gender sensitisation which include talks on gender roles, sexual orientation, the difference between gender and sex, media portrayal of the LGBTQ community, how transgender history has existed since the beginning of time, the Mughal empire, about Khajuraho temple and its carvings. We also conduct gender sensitisation workshops with teachers from nursery to class five.

'Throughout the year, we invite speakers from the community to share their knowledge and experience with us. We have hosted Prince Manvendra, Miss TransQueen beauty pageant founder Reena Rai, YouTuber Amrita Singh and academic Vqueeram Aditya Sahai. These talks are open for everyone in the school to attend. Next year onwards, we plan to introduce the concept of gender fluidity among the younger lot in classes three, four and five.

'Our larger aim is to reach out to other schools and motivate them to start something like this and also become inclusive. We have visited Doon Public School, DAV School, Shiv Nadar School in both Gurgaon and Noida. We have also reached out to government schools like Ramjas and Maharaja Agrasen. We partnered with the radio station Red FM for a ten-day mini campaign where our students went live every day on the radio station and talked about bullying. We also visited a different school each day with the RJ team for conducting sensitisation workshops.'

The radically inclusive agenda of Tagore International School would not have been possible without the wholehearted support of the parents. Vedica told me, 'When we started in 2013, we sent out letters and circulars to parents clearly informing them that we are going to start something like this in our school. None of them reverted with a negative response because they know what we believe in and what we stand for; that's how we go forward.'[33]

In September 2018, I read an article in the *Indian Express* about the creation of India's first gender-neutral hostel at TISS in Mumbai. 'Rainbow-coloured flags, scarves and posters adorn the walls of most of the 10 two-seater rooms occupied by transgender, gender non-conforming students and their allies.' The article goes on to describe how earlier, in 2018, TISS had given graduating students the option to choose from the titles 'Ms', 'Mr' or a gender-neutral 'Mx' in their certificates, and quotes Asha Bano, the dean of student affairs, as saying: 'The hostel is a collective effort by students, faculty and administration. It was a felt demand by students that was put forth to the administration through the union.'[34]

Isn't it wonderful to see how school and college authorities, teachers, students and parents are collectively creating these nurturing spaces? In Queeristan, schools like Tagore International and colleges like TISS will be the norm and not the exception.

Sparks of change are already visible at the level of individual schools and colleges as well as at a broader level of educational boards in different states like Chhattisgarh and Maharashtra, which have included trans rights in their curricula. Chhattisgarh schools have introduced chapters on what it means to be transgender in their curriculum for classes six to ten.[35] In Maharashtra, the class eleven sociology textbook includes single parents and same-sex families. The textbook published by the state's publishing bureau, Balbharti, was introduced in the academic year 2019–2020 as part of the curriculum revision exercise for class eleven.[36] Hoshang Merchant has been including queer texts in his literature classes at the University of Hyderabad since the mid-1980s, and R. Raj Rao has been teaching his 'LGBT Writing in India' course at the University of Pune since 2007. In 2015, Delhi's Ashoka University started its path-breaking Centre for Studies in Gender and Sexuality, with a focus on scholarly research combined with activism and outreach, and one of the many programmes they conduct is the monthly 'Issues in Society, History and Queerness' lecture series.[37]

On the International Day Against Homophobia, Biphobia, Intersexism and Transphobia in May 2019, Keshav Suri launched a children's book series featuring Elphie—the Lalit's elephant mascot dressed in rainbow colours, designed to be gender non-binary. These stories aim to sensitise children as well as parents to concepts of gender fluidity, inclusivity and diversity. Keshav launched the *Elphie* book series with the unique concept of Drag Queen Story Hour at their hotel properties across the country, during which fabulous drag queens from Kitty Su read out stories from *Elphie*,[38] and the books are kept in the room of every Lalit property in the country.

Twenty-six-year-old LGBTQ activist Ankit Bhuptani has been working to provide support to children in their vulnerable adolescent years through the non-profit VIDYA. Ankit is the founder of the India chapter of the Gay and Lesbian Vaishnava Association (GALVA) and the convener of the Queer Hindu Alliance, a collective which provides consultation and assistance on understanding homosexuality to faith leaders as well as to families of queer Hindus. He told me about his work at VIDYA:

'Most of the work done in LGBTQ rights by NGOs targets people who are eighteen and above. When a child discovers their sexuality, maybe between the sixth to ninth grade, there's no help available, not till they are eighteen years old. For a child to face rejection in the form of not being allowed to sit on their preferred bench because of their sexuality or being bullied by teachers, it creates a lot of emotional pain that is very difficult to overcome later. Personally, I felt it is very important to talk about LGBTQI when the child discovers it, so that they don't consider themselves as lesser than others.

'This is also when bullying starts. If your gender expression is different, then bullying is directed at you. It's not like how they show it in US television shows. It happens in slums, in municipal schools, every place that the child occupies, but no one really talks about it. Often, the child will give up on studying. Now, because it's a two-fold issue where there's marginalisation because of both queerness and class, it is often assumed that the latter is responsible for the child dropping out. It is not seen as a case of homophobia, but of class disparity.

'Over and above this, a child may face severe mental health issues, and the rejection and bullying might lead to suicidal tendencies. We must avoid that at all costs, and my work at VIDYA is dedicated to these causes.

'Along with working for LGBTQ children, I also do teacher training, both through VIDYA, where we have sensitised around fifty teachers, and also through independently hosted workshops, in my own capacity, through which I have reached out to seventy teachers. I also reach out to municipal-run schools in Maharashtra and Gujarat, under the guise of doing a diversity workshop or a peace-building and social justice lecture, and then I make it about LGBTQ rights and inclusion. This is how I've been able to be invited into spaces that might not be so welcoming initially of discourse around LGBTQ.'[39]

Do you see how Ankit is performing his own version of cultural acupuncture? While I admire Ankit's ingenuity, I also want to acknowledge the schools and colleges he works with for having been open to these workshops. The Padma Shri awardee Narthaki Nataraj told the media that whenever she was invited to speak to young students, she used the occasion to sensitise them to inclusion. 'They see me as a star and an inspiration. I stand as an answer to their question for the gender identity crises. There may be children among them who might be facing the same situation as I did. I did not have any exposure or an example to look up to. But today, these kids have me, and they will understand that it's not wrong if their classmate or a friend behaves more like their opposite gender.'[40]

In Queeristan, There Is an Explosion of Positive Media About Our Queer Lives and Experiences

Weekday mornings are quite crazy in our home. While my partner takes his shower, I run around getting his tiffin dabba ready, laying out his clothes on the bed and making sure his shoes are all shiny. (Yes, I'm very gharelu that way. Total pati-parmeshwar type, although given my name, he should be doing my seva, right? Let it be now. *Jo hai so hai.*)

Finally, we have our bowls of granola and milk together over ten minutes of quality time before he leaves to catch his train. Can I tell you a secret? We do something very bad in this quality time. We watch TV as we eat. No, we don't watch the news! It's 2020, darlings. There's Twitter for that. Instead, we watch our guilty pleasure—gay TikTok video compilations beamed from his phone on to our TV screen in the living room.

TikTok, as you might know, is an app owned by the Chinese start-up ByteDance. As of May 2019, it had 200 million users in India as compared to Facebook's 300 million, and is growing much more rapidly than Facebook in our country.[41] The writer Snigdha Poonam explains the compelling nature of TikTok, in her 2019 essay in the *1843 Magazine* from the *Economist*:[42] 'Unlike YouTube, its videos are a maximum of a minute long, although many are much shorter. This encourages its users, predominantly teenagers and twenty-somethings, to catch people's attention as quickly as possible: the sillier or more extreme the stunt, the better. When you open the app, the first thing you see is not what people you follow have posted, but a video that is currently going viral, in an algorithm-powered feed called "For You". If you enjoy it, you can double-tap to "like" it, like on Instagram, or follow the user—actions which bump it up to the top of other people's "For You" feed. If you're bored by it, you swipe up to see the next video. The longer people spend watching videos, the higher up the charts they climb. You could describe TikTok as an unholy marriage between Instagram, YouTube and Tinder. It has taken the most addictive components from each of them and used them to create a platform that is hard to look away from.'

Snigdha elaborates, 'TikTokers don't need a fancy phone, camera skills, editing software or fast internet. All they have to do is fill up 15 seconds with something people can't stop watching. These lower barriers to entry mean that TikTok influencers come from a wider variety of backgrounds than influencers on other platforms. A quarter of TikTok's global downloads come from India, compared with just 10% of Instagram users. ... Many of India's TikTok stars live in small towns or villages, have either never made it to college or dropped out, and speak their vernacular language.'

In February 2020, an article in *Mint* talked about the pervasiveness of TikTok across the country—from brands like the e-commerce platform Flipkart that ran a campaign called #BigBillionStar which got sixteen billion views and Pepsi's #SwagStepChallenge that got fifty-two billion views, to organisations like the central government's National Skill Development Corporation which partnered with TikTok to educate its users about its government-driven skill development programmes and vocational training opportunities.[43]

TikTok is so popular in India that there are now YouTube channels completely dedicated to tracking TikTok stars. My partner and I are huge fans of the brilliant cross-dressing sassy queen @jigarrathod169, and as we watch Jigar's captivating videos and also those of others, we often stop mid-breakfast and turn towards each other in total awe at how the app is being creatively co-opted by small town and rural Indian youth to perform queerness.[44]

Just consider the range of representations made in the video compilation 'Friendships in TikTok Part 12' that premiered on the YouTube channel Entertaining Video on 14 November 2019.[45] Most of the clips have Bollywood songs as their background. In each clip, the cell phone camera captures male couples using a range of popular TikTok visual tropes to demonstrate their affection for each other. The lip synch, the comedy sketch, the split screen, the selfie-stick camera angle, the pan shot, the camera running along with the performer, the heart and star filters—it is all there! The men are constantly kissing and hugging each other. The first flush of love. Domestic bliss. Fights. Jealousy. All the possible heteronormative scenarios are performed to perfection.

Some of these men have facial hair, as is the fashion these days, courtesy Virat Kohli and the Indian cricket team, while others are clean shaven. Some are older, but most of them are young. There is a wide range of body types on display. You could pass any of these men in the street without realising that they are online superstars. This complete normalcy is what excites my partner and me. The TikTok video backgrounds also interest us. These videos are shot in regular homes. There are kitchens with utensils piled up in the sink. Dorm rooms with messed-up blankets and piles of books. Bathrooms where men are wiping their heads with a towel together after a shower. Sometimes, the videos are shot in public places in the towns that the TikTok stars are from, a park or a parking lot, spaces that are full of knowing bystanders, hyper-aware that a TikTok is being shot.

In one of my favourite videos, the camera first zooms in on a man's abs being caressed by a sprig of flowers, then goes wide for the frame to include his male partner, as they embrace and seductively dance together. In another, the soundtrack is that of the *Karan Arjun* title song that was originally pictured on the veteran actress Rakhee Gulzar crooning about her two sons: '*Yeh bandhan toh pyaar ka bandhan hai*.' The on-screen video shows two shirtless men under the sheets in a bedroom!

While the videos I have described above feature gay men, Aniket Chitnawis, who works at BuzzFeed India, has started compiling a Twitter thread of diverse queer Indian TikTok videos, and it's great fun to go through these.[46]

I read this TikTok co-option by queer Indian youth as a form of mimicry and hybridity—to use two popular terms from the cultural theorist Homi Bhabha.[47] I started this chapter by saying that we first need to imagine Queeristan and then live in it. I see the different acts of heteronormative mimicry being performed by the men in the videos as both a homage to heteronormative romance as well as the articulation of a radical queer agenda. Over the course of repeated viewing, and because there are so many of these videos being produced and circulated, this performed queerness gets delinked from the heteronormative homage it started off as and becomes valid on its own terms.

I consider this ubiquitous normalisation of queer desires to be super exciting. We are no longer a 'miniscule minority'. Through TikTok, we are showing ourselves and being seen all across India, with every right swipe.

~

Just a few years ago, playing a queer character was something that only a bold Manoj Bajpai would have taken on, like when he portrayed the real-life Dr Siras in the 2015 biopic *Aligarh*.[48] Today, some of the biggest stars in the country are lining up to play explicitly queer characters on-screen. Here, I am thinking of Ayushmann Khurrana who plays a gay man in Bollywood's *Shubh Mangal Zyada Saavdhan*,[49] Akshay Kumar who plays a trans woman in *Laxmmi Bomb*,[50] Vijay Sethupathi who portrays a trans woman in the Tamil hit *Super Deluxe*,[51] Jayasurya who portrays the journey of a trans woman after her gender reassignment surgery in the Malayalam film *Njan Marykutty*,[52] and Nivin Pauly who plays a gay character, quite naturally, in the critically and commercially acclaimed Malayalam film *Moothon*.[53] I have already written about Sonam Kapoor playing a lesbian in the 2019 *Ek Ladki Ko Dekha Toh Aisa Laga*.[54]

These films are just the tip of the iceberg. There are going to be lots more. Also, from ridicule or humour or tragedy, our queer mainstream storylines have become much more nuanced. Love, parenting, self-actualisation—these are just some of the themes that the films listed above explore.

The commercial success of *Shubh Mangal Zyada Saavdhan,* in early 2020, is going to be a huge instigator in the production of more mainstream queer-positive content. I can't tell you how wonderful it felt, sitting in a cinema hall with my partner and having the audience all around us laugh at the homophobic family in the film, not at the gay characters. 'When did you realise you were straight?' Ayushmann's character asks his partner's uncle in one scene, in a reversal of the trite and patronising question queer people are often asked about when we 'came to know' about our sexuality.

When the two heroes kissed on-screen, perhaps within the first ten minutes of the film starting, I held my partner's hand tightly in anxiety, but no one, I repeat, no one in the audience booed or hooted. Instead, the derision was reserved for the dad character, who couldn't accept his child for being who he was and was trying to 'cure' him by doing absolutely ridiculous things like organising a name-changing ceremony. In a key moment in the film, Ayushmann's character wears the rainbow flag as a cape and shouts from the rooftop of his partner's home that his partner's father has a disease and the name of the disease is homophobia.

At the end of the film, as the two heroes finally got on to the train together, to live happily ever after of course, everyone around us clapped. Then we all trooped out of the cinema humming Bappi Lahiri's 'Yaar Bina Chain Kahan Re' that was being performed by the film's entire star cast during the closing credits, in the most camp and glitter-filled rendition possible.

Yes, Indian audiences are changing, and our filmmakers have realised this.

A key inflection point in this explosion of mainstream queer content has been the opening up of digital and online platforms like ALTBalaji, Netflix and Amazon. Kukoo, a trans woman character in Netflix's 2018 *Sacred Games*, is monumental,[55] as are ALTBalaji's eponymous gay couple Romil and Jugal in the 2017 series by the same name[56] and the lesbian couple Umang and Samara in the 2019 Amazon Prime series *Four More Shots Please*, a *Sex and the City* rip-off.[57] YouTube is fertile ground for queer content too. The 2016 Kannada web series *The Other Love Story* that features two lesbian protagonists found huge audiences.[58] So did *All About Section 377*, released in the same year, and its 2018 sequel *Still About Section 377*.[59]

The National Award–winning filmmaker Apurva Asrani—an out and proud gay man who worked as editor on the *Made in Heaven* Amazon Prime web series that features a gay wedding planner as one of its lead characters[60]—writes, '[Director] Zoya [Akhtar] had asked me to read the script and give her feedback. I remember reading the script at midnight and bursting into tears. When Sid, my partner, asked me if I was crying because the story made me sad, I turned to him and said, "No, I'm crying because I'm happy." We are finally telling our stories.'[61]

The digital platforms have broadened the contours not only for the production of new queer content but also for the recirculation of old, overlooked content. So *Do Paise Ki Dhoop, Chaar Aaney Ki Baarish* from 2009,[62] which features a group of people—a gay man, a commercial sex worker and her disabled son—who have come together as a family, can now be streamed widely and appreciated. We can watch *Evening Shadows*, Sridhar Rangayan's 2018 film about a son coming out to his mother on a road trip,[63] alongside the 2016 *Dear Dad*, which reverses the gaze and has a gay father who comes out to his high-school-going son on a road trip.[64] Both these films disappeared from our cinemas in a flash, but online, they have a much longer life.

The actor Huma Qureshi spent a day with me and my team at our Culture Lab in November 2019. She was playing a lesbian character in director Dibankar Banerjee's next project, for a digital platform, and I was impressed at how eager both Dibankar and Huma were to gather my point of view as well as that of my queer colleagues at the lab. At around the same time, the filmmaker Ashim Ahluwalia told me that he was making a cinematic version of R. Raj Rao's novel *The Boyfriend*,[65] while Sachin Kundalkar called me excitedly to share that he was adapting his own Marathi queer novel *Cobalt Blue* into a feature film, again for a digital platform.[66]

~

As someone who has been seeing and curating Indian queer cinema over the years, I am also thrilled at how we queers are becoming better at telling our own stories. I just have to look back at my favourite Indian short films from Kashish over the years, all of which offer compelling, rich, textured narratives of being queer and Indian in settings that span rural as well as urban India.

The National Award–winning *Daaravtha: The Threshold*, a 2016 film by Nishant Roy Bombarde, is a simple story about a confident, young boy Pankaj, who is different from his peers because of his love for dance, henna and jewellery.[67] Pankaj has a massive crush on his next-door neighbour, an older boy studying in his school, who is cast in the annual-day dance alongside him. *Daaravtha* is also a story about parenting. What does it mean to be a parent and love your child when they are different from what you might have expected? The fact that Pankaj is comfortable in his skin frees his mother to rethink her own life, dreams and aspirations.

In Rohan Parashuram Kanawade's *U Ushacha* that released in 2019, Usha, a single mother and farm labourer in Maharashtra, encounters the new English primary school teacher assigned to her village.[68] As Usha starts taking English tuitions from the teacher, love blossoms between the two women. Both *Daaravtha* and *U Ushacha* are in Marathi. We have been craving films like these for years, and, finally, they are here, in Queeristan.

Rohin Raveendran Nair's 2019 short film *The Booth* is a tender love story between an older woman who works as a security guard at the entrance of an urban Indian shopping mall and a younger woman (perhaps college-going) who spends all day ambling around the mall, waiting to go back into the security booth and get frisked again.[69] In those moments inside the booth, sparks fly between the two women. The mall and, by extension, the urban cityscape that surrounds it are an impersonal and alienating space, but also a space of possibilities, where attraction can overcome the barriers of class and age for a few stolen moments.

This desperate clinging for connection is something that Faraz Ansari also explores evocatively in his 2018 silent short film *Sisak*.[70] It plays out as an operatic love story of attraction between two men who meet each other regularly on a Mumbai local. As their hands come closer to each other on the handle of the compartment door one evening, the music reaches its crescendo, and one gets goosebumps. Faraz's next film is *Sheer Qorma*, a lesbian Muslim love story that stars heavy-hitting Bollywood actresses like Shabana Azmi, Swara Bhaskar, Divya Dutta and Surekha Sikri.[71]

All the above are fictional films. A multitude of queer Indian documentary films about our experiences are also being made and shown each year. The 2018 *Yeh Freedom Life* was filmed by Priya Sen over the course of a year in Ambedkar Nagar, a dense, largely working-class area in South Delhi.[72] It shows us the two very different worlds of its protagonists, Sachi and Parveen. Sachi works at a local beauty parlour; Parveen runs the family's small cigarette counter at a crowded intersection. They are both in love with other women. The film is as much about their lives as it is about metropolitan Delhi. In a similar vein, *Please Mind the Gap*—released in 2019 and also set in Delhi—chronicles the life of Anshuman, a trans man who commutes in the Delhi Metro every day and negotiates the public perception of his gender identity.[73]

In Queeristan, Various Books Chronicle Our Multifaceted Lives

There is a rich body of queer Indian literature by now. Instead of giving you a comprehensive listing, I am going to take you on a selective ride through some of my favourite books.

To me, non-fiction books like the anthology *Out!* edited by Minal Hajratwala and released in 2012 at the Culture Lab[74] or the Ashwini Sukthankar–edited, path-breaking 1999 anthology *Facing the Mirror: Lesbian Writing from India*[75] should be part of every queer canon, among a long list of other titles that would typically include R. Raj Rao's novels, Hoshang Merchant's memoirs as well as Ruth Vanita's and Saleem Kidwai's historical research. I would also add Amruta Patil's dark, dreamy and sexy *Kari* to this list. 'Whatever love laws have to be broken, the first few seconds suffice. After that everything is a matter of time and incident.'[76] Hailed as India's first lesbian graphic novel in 2008, it is both a love story—between the protagonist Kari and her girlfriend Ruth—as well as Kari's individual exploration of what it means to live in, love in and form bonds of intimacy with Mumbai.

Of late, there have been many powerful autobiographies by hijra writers like Priya Babu's *Naan Saravanan Alla*,[77] Living Smile Vidya's *I Am Vidya*[78] and A. Revathi's *The Truth About Me: A Hijra Life Story*[79] that have expanded the queer Indian literary canon.

A celebrated trans activist and the former director of the queer NGO Sangama, Revathi became a lit-fest sensation when *The Truth About Me* was published in 2010. She wrote with unflinching honesty about her childhood, her life in a hijra community and her journey of becoming her own self. In her second book, *A Life in Trans Activism*, I was especially thrilled to read the personal stories of Mookan, Charu, Kiran, Sonu, Christy, Satya and Gee, seven trans men she had invited to be a part of her narrative, who tell their stories in their own words.

Towards the end of the book, Revathi writes: 'My prime concern is that the next generation of transgender people should not go through what I have undergone. ... No legislation can restore the lost lives of trans people of my generation. Can I go back to being a twelve-year old? Can I live the life I longed for? Twenty years back, I wanted to be a lawyer. Is that possible? But for the present and future generations of trans people, I dare to dream of an equitable and accepting world—a world in which legislation and acceptance mutually support each other.'[80]

Revathi's was one of the voices that editors Arvind Narrain and Gautam Bhan had invited to contribute to their important 2005 anthology *Because I Have a Voice: Queer Politics in India*.[81] Many of the people you have encountered in *Queeristan*, like Devdutt Pattanaik, Ali Potia, Pawan Dhall, Sandip Roy and Maya Sharma, were also contributors to this anthology.

While writing this book, I re-read some of my favourite books like Maya Sharma's 2013 *Loving Women: Being Lesbian in Unprivileged India*, which documents the stories of ten working-class queer women, and in doing so, dispels the myth that all lesbians in India are urban or that they belong to the upper and middle classes. In the book's introduction, Maya writes that 'one after the other, these stories remind us that in the midst of intersecting oppressions, each of our subjects is a political radical, a cultural rebel and a potential/actual agent for sexual autonomy and social change.'[82]

When I read this sentence about cultural rebels by Maya, I was reminded of the 2019 anthology *Gulabi Baaghi*, which I enjoyed greatly.[83] The book brings together deeply personal recollections by queer social rights activists like its Hyderabad-based editor Owais, Kolkata-based trans woman Ranjita Sinha and Mumbai-based trans man Siddhant More. Many of these narratives in the book would be inaccessible without translation. Siddhant's story, for instance, first appeared in the Bindumadhav Khire–edited Marathi collection *Antarang: Samalingi Mula Mulincha Atmakatha*, or *Anthology of True Stories of Lesbians and Gays*, in 2013.[84]

In non-fiction, there are wonderful essays that explore the intersection of caste, class and sexuality, like Dhrubo Jyoti's 'A Letter to my Lover(s)', part of the 2018 intersectional anthology *Eleven Ways to Love*. Here is a powerful passage from the essay:

> You see, caste taught me everything I knew about sexuality, it was the bank from which this currency flowed. It taught you everything too, but you had denial and I had Ambedkar. When I came out, your friends asked me how I spoke such good English, wore good clothes or had a good job. I laughed, Ambedkar had warned me. So I didn't panic.
>
> You know, many of us don't think we deserve happiness. Caste broke our hearts and love cannot put them back together. Your forefathers taught us that our skins were blighted, our bodies foul and our colours dark. We have long memories—your forefathers crossing rivers on full-moon nights, armed with sticks, torching our huts, raping my foremothers. Our relationship with feeling less than human spans centuries. What is our love in front of this?
>
> When I first saw your gorgeous, luminous smile on my phone, I knew that my desire had already been fixed by caste. I had been trained to know what good looks are (brahmin), what good queerness is (English-speaking), and what attractive background is (urban rich). You were casteless because you had all of these. I just had my ankles.
>
> You know, I have loved this past month because I don't know your caste, or you mine. But I worry that when we lie in bed together, I will fear how much you will recoil from my body if you knew my caste, or whether you are already recoiling because you already do.
>
> And if we aren't ever to meet after that, will you do something for me? Will you buy me a pair of shorts, the cream-coloured flower patterned ones you are wearing?[85]

When it comes to queer fiction, while I have loved recent books like Sandip Roy's Calcutta-to-California family opus *Don't Let Him Know* and Amrita Mahale's post-liberalisation, nostalgic *Milk Teeth*, lovingly set in the Matunga suburb of Mumbai, I am drawn more and more to stories from non-urban or small-town India, translated into English from other languages. The celebrated artist Bhupen Khakhar's rare collection of Gujarati short stories (translated into English in 2001) is something that I have kept going back to for years, not only for the brilliant writing but also for the illustrations of male intimacy, done by Bhupen himself, that accompany the stories. How naturally he draws his male lovers, who embrace each other, bespectacled, with grey hair and sagging skin, a lifetime of experience in their eyes, and how tenderly he writes about his queer universe of Baroda in the 1970s. It is a universe that is populated by Gujarati characters like Maganbhai, Manilal, Sunderlal and Jeevanlal, and rife with the desire for sweet-smelling 'phoren soap'.[86]

The 2013 translation into English by Jerry Pinto of Sachin's *Cobalt Blue* hit me—to use an obvious metaphor here—like a bolt from the blue, when I first encountered it. The simple story of young love and loss is poised on a knife's edge of yearning-heartbreak-hope. It's our very own desi *Call Me By Your Name*, set in a middle-class Maharashtrian family in Pune, although *Cobalt Blue* was released a year before André Aciman released his novel. In this slim, sparse book, Sachin paints us a world that is familiar and intimate, with monsoons, Ganpati visarjan, board exams and marriage preparations, serving as the background score to the inner monologues of Tanay, a homosexual man, and Anuja, his heterosexual sister, who are both seduced and then abandoned by the paying guest who moves into their home. Here is a passage from the book that always has me in tears when I read it, just as Dhrubo's letter does:

> It's recently come to my attention that when I'm listening to someone, I cock my head. On the phone, I hold the receiver between my head and shoulder as Anuja does, playing a rhythm on the table in front of me. When I watch a film, I run my fist over my face, as Shrikrishna used to. When I shave, I bring my face close to the mirror as Baba does. When the milk boils over, I walk to the gas calmly, turn it off and wipe the counter down, without a word—as Aai does.
>
> How did I acquire these habits? Perhaps that's what happens during the forging of a relationship if nothing else, you adopt some of the other person's habits. It makes you feel those small adaptations, those adoptions, make him one of you.
>
> Have you picked up some habits from me? Do you draw circles with a finger on your thali when you've finished eating? Do you, every once in a while, squeeze shaving cream on your toothbrush. Do you sleep with a knee drawn to you, the bedclothes kicked away?[87]

A book like *Mohanaswamy*, which had a huge impact on queer people in Karnataka, was also transformational to my understanding of Indian queerness. The book's celebrated author, Vasudhendra, is the only out gay Kannada author today. He wrote thirteen books that dealt with non-queer subjects before writing *Mohanaswamy* as a semi-autobiographical tale about a gay man from rural Karnataka. The book's publication in Kannada in 2013 created quite a storm. Again, I am grateful that it was translated from Kannada to English by Rashmi Terdal and released in 2017, so that non-Kannada readers could also enter Mohanaswamy's world.[88]

From Karnataka to Jharkhand. *My Father's Garden*, the fourth novel by Hansda Sowvendra Shekhar, was on the shortlist for the JCB Literature Prize in 2019. Hansda is from the advisai Santhal community and he writes extensively about his adivasi background in all his books. When I met Hansda in Jaipur on the sidelines of the JCB Prize event in 2019, he told me that he was a qualified medical doctor and continues to work as a medical officer with the government of Jharkhand, in Pakur, where, incidentally, a part of *My Father's Garden* is set. This dual life—writer and doctor—adds a rich texture to his writing.

My Father's Garden is divided into three sections, titled 'Lover', 'Friend' and 'Father', and each section deals with a different aspect of toxic masculinity. Like with *Mohanaswamy*, what makes the novel special is its attention to detail and a description of a milieu that I have never encountered in queer Indian literature before.

Consider this excerpt, which Hansda ends the first chapter with:

> I wanted Samir, entire. Not his words but him. His body, his breath, his entire being. I wanted a completion that I would find nowhere, with no one. I was meant to sink, I was sinking. As I made my way back to Pakur, I found myself crying on the train. I was tortured by my inability to tell my parents about my choices, by the thought of the pain and disappointment I would cause them if I spoke the truth, by my inability to accept what I did not want to accept. All of it, everything that I felt and was yet to feel, was flowing out of my eyes. I must have known a storm was coming, because I had worn dark glasses that morning. And I took care to see that my face did not contort. I made no sound. The group of hijras came into the coach I was in. They came near my seat but did not ask me for money. Maybe they still remembered that I was a regular passenger. Maybe they recognized me despite the shades on my eyes. Something came to my mind then: I took out my wallet and handed over the first currency note I could grab. I realized that it was a hundred-rupee note only when a hijra began counting change. They held ninety rupees before me. Ten rupees was what they took from people. I looked at the money but did not look up, afraid

> that they might see me crying. 'No, keep it all,' I said. 'Should I?' 'Yes.' The hijra was perhaps surprised, but they took the note. At a connecting station, I was standing near an Uber pick-up point. A driver passed me by lugging two huge bags. A young woman followed him. She had a bag slung from her shoulder and was dragging a large suitcase with wheels. Following that woman was a couple: a man and a woman, frail with age, walking slowly, cautiously. The man was holding the arm of the woman and it was hard to tell who was supporting whom. It was a reality I felt I could only aspire to, growing old with someone whom I could trust. Who would offer me an arm when I was sixty? Whom would I offer mine? Standing beside that Uber pick-up point I felt like bawling my heart out. My parents' faces flashed in my mind, Samir's face flashed in my mind. Time passes and things get better; wounds heal and some things are forgotten. After four months, I had some official work in Jamshedpur, after which I was going back home. I boarded the train. Once again, I couldn't find a vacant seat so I stood near a door. The same group of hijras passed me, asking people for money. I immediately took out my wallet, though they hadn't asked me for money, and handed over a ten-rupee note to the hijra standing close to me. It was the same hijra I had given the hundred-rupee note to. I wasn't crying this time. I wasn't wearing shades. I was as happy and peaceful as I could reasonably be. The hijra took the note from me and asked, '*Poora hai?*' I think I knew what that question meant. But I did not know what to say. They waved their hand vertically, twice, before my body, and asked again, '*Sab poora hai?* Complete *hai*? *Kuch* missing *toh nahin hai*?' 'Na, na, kuch missing *nahin hai. Sab* complete *hai,*' I said with a start. 'All okay. Nothing missing,' I added in English, as if that would convince her. With great tenderness on her face, they placed a hand on my head, touched my cheek and walked away. I stood there wondering if everything was really complete, if I was whole.[89]

In Queeristan, we will be hearing more and more voices like Revathi, Maya, Dhrubo, Sachin, Hansda and Vasudhendra, voices that speak to us directly.

There is so much new and exciting queer scholarship in academia as well. In Pawan Dhall's much-awaited *Out of Line and Offline: Queer Mobilizations in '90s Eastern India*, released at the Rainbow Literature Festival in Delhi in December 2019, Pawan traces the early history of internet-empowered community formation in the eastern part of the country, through in-depth interviews of about a dozen queer individuals and their allies, as well as archival research into early internet support forums.[90] *Queer Potli: Memories, Imaginations and Re-imaginations of Urban Queer Spaces in India,* also edited by Pawan, contains twelve pieces—academic essays, memoirs, poems—that explore different Indian 'urban queer spaces' such as an NGO walk-in centre, a gay bar, a bodybuilding gym and a metro.[91]

I read both these books as companion pieces to my earlier book *Gay Bombay*.[92] I also see linkages between *Gay Bombay* and Dhiren Borisa's yet unpublished doctoral work on the queer cartographies of desire in Delhi. For his research, Dhiren, who has completed probably the first-ever geographies of sexualities PhD from an Indian university, studied different queer Delhi spaces such as cruising parks, nightclubs, massage parlours, LGBTQ forums and dating apps like Grindr. His research highlights the negotiations that dalit and queer individuals have to make while navigating these spaces both physically as well as online. Dhiren shows us that there are caste, class and gendered hierarchies implicit in all of these queer spaces.

Besides technology, another connecting thread running through the work of Dhiren, Kareem Khubchandani, Brian Horton as well as mine, is the dance floor. Kareem's new book *Ishtyle* is set in the gay party scene in Bengaluru, just as *Gay Bombay* was partly set in Mumbai's gay social circuit, more than a decade ago. In the book, Kareem, who has trained in performance studies, focuses on dance as a way of mapping relationships between media, labour, class, sexuality and gender in queer Bengaluru.[93]

In Brian's PhD dissertation from Brown University, *Shimmers of the Fabulous: Reinventions of Queer Life and Politics in Mumbai*, he asks: What do queer people do when they are not 'suffering'? He spoke about his paper with me: 'My work is primarily on queer social and activist spaces in urban India, specifically Bombay. The facetious question I ask is: What do queer people do when they are not suffering? My argument is that the kind of gaze that is put on to places like India, like the rest of the Global South, is one that demands queer people speak in the language of suffering or crisis or precarity in order to be intelligible. The only way queer life comes to matter is through illegality—so we look at 377. My argument is: What would it mean if we look at spaces that have existed for a long time—cruising sites, parties, Pride parades to some extent—as ordinary spaces? Looking at them as spaces of queer sight and queer pleasure. What if we emphasise these spaces; in doing so, can we make the argument that queer subjects can be imagined to be fabulous, and what would that entail, and what kinds of ethical, political, aesthetic features would be creatable in a world where we do not take precrarity as the primary form of recognition.'[94]

I have only named some of the works out there, those that are deeply connected to my own research interests. There is a lot more to read. But even from this tiny glimpse, I do hope you realise that we are studying ourselves extensively and telling our own stories in Queeristan. It is exhilarating to be part of this contemporary chronicling.

In Queeristan, There Are Many Intersectional Projects That Advance the Dignity of All

When I was in Cape Town in June 2015 to attend the World Economic Forum in Africa, I came across the word '*ubuntu*' from the Zulu and Xhola languages. It broadly refers to the idea of interconnectedness. 'I am because you are.'

One year after the Supreme Court's Section 377 verdict, lawyer Menaka Guruswamy wrote about the importance of intersectionality for the Indian queer movement as it marches ahead:

> Our freedoms do not exist in silos, they exist in tandem with each other. In constitutional litigation, we use existing rights of freedom and dignity of one marginalised group to extend it to another, arguing that such rights are due to every citizen. Similarly, diverse movements must recognise that in standing with each other, in ensuring the freedoms and equality of each group, they shore up their own. It is also time for movements working on gender, caste and labour issues to embrace their LGBT brethren within and outside. Similarly, queer citizens in India must also realise that a national register used against one community can well be extended to another. German history teaches us this. In isolated communities, we have little power. But in coalitions, we have the ability to fight for the fulfilment of the promises of our Constitution.[95]

Intersectional coalition building is finally happening in Queeristan. Whether online or on the ground—in the midst of the protests taking place across the country against the Citizenship Amendment Act in the winter of 2019–20 or in the community responses to the COVID-19 pandemic—I encounter the spirit of ubuntu more and more. LGBTQ community events like the Delhi Queer Pride are making their space as accessible as possible and are supporting dalit rights, disability rights, elder rights and feminism, alongside the rights of the queer community. An organisation like Solidarity Foundation has chosen to situate itself at the intersection of class, sexuality and sex work. It is thrilling to witness this.

Here are just some of the exciting online-offline intersectional projects that have recently sprung up in Queeristan, and whose work I admire:

i. The Queer Muslim Project[96]

Rafiul Alom Rahman formally started the Queer Muslim Project (TQMP) in March 2017, although the seeds of it were sown in the preceding years. In April 2015, he had presented the paper 'Can the Muslim Queer Speak?: Sexuality, Masculinity and the "Problem" of Being a Minority within a Minority in India' at an international conference on masculinities at St Stephen's College, Delhi University. I have known Rafiul since he was part of the MINGLE youth leadership cohort in 2014 that we hosted at Godrej. I wrote one of his recommendations for his PhD application to the University of Texas, Austin, which he began in 2016 but discontinued soon after to return to India.

In December 2019, Rafiul and I were together at the colony club in Delhi's Gulmohar Park for the inaugural Rainbow Literature Festival. There were two parallel festival stages, and both featured writers and also other performers like the classical singer Shubha Mudgal and a puppeteer reinterpreting an Oscar Wilde tale. As the novelist Sandip Roy told the listeners of his San Francisco public radio KALW 91.7 FM show that month, summarising his experience at the literature festival, 'The real wonder of the festival is not just what's happening on stage. The real miracle is the people. The activist telling the story of the first Pride walk in India twenty years ago. The blonde drag queen. The older lesbian in a plaid shirt. The intersected activist. The young Mr Gay India in a flowing coat talking to the grey-haired feminist publisher about coming out to his mother. Human encounters in a world of apps. That is the pot of gold at the end of the rainbow.'[97]

It was the end of day one at the literature festival, and the Nizami Brothers were regaling us with qawali. The 'debate' over the Citizenship (Amendment) Bill, 2019, was playing itself out in parliament. What does it mean for a Sufi song to be sung at a queer festival in today's India? As the brothers shifted from Amir Khusro to Bollywood, one of my favourite songs came up. I wrapped my shawl a little more tightly. It was from *Bajrangi Bhaijaan*, which I have sobbed over, thrice. *'Jab talak tu sunega na dil ki, dar se tere na jaayega aashiq.'*[98] The lover will not leave your shrine, until you listen to his heart's plea.

Do all higher powers have empathy, I wondered.

I sat back with Rafiul in a tepee-like tent on the lawns, and he reminisced about his journey with TQMP over the past few years.

'While I was in the US, I got the opportunity to attend interfaith queer events and also engage with activists who were using faith in a more affirmative manner, you know, across faiths actually—Christian and Jewish folks. I also learnt about the kind of work that was happening in Muslim communities, with groups like MASGD, which is Muslim Alliance for Sexual and Gender Diversity. There is such amazing work happening with more feminist interpretations of Islamic theology and rethinking Islam from the perspectives of marginalised communities like women and LGBTQ people, and I felt that this wealth of knowledge was not available here.

'When I came back to India, I decided that the first thing was to disseminate this information and say that there are possibilities to find meaning even in Islam, because too often, queer Muslims are expected to be either queer or Muslim. For me, that wasn't the case because while I wasn't myself very religious, I felt that Islam was the place where I found peace and spiritual healing, and there were many people like me. But there wasn't enough acceptance within Muslim communities that tell you that Islam condemns homosexuality, or in queer spaces where any kind of expression of faith is seen as, almost, you know, not in a very nice way.

'So that's how I started a Facebook page called the Queer Muslim Project, and the idea was to share all this information—the YouTube lectures, the articles, the community building work that was happening abroad, be it in the US or Canada or the UK, with the Inclusive Mosque Initiative or the kind of conversations that feminist activists and scholars were having within Islamic theology. By the end of 2017, I remember a couple of people writing to me—"Hey, why don't you go offline?" "Why don't we do this event?" "Why don't you come to Bangalore?" "Why don't you come to Mumbai?" and so on.

'There is an organisation called Aneka, which is based out of Bangalore, that had been doing some bit of work on faith and sexuality, but primarily in the space of Christianity. We partnered with them and organised a one-day national consultation in Bangalore in May 2018, and it was focused on LGBTQ Muslims and their experiences, but we had a few allies too. We had around thirty participants. A lot of people mentioned how they felt really lonely, how there wasn't enough representation, how they often felt that they were the only people, there wasn't enough support or even community sometimes, and how we constantly had to navigate Islamophobia as well as homophobia and transphobia.

'In January 2019, we finally got a grant from the PlanetRomeo Foundation and organised our first LGBTQI retreat in India. Here, we had twenty-five participants from across India—queer and trans folks and Muslims. It was very emotionally charged. People felt that it was a rare space that they could be themselves without ever being questioned about how Muslim are you or how queer are you. We had consciously created a space on the side, and we had said that there is no compulsion in prayer, but anybody who wants to pray can pray, and it was meant to be an inclusive prayer space so anyone could stand wherever they liked irrespective of their gender or dressing, because the focus was on intent—with what intention are you coming to pray? A lot of people who had not prayed for a long time found that space to be very healing.

'Towards the end of 2018, we started using Instagram in a more focused way because we felt that somewhere what really works for us and what a lot of people were sharing were their own stories. We often don't get to tell these stories; it is other people who write our stories. Representation in media is really skewed. We don't have role models. So we thought, how about if we change that narrative, how about if we tell our stories? Today, TQMP is a global project. We have an online community of over 14,000 people, and at the heart of this community are these stories of people and their courage and hope.

'After operating as a collective for the past two years, this year we have registered as a non-profit company. The idea is to now broaden the conversation through TQMP, of course, but also take some of the learnings from TQMP into the larger LGBTQI movement, build cross-movement dialogues and really engage with young people on the questions of faith, gender and sexuality, and justice. We want to go offline and develop resources in local languages like Hindi, Urdu and Bangla. We want to do focused webinars with scholars abroad, and we want to build inter-faith dialogue and really create space for more interfaith conversations. Another thing we want to do is build life skills for LGBTQI youth—which will be open to all faiths.'

ii. The Chinky Homo Project[99]

Pavel Sagolsem and Kumam Davidson began the Chinky Homo Project (TCHP) together as a WordPress blog and Instagram account in 2018, alongside the publication of their co-written article 'Do Queer Migrants From the Northeast Find Indian Cities Alienating or Empowering?'[100] published by *In Plainspeak*, the digital magazine of the not-for-profit TARSHI (Talking about Reproductive and Sexual Health Issues). TCHP aims at exploring the diversity of queer narratives from India's northeastern states through writing, cinema, music, painting, photography and other collaborative experiments.

Pavel, whom I had met when they spoke at the Culture Lab in 2019, told me more about the project's origin story.

'It is a very personal journey of anxiety and self-reclamation at the same time. Both David and I had been active in the respective cities we migrated to for our studies. My journey started from Baroda, where I landed after my twelfth standard for my graduation. Then, I went on to Hyderabad Central University for my master's and started my activism after getting in touch with a few groups there. For David, it happened to be Delhi because that's where he completed his graduation and also his masters in JNU.

'Politics and discourse go hand in hand, and becoming part of the discourse meant that as persons from the Northeast, we had to assimilate ourselves in the culture and way of thinking of those people who we were with because we were a minority in whichever group we went into. During my Hyderabad University days, out of the twenty people who were active in the city, I was one out of two or three persons from the Northeast. When I say I was a minority, I want to speak in terms of the regional imagination of identities and also how the Northeast is a bit disconnected from the rest of the country. So, even though North Indians or Central Indians or South Indians all have different cultures, when it comes to imagining ourselves as a citizen of this nation, there is a certain discourse which is similar for all of them.

'That was very interesting and exciting for me, to sort of adopt to assimilate oneself and one's identity. I didn't really strategise, but as it turns out, it was for my own advantage because now I can speak the language of "them", and even when I voice my concern, I can voice it in such a way that my concern is not seen as coming from a different person from a different land but coming from within them.

'The first anxiety was to find access to and getting a place in the LGBTQI movement or community outside of Manipur. So the assimilation bit helped me to find that acceptance, and I was very happy about it, but there was still an "othering". In political spaces, when I would speak as a Northeast person, there would be dissonance with the rest of the people because they can't really tell where we're coming from. David and I got on the same page about our anxieties and dissonance within the larger LGBTQI movement when we were in Delhi, where we became close friends and almost like family. We both had gone back home to Manipur for a year, on separate trips. Between the two of us, I go to protests, I scream and shout, but writing about it and media engagement is really not my forte.

'David started using social media to let out his angst on various platforms. Gender, patriarchy and family were the things he was lashing out about. One day, I saw an Instagram account on my feed called Chinky Homo. Then I found out that it was David's account! For a long time, we had been talking about doing something to bring together friends from the Northeast who were queer or politically active in their own ways. I messaged that account immediately. David was online. And he said I could share my own posts on that page too. And I was like, wow, but I have another idea. "Do you want to do this as a project?" That is the genesis of the Chinky Homo Project.

'The Chinky Homo Project is not just targeted to audiences outside the Northeast. It also aims to create these conversations within the Northeast. Any queer person who is growing up in Manipur or any part of the Northeast right now, when they need to get out of the state for education and other things, we want them to have read about other northeastern queer people's experiences. We don't want them to feel obliged, isolated or to assimilate or agree to stereotypes which will be imposed on them when they step out of that region. When David and I came out of Manipur, when the LGBTQI community imposed these on us, we accepted it because that was the first sign of an acknowledgement of us. We needed that because we were very apolitical, and in order to get into that space and learn how to be political, we had to accept it. This became detrimental to us later, and we were not able to get out of it. But for young people back at home, we did not want that to be the entry point. We want self-determination.'

iii. The Dalit Queer Project[101]

Aroh Akunth—who moderated a panel on the 'Caste and Queerness' event at the Culture Lab in January 2019 and is now an MA student of Modern Indian Studies at Universität Göttingen in Germany—is one of the founders of the Dalit Queer Project on Instagram, and they told me more about the project's path-breaking work as well as their future plans, over a phone call from Germany:

'We don't define ourselves as a collective or organisation. Clearly, there are people working on the project, but our functioning within the project is defined by the kind of work we are doing. For example, I'm the people's person, so my work is to reach out to as many dalit queer people as possible; the parameters of them being dalit queer is that they have to self-identify as dalit queer, even if they're not "out" on either of those identities. Then we take it from there.

'So then, there's me, there's Prateek [Prateek Draik is an architect, urban designer and artist, who does most of the art for the profiles featured on the Instagram account], who looks at the visual art submitted, and there are people who contribute pieces to us, everything from stories to articles to poems. The reason we are on Instagram as opposed to Facebook is because Instagram relies a lot on visual narratives, which makes sense for something as varied as the dalit community. We are 17.5 per cent of India, we are millions of people, and we speak hundreds of languages, if not thousands. Visual representation is something we can still connect to. Right now in the project, our centring is of queer, trans and intersex people within the project. Nearly half of us identify as queer, non-binary or intersex, which is something one does not see in a lot of queer organisations.

'We want to de-establish the idea that "Oh, dalit queers are only urban," because there are so many dalit queer people on the project who are rural and work in rural areas. It was also important for us to say that dalit queer people are not these people who are "taking up spaces in activism, academia and art", because while we are there, there are also people like Grace Banu who was a part of the Tuticorin protests; it's not a very glamorous place to be in. If somebody is contesting in the Lok Sabha elections, it's not a small deal. Even if they are just contesting. Because it takes a certain level of mobilisation of resources, which we feel is unprecedented for someone like a dalit intersex person. Also, you wouldn't imagine a dalit queer person leading a union—like a union of workers in a central university—and that is also something we're changing. I think one way in which the project is challenging the existing queer politics is that it is showing that dalit queers do not need anybody else to exist and collectivise.

'We are carving a niche for ourselves within anti-caste politics, which is a precarious position, right? It can't be like: *Aap apne* anti-caste *sangathan mein* sexual harassment policy *layien. Aap apne* anti-caste *sangathan mein* gender sensitisation *karien.*

'Aap unko bataien ki dono communitites *ek dusre ke* experience *se kya seekh sakte hain. Aap* rights *ke liye* demand *karein, jab* Trans Bill *ke liye* protest *karte hain, tab aap sadakon pe utariye.* Make your involvement felt, because we are not your tokens, and vice versa for queer politics.

'Other than the online curation that you see, there are workshops being designed to talk about things like identity formation. So on panels when we talk about dalit queer, people have no idea what either dalit or queer means, or they have a pre-existing notion that makes them anti to the ideas which will be coming from the panel. But what if we begin with what is the understanding of caste for an "upper-caste" person? Because it is not like they don't have an understanding of caste. Of course they do. How does someone feel proud about their name from birth whereas another person feels ashamed?

'They wouldn't know of entitlement—for them that is the norm. This is precisely why when something like reservation happens, they have a sense of woundedness. This woundedness is created, it doesn't exist. It's created with respect to the State because these people, these franchised people—as opposed to disenfranchised people—do not want to ask of the State, that "Okay, give us jobs", "Have free education for everybody", "Have free water for everybody". They're used to somebody living lesser, so that they can live completely. So we are doing workshops around identity formation, intimacy, intimate partner violence.

'Largely, the problem with the project is that it's a non-funded project. Which is the problem of every project ever, but I'm guessing not so much for the projects which have been sustained by caste capital over the years or have some big corporate players in it. PlanetRomeo has been really kind, they are our community partner. They specifically work with the Global South. They just care about community and community generation. The Queer Muslim Project, Bi Collective, Ace Collective, all of them got their funding from them. There's many more, I'm sure.

'They are community partners in the sense that they help us design whatever workshops and resources are needed. It's not like they play a role in it, but they pay for it. It doesn't make sense for dalit queers to work for free. A lot of us are researchers. It is just labour going unpaid at the end of the day, and it doesn't provide any incentive. And we were also clear when we came up with something like the Dalit Queer Project that it's okay if we are paid less, but it doesn't make sense for us to work for free because, at the end of the day, this is hard community work. This fund is a sort of a start-up fund, but otherwise it's a non-funded project in the sense that we don't have any income. So something like a potluck really depends on some members opening their house to other members, or a meeting depends on us finding a free place like a park.

'Our meetups largely happen in metros. At our meetup in Delhi, we had around twenty-two people who responded positively to it, which is a huge number for dalit queer people. Even if people are not from Delhi and they're visiting Delhi, they can still make it to the meetup. But now, we are also thinking of meetups in a different way. For example, if I happen to be dalit queer and if I'm in, say, a university in Gujarat, then all I have to do is put up posters and say a dalit queer meetup is happening, and maybe through those posters I'll find people who are interested, curious or are from our community, right?

'We're very specific that we limit the project clearly to scheduled castes. Of course, we want to be there in any political capacity and in support of anybody who is marginalised and queer. But then, our resources cannot be opened up for other positionalities because there are no resources for *our* positionalities. This is our understanding of it. So that's what we work with. This is the reason it's called just the Dalit Queer Project, because people were like, "*Aapne ise bahujan queer kyon nahi kaha*?" or "*Aapne ise anti-caste kyon nahi kaha*?" And on the other side of the spectrum of voices which don't want such collectivisation in the name of caste at all, *kyunki nahi ho raha hain na*, *matlab*, bahujan is some 85 per cent, queer is untraceable, it seems everybody under the sun is either bahujan or queer in India. It's just impossible to focus and work on that paradigm because it's just like … okay, maybe I can work with an OBC [Other Backward Castes] queer person, but does it mean I have to open the project to them? This kind of imposition of either bahujan or queer on a doubly marginalised community like ours is nothing but an erasure of our continuing histories of violence. We would love to facilitate, and we do, but it's not something that can be asked of us, because that is where the entitlement lies.

'Another thing we have been very careful of is regional representation and the representation of women within the project. So most of our Instagram series either would be just about trans and intersex people or we would definitely have dalit women in it. Also, the positionality of a dalit queer woman cannot be pitted against that of a dalit queer man the same way it is done between savarna women and savarna men. Of course, dalit queer men are getting the privileges of being a man and identifying as a man, and that grants them visibility, but because they carry caste and sexuality markers on them, and if they're out especially, it's not like they are … intentionally delaying the discourse of dalit queer women. This is too big a weight to place on the first-generation of people who identify as dalit queer. In fact, in our experience, there have been dalit queer researchers who have historically worked with dalit women, and they have also centred narratives of dalit queer women within their work. How gay men have historically delayed and hampered the lesbian discourse in the mainstream, right? That's not been the same for dalit queer men, because when we're talking to a lot of dalit queer men, again only talking on the basis of experience within the project, their idea of the journey to becoming DQ was not "Oh, I'm dalit and I'm queer"; it was originally coming from a strong feminist leaning and scholarship.

'We also intend to create resources around how we see intersectionality, how we see sexual harassment or the discourse around it. For example, if a man stares and whistles at a woman, which is horrible, *abhi woh ladka ghoor raha hai* or *seeti maar raha hai, toh*, we have to all condemn it. At the same time, if say, a woman calls somebody a "chamar" or calls somebody "downmarket" or "*yeh toh* SC/ST crowd *hai*," *matlab* any casteist remark, that is not treated with the same severity.

'Another project that I have been working on seeks to develop transnational perspectives on caste and queerness. In India, both—in whatever limiting ways—dalits and queers are addressed by the State in the Constitution, and that has enabled some kind of representation and assertion. In a lot of other South Asian countries where dalit populations exist—like Sri Lanka, Bhutan, Nepal, Pakistan, Bangladesh—either they are not addressed or there is codified discrimination within the constitution which leads to erasure and them not becoming part of the discourse at all. This project seeks to capture how the realities of caste and queerness mutate across borders and what is changing there. Then, we want to develop resources on mental health, provide legal aid; so the scope is really huge.'[102]

~

As I finish this book in March 2020, charged with enthusiasm after learning about projects like the ones described above, the COVID-19 pandemic has struck India, and I am getting to see more glimpses of the solidarity within the queer movement. So many of the names that you have read about earlier in the book have galvanised and come together to organise food and supplies for those most hit by the lockdown within the country.

Grace Banu is spearheading a programme to provide food assistance for 150 trans families in Tuticorin, Tamil Nadu, and similar campaigns are organised in cities like Hyderabad and Chennai. In Bengaluru, the NGO Sangama has galvanised online support to help sustain the homes of 500 sex workers and trans people,[103] while S. Veena, a dalit trans person and programme manager at the Solidarity Foundation, volunteers with the sociopolitical collective Swaraj Abhiyan to distribute free rations to 300 households in the basti that she resides in.[104] In Mumbai, young girls from the NGO Kranti are distributing fresh food cooked in their own home kitchen to 85 cancer patients and their families trapped on the street outside the Tata Memorial Hospital, unable to go back to their hometowns because of the lockdown.[105] One of my mentees Anish Gawande, as part of the collective Youth Feed India, is helping provide emergency ration supplies for 2,500 families of powerloom workers, head loaders and rickshaw drivers in Bhiwandi, located just outside Mumbai.[106] Another mentee Anudeep Kanneganti, one of Ashoka University's Young India Fellows for 2020, is collaborating with his batchmates to provide essential supplies to migrant workers in North Delhi.[107] The Keshav Suri Foundation and the Lalit Suri Hospitality Group are providing food and ration supplies to NGOs working with marginalised transgender groups across the country, like the Saksham Trust in Chandigarh, Aarohan in Delhi and Payana in Bengaluru.[108] My own company Godrej has joined so many other corporations you have read about in this book, like Wipro and Tata, in giving funds and other resources to a range of efforts aimed at providing relief to our country's citizens.

Seeing our community—individuals, NGOs and corporates—all coming together during the COVID-19 crisis, gives me hope during the dark days of the pandemic. The world has changed so much in the time between when I started writing this book and this moment, when I am wrapping it up. The title of this chapter—'Other Worlds Are Possible'—a mantra that has guided me over the course of this book, feels so much more urgent. This is a time for *all of us* to step up, gravitate towards hope, use our agency and participate—in the re-imagination and co-creation of a more just and equal world. It is our collective action right now that is going to eventually determine Queeristan's future.

20

Get Started Jaldi

Your Roadmap to Queeristan

Speaking of stepping up and participating—now that you know nearly everything there is to know about my imagining of Queeristan, here are the people and organisations you can reach out to, and build this wonderful queer world of opportunity and change alongside us. This chapter has a list of experts on everything you could possibly need—legal help, job databases, community NGOs, support for persons living with HIV, mental health helplines; you name it, it's there! A caveat—this list is not exhaustive. These are just people and organisations I have come across in one year of research, information about whom was either available publicly or was given to me by them.

D&I Consultancies, Forums and Organisations

These are the corporate experts you can invite into your companies to help you on your inclusion journey.

1. **Community Business** has published various research papers on LGBTQ inclusion in India. If you want to be an inclusive company, Community Business can help with training modules and also hold webinars and conferences. communitybusiness.org.
2. **Pride Circle**, besides organising meetups, celebrations and seminars, also works on hiring, skilling, placement and mentoring. One of its biggest successes has been the RISE job fair. thepridecircle.com.
3. **Periferry** is a social inclusion start-up focused on training, skilling and placing trans people. Periferry also sensitises workplaces to make them more inclusive. periferry.com.

4. **Beyond Diversity Foundation** collaborates with institutions to create strategies towards inclusion, training leadership, sensitisation in the workplace, assessment of an organisation's unconscious bias and more. beyondiversity.com.
5. **Interweave Consulting** specialises in D&I consulting such as sensitisation of leadership, bias-free hiring and more. interweave.in.
6. **Serein** uses the latest research in behavioural economics, sociology, cognitive science and psychology to develop D&I solutions that are specific to the Indian context. serein.in.
7. **Diversity Dialogues** is a group of Bengaluru-based D&I professionals with more than thirty years of combined corporate experience who advise companies on inclusion across the pillars of gender, disability, LGBTQ and generational inclusion. dialogues.diversity@gmail.com.
8. **Working with Pride** is a community of D&I professionals, along with LGBTQ employees and allies. Their programming includes transformational leadership training programmes for LGBTQ professionals across the country. workingwithpride.org.
9. **Belongg** is an online and offline community platform that aims to provide useful services to people who face bias because of their gender, sexuality, caste, religion or ability. These services include research reports, web series, a diversity library service and listings of inclusive landlords. belongg.net.

Legal Resources

Should you need to understand the legalities of hiring LGBTQ persons or anything else in connection with the law and being queer in India, these are some organisations whose resources and expertise might help.

1. **Alternative Law Forum** is a collective of lawyers in Bengaluru, who believe in an interdisciplinary practice of law that specifically targets social and economic injustices with critical research, advocacy and pedagogic interventions. altlawforum.org.
2. **Centre for Law and Policy Research** is a not-for-profit legal research organisation in Bengaluru that has been leading litigation efforts and providing legal support for the trans rights movement. clpr.org.in.
3. **Samāna Centre for Gender, Policy and Law** in Delhi is a consultancy that provides services and advocacy on gender, LGBTQ and related aspects to corporates in India. samanacentre.com.

4. **Majlis**, based in Mumbai, works towards evolving innovative legal practices to defend women's rights. Gender-just ideology guides the group's campaigns, legal representation and advocacy. majlislaw.com.
5. **Vidhi Centre for Legal Policy** in Delhi is an independent think tank doing legal research to make better laws and improve governance. The centre has released a series of reports on queering the law. vidhilegalpolicy.in.
6. **Lawyers Collective** is a group of lawyers working to empower marginalised sections of society through their engagement in human rights advocacy, legal aid and litigation. The collective has been instrumental in many key judgements involving the LGBTQ community. lawyerscollective.org.

Mental Health Resources

In this section, you will find safe spaces and trusted mental health professionals I have crowdsourced from queer people on the internet. If you work in a company, this list is something you should consider going through, should you want to take another look at the services offered by your employee assistance programme.

1. **Anjali Sexuality and Mental Health Institute** in Kolkata studies the intersectionality of mental health and sexuality. anjalimentalhealth.org.
2. **iCALL** is an LGBTQIA-friendly psychosocial helpline, initiated by TISS in Mumbai, that provides emotional support and psychological interventions to those in psychosocial distress. iCALL's crowdsourced list of 'Mental Health Professionals We Can Trust' is an exhaustive resource.[1] icallhelpline.org.
3. **Mariwala Health Initiative** is a funding agency for innovative mental health initiatives, with a particular focus on making mental health accessible to marginalised persons and communities. The group has created a six-day certificate course that provides tools to address distress and promote the well-being of LGBTQ persons. Its website has loads of resources, including an excellent mental health starter kit as well as multiple papers on queer mental health. mhi.org.in.
4. **Saahas** is a free support group in Mumbai for individuals who identify as being on the LGBTQ spectrum. It is run by two queer clinical psychologists using LGBTQ-affirmative therapy approaches. instagram.com/saahastherapygroup.

5. **Health Professionals for Queer Indians** is a group of healthcare professionals working to sensitise healthcare professionals to the healthcare needs of the LGBTQ community. facebook.com/HPFQI.
6. **The Blue Dawn** is a support group and a community initiative which connects bahujan people—dalits, adivasis, OBCs, pasmandas, nomadic tribes—with counsellors who understand the intersection of mental health and caste/minority issues and with sponsors who can help make mental health counselling accessible to the community. facebook.com/thebluedawn56.
7. **Varta Trust Online Locator for Queer Friendly Services** aims to bridge the gap between legal, sexual health and mental health services and the queer community in various sectors. vartagensex.org/reachout.php.
8. **Safe Access** is a not-for-profit organisation based in Delhi that aims to create awareness among healthcare providers on LGBTQ health challenges and provides a listing of LGBTQ-friendly doctors, clinics and labs on its website. safeaccess.co.in.

Queer Community-Based Organisations (CBO) and Support Groups

These are LGBTQ community experts with deep knowledge about queer people. They also provide the infrastructure of support and community a queer person might require. So as an employer, colleague, friend or even as a queer person, you should reach out to these groups, if needed. Since I am based in Mumbai, I'll start this list from the West, and then we will move across other parts of the country.

In West India

1. **Humsafar Trust** in Mumbai is one of the oldest LGBTQ health and human rights organisations in the country offering everything from legal support to crisis management, support groups and counselling for the LGBTQ community. humsafar.org.
2. **Yaariyan** is a voluntary LGBTQ youth initiative and one of the support groups of the Humsafar Trust. facebook.com/YaariyanMumbai.
3. **Umang** is the LBT (lesbian, bisexual and trans persons) support group of the Humsafar Trust. facebook.com/umanglbt.
4. **Sweekar: The Rainbow Parents** is a support group formed in Mumbai for parents of Indian LGBTQ children. Sign up by using this form: tinyurl.com/ParentsSupportGroup.

5. **Lesbians and Bisexuals in Action (LABIA)** in Mumbai is the oldest-surviving queer women's group in India, working on gender, sexuality and social justice. labia.collective@gmail.com.
6. **Gay Bombay** is one of Mumbai's longest-running gay support groups. My first book *Gay Bombay* describes the early days of the group's formation and activities. facebook.com/GBGayBombay.
7. **6 Degrees** organises events where members of the community can network professionally, recruit, share ideas or hone new skills. facebook.com/6DegreesGN.
8. **Sakhi Char Chowghi Trust** in Mumbai promotes safe sex and counselling among the transgender and MSM populations. It was started by the trans rights activist and NALSA petitioner Gauri Sawant, who now focuses on the Sai Sawali Trust project Aaji Cha Ghar. This intersectional project seeks to give shelter to numerous trans people, particularly the aged, as well as children of sex workers. aajichaghar.com/all-project-list/aajicha-ghar.
9. **GAURAV (Greater Action of Unity Rights Advocacy and Visibility)** is a CBO in Mumbai promoting positive health-seeking behaviour among the MSM population. gauravcbo.org.
10. **Thane Queer Collective** is a safe space for queer people in Thane, Maharashtra. facebook.com/thanequeercollective.
11. **Sarathi Trust** in Nagpur and Vidarbha in Maharashtra is a sexual health organisation for the MSM and transgender populations. sarathitrust_2005@yahoo.in.
12. **Abhimaan**, the first CBO for the LGBTQ community in Kolhapur, Maharashtra, is a group of 'Rainbow Warriors' who aim to make Kolhapur a queer-friendly city. instagram.com/abhimaan.kolhapur.
13. **Samapathik Trust** in Pune, Maharashtra, founded by activist Bindumadhav Khire, works on issues of advocacy and health of LGBTHI communities. samapathik@hotmail.com.
14. **QueerAbad** is a community space for the LGBTQ community in Ahmedabad, Gujarat, family members and allies. instagram.com/queerabad.
15. **Foram Foundation** in Vadodara, Gujarat, works for the LGBT community by conducting health, rights and education programmes. facebook.com/foramfoundation.
16. **Lakshya Trust**, founded by Prince Manvendra Singh Gohil, works on HIV/AIDS awareness and prevention among MSM and GBT (gay, bisexual and transgender people) in Vadodara, Surat and Rajkot in Gujarat. lakshyatrust.com.

17. **Vikalp Women's Group** is an LBT group based in Baroda. facebook.com/vikalpwomensngo.
18. **Goa Rainbow Trust** is an NGO that hosts a range of events for the Goa LGBTQ community. goarainbowtrust.com.

In North India

19. **Alliance India**, Delhi, works with the government and with HIV/AIDS-affected communities to build capacity, provide technical support and advocate to strengthen the delivery of community-based HIV programmes. info@allianceindia.org.
20. **Nazariya** is a queer feminist resource group in Delhi that works in capacity building and training on gender and sexuality. nazariyaqfrg.wordpress.com.
21. **Nazariya** (yes, a second one, again in Delhi. Remember, there are so many nazariyas to look at the world from!) is a grassroots LGBTQ straight alliance, which is an intersectional, feminist, social justice advocacy group. nazariyalgbt.org.
22. **Naz Foundation** in Delhi works in the area of sexual health. They raise awareness about HIV/AIDS and how to prevent it. They also help LGBTQ persons with getting access to doctors, lawyers and counsellors. naz@nazindia.org.
23. **The Transgender Welfare Equity and Empowerment Trust (TWEET) Foundation** in Delhi works on trans employment and upliftment. The foundation also works towards the establishment and maintenance of group care homes for elderly trans persons and trans persons with physical disabilities. tweetindia.org.
24. **Nirantar: A Centre for Gender and Education** in Delhi is a non-profit organisation that develops teaching-learning materials for organisations that work on issues of gender and sexuality with young people, NGOs and government programmes. nirantar.net.
25. **Talking About Reproductive and Sexual Health Issues (TARSHI)**, Delhi, works on freedom in sexual and reproductive choices in people's lives by conducting trainings, developing publications, participating in public awareness and education initiatives, and running an info-line. tarshi.net.
26. **Harmless Hugs** is a collective based in Delhi, and they organise a Queer Holi event, an international queer theatre and film festival called Tarang and an annual Delhi LGBTQ flash mob. facebook.com/harmlesshugs.

27. **Bi Collective Delhi** is a resource group and support group that provides a safe space for people attracted to those of their own gender and other genders. facebook.com/bidelhi.
28. **The Keshav Suri Foundation for LGBTQ Empowerment**, Delhi, seeks to provide a platform to the LGBTQ community, helps with employment and skilling of the LGBTQ workforce, and also sensitises workplaces about D&I practices. keshavsuri.foundation.
29. **Sonzal Welfare Trust** works for the psychosocial welfare of gender and sexual minorities in Jammu and Kashmir. facebook.com/sonzalwelfare.
30. **Saksham Trust**, Chandigarh, advocates for the rights and well-being of transgender communities through counselling and sensitisation. facebook.com/SakshamTrustNGOChandigarh.
31. **Queer Collective Dehradun** in Uttarakhand has provided a space for the LGBTQ community to advocate for their rights and express their views. It has been instrumental in the Dehradun Pride walks that have taken place. facebook.com/LGBTDehradun.

In East India

32. **Solidarity and Action Against the HIV Infection in India (SAATHI)** works in advocacy, capacity building and research for the prevention of HIV. saathii.org.
33. **Sappho for Equality** in Kolkata is an advocacy group working for the rights of lesbian, bisexual women and trans men. It provides a range of services including mental health counselling, legal aid, crisis intervention and a wide range of resources. sapphokolkata.in.
34. **The Pratyay Gender Trust** in Kolkata is a sexuality rights initiative that provides counselling, healthcare referrals, vocational training, crisis management, legal aid and advocacy for the protection of trans rights. facebook.com/PratyayGenderTrust.
35. **Amitie Trust** in Howrah, West Bengal, organises health camps and conducts research in collaboration with the Integrated Network for Sexual Minorities (INFOSEM) to tackle issues faced by the hijra, kothi and intersex community. facebook.com/amitie.trust.
36. **Miitjyu Foundation** in Darjeeling, West Bengal, works for advocacy and sensitisation for the upliftment of the MSM community. facebook.com/Miitjyu-1944748808979142.
37. **Parichay Collective** in Bhubaneswar, Odisha, is a co-organiser of Bhubaneswar Pride. The collective offers peer counselling and support to

the Odia LGBTQ community as well as organises events such as poetry readings and meetups. instagram.com/the_parichay_collective.

38. **Utthan JSR** in Jamshedpur, Jharkhand, has organised health camps and sensitisation sessions for the LGBTQ community. facebook.com/groups/2180763305511985.
39. **Dostana Safar** is a CBO in Patna, Bihar, working mainly towards the upliftment of the transgender and hijra communities. facebook.com/dostanasafar.bihar.

In Central India

40. **Queergarh** in Raipur, Chhattisgarh, has organised discussions, the Raipur Pride and multiple flash mobs in Raipur and Bhilai. facebook.com/LGBTQ-Chhattisagarh-104425607565159.
41. **Anmol Samaj Sevi Sansthan CBO** is based in Bhopal, Madhya Pradesh. It is one of the groups in Bhopal that co-organises Bhopal Pride. facebook.com/anmolsamajsevi.sansthan.
42. **Queermitra** is a community of people in Bhopal working towards equality and LGBTQ rights. facebook.com/Queermitra.

In Northeast India

43. **Ya-All Manipur** ('Yawol' in Manipuri means 'revolution') is the first queer-led and queer-focused registered youth network in Manipur. facebook.com/manipur.youthnetwork.
44. **All Manipur Nupi Manbi Association (AMaNA)** is a collective that works towards the upliftment of the trans community in Manipur through free legal aid, sensitisation sessions with various stakeholders and spoken English courses. facebook.com/AMANAMANIPUR.
45. **Empowering Trans Ability (ETA)** is a collective for the trans, bisexual and lesbian community in Manipur which works in peer counselling, crisis response and the sensitisation of legal professionals and community members. facebook.com/Empowering-Trans-Ability-ETA-Imphal-Manipur-1007664919312869.
46. **Xukia** is an informal youth-led LGBTQ organisation in Guwahati, Assam. facebook.com/xukia.assam.
47. **Xomonnoy** is an intersectional queer feminist support group based in Guwahati. instagram.com/xomonnoy.
48. **All Assam Transgender Association** provides free legal counselling and sensitisation sessions on trans rights. allassamtransgenderassociation.com/facebook.com/forTgirls.

49. **Rainbow Hills Association** in Gangtok, Sikkim, is an organisation working towards equality and acceptance of the LGBTQ community. rainbowhills19@gmail.com.
50. **Shillong LGBTQ Community** in Meghalaya organises meetups and celebrations for Shillong's LGBTQ community and also organised Shillong's first Pride march in 2018. facebook.com/LGBTQShillong.

In South India

51. **Telangana Hijra Transgender Samiti** is a collective of transgender, hijra, non-hijra intersex, trans women, trans men and gender queer people. facebook.com/telanganahijratrans.
52. **Sangama** is an activist space working in Bengaluru on sexual minorities' issues and rights. It works as a documentation, drop-in resource and crisis-intervention centre. sangama.org.
53. **All Sorts of Queer (ASQ)** is a support group and safe space in Bengaluru. asq.blore@gmail.com.
54. **Swabhava Trust** in Bengaluru is working towards providing health, legal and counselling services to the LGBTQ community. It also provides training support on diversity policies. swabhava.org.
55. **Aravani Art Project** is an artistic collective of trans women who use public art as a form of collaborative social intervention. aravaniartproject.com.
56. **Payana** in Bengaluru is working for the betterment of working-class non-English-speaking sexual minority community members in Karnataka, particularly the MSM and transgender communities. payanablr.in.
57. **Ondede** is an advocacy and social justice group in Bengaluru, co-founded by activist Akkai Padmashali, that is committed to work for the rights of children, women and sexual minorities. The group focuses on research, documentation, community media, engaging with the State and increasing evidence-based advocacy in policy and practice. facebook.com/Ondede-Dignity-Voice-Sexuality-1421467274812188.
58. **Solidarity Foundation** in Bengaluru seeks to provide support to sex workers and sexual minorities in the country through fellowships, grants, corporate involvement, livelihood support, skilling and empowerment. solidarityfoundation.in.

50. **South India AIDS Action Programme** in Chennai works in developing CBOs, collaborating to co-create, design programmes and raise funds, as well as in prevention and treatment of HIV and other sexually transmitted infections (STIs). siaapindia.org.

60. **Sahodaran** in Chennai works on sexual health awareness and STI/HIV/AIDS prevention among members of the LGBTQ community. sahodaran.org.
61. **Sahodari** in Coimbatore works for the rights of transgender, intersex and gender non-binary people. The group uses education, art and creativity as a means of empowerment. sahodari.org.
62. **Orinam** is a collective in Chennai that creates resources and organises events such as meetups and film festivals. It also has an incredible archive of material on the Section 377 journey, the Trans Act and other legal milestones in India. orinam.net.
63. **Srishti Madurai** is an intersex, gender queer and LGBTQ student volunteer group designed to target the problems of queer people in the non-metro cities of Tamil Nadu. srishtimadurai.blogspot.com.
64. **Queerhythm** in Trivandrum, Kerala, is a support group for queer individuals. queerythm.wordpress.com.
65. **Sahayatrika** in Thrissur, Kerala, works for lesbian, bisexual, female-to-male transgender, queer, intersex and asexual persons in the state. facebook.com/Sahayatrika-715674861851052.
66. **Queerala** in Kochi, Kerala, is an organisation for Malayali LGBTQ people. It provides necessary counselling services, acts as a resource as well as spreads awareness about and supports LGBTQ individuals facing physical and mental health issues. queerala.org.
67. The **Trans Rights Now Collective** in Tamil Nadu is a dalit-bahujan-adivasi-centred collective of trans people who are working across India to build trans leaders, support trans education and build trans job opportunities. It is coordinated by the activist Grace Banu, the first known transgender person to be admitted to an engineering college in Tamil Nadu. transrightsnowcollective@gmail.com

Digital Resources

These are just some of the online resources you could access to learn more about the diversity that exists in queer India.

1. **Agents of Ishq** is a multi-media project around sex, love and desire in India. agentsofishq.com.
2. **Being LGBTI in Asia** is a regional programme aimed at addressing discrimination on the basis of sexual orientation, gender identity or intersex status. medium.com/being-lgbti-in-asia.

3. **Chinky Homo Project** is a digital and print anthology that aims to capture the subjectivity and experience of queer persons from the Northeast. thechinkyhomoproject.wordpress.com.
4. **Dalit Queer Project** is a platform and community that explores what it means to be dalit and queer through online curation of art and writing, meetups, workshops and more. instagram.com/dalitqueerproject.
5. **Fifty Shades of Gay** is an LGBTQ portal that serves as a resource to understand alternative sexualities, gender identity and expression in a non-judgemental environment. fiftyshadesofgay.co.in.
6. ***Gaylaxy*** is an LGBTQ magazine that serves as a resource for queer news and events. gaylaxymag.com.
7. ***Varta***, a webzine from the Varta Trust, provides a platform for dialogue on gender and sexuality across diverse queer lived experiences. vartagensex.org/index.php.
8. ***In Plainspeak*** by TARSHI is a creative and educational digital magazine on sexual and reproductive health and rights in the Global South. tarshi.net/inplainspeak.
9. **Orinam** is a bilingual site in Tamil and English that serves as an online resource for the LGBTQ community. orinam.net.
10. ***Scripts*** is the queer zine published by LABIA. scripts.labiacollective.org.
11. **'Pink List'** is a list of candidates who contested the 2019 Lok Sabha elections and who publicly supported LGBTQ rights. pinklistindia.com.
12. ***Qitaab*** is an intersectional feminist zine that publishes opinions, artwork, written work and other creative pieces to explore relevant LGBTQ issues. qitaabzine.com.
13. ***Swakanthey*** is Sappho for Equality's bilingual—Bengali and English—biannual magazine. It consists of fiction, poetry, interviews, art, comic strips and articles revolving around queer issues. sapphokolkata.in/magazine.
14. **Queer Chennai Chronicles** records individual and collective narratives of queer people in Chennai. queerchennaichronicles.com.
15. **Queer Ink** is an organisation that curates, develops and promotes Indian LGBTQ works across several mediums—print, film, theatre and more. queer-ink.com.
16. **Queer Muslim Project** is a digital platform that creates visibility and awareness about LGBTQ Muslim issues in India and South Asia through online advocacy. facebook.com/thequeermuslimproject.

17. **Sexuality and Disability** is a joint venture by Point of View and CREA. It uses art, writing and media to create resources at the intersections of sexuality, disability and violence. blog.sexualityanddisability.org.
18. **Point of View**'s incredible work focuses on sexuality, disability and technology. pointofview.org.
19. ***Gaysi Zine*** presents stories and resources that explore what it means to be queer and desi. gaysifamily.com/tag/gaysizine.
20. **TransVision** is a YouTube channel that creates content written as well as directed by trans people, and is meant to serve as a resource that busts common stereotypes and misconceptions about the trans community. youtube.com/channel/UCYjwx0gcDp-C-uPZITPrbJg.

Cultural Festivals

Come hang out with us. Attend one of these festivals in a city near you. Also, if you head a company, consider sponsoring one of these or any other queer festival that you know about.

1. **Awadh Queer Literature Festival** provides a platform for queer literature in Lucknow through workshops, book readings, theatre performances, film screenings and exhibitions. facebook.com/aqlfest.
2. **Bangalore Queer Film Festival** focuses on screening films from non-Western locations, films by independent filmmakers, popular cinema that experiments with LGBTQ concerns and experimental films that push aesthetic limits. The festival also includes dance, music, theatre, photography and art. bqff.in.
3. **Chennai Queer LitFest** by Queer Chennai Chronicles curates conversations about queer Indian literature and queerness in India—particularly how the queer literary imagination affects the lives of queer people. queerlitfest.com.
4. **Rainbow Literature Festival** held in Delhi every year is a mix of different forms of expression such as prose, poetry, art, performance, films and discussions. rainbowliteraturefestival.com.
5. **Delhi Queerfest**, held annually, explores queerness as an identity, politics or process that challenges dominant norms, as a way of seeing not just LGBTQ lives but also the world itself. facebook.com/delhiqueerfest.
6. **Dialogues: Calcutta International LGBT Film and Video Festival** in Kolkata celebrates national and international writers, directors, actors

and their work, and screens feature films, shorts and videos dealing with LGBTQ themes and issues. sapphokolkata.in/events.

7. **Kashish Mumbai International Film Festival**, South Asia's biggest queer film festival, encourages greater visibility of queer cinema among wide audiences as a means to foster better understanding of queer desires and expressions. mumbaiqueerfest.com.
8. **Likho India LGBTQ Media Summit** aims to nurture writers who write on LGBTIQ themes and to promote fair and inclusive portrayal of LGBTQ communities in the media. facebook.com/likho.hst.
9. **Queer and Allies Art Festival** brings together artists, craftspeople and performers from all over the country. It takes place in various cities in India, such as Pune, Chennai, Bengaluru and Hyderabad. lgbtq.co.in/qaaf.
10. **Reel Desire: Chennai International Queer Film Festival** is an annual festival addressing stigma-free inclusion of LGBTQ people within families, educational institutions, healthcare facilities, workplaces and the media and film industries. ciqff.org.
11. **Tarang: Delhi International Queer Theatre and Film Festival** by Harmless Hugs spotlights social problems, aspirations and concerns of the LGBTQ community in India through the medium of art, theatre and movies. facebook.com/harmlesshugs.
12. **The Out and Loud Pune International Queer Film Festival** by the online collective Mist is an annual event with screenings of films from the world over. It also includes performances and panel discussions. facebook.com/outloudpiqff.

This list could go on forever. Some amazing folks have compiled useful resources as well. *Feminism in India* has compiled an incredible resource of intersectional social justice collectives across campuses in India. If you are a student, check it out; you are bound to find queer collectives here, too.[2] Agents of Ishq's list of queer support resources of all kinds is also really comprehensive—from digital resources to NGOs.[3]

Bas, enough for now. I have tried to give you everything I could—now you really have no excuse, *haan*? Come, co-create Queeristan with us.

Endnotes

Prologue: If the BBC Says I'm Gay, It Must Be True

1. Bhupen Khakhar, *Maganbhai's Glue, Pages from a Diary, Vadki, Phoren Soap and Maujila Manilal*, trans. Ganesh Devy, Naushil Mehta and Bina Srinivasan (New Delhi: Katha Books, 2001).
2. Parmesh Shahani, *Gay Bombay: Globalization, Love and (Be)Longing in Contemporary India* (New Delhi: Sage Publications, 2008).
3. Chhavi Dublish, 'South Asian Gays Find US Voice', *BBC*, 13 April 2004, news.bbc.co.uk/2/hi/south_asia/3620417.stm.
4. Naz Foundation vs Government of NCT of Delhi and Ors. Civil, paragraph 130, 131, appeal no. 7455 of 2001, 2 July 2009.
5. Kumar Kunal Jha and Sasmita Palo, *Queer at Work* (Singapore: Palgrave Macmillan, 2019).
6. Lewis Griggs and Lente-Louise Louw, eds., *Valuing Diversity: New Tools for a New Reality* (New York: Mcgraw-Hill, 2019).
7. Janice Gassam, '10 Books to Help You Foster a More Diverse and Inclusive Workplace', *Forbes*, 25 August 2019, forbes.com/sites/janicegassam/2019/08/25/10-books-to-help-you-foster-a-more-diverse-and-inclusive-workplace/#666eb6cf220c.
8. Leighton Brown and Matthew Riemer, *We Are Everywhere: Protest, Power, and Pride in the History of Queer Liberation* (Berkeley: Ten Speed Press, 2019).
9. Saundarya Rajesh, *The 99 Day Diversity Challenge: Creating an Inclusive Workplace* (New Delhi: Sage Publications, 2018).
10. Mahzarin Banaji and Anthony Greenwald, *Blindspot: Hidden Biases of Good People* (New York: Delacorte Press, 2013).
11. Laura Liswood, *The Loudest Duck: Moving Beyond Diversity While Embracing Differences to Achieve Success at Work* (New Jersey: Wiley, 2009).
12. Mark Kaplan and Mason Donovan, *The Inclusion Dividend: Why Investing in Diversity and Inclusion Pays Off* (Massachusetts: Bibliomotion, 2013).
13. Marc Benioff and Monica Langley, *Trailblazer: The Power of Business as the Greatest Platform for Change* (Redfern: Currency, 2019).

1
Jugaad Resistance

1. Naz Foundation vs Government of NCT of Delhi, paragraphs 130–131.
2. Suresh Kumar Koushal and Anr vs Naz Foundation and Ors, WP (civil) no. 10972 of 2013 (11 December 2013), paragraph 43.
3. 'The arc of the moral universe may bend toward justice, but it doesn't bend on its own.' Martin Luther King Jr., *I Have a Dream: The Quotations of Martin Luther King Jr.* (New York: Grosset & Dunlap, 1968).
4. Danish Sheikh, 'Short Dispatches from the 377 Courtroom', Orinam, 11 July 2018, orinam.net/377/wp-content/uploads/2018/07/s377_sc18_day2_danish.pdf.
5. Live Law (@LiveLawIndia), 'It is not just consensual sex between ...', Twitter, 11 July 2018, twitter.com/LiveLawIndia/status/1016944944295002115.
6. Priyanka Chopra Jonas, 'TIME 100 Most Influential People 2019', *Time*, time.com/collection/100-most-influential-people-2019/5567711/arundhati-katju-menaka-guruswamy.
7. Akhil Kang, 'Casteleess-ness in the Name of Caste', *Round Table India*, 4 March 2016, roundtableindia.co.in/~roundta3/index.php?option=com_content&view=article&id=8491:casteless-ness-in-the-name-of-caste&catid=119:feature&Itemid=132.
8. Navtej Singh Johar vs Union of India, W (Crl) no. 76 of 2016 (2018), paragraph 20.
9. Richa Taneja, ed., 'Homosexuality Not a Disorder, Says Indian Psychiatric Society', NDTV, 10 July 2018, ndtv.com/india-news/homosexuality-not-a-disorder-says-indian-psychiatric-society-1880806.
10. 'Indian Activist Jailed for Being Gay', *BBC*, 8 September 2018, bbc.com/news/world-asia-india-45444652.
11. 'Won't Tolerate Adultery, Homosexuality: Army', *Times of India*, 1 November 2019, timesofindia.indiatimes.com/india/army-will-not-tolerate-homosexuality-adultery-in-its-ranks/articleshow/71840741.cms.
12. 'The SC Judgment on Section 377 Opens the Doors for Further Legal Victories', *Hindustan Times*, 22 September 2018, hindustantimes.com/analysis/the-sc-judgment-on-section-377-opens-the-doors-for-further-legal-victories/story-yviHhGYjP29OGzZ15rrAPL.html.
13. Vallabh Ozarkar, '25-year-old MBA Graduate Ends Life over "Gay" Jibes, Suicide Note Alleges He Was Taunted at Workplace', *Mumbai Mirror*, 24 July 2019, mumbaimirror.indiatimes.com/mumbai/crime/man-commits-suicide-over-gay-jibes/articleshow/70355044.cms.
14. 'Sir Ian McKellen in Conversation with Parmesh Shahani', produced by India Culture Lab, video, 30 May 2016, youtube.com/watch?v=pzLLNShQSC4.
15. 'Sonam Kapoor Discusses What's Changed for the LGBTQ Community After the 377 Verdict', Twitter Blue Room Video, Twitter, 28 June 2019, twitter.com/i/events/1144580369070489601.
16. 'Indians aren't doing jugaad because it makes them more creative—they are doing it because of lack of opportunity ... we make do with less, we manage, but it is not celebrated as a badge of resourcefulness in India—people have a jugaad mindset to survive.' Parmesh Shahani, in Helen Russell, *The Atlas of Happiness: The Global Secrets of How to be Happy* (London: John Murray Press, 2018).

17. Dharmesh Shah, 'Lessons From Clayton Christensen: The Software Innovator's Dilemma', *Onstartups*, 10 May 2006, onstartups.com/tabid/3339/bid/173/Lessons-From-Clayton-Christensen-The-Software-Innovator-s-Dilemma.aspx.
18. C.K. Prahalad and Venkat Ramaswamy, 'Co-Opting Customer Competence', *Harvard Business Review* (January–February 2000).
19. Mary L. Gray, *Out in the Country: Youth, Media, and Queer Visibility in Rural America*, (New York: New York University Press, 2009).
20. Snigdha Poonam, *Dreamers: How Young Indians Are Changing Their World* (New Delhi: Penguin Random House, 2018).
21. Suraj Yengde, *Caste Matters* (New Delhi: Penguin Random House, 2019).
22. Dipankar Gupta, *Mistaken Modernity: India Between Worlds* (New Delhi: HarperCollins, 2000).
23. Akshay Pathak, 'Brahmins Preferred: The Caste of Sexuality', *Round Table India*, 22 May 2015, roundtableindia.co.in/~roundta3/index.php?option=com_content&view=article&id=8186:brahmins-preferred-the-caste-of-sexuality&catid=119:feature&Itemid=132.
24. 'The Role of Caste in the LGBTQ Community', *India Culture Lab* (blog), 5 February 2019, indiaculturelab.org/blog/the-role-of-caste-in-the-lgbtq-community.
25. Anjali Arondekar, 'Borderline Sex', in Donald E. Hall and Annamarie Jagose, eds., *The Routledge Queer Studies Reader* (Oxon: Routledge, 2012), 547–557.

2
Cultural Acupuncture: My Godrej Journey

1. 'Vicks—Generations of Care #TouchOfCare', produced by Vicks India, video, 29 March 2017, youtube.com/watch?v=7zeeVEKaDLM.
2. 'Making India', produced by Godrej, video, 13 August 2018, youtu.be/LzIafPDliLM.
3. Henry Jenkins, '"Cultural Acupuncture": Fan Activism and the Harry Potter Alliance', *Transformative Works and Cultures* (15 June 2012), 10, doi.org/10.3983/twc.2012.0305.
4. Andrew Slack, 'Cultural Acupuncture and a Future for Social Change', *HuffPost*, 25 May 2011, huffpost.com/entry/cultural-acupuncture-and_b_633824.
5. Slack, 'Cultural Acupuncture'.
6. 'Protego', Harry Potter Alliance, thehpalliance.org/success_stories_protego.
7. Henry Jenkins, Sangita Shresthova, Liana Gamber-Thompson, Neta Kligler-Vilenchik and Arely Zimmerman, *By Any Media Necessary: The New Youth Activism* (New York: New York University Press, 2016).
8. 'Police Battle Protesters as They Set Streets Ablaze in Central Hong Kong', *South China Morning Post*, 20 September 2019, scmp.com/news/hong-kong/politics/article/3030862/police-battle-protesters-they-set-streets-ablaze-central.
9. Godrej Industries Limited and Associate Companies, *Godrej Code of Conduct*, 29.
10. Nisaba Godrej, 'Nisaba Godrej's Message on International Day Against Homophobia', *India Culture Lab* (blog), 18 May 2015, indiaculturelab.org/blog/nisaba-godrejs-message-to-godrej-employees-on-international-day-against-homophobia/.
11. Nisaba Godrej, LinkedIn, 7 September 2018, linkedin.com/posts/nisaba-godrej-08507a79_where-the-mind-is-without-fear-and-the-head-activity-6443716778609696768-i2Ko/.

12. Homi K. Bhabha, 'Signs Taken for Wonders', *The Location of Culture* (Oxon: Routledge, 1994).
13. Jeff Roy, 'Configuring Transgender Hijra Music and Dance', in Gregory Bartz and William Cheng, eds., *Queering the Field: Sounding Out Ethnomusicology* (Oxford: Oxford University Press, 2019), 161–184.
14. Being LGBTI in India, 'Watch the Trans*forming Asia—A Facebook Live Event …', Facebook, video, 13 October 2017, facebook.com/beinglgbtiinasia/videos/watch-the-transforming-asia-a-facebook-live-event-with-india-culture-lab-and-und/865678010255286.
15. Prasenjit Bhattacharyya, LinkedIn, 9 December 2019, linkedin.com/posts/prasenjit-bhattacharya-2a56215_diversity-inclusion-diversityandinclusion-activity-6609865584614182912-Yc8i.
16. Open For Business, *Why Fast-Growing Companies from Emerging Markets Are Embracing LGBT+ Inclusion*, open-for-business.org/new-global-champions.
17. 'Parmesh Shahani', *The Canada in India Show*, canadainindia.libsyn.com/parmesh-shahani.
18. 'Episode 2', *Gaycation Season 2,* Viceland, 14 September 2016.
19. United Nations Human Rights Office of the High Commissioner, *Tackling Discrimination Against Lesbian, Gay, Bi, Trans, and Intersex People: Standards of Conduct for Business* (2017), unfe.org/wp-content/uploads/2017/09/UN-Standards-of-Conduct.pdf.
20. Nayanika Nambiar and Parmesh Shahani, *A Manifesto for Trans Inclusion in the Indian Workplace*, India Culture Lab (December 2018).

3
Mumbai Meri Jaan: Circulatory Queerness

1. Rahul Mehrotra, 'The Architectural Wonder of Impermanent Cities', TED, presentation, April 2019, ted.com/talks/rahul_mehrotra_the_architectural_wonder_of_impermanent_cities?language=en.
2. 'Circulatory Urbanism', Urbz, urbz.net/projects/circulatory-urbanism.
3. Shahani, *Gay Bombay*.
4. Lana Wachowski, Lily Wachowski, dirs., *The Matrix* (Warner Bros, 1999).
5. Nadeem Shravan, music dir., 'Pardesi Pardesi' (Tips Music), in Dharmesh Darshan, dir., *Raja Hindustani* (Cineyugg Entertainment and Tips Films, 1996).
6. Norah Jones, 'Come Away with Me Tonight', *Come Away with Me Tonight* (Blue Note Records, 2002).
7. Michel Foucault, *Discipline and Punish: The Birth of the Prison* (New York: Pantheon Books, 1977).
8. Sridhar Rangayan, dir., *Yours Emotionally!* (Solaris Pictures and Wise Thoughts, 2007).
9. Sridhar Rangayan, phone conversation with the author, 28 June 2019.

4
Some Thoughts on Privilege

1. Grace Banu at 'Queeristan: Caste and Queerness', event hosted by India Culture Lab, 18 January 2019.
2. 'Divya Kandukuri on Intersectional Feminism', produced by India Culture Lab, video, 13 March 2019, youtube.com/watch?v=niatQ2aYNOk.

3. Nisaba Godrej, 'Nisaba Godrej: The "Ovarian Lottery"', *Mint*, 2 October 2015, livemint.com/Opinion/vWuXDdaZ7k186vL1efFBEL/Nisaba-Godrej-The-ovarian-lottery.html.
4. Godrej, 'The "Ovarian Lottery"'.
5. 'Baba Amte—The Journey', Anandwan, anandwan.in/baba-amte-the-journey.html.
6. Joseph B. Soloveitchik, *The Lonely Man of Faith* (New York: Toby Press, 2018).
7. Parmesh Shahani, 'Parmesh's Viewfinder: Meet the Amtes', *Verve*, 3 June 2016, vervemagazine.in/arts-and-culture/parmeshs-viewfinder-meet-the-amtes.
8. Pierre Bourdieu, *Outline of a Theory of Practice* (Cambridge: Cambridge University Press, 1977).
9. Parmesh Shahani, 'Parmesh's Viewfinder: Other Worlds Are Possible', *Verve*, 21 June 2018, vervemagazine.in/arts-and-culture/other-worlds-are-possible.
10. Parmesh Shahani, 'Parmesh's Viewfinder: Cape of Good Hope', *Verve*, 20 July 2015, vervemagazine.in/arts-and-culture/parmesh-viewfinder-the-cape-of-good-hope.
11. 'Meet Divyanshu Ganatra, India's First Blind Solo Paraglider', *YourStory*, 26 February 2018, yourstory.com/2018/02/divyanshu-ganatra-blind-solo-paraglider.
12. 'The Barefoot Story', Barefoot College, barefootcollege.org/about.
13. 'Women's Empowerment', Mann Deshi Foundation, manndeshifoundation.org/women-empowerment.
14. Palagummi Sainath, *Everybody Loves a Good Drought* (New Delhi: Penguin Books, 1996).
15. 'Why We Need To Talk About Rural India?', produced by India Culture Lab, video, 11 April 2018, youtube.com/watch?v=_-J9gT4_ouY.
16. 'About', People's Archive of Rural India, ruralindiaonline.org/pages/about.
17. Shonali Bose, dir., *The Sky Is Pink* (Ivanhoe Pictures, Purple Pebble Pictures, RSVP, Roy Kapur Fims, Tencent Pictures and Zee Music Company, 2019).
18. Kath Weston, *Families We Choose: Lesbians, Gays, Kinship* (New York: Columbia University Press, 1997).

5
The Queer Alphabet Soup and Why It Matters

1. Alfred Kinsey, Wardell Pomeroy and Clyde Martin, *Sexual Behavior in the Human Male* (Bloomington: Indiana University Press, 1998).
2. LGBT Foundation, *Using Blockchain Technology to Advance Equal Rights and Acceptance for the LGBT* (2018), 5, lgbt-token.org/wp-content/uploads/2018/04/180415-LGBT-Whitepaper.pdf.
3. AIDS Bhedbhav Virodhi Andolan (ABVA), *Less Than Gay: A Citizen's Report on the Status of Homosexuality in India* (1991), 6.
4. ABVA, *Less Than Gay*.
5. Human Rights Campaign (@HRC), '4/ #Pansexual: Describes someone …', Twitter, 28 April 2018, twitter.com/hrc/status/989979634753331201?lang=en.
6. Akshat Agarwal, Namrata Mukherjee and Diksha Sanyal, *Queering the Law: Making Indian Laws LGBT+ Inclusive* (Vidhi Centre for Legal Policy: 2019) 6,10, vidhilegalpolicy.in/2019/07/31/queering-the-law-making-indias-laws-lgbt-inclusive.
7. The Transgender Persons (Protection of Rights) Bill, 2016, Lok Sabha.
8. The Transgender Persons (Protection of Rights) Bill, 2019, Lok Sabha.

9. 'Gender Dysphoria', *Diagnostic and Statistical Manual of Mental Disorders (DSM-5)* (Philadelphia: American Psychiatric Association, 2013).
10. GLAAD, 'Glossary of Terms: Transgender', *GLAAD Media Reference Guide: 10th Edition* (October 2016), glaad.org/reference/transgender.
11. Akhil Katyal, *The Doubleness of Sexuality* (New Text, 2016), 269–270.
12. United Nations High Commissioner for Refugees, 'Frequently Asked Questions', *Sexual Orientation, Gender Identity and Intersex Status in the Pacific* (2015), ohchr.org/Documents/Publications/UNFE_PacificCampaignInfoSheet-Aug2015.pdf.
13. Beyond Diversity, *Understanding LGBTQ: An Ally's Perspective* (2018), 3, beyondiversity.com/understanding-lgbt-an-allys-perspective.
14. 'Tinder India Allows 23 New Gender Identity Options—Here's What They Are', *Scroll.in*, 14 November 2018, scroll.in/article/901962/tinder-india-allows-23-new-gender-identity-options-heres-what-they-are.
15. NALSA vs Union of India and Others, Writ petition (civil) no. 400 of 2012 (2012), paragraph 108.
16. Lawrence Cohen, 'Kothi Wars: AIDS Cosmopolitanism and the Morality of Classification', in Vincanne Adams and Stacy Leigh Pigg, eds., *Sex in Development: Science, Sexuality, and Morality in Global Perspective* (Durham: Duke University Press, 2005).
17. Cohen, 'Kothi Wars'.
18. Nambiar and Shahani, *Manifesto for Trans Inclusion.*
19. Brian Horton, Skype conversation with the author, 29 June 2019.
20. Judith Butler, 'On Linguistic Vulnerability', *Excitable Speech: A Politics of the Performative* (New York: Routledge, 1997), 2.
21. Katyal, *The Doubleness of Sexuality*, 271.
22. ABVA, *Less Than Gay*, 8.
23. Herman G. Weinberg, *Society and the Healthy Homosexual* (New York: St Martin's Press, 1972).
24. Siddharth Dube, *No One Else: A Personal History of Outlawed Love and Sex* (New Delhi: HarperCollins, 2015), 130–131.
25. Shubham Singhal, 'Development of the Acceptance towards Lesbian, Gay, Bisexual and Transgender Scale', *International Journal of Science and Research* 8, no. 2 (2019).
26. Singhal, 'Development of the Acceptance.'
27. Gregory M. Herek, 'Beyond "Homophobia": Thinking About Sexual Stigma and Prejudice in the Twenty-First Century', *Sexuality Research and Social Policy* 1, no. 2 (2004), 6–24.
28. Singhal, 'Development of the Acceptance'.
29. MINGLE, *In & Out: The Indian LGBT Workplace Climate Survey 2016* (2016), 4, 11, gaystarnews.com/wp-content/uploads/2016/06/Indian-LGBT-Workplace-Climate-Survey-2016.pdf/
30. 'Glossary of Terms', Human Rights Campaign, hrc.org/resources/glossary-of-terms.

6
Historicising Queer India

1. Pawan Dhall, 'To CC with Love!', *Varta* (blog), 22 August 2015, varta2013.blogspot.com/2015/08/to-cc-with-love.html.

2. Dhall, 'To CC with Love'.
3. 'How Stonewall Came to India via Coffee House in Connaught Place', *Times of India*, 24 June 2019, timesofindia.indiatimes.com/india/how-stonewall-came-to-india-via-coffee-home-in-connaught-place/articleshow/69920054.cms.
4. Pawan Dhall, *Out of Line and Offline: Queer Mobilizations in '90s Eastern India* (Kolkata: Seagull Books, 2020).
5. Pawan Dhall, phone conversation with the author, 1 September 2019.
6. 'Qatha: Queer Kolkata Oral History Project', Varta, vartagensex.org/kolkata.php.
7. Dhall, phone conversation with the author.
8. Smita Vaniyar, '(R)evolution: How India's Women Carve out Communities Online', *Swaddle*, 25 January 2018, theswaddle.com/indias-women-carve-out-communities-online.
9. Zaid Al Beset, 'Letters of Desire', *Varta* (blog), 1 October 2013, varta2013.blogspot.com/2013/10/letters-of-desire.html#more.
10. Sridhar Rangayan, dir., *Project Bolo* (Humsafar Trust and Vivek Anand: 2011).
11. Vinay Chandran and Arvind Narrain, eds., *Nothing to Fix: Medicalisation of Sexual Orientation and Gender Identities (Sexualities)* (New Delhi: Sage Yoda Press, 2015).
12. Qamra, qamra.in.
13. Gautam Bhan and Arvind Narrain, *Because I Have a Voice: Queer Politics in India* (New Delhi: Yoda Press, 2005).
14. 'Dr Anjali Arondekar's Keynote Speech', Queer Futures Workshop organised by the Saida Waheed Gender Initiative, 11 June 2019, youtube.com/watch?v=XVme0p3Zgkw.
15. İrvin Cemil Schick, 'What Ottoman Erotica Teaches Us About Sexual Pluralism', *Aeon*, 23 March 2018, aeon.co/ideas/what-ottoman-erotica-teaches-us-about-sexual-pluralism.
16. Devdutt Pattanaik, *Shikhandi and Other Tales They Don't Tell You* (New Delhi and Gurgaon: Zubaan and Penguin, 2014), 176.
17. Pattanaik, *Shikhandi*, 166–167.
18. Pattanaik, *Shikhandi*, 40–48.
19. Pattanaik, *Shikhandi*, 12.
20. Sampad Patnaik, 'Explained: How ASI Conserves, Why Odisha Is Upset', *Indian Express*, 19 November 2018, indianexpress.com/article/india/how-asi-conserves-why-odisha-is-upset-over-konark-sun-temple-restoartion-naveen-patnaik-5452632.
21. ABVA, *Less Than Gay*, 4.
22. Pattanaik, *Shikhandi*, 126–127.
23. Laxmi Tripathi, *Red Lipstick: The Men in My Life* (New Delhi: Penguin Random House, 2016).
24. Tripathi, *Red Lipstick*, 6–7.
25. NALSA vs Union of India, paragraph 15.
26. Adrija Roychowdhury, 'When Eunuchs Were the Mid-Rung of Power in the Mughal Empire', *Indian Express*, 19 July 2018, indianexpress.com/article/research/eunuch-security-guards-bihar-mughal-empire-history-5266102.
27. Danish Hussain, 'Very Queer Qissas', *Mint*, 11 October 2017, livemint.com/Leisure/5H6y0jHdjrq8IGuHwQO8aO/Very-queer-qissas.htmll.

28. 'Dalai Lama Supports Gay Marriage', *Telegraph*, 7 March 2014, telegraph.co.uk/news/worldnews/asia/tibet/10682492/Dalai-Lama-supports-gay-marriage.html.
29. Devdutt Pattanaik, 'Introduction to the Karmic Faiths', *I Am Divine. So Are You : How Buddhism, Jainism, Sikhism and Hinduism Affirm the Dignity of Queer Identities and Sexualities* (Noida: HarperCollins, 2017), 33–34.
30. Devdutt Pattanaik and Loraine Tulleken, eds., *Behold, I Make All Things New: How Judaism, Christianity and Islam Affirm the Dignity of Queer Identities and Sexualities* (Noida: HarperCollins, forthcoming in 2020).
31. Leonard Zwilling and Michael J. Sweet, 'Like a City Ablaze: The Third Sex and the Creation of Sexuality in Jain Religious Literature', *Journal of History of Sexuality* 6, no. 3 (1996).
32. Maya Sharma, *Loving Women: Being Lesbian in Unprivileged India* (New Delhi: Yoda Press, 2006).
33. 'Queeristan: Pride Pan India', *India Culture Lab* (blog), 4 February 2019, indiaculturelab.org/blog/queeristan-pride-pan-india.
34. Ruth Vanita and Salim Kidwai, eds., *Same Sex Love in India* (New Delhi: Penguin Books, 2000).
35. Vanita and Kidwai, *Same Sex Love in India.*
36. 'Dhiren Borisa on Dalit Queerness', produced by India Culture Lab, video, 1 February 2019, youtube.com/watch?v=Z2bJUpFLYrw.
37. Yengde, *Caste Matters*, 54.
38. moulee, '"Safe" Queer Spaces: How Inclusive Is Inclusive?', *Round Table India*, 13 March 2016, roundtableindia.co.in/index.php?option=com_content&view=article&id=8502:safe-queer-spaces-how-inclusive-is-inclusive&catid=119:feature&Itemid=132.
39. moulee, 'Dear Savarna Queer Men, Let's Talk About Casteism Within Our Movement', *News Minute*, 16 June 2016, www.thenewsminute.com/article/dear-savarna-queer-men-lets-talk-about-casteism-within-our-movement-44951.

7
LGBTQ India and the Law

1. Community Business, *LGBT+ Workplace Inclusion in India: The Definitive Guide* (2019), 26, communitybusiness.org/latest-news-publications/lgbt-workplace-inclusion-india-definitive-guide-0.
2. Thomas Babington Macaulay, 'Minute by the Honourable T.B. Macaulay, Dated the 2nd February 1835', columbia.edu/itc/mealac/pritchett/00generallinks/macaulay/txt_minute_education_1835.html.
3. 'What Is Section 377?', *India Today*, 6 September 2018, indiatoday.in/india/story/what-is-section-377-1333115-2018-09-06.
4. 'Prathyush Parasuraman: Do Homosexuals Cause Earthquakes? Reframing the Queer Disposition', symposium by Institute for South Asia Studies Departmental, video, 3 May 2018, youtube.com/watch?v=SObA9fUDBcU.
5. Nandita Singh, 'Why 13 Crore Indians Are Celebrating Their "Independence Day" Today', *Print*, theprint.in/india/governance/why-13-crore-indians-are-celebrating-their-independence-day-today/109449/.

6. Shobha Aggarwal, 'Reminiscing ABVA's Struggle for Gay Rights in the Twentieth Century: A Brief History of That Time', *AIDS Bhedbhav Virodhi Andolan* (blog), 1 July 2019, aidsbhedbhavvirodhiandolan.blogspot.com/2018/09/reminiscing-abvas-struggle-for-gay.html.
7. Geeta Pandey, 'The Woman Who Discovered India's First HIV Cases', *BBC News*, 30 August 2016, bbc.com/news/magazine-37183012.
8. 'Sexuality and Queer Politics in India: The Indian Experience—Part One: Naisargi N. Dave', panel organised by Envisioning Global LGBT Human Rights, video, 7 October 2011, vimeo.com/76565704.
9. Dube, *No One Else*, 205.
10. 'Tracing the Journey and Struggles of ABVA: The Organisation That Laid the Foundation of LGBT Rights in India', *Gaylaxy*, 22 December 2018, gaylaxymag.com/exclusive/tracing-the-journey-and-struggles-of-abva-the-organisation-that-laid-the-foundation-of-lgbt-rights-in-india/#gs.2ws7fy.
11. Naz Foundation vs Government of NCT of Delhi.
12. Jyoti Panday, 'India's Supreme Court Upholds Right to Privacy as a Fundamental Right—and It's About Time', *EFF*, 28 August 2017, eff.org/deeplinks/2017/08/indias-supreme-court-upholds-right-privacy-fundamental-right-and-its-about-time.
13. Justice K.S. Puttuswamy vs Union of India, WP (Crl) no. 494 of 2012 (26 September 2018), paragraph 169.
14. Sharma, *Loving Women*, 22.
15. Sharma, *Loving Women*, 23–25.
16. Sharma, *Loving Women*, 25.
17. Sharma, *Loving Women*, 25–26.
18. 'Sexuality and Queer Politics in India: The Indian Experience—Part Two: Gautam Bhan', panel organised by Envisioning Global LGBT Human Rights, video, 7 October 2011, vimeo.com/76567393.
19. Cohen, 'Kothi Wars'.
20. 'Sexuality and Queer Politics in India—Part Two'.
21. Jyoti Puri, *Sexual States: Governance and the Struggle over the Antisodomy Law in India* (Durham: Duke University Press, 2016).
22. 'Sexuality and Queer Politics in India—Part Two'.
23. Tanu Sharma, 'MHA Justifies Retention of Section 377, but Health Ministry Cites NACO Studies', *Indian Express*, 3 July 2009, archive.indianexpress.com/news/mha-justifies-retention-of-section-377-but-health-ministry-cites-naco-studies/484404.
24. Shalini Nair, 'Many Ups and Downs in Battle Against 377', *Indian Express*, 11 January 2018, indianexpress.com/article/explained/many-ups-and-downs-in-battle-against-ipc-section-377-homosexuality-lgbtq-5019604.
25. *Notes of Proceedings in Suresh Kumar Kaushal vs Naz Foundation*, Orinam, April 2012, orinam.net/content/wp-content/uploads/2012/04/Naz_SC_Transcript_2012_final.pdf.
26. 'Sexuality and Queer Politics in India—Part One'.
27. Sangeeta Barooah Pisharody, 'It Is Like Reversing the Motion of the Earth', *Hindu*, 20 December 2013, thehindu.com/features/metroplus/society/it-is-like-reversing-the-motion-of-the-earth/article5483306.ece.

28. 'Naz Foundation Files Review Petition Against the Supreme Court Judgment on Section 377', Lawyers Collective, 24 December 2013, lawyerscollective.org/2013/12/24/naz-foundation-files-review-petition-supreme-court-judgment-section-377.
29. Koushal vs Naz Foundation.
30. 'Stories Can Change the Law: Arundhati Katju; TEDx Ferhadija', produced by TedxTalks, video, 11 April 2019, youtube.com/watch?v=r-KAKdpEWNo.
31. 'SC Agrees to Review Section 377, Refers Matter to Larger Constitution Bench', *Economic Times*, 8 January 2018, economictimes.indiatimes.com/news/politics-and-nation/sc-agrees-to-review-section-377-refers-matter-to-larger-constitution-bench/videoshow/62416465.cms.
32. 'Stories Can Change the Law'.
33. NALSA vs Union of India, paragraph 11.
34. NALSA vs Union of India, paragraph 60.
35. Danish Sheikh, 'The Supreme Court Judgement on Transgender Rights (NALSA vs Union of India): A Summary of the 15th April 2014 Judgement', Orinam, April 2014, orinam.net/content/wp-content/uploads/2014/04/nalsa_summary_danish.pdf.
36. YP Foundation, *Trans Rights in India* (2018), static1.squarespace.com/static/5837d4b3725e25680b8b758e/t/5ac3021b758d46d5fbdb41c8/1522729539201/Longformat%2Billustrations+web.pdf.
37. Sampoorna Working Group, 'Sampoorna's Response to MSJE Transgender Rights Bill', *Orinam* (blog), 13 January 2016, orinam.net/sampoorna-response-msje-trans-rights-bill.
38. 'TG Bill 2016 Factsheet: Bill Provisions and Community Demands', *Sampoorna* (blog), 23 November 2017, sampoornaindiablog.wordpress.com/2017/11/23/tg-bill-2016-factsheet-bill-provisions-community-demands.
39. Shreya Ila Anasuya, 'Why We Should Pay Urgent Attention to a Campaign to Stop the Trans Bill 2016', *Wire*, 2 December 2017, thewire.in/gender/pay-urgent-attention-campaign-stop-trans-bill-2016.
40. NALSA vs Union of India, paragraph 11.
41. 'The Transgender Persons (Protection of Rights) Bill 2016', Orinam, orinam.net/resources-for/law-and-enforcement/nalsa-petition-tg-rights-india/trans-persons-protection-rights-bill-2016.
42. 'All India Coalition Against the Transgender and Anti Trafficking Bill, 2018', Orinam, orinam.net/content/wp-content/uploads/2019/01/2.-AT-BILL-PARCHA_English_Delhi-Protest_28th-December_Colored.pdf.
43. Ministry of Women and Child Development, 'Comprehensive Legislation on Child Abuse', Press Information Bureau, 12 July 2019, pib.gov.in/PressReleasePage.aspx?PRID=1578559.
44. Sanyukta Dharmadhikari, 'Trans Bill 2019 Passed in Lok Sabha: Why the Trans Community in India Is Rejecting It', *News Minute*, 5 August 2019, thenewsminute.com/article/trans-bill-2019-passed-lok-sabha-why-trans-community-india-rejecting-it-106695.
45. 'Lok Sabha Passes Surrogacy Bill', *Economic Times*, 5 August 2019, economictimes.indiatimes.com/news/politics-and-nation/lok-sabha-passes-surrogacy-bill/articleshow/70538473.cms?from=mdr.
46. 'Despite Massive Protests, Trans Bill Gets President's Assent, Becomes Law', *News Minute*, 7 December 2019, thenewsminute.com/article/despite-massive-protests-trans-bill-gets-president-s-assent-becomes-law-113643.

47. Gaurav Das, 'Assam's First Transgender Judge Awaits Centre's Response to SC Plea Against "Humiliating" Act', *Wire*, 3 February 2020, thewire.in/lgbtqia/swati-bidhan-baruah-transgender-act.
48. YP Foundation, *Trans Rights in India.*
49. United Nations Development Programme, India, *The Case of Tamil Nadu Transgender Welfare Board: Insights for Developing Practical Models of Social Protection Programmes for Transgender People in India* (2012), undp.org/content/dam/india/docs/HIV_and_development/the-case-of-tamil-nadu-transgender-welfare-board--insights-for-d.pdf.
50. Rajvi Desai, 'Tamil Nadu Becomes First State to Ban So-Called Corrective Surgery on Intersex Babies', *Swaddle*, 30 August 2019, theswaddle.com/tn-first-state-to-ban-sex-reassignment-surgery-on-intersex-babies.
51. 'Breaking New Ground: Transgender Persons' Fundamental Right to Marry', *Centre for Law and Policy Research* (blog), 24 June 2019, clpr.org.in/blog/breaking-new-ground-transgender-persons-fundamental-right-to-marry.
52. 'Kerala Becomes First State to Unveil Transgender Policy', *Indian Express*, 12 November 2015, indianexpress.com/article/india/india-news-india/kerala-becomes-first-state-to-unveil-transgender-policy.
53. 'Pinarayi Government's First Budget: Thomas Isaac to Play Diligent Taxman', *News Minute*, thenewsminute.com/article/pinarayi-governments-first-budget-thomas-isaac-plays-diligent-taxman-46127.
54. YP Foundation, *Trans Rights in India.*
55. United Nations Development Programme, India, *Good Practices Following the Supreme Court Judgement* (2017), in.undp.org/content/india/en/home/library/poverty/good-practices-following-the-supreme-court-judgement.html.
56. Bindu N. Doddahatti, 'Karnataka Trans Policy May Be a Step in the Right Direction, But Needs Work', *Wire*, 20 March 2018, thewire.in/lgbtqia/karnataka-trans-policy-may-be-a-step-in-the-right-direction-but-needs-work; Rahul Chiranjit Sen, 'Karnataka Government Launched Pension Scheme "Mythri" for Transgender People', *Gaylaxymag*, 22 February 2014, gaylaxymag.com/latest-news/karnataka-government-launches-pension-scheme-mythri-for-transgender-people; Government of Karnataka, *Karnataka State Policy on Transgenders*, translaw.clpr.org.in/wp-content/uploads/2018/10/karnataka-state-transgender-policy-3.pdf.
57. United Nations Development Programme, *Good Practices.*
58. Priya Ranjan Sahu, 'Odisha Becomes First State to Include Transgenders in BPL Category', *Hindustan Times*, 3 June 2016, hindustantimes.com/india-news/odisha-becomes-first-state-to-include-transgenders-in-bpl-category/story-JGXrji3vjRyJUMCDueZCtK.html.
59. Vivek Trivedi, 'Madhya Pradesh Appoints Its First Transgender Government Officer', *News18*, 12 March 2019, news18.com/news/india/madhya-pradesh-appoints-its-first-transgender-government-officer-2064805.html.

*The legal struggle against Section 377—fragments of which have been mentioned in this chapter—over the past three decades has been fascinating. For a detailed timeline of how the 377 case progressed through the courts over the years, I highly recommend that you visit 377.orinam.net.

8
It's All About Loving Your Children

1. Kusuma Krishna, phone conversation with the author, 27 June 2019.
2. 'Episode 3: Accepting Alternative Sexualities', *Satyamev Jayate: Season 3*, television programme on Star Network, 19 October 2014.
3. Shelly Chopra, dir., *Ek Ladki Ko Dekha Toh Aisa Laga* (Vidhu Vinod Chopra Films, 2019).
4. Tarun Manushkani, dir., *Dostana* (Dharma Productions, 2008).
5. Gérard Genette, *Paratexts: Thresholds of Interpretation* (Cambridge: Cambridge University Press, 1997), 1–2.
6. Anupama Chopra, 'Opening India's Closet', *Los Angeles Times*, 9 November 2008, latimes.com/archives/la-xpm-2008-nov-09-ca-bollywood9-story.html.
7. 'Shubh Mangal Zyada Saavdhan', produced by Film Companion, video, 12 February 2020, youtu.be/w1WHeBOH2jc.
8. 'Being Gay: The Parents' Story', *We The People*, television programme on NDTV, 17 April 2011.
9. Sandeep Nair, phone conversation with the author, 11 June 2019.
10. Debarati Sen, 'LGBTQAI Support Group for the Parents, by the Parents', *Times of India*, 29 May 2019, timesofindia.indiatimes.com/life-style/parenting/moments/lgbtqai-support-group-for-the-parents-by-the-parents/articleshow/69538352.cms.
11. 'Pride Now', *The Urban Debate*, television programme on Mirror Now, 6 September 2018.
12. 'Dancing Queens: A Celebration of India's Transgender Communities', performance hosted by India Culture Lab, 2 February 2016, youtube.com/watch?v=pOcsx Hehkfc&feature=emb_logo.
13. Shankar Mahadevan, Ehsaan Noorani and Loy Mendonca, music dir., 'Maa' (T-series), in Aamir Khan, dir., *Taare Zameen Par* (Aamir Khan Productions, 2007).
14. Neville Bhandara, 'Manvendra Singh Gohil on Being India's First Openly Gay Prince', *HomeGrown*, 13 March 2017, homegrown.co.in/article/36075/in-conversation-with-indias-gay-prince-manvendra-singh-gohil.
15. 'What We Do', Lakshya Trust, lakshyatrust.com/what-we-do.
16. 'Bidisha: A Rebel with a Cause', *India's Got Talent Season 8*, television programme on Colours TV, 2018.
17. 'The Gay Sex Debate', *The Newshour Debate*, television programme on Times Now, 11 December 2013.

9
LGBTQ Inclusion Is Fundamentally a Good Thing to Do

1. Gregory Mankiw, 'Earnings and Discrimination', *Principles of Microeconomics* (San Diego: Harcourt College, 2013).
2. Horton, Skype conversation with the author.
3. '100 LGBT+ Executives 2019, LGBT+ Role Model Lists 2019', Outstanding, 2019, out-standing.org/nominations/100-lgbt-executives-2019.
4. Ali Potia, phone conversation with the author, 28 June 2019.

5. Fabrice Houdart, 'Is LGBTI Equality Good for Business or the Right Thing to Do?', *Out Leadership* (blog), 24 January 2020, outleadership.com/insights/is-lgbti-equality-good-for-business-or-the-right-thing-to-do.
6. 'Tata Steel Launches WINGS: An Employee Resource Group for LGBTQ Employees', *Gaylaxy*, 22 May 2018, gaylaxymag.com/latest-news/tata-steel-launches-wings-an-employee-resource-group-for-lgbtq-employees.
7. Anubhuti Banerjee, phone conversation with the author, 4 July 2019.
8. Madonna, 'More', *I'm Breathless* (Sire Records: 1990).

10
LGBTQ Inclusion Can Make You Money

1. LGBT Capital, *Estimated LGBT Purchasing Power: LGBT-GDP—2018* (2018), lgbt-capital.com/docs/Estimated_LGBT-GDP_(table)_-_2018.pdf; LGBT Foundation, *Using Blockchain Technology*, 5.
2. PricewaterhouseCoopers, *Out to Succeed: Realising the Full Potential of LGBT+ Talent* (2018), 3, pwc.com/gx/en/people-organisation/pdf/outnext-survey.pdf.
3. LGBT Foundation, *Using Blockchain Technology*, 6.
4. 'Lure of the "Pink rupee": Why Indian Firms Are Investing in LGBT Events', *Firstpost*, 20 December 2014, firstpost.com/business/lure-of-the-pink-rupee-why-indian-firms-are-investing-in-lgbt-events-797413.html.
5. McKinsey, *Delivering Through Diversity* (January 2018), 8,14, mckinsey.com/-/media/McKinsey/Business%20Functions/Organization/Our%20Insights/Delivering%20through%20diversity/Delivering-through-diversity_full-report.ashx.
6. Juliet Bourke, *Which Two Heads Are Better Than One? How Diverse Teams Create Breakthrough Ideas and Make Smarter Decisions* (Australian Institute of Company Directors, 2016).
7. Katie Abouzahr, Matt Krentz, Rocío Lorenzo, Miki Tsusaka and Nicole Voigt, *How Diverse Teams Boost Innovation* (Boston Consulting Group, 2018), bcg.com/en-in/publications/2018/how-diverse-leadership-teams-boost-innovation.aspx.
8. American Chamber of Commerce (AMCHAM), *Companion Paper: Increasing Innovation and Productivity in Singapore: The Role of Diversity and Inclusion* (2019).
9. Atish Patel, 'Homophobia May Cost India's Economy Billions of Dollars', *Wall Street Journal* (blog), 2014, blogs.wsj.com/indiarealtime/2014/06/10/how-homophobia-hurts-indias-economy.
10. Patel, 'Homophobia'.
11. 'Tim Cook Speaks Up', *Bloomberg Businessweek*, 31 October 2014, bloomberg.com/news/articles/2014-10-30/tim-cook-speaks-up.
12. Ajit Shashidhar, 'Baggage Queen', *Business Today*, 8 October 2017, businesstoday.in/magazine/features/vip-industries-radhika-piramal-managing-director-luggage-brand-skybags-caprese-indian-luggage-maker-luggage-industry/story/260431.html.
13. Center for Talent Innovation, *Diversity, Innovation, and Market Growth*, talentinnovation.org/_private/assets/IDMG-ExecSummFINAL-CTI.pdf.
14. Community Business, *LGBT+ Workplace Inclusion*, 14.
15. Jon Miller and Lucy Parker, *Open for Business: The Economic and Business Case for LGB&T Inclusion* (Open for Business: 2015), 5.

16. Ritesh Rajani, phone conversation with the author, 18 June 2019.
17. Srinivas Muktha, Ritesh Rajani and Madhumitha Venkataraman, 'LGBTIQ+ Inclusion at the Workplace', Orinam, July 2016, orinam.net/content/wp-content/uploads/2011/10/Basic_guide_to_building_LGBTIQA_inclusive_workplaces_05072016.pdf.
18. US Chamber of Commerce Foundation, *Business Success and Growth Through LGBT-Inclusive Culture* (9 April 2019), uschamberfoundation.org/sites/default/files/Business-Success-Growth-LGBT-Inclusive-Culture-FINAL-WEB.pdf.
19. Rajani, phone conversation with the author.
20. Sylvia Hewlett and Kenji Yoshino, 'LGBT Inclusive Companies Are Better at 3 Big Things', *Harvard Business Review*, 2 February 2016, hbr.org/2016/02/lgbt-inclusive-companies-are-better-at-3-big-things.

11
LGBTQ Inclusion Can Make Your Company More Innovative, and Help Attract and Retain Talent

1. 'Breaking Free: Discussion with Radhika Piramal, Joe Zachariah and Padma Iyer', panel discussion hosted by India Culture Lab, 3 February 2016, youtube.com/watch?v=Pm_xUeKJOzY&feature=emb_logo.
2. 'Diversity as the Engine of Innovation', *Deloitte Review*, no. 8, 2011, deloitte.com/content/dam/insights/us/articles/diversity-as-an-engine-of-innovation/US_deloittereview_Diversity_as_an_Engine_of_Innovation_Jan11.pdf.
3. Katie A. Liljenquist, Katherine W. Phillips and Margaret A. Neale, *Better Decisions Through Diversity*, KelloggInsight, 1 October 2010, insight.kellogg.northwestern.edu/article/better_decisions_through_diversity.
4. Miller and Parker, *Open for Business*, 42.
5. Joshua Muyiwa, 'How Corporate India Can Make Inclusion of Transgender Persons a Reality', *News Minute*, 22 July 2019, thenewsminute.com/article/how-corporate-india-can-make-inclusion-transgender-persons-reality-105879.
6. Banerjee, phone conversation with the author.
7. Vodafone, *LGBT+ Research* (4 July 2018), outnowconsulting.com/media/51271/finalreport-vodafone-final-04jul18asm.pdf.
8. MINGLE, *In & Out*, 12.
9. Sylvia Ann Hewlett and Kenji Yoshino, *Out in the World: Securing LGBT Rights in the Global Marketplace* (Center for Talent Innovation: 2016), talentinnovation.org/_private/assets/OutInTheWorld_Infographic-CTI.pdf.
10. Miller and Parker, *Open for Business*, 40.
11. 'Godrej LOUD: Find Out the Power of Dream', *Money Control*, 20 August 2014, moneycontrol.com/news/trends/features-2/godrej-loud-find-outpower dream-1369403.html.
12. Nair, phone conversation with the author.
13. MINGLE, *In & Out*.
14. Christina Merhar, 'Employee Retention: The Real Cost of Losing an Employee', *PeopleKeep*, 4 February 2016, peoplekeep.com/blog/bid/312123/employee-retention-the-real-cost-of-losing-an-employee.

15. Sai Balakrishnan, *Shareholder Cities: Agrarian-Urban Land Commodification in India's Corridor Regions* (Philadelphia: University of Pennsylvania Press, 2019).
16. Sameer Samudra, phone conversation with the author, 19 June 2019.
17. Richard Florida, 'The Global Map of Homophobia', *Citylab*, 7 February 2014. citylab.com/equity/2014/02/global-map-homophobia/8309.
18. Richard Florida, 'The Rise of the Creative Class: And How It's Transforming Work, Leisure, Community and Everyday Life', *Canadian Public Policy* 29 (2003).
19. Deloitte, *Foreign Direct Investment and Inclusive Growth: The Impacts on Social Progress* (2014).
20. AMCHAM, *Companion Paper*.
21. Miller and Parker, *Open for Business*, 35.
22. Waverly Deutsch, Vivienne Ming, Mary E. Shea and Chris Sinton, 'The State of LGBT Entrepreneurship in the U.S', *Startout*, July 2016.
23. 'The Unbearable Wrongness of Koushal: IITians Move Supreme Court Against Sec 377', *Orinam* (blog), 14 May 2018, orinam.net/377/wrongness-of-koushal-iit-petition-may-2018.
24. Tony Christopher, 'I Am a Gay Infosys Techie. What It Took for Me to Come Out', *NDTV*, 15 January 2018, ndtv.com/blog/i-am-a-gay-infosys-techie-what-it-took-for-me-to-come-out-1797931.

12
LGBTQ-Inclusive Messaging Helps You Improve Your PR and Keep Up with the Millennials

1. Humsafar Trust, 'List of Brands Supporting the LGBTQ'.
2. U. Urvi Malvania, '#LoveIsLove: India's Top Brands Go All Out with "Pride" Campaign', *Business Standard*, 10 September 2018, business-standard.com/article/current-affairs/loveislove-india-s-top-brands-go-all-out-with-pride-campaign-118091000030_1.html.
3. Tata Group (@TataCompanies), 'We welcome the landmark judgement ...', Twitter, 7 September 2018, twitter.com/tatacompanies/status/1037981853632741376; Rekha M Menon (rekha_m_menon), '#Inclusion is the bedrock of ...', Twitter, 6 September 2018, twitter.com/rekha_m_menon/status/1037654786106171393.
4. Vandana, 'Why We Should Welcome Brands to Celebrations over Striking Down of Section 377', *Dailyo.in*, 10 September 2018, dailyo.in/variety/section-377-section-377-verdict-homosexuality-homophobia-lgbt-community-corporate-india/story/1/26558.html.
5. Ritesh Rajani, 'LGBTQ+ Inclusion at Indian Workspaces', *The Investigator* 2, no. 4 (2016).
6. Ralco Tyres, 'Independence Day—Ralco', Facebook, 2019. facebook.com/ralcotyres/posts/1668218956644034.
7. '#Freetheroads', produced by Ralco Tyres, video, youtube.com/watch?v=RJdM2mvEFEs.
8. 'How Deeply Has Kaun Banega Crorepati Impacted India's TV Viewing Landscape?', *Zapr* (blog), 2017, blog.zapr.in/tv-analytics/kaun-banega-crorepati-amitabh-bachchan-impact-india-tv-viewing-landscape.
9. Procter & Gamble, *Procter & Gamble Hygiene and Healthcare Limited Annual Report 2016-2017* (2017), pg.com/en_IN/downloads/investor_relations/pghh/annual_reports/annual_report_2017.pdf.

10. 'Fastrack Challenges Taboos Ask People to Let Go of Societal Norms with Its Latest Ad Campaign', *Economic Times*, 17 April 2013, economictimes.indiatimes.com/fastrack-challenges-taboos-ask-people-to-let-go-of-societal-norms-with-its-latest-ad-campaign/articleshow/19577826.cms?from=mdr.
11. Titan Industries, *Titan Industries Limited Annual Report 2012–2013* (2013), titancompany.in/sites/default/files/Annual%20Report%202013.pdf.
12. 'Almost Half Indian Millennials Favour Marriage Equality', *Business Standard*, 28 June 2015, business-standard.com/article/news-ians/almost-half-indian-millennials-favour-marriage-equality-115062800542_1.html.
13. Debra Donston-Miller, 'Workforce 2020: What You Need to Know Now', *Forbes*, 5 May 2016, forbes.com/sites/workday/2016/05/05/workforce-2020-what-you-need-to-know-now.
14. Christine Barton, Christine Beauchamp and Lara Koslow, *How Millennials Are Changing the Face of Marketing Forever* (Boston Consulting Group: 15 January 2014), bcg.com/publications/2014/marketing-center-consumer-customer-insight-how-millennials-changing-marketing-forever.aspx.
15. S. Rukmini, 'Homosexuality in India: What Data Show', *Mint*, 14 Sep 2018, livemint.com/Politics/nLQiPpl5UICajLDXETU3EO/Homosexuality-in-India-What-data-shows.html.
16. Suneera Tandon and Maria Thomas, 'Indian Brands Are Suddenly Discovering Feminism and Gay Rights. Not the Least Because They Sell', *Quartz India*, 20 February 2017, qz.com/india/913694/indian-brands-are-discovering-feminism-and-gay-sex-rights-like-never-before-not-the-least-because-they-sell.
17. Nambiar and Shahani, *Manifesto for Trans Inclusion*.
18. 'The Visit', produced by Myntra, video, 28 May 2015, youtube.com/watch?v=Ef27m5ocK6Q.
19. 'Diversity as the Engine of Innovation', *Deloitte Review*.
20. Rajani, 'LGBTQ+ Inclusion at Indian Workspaces'.
21. Rajani, phone conversation with the author.
22. Alex Mayyasi and Priceonomics, 'How Subarus Came to Be Seen as Cars for Lesbians', *Atlantic*, 2016, theatlantic.com/business/archive/2016/06/how-subarus-came-to-be-seen-as-cars-for-lesbians/488042.
23. Alex Mayyasi, 'How an Ad Campaign Made Lesbians Fall in Love with Subaru', *Priceonomics*, 2016, priceonomics.com/how-an-ad-campaign-made-lesbians-fall-in-love-with.
24. 'Diversity as the Engine of Innovation', *Deloitte Review*.
25. Human Rights Campaign Foundation, *Corporate Equality Index 2019: Rating Workplaces on Lesbian, Gay, Bisexual, Transgender, and Queer Equality* (2019), 4, assets2.hrc.org/files/assets/resources/CEI-2019-FullReport.pdf?_ga=2.135715764.443426457.1572437516-1088122530.1572437516.
26. Human Rights Campaign Foundation, *Corporate Equality Index 2002* (2002), 3, assets2.hrc.org/files/assets/resources/CorporateEqualityIndex_2002.pdf?_ga=2.67973396.443426457.1572437516-1088122530.1572437516.
27. 'Rainbow Tick Standards', Quality Innovation Performance, qip.com.au/standards/rainbow-tick-standards.

28. Jiby Joyce, phone conversation with the author, 11 October 2019.
29. Nair, phone conversation with the author.
30. Miller and Parker, *Open for Business*, 34.
31. Liz Flora, 'Dolce & Gabbana: Still Canceled in China', *Gartner*, 17 July 2019, gartner.com/en/marketing/insights/daily-insights/dolce-gabbana-still-canceled-in-china.
32. Gaurav Probir Pramanik (@gauravpramanik), 'As promised, I wrote an email …', Twitter, 9 September 2018, twitter.com/gauravpramanik/status/1038700905216929792?s=20.
33. Tech Mahindra (@tech_mahindra), 'Hi Gaurav, This is indeed disturbing …', Twitter, 11 September 2018, twitter.com/tech_mahindra/status/1039377927421534208.
34. Open for Business, *New Global Champions: Why Fast-Growing Companies from Emerging Markets Are Embracing LGBT+ Inclusion* (2019), 11.
35. Gaurav Pramanik, phone conversation with the author, 13 June 2019.

13
Step One: Set in Place Strong Policies and Specific Benefits for LGBTQ Employees

1. Godrej Industries Limited, 'Diversity and Equal Opportunity', *Godrej Industries Limited Policies and Guidelines*, godrejite.com/Godrejite/PolicyDocuments/Policies/GIL_Policy%20Manual_Officers.pdf.
2. Humsafar Trust, *Humsafar Trust Manual for Corporates* (2018).
3. 'IBM Policies: Workforce Diversity', IBM.com, ibm.com/ibm/responsibility/policy4.shtml.
4. 'IBM Policies and Principles', IBM.org, ibm.org/responsibility/policies#workforceDiversity.
5. UN Globe, *Recommendations for an Inclusive Workplace for Trans and Gender Nonconforming Staff Members, Dependents, and Other Stakeholders of the UN System* (2018), static1.squarespace.com/static/5367af22e4b0915380a1eb0a/t/5a86fcacf9619a7edf05abc5/1518795949343/UN-GLOBE+recommendations+for+inclusive+workplaces+for+trans+and+gender+non-conforming+staff%2C+February+2018.pdf.
6. Rajdutt S. Singh, 'India: Overview of the Sexual Harassment of Women at Workplace', *Mondaq*, 21 October 2014, mondaq.com/india/x/348338/ employment+litigation+tribunals/Overview+Of+The+Sexual+Harassment+ Of+Women+ At+Workplace.
7. Ashwaq Masoodi, 'What Is Sexual Harassment under Indian Laws', *Mint,* 2 July 2015, livemint.com/Politics/XgRdygHg297gwYMYPjNSuI/What-is-sexual-harassment-under-Indian-laws.html.
8. Nitesh Desai Associates, *India's Law on Prevention of Sexual Harassment at the Workplace*, (November 2019), nishithdesai.com/fileadmin/user_upload/pdfs/Research%20Papers/Prevention_of_Sexual_Harassment_at_Workplace.pdf.
9. Godrej Industries Limited, 'Prevention of Sexual Harassment', *Policies and Guidelines*, 25.
10. Madhumitha Venkataraman, phone conversation with the author, 12 October 2019.
11. Rajani, phone conversation with the author.
12. Venkataraman, phone conversation with the author.
13. Richa Singh, email correspondence with the author, 20 February 2020.

14. Samudra, phone conversation with the author.
15. Bindumadhav Khire, *Considerations in Framing LGBTI Inclusive Policies for Corporates*, (Samapathik Trust: September 2018).
16. 'Citigroup Embraces LGBT, Live-In Partners of Its Staff', *Economic Times*, 16 July 2019, economictimes.indiatimes.com/news/company/corporate-trends/citigroup-embraces-lgbt-live-in-partners-of-its-staff/articleshow/70237694.cms.
17. Jiby Joyce, email correspondence with the author, 10 February 2020.
18. 'Diversity and Inclusion at Godrej', produced by India Culture Lab, video, 16 May 2016, youtube.com/watch?time_continue=87&v=lo3IrFprZKA.
19. Community Business, *LGBT+ Workplace Inclusion*, 51.
20. Udit Prasanna Mukherji and Namrata Singh, 'TCS First Tata Company to Include LGBT Staff for Health Cover', *Times of India*, 7 December 2019, timesofindia.indiatimes.com/business/india-business/tcs-first-tata-co-to-include-lgbt-staff-for-health-cover/articleshow/72411005.cms.
21. Brinda Sarkar, 'Intuit India Employees to Get Gender Affirmation-Related Support Benefits', *Economic Times*, 2 August 2019, economictimes.indiatimes.com/jobs/intuit-india-employees-to-get-gender-affirmation-related-support-benefits/articleshow/70543926.cms?sf107559915=1&from=mdr.
22. Singh, email correspondence with the author.
23. Amita Karadkhedkar, phone conversation with the author, 12 October 2019.
24. Banerjee, phone conversation with the author.
25. Venkataraman, phone conversation with the author.
26. World Professional Association for Transgender Health (WPATH), *Standards of Care for the Health of Transsexual, Transgender, and Gender Nonconforming People* (2011), wpath.org/media/cms/Documents/SOC%20v7/SOC%20V7_English.pdf.
27. Nambiar and Shahani, *Manifesto for Trans Inclusion*.
28. Rajani, phone conversation with the author.
29. Ramkrishna Sinha, phone conversation with the author, 15 June 2019.
30. Shilpa Phadnis, 'Tech Mahindra Offers Same-Sex Adoption Leave', *Times of India*, 27 December 2019, timesofindia.indiatimes.com/business/india-business/techm-offers-same-sex-adoption-leave/articleshow/72987808.cms.
31. Godrej Industries Limited, 'Adoption Leave and Benefits', *Policies and Guidelines*, 145.

14
Step Two: Actively Recruit LGBTQ Employees

1. 'The OUTstanding Lists: LGBT Leaders and Allies Today', *Financial Times*, 26 October 2017, ft.com/content/b6a08ba0-b40c-11e7-aa26-bb002965bce8.
2. Sangeeta Tanwar, 'Swiggy's First Transgender Employee Is Leading a Diversity Drive at the Indian Foodtech Unicorn', *Quartz India*, 17 July 2019, qz.com/india/1667648/ex-amazon-techie-is-leading-a-diversity-drive-for-lgbtq-at-swiggy.
3. We Are Swiggy, 'We just launched the Swiggy Pride Network …', Facebook, 5 November 2019, facebook.com/weareswiggy/posts/554958118405449?__tn__=-R.
4. 'Project Vayati', Solidarity Foundation, solidarityfoundation.in/post/project-vayati.
5. 'Why Us', PeriFerry, periferry.com/why-us.

6. PeriFerry (periferry), 'Our FIRST COHORT is here ...', Instagram, 4 October 2019, instagram.com/p/B3L0rSLjoOC.
7. PeriFerry (periferry), '100% JOB PLACEMENT ...', Instagram, 5 November 2019, instagram.com/p/B4fdmkyDFOx.
8. Rajani, phone conversation with the author.
9. Community Business, *Creating Inclusive Workplaces for LGBT Employees in India: The Definitive Guide* (2012).
10. Potia, phone conversation with the author.
11. Community Business, *Creating Inclusive Workplaces.*
12. Nambiar and Shahani, *Manifesto for Trans Inclusion.*
13. UN Globe, *Recommendations for an Inclusive Workplace.*
14. Karadkhedkar, phone conversation with the author.
15. Zainab Patel, phone conversation with the author, 15 June 2019.

15
Step Three: Create an LGBTQ-Friendly Work Culture Within the Company

1. Neelam Jain, phone conversation with the author, 25 June 2019.
2. MINGLE, *India Workplace Climate Study* (2016), 7.
3. MINGLE, *India Workplace Climate Study*, 7.
4. Nair, phone conversation with the author.
5. Nambiar and Shahani, *Manifesto for Trans Inclusion*, 41.
6. Nambiar and Shahani, *Manifesto for Trans Inclusion*, 40.
7. Jain, phone conversation with the author.
8. Swagato Mallick, email correspondence with the author, 22 January 2020.
9. Mallick, phone conversation with the author, 8 March 2020.
10. Rashmi Vikram, phone conversation with the author, 11 June 2019.
11. Nambiar and Shahani, *Manifesto for Trans Inclusion*, 40.
12. Nair, phone conversation with the author.
13. Aritra Kinjal, phone conversation with the author, 12 June 2019.
14. Sinha, phone conversation with the author.
15. Humsafar Trust, *Humsafar Trust Manual for Corporates.*
16. Shubha Chacko, phone conversation with the author, 26 July 2019.

16
Step Four: Address the Specific Circumstances of Trans Employees

1. Nambiar and Shahani, *Manifesto for Trans Inclusion.*
2. Karadkhedkar, phone conversation with the author.
3. Nambiar and Shahani, *Manifesto for Trans Inclusion*, 42.
4. Nambiar and Shahani, *Manifesto for Trans Inclusion*, 43.
5. Venkataraman, phone conversation with the author.
6. 'In a First, Kochi Metro Appoints Transgenders as Its Staff', *Times of India*, 20 May 2017, economictimes.indiatimes.com/news/politics-and-nation/in-a-first-kochi-metro-appoints-transgenders-as-its-staff/breaking-new-grounds/slideshow/58764418.cms.

7. 'Transgenders Make Kochi Metro Trendy', *Hindu*, 28 June 2017, thehindu.com/news/national/kerala/transgenders-in-kochi-metro-a-symbol-of-modernity-isaac/article19155139.ece.
8. 'Kerala Becomes First State to Unveil Transgender Policy', *Indian Express*, 12 November 2015, indianexpress.com/article/india/india-news-india/kerala-becomes-first-state-to-unveil-transgender-policy.
9. R. Babu, 'In One Week, Eight Transgender Employees Quit Working for Kochi Metro', *Hindustan Times*, 25 July 2017, hindustantimes.com/india-news/in-one-week-eight-transgender-employees-quit-working-for-kochi-metro/story-XDp6xgnA2Y6dhaAYcs8abP.html.
10. 'Nine Trans People Quit Kochi Metro Job', *Deccan Chronicle*, 25 June 2017, deccanchronicle.com/nation/in-other-news/250617/nine-transgenders-quit-kochi-metro-job.html.
11. Nambiar and Shahani, *Manifesto for Trans Inclusion*, 51.
12. Nambiar and Shahani, *Manifesto for Trans Inclusion*, 51.
13. Nambiar and Shahani, *Manifesto for Trans Inclusion*, 52.
14. Nambiar and Shahani, *Manifesto for Trans Inclusion*, 51.
15. 'Project Vayati', Solidarity Foundation.
16. Solidarity Foundation, email correspondence with the author.
17. Amit Kekre, email correspondence with the author, 19 January 2020.
18. Nambiar and Shahani, *Manifesto for Trans Inclusion*, 52.
19. Human Rights Campaign Foundation, *Transgender Inclusion in the Workplace: A Toolkit for Employers* (2016).
20. Humsafar Trust, *Humsafar Trust Manual for Corporates.*
21. WPATH, *Standards of Care.*
22. Out and Equal Workplace Advocates, *Workplace Gender Identity and Transition Guidelines* (2015).
23. Nambiar and Shahani, *Manifesto for Trans Inclusion*, 47.
24. Out and Equal Workplace Advocates, *Workplace Gender Identity.*
25. Human Rights Campaign Foundation, *Transgender Inclusion.*
26. Out and Equal Workplace Advocates, *Workplace Gender Identity.*
27. Humsafar Trust, *Humsafar Trust Manual for Corporates.*

17
Step Five: Become an Advocate for LGBTQ Issues Outside the Company

1. Kenji Yoshino, *Covering: The Hidden Assault on Our Civil Rights* (New York: Random House, 2006).
2. Hewlett and Yoshino, 'LGBT Inclusive Companies Are Better at 3 Big Things.'
3. US Chamber of Commerce Foundation, *Business Success and Growth.*
4. US Chamber of Commerce Foundation, *Business Success and Growth*, 27, 29.
5. Richard Fausset, 'Bathroom Law Repeal Leaves Few Pleased in North Carolina', *New York Times*, 20 March 2017, nytimes.com/2017/03/30/us/north-carolina-senate-acts-to-repeal-restrictive-bathroom-law.html.
6. Jason Hanna, Eliott C. McLaughlin and Madison Park, 'North Carolina Repeals "Bathroom Bill"', *CNN*, 31 March 2017, edition.cnn.com/2017/03/30/politics/north-carolina-hb2-agreement/index.html.

7. Open for Business, *New Global Champions.*
8. 'Talking LGBT Diversity in India', panel discussion at the Out and Equal 2017 Workplace Summit, 10 October 2017, outandequal.org/app/uploads/2017/11/C-Moulee-Talking-LGBT-Diversity-in-India-.pdf; Partha Sarathi Biswas, 'Corporate Sector Marks Its Presence in Pride March in Pune', *Indian Express*, 8 August 2016, indianexpress.com/article/cities/pune/corporate-sector-marks-its-presence-in-pride-march-in-pune-2960693.
9. Rujuta Parekh, 'Mega Job Fair "RISE" to Be Held in City', *Times Of India*, 2 May 2019, timesofindia.indiatimes.com/articleshow/69151811.cms?utm_source=contentofinterest&utm_medium=text&utm_campaign=cppst.
10. 'Out and Equal Workplace Advocates India Forum 2018: Agenda', Out and Equal, outandequal.org/app/uploads/2018/06/India-Forum-Agenda-Web-2.pdf.
11. 'Episode 3: Accepting Alternative Sexualities', *Satyamev Jayate: Season 3.*
12. Suresh Ramdas (sr81_mgwi), 'Thrilled to be in the list of ...', Instagram, 30 October 2019, instagram.com/p/B4PEf8_lRcZ.
13. 'Chapter 0040', Aravani Art Project, aravaniartproject.com/gs.
14. Mona Thangaraj, email correspondence with the author, 22 January 2020.
15. Singh, email correspondence with the author, 3 February 2020.
16. Rangayan, phone conversation with the author, 28 June 2019.
17. Pallav Patankar, phone conversation with the author, 28 June 2019.

18
But No Token Rainbows, Please. We Want Jobs, Not Your Instagram Filters!

1. Paige Horton, 'Pinkwashing Pride: How Can Companies Get LGBT+ Engagement Right?', LinkedIn, 27 August 2019, linkedin.com/pulse/pinkwashing-pride-how-can-companies-get-lgbt-right-paige-horton.
2. Yatra.com (@YatraOfficial), 'Yes it's for real ...', Twitter, 7 September 2018, twitter.com/yatraofficial/status/1038075673267462150?lang=en.
3. 'Yatra.com TV Advert', produced by Yatra, video, 23 December 2006, youtube.com/watch?v=75nkocSxyeo.
4. Rajani, phone conversation with the author.
5. Hidesign (@hidesign), 'Every colour, every shape, every size is BEAUTIFUL ...', Facebook, 12 December 2013, facebook.com/hidesign/photos/every-colour-every-shape-every-size-is-beautiful-in-a-world-full-of-diversities-/10151801689852864.
6. Hidesign (@hidesign), '#StorytellingSaturdays—Castro Street's Favourite', Facebook, 6 July 2019, facebook.com/hidesign/photos/a.10151714984402864/10156485495707864/?type=3&theater.
7. Karan Johar, *An Unsuitable Boy* (New Delhi: Penguin Random House, 2016).
8. 'Knorr—One Night with Karan #WhatsCooking?', produced by Knorr India, video, 31 October 2019, youtube.com/watch?v=YWjBs5CiUfE&feature=emb_title.
9. Hansda Sowvendra Shekhar, *My Father's Garden* (New Delhi: Speaking Tiger Books, 2018).
10. Anurag Kashyap, dir., *Bombay Velvet* (Phantom Films: 2015).

11. Anindita Ghose (@aninditaghose) and Parmesh Shahani (@parmeshs), 'This ad could have been more …', Twitter, 5 November 2019, twitter.com/aninditaghose/status/1191727362976694272?s=20.
12. Anuradha SenGupta (@anuradhasays) and Parmesh Shahani (@parmeshs), 'Wonder what folks think about this …', Twitter, 5 November 2019, twitter.com/anuradhasays/status/1191717091881013248?s=20.
13. Bajaj Allianz General (@bajajallianzgeneral), 'Care is all inclusive …', Instagram, 10 August 2019, instagram.com/p/B0_O9EcF582/?igshid=4148oe6sxkn8; Harish Iyer (@iyeharish), 'Equality is a right not a privilege …', Instagram, 10 August 2019, instagram.com/p/B0_S5zdFmUD/?igshid=ulezb7p4xv9g.
14. Neville Bhandara, 'Meet Queer India's Torchbearers Who Are Working Towards a Truly Equal Future', *Elle India*, 10 June 2019, elle.in/article/forward-march-levis.
15. '#ProudToBeMore: Levi's® India Campaign Celebrates Equality', Levi Strauss & Co., 9 December 2019, https://www.levistrauss.com/2019/12/09/proudtobemore-levis-india-campaign-celebrates-equality.
16. IndraJeet Ghorpade, 'At a Pub in Hyderabad, I Saw How Zomato Is Helping Homophobic Businesses Flourish', *Youth Ki Awaaz*, 17 April 2019, youthkiawaaz.com/2019/04/zomato-is-supporting-homophobic-businesses-flourish.
17. Zomato (@ZomatoIN), '#Section377 #LoveIsLove …', Twitter, 6 September 2018, twitter.com/zomatoin/status/1037602633190703104?lang=en.
18. Vaishnavi Singh, 'Zomato Starts "LGBT Friendly" Tag For Restaurants, But What Is It?', *Quint*, 16 June 2019, thequint.com/neon/gender/zomato-launches-lgbtqia-friendly-tags-for-restaurants.
19. Rachelle Bharathi Chandran, 'Caste in Liberal Feminist Spaces', *Round Table India*, 26 April 2018, roundtableindia.co.in/~roundta3/index.php?option=com_content&view=article&id=9362:shallow-savarna-feminist-media-spaces-and-why-we-must-fight-it&catid=119:feature&Itemid=132.
20. Venkataraman, phone conversation with the author.

19
Queeristan: Other Worlds Are Possible

1. Nuzhat Aziz, 'Seeking: Love, Acceptance, and the Right to Live Life Without Apologies', *Times of India*, 19 May 2019, timesofindia.indiatimes.com/life-style/spotlight/seeking-love-acceptance-and-the-right-to-live-life-without-apologies/articleshow/69375398.cms.
2. Shree Gomes Gupta, 'Dutee Chand on the Backlash She Faced After Coming Out: "I Was Made to Feel Like I Did Not Deserve to Live"', *Vogue*, 5 November 2019, vogue.in/culture-and-living/content/dutee-chand-vogue-india-interview-backlash-after-coming-out-as-lesbian-lgbtqi.
3. Lalit Salve, 'From Lalita to Lalit: A Cop's Journey of Acceptance and Peace', *Thrive Global*, 18 March 2019, thriveglobal.in/stories/from-lalita-to-lalit-a-cops-journey-of-acceptance-and-peace.
4. 'Assam Gets Its First Transgender Judge in Swati Bidhan Baruah', *Mirror Now*, 14 July 2018, timesnownews.com/mirror-now/society/article/assam-gets-its-first-transgender-judge-in-swati-bidhan-baruah/254507.

5. Apoorva Mandhani, 'Sathyasri Sharmila Becomes First Transgender Lawyer to Register with Bar Council of Tamil Nadu and Puducherry', *Live Law*, 1 July 2018, livelaw.in/sathyasri-sharmila-becomes-first-transgender-lawyer-to-register-with-bar-council-of-tamil-nadu-and-puducherry.
6. 'A First: LGBT Member Joins Secretariat as Full-Time Staffer', *Times of India*, 6 December 2018, m.timesofindia.com/city/bengaluru/a-first-lgbt-member-joinssecretariat-as-full-time-staffer/amp_articleshow/66960531.cms.
7. YP Foundation, *Trans Rights in India*.
8. Pierre Bordieu, *Distinction: A Social Critique of the Judgement of Taste* (Oxon: Routledge, 1984), 170.
9. Gargi Chaudhry, 'Awarded Padma Shri for My Talent; Not Physical Differentiation: Narthaki Nataraj', *Asian Age*, 6 February 2019, asianage.com/newsmakers/060219/awarded-padma-shri-for-my-talent-not-physical-differentiation-narthaki-nataraj.html.
10. Sushant Divgikr, 'I am in LOVE with Raipur ...', Facebook, 30 September 2019, facebook.com/sushant.divgikar/posts/10220706035787919.
11. Sidhant Kumar Behera, 'Queergarh: We're Organising Chhattisgarh's First Pride March and It's Not Easy', *HuffPost India*, 6 September 2019, huffingtonpost.in/entry/section-377-chhattisgarh-gay-rights_in_5d716559e4b0ed33e1aac9cf.
12. Ejaz Kaiser, 'In a First-of-Its-Kind Event, 15 Transgender Couples Tied the Knot in Raipur', *New Indian Express*, 31 March 2019, newindianexpress.com/nation/2019/mar/31/transgenders-transcend-social-barriers-get-married-in-raipur-1958313.html.
13. Kai Schultz, 'A Drive to Recruit Transgender Police in India Raised Hopes—Then Dashed Them', *New York Times*, 10 September 2019, nytimes.com/2019/09/10/world/asia/india-transgender-police.html.
14. Kai Schultz, '"My Loneliness Keeps Me Going": Fighting for Equality in India', *New York Times*, 29 November 2019, nytimes.com/2019/11/22/world/asia/india-transgender.html.
15. Neethu Joseph, 'When Chants of "Happy Pride" and "My Body, My Right" Broke Silence of Hot Noon in Kochi', *News Minute*, 18 November 2019, thenewsminute.com/article/when-chants-happy-pride-and-my-body-my-right-broke-silence-hot-noon-kochi-112519.
16. 'Kerala Govt. Gives Wings to Nation's First Transman Pilot's Dreams', *Hindu*, 12 October 2019, thehindu.com/news/national/kerala/govt-gives-wings-to-nation-s-first-transman-pilots-dreams/article29660675.ece.
17. Ashwini M. Sripad, 'In a First, a Transwoman to Head Karnataka Janapada Academy', *New Indian Express*, 17 October 2019, newindianexpress.com/states/karnataka/2019/oct/17/in-a-first-a-transwoman-to-head-karnataka-janapada-academy-jogati-manjamma-2048819.html.
18. K. Sambath Kumar, 'In Tamil Nadu, a Hostel for Transgender Kids', *Times of India*, 28 July 2019, timesofindia.indiatimes.com/india/in-tamil-nadu-a-hostel-for-transgender-kids/articleshow/70415589.cms.
19. '#GoodNews: First Transgender Nurse Appointed in Tamil Nadu', *Quint*, 3 December 2019, thequint.com/news/india/first-transgender-nurse-appointed-in-tamil-nadu-government-hospital.

20. 'Maharashtra Govt Sets Up Transgender Welfare Board', *Business Standard*, 23 February 2019, business-standard.com/article/pti-stories/maharashtra-govt-sets-up-transgender-welfare-board-119022300350_1.html.
21. '#LettersfromQueeristan: 4 LGBTQ Individuals Pen Their Hopes for the Future', *India Culture Lab* (blog), 21 January 2019, indiaculturelab.org/blog/letters-from-queeristan-lgbtq-activists-pen-letters-to-state.
22. Agarwal, Mukherjee and Sanyal, *Queering the Law*.
23. International Commission of Jurists, *Living with Dignity: Sexual Orientation and Gender Identity Based Human Rights Violations in Housing, Work, and Public Spaces in India* (June 2019), icj.org/wp-content/uploads/2019/06/India-Living-with-dignity-Publications-Reports- thematic-report-2019-ENG.pdf.
24. Gaurav Das, 'Assam's First Transgender Judge Awaits Centre's Response to SC Plea Against "Humiliating" Act', *Wire*, 3 February 2020, thewire.in/lgbtqia/swati-bidhan-baruah-transgender-act.
25. 'Gay Couple Moves Kerala HC to Strike Down Provisions of Special Marriage Act', *India Today*, 28 January 2020, indiatoday.in/india/story/gay-couple-moves-kerala-hc-to-strike-down-provisions-of-special-marriage-act-1640863-2020-01-28.
26. Meera Emmanuel, 'How the Madras HC Upheld the Right to Marry for Transgender Persons', *Bar and Bench*, 23 April 2019, barandbench.com/news/madras-hc-right-to-marry-transgender.
27. ETB Sivapriyan, 'Marriage Between Man and Transwoman Is Valid: Madras HC', *Deccan Herald*, 23 April 2019, deccanherald.com/national/marriage-between-man-and-transwoman-is-valid-madras-hc-730260.html.
28. 'About', Pink List India, pinklistindia.com.
29. 'Trailblazers', Pink List India, pinklistindia.com/trailblazers.
30. 'Outspoken Allies', Pink List India, pinklistindia.com/outspokenallies.
31. Samyuktha Vijayan, phone conversation with the author, 12 November 2019.
32. Aditya Tiwari, *April Is Lush* (New Delhi: Blue Rose Publishers, 2019).
33. Vedica Saxena, phone conversation with the author, 4 December 2019.
34. 'At TISS, India's First Gender-Neutral Hostel: "All Students Can Come, Chill"', *Indian Express*, 15 September 2018, indianexpress.com/article/india/at-tiss-indias-first-gender-neutral-hostel-all-students-can-come-chill-5357408.
35. United Nations Development Programme, *Good Practices*, 27.
36. Ankita Bhatkhande, 'Maharashtra Sociology Textbook Includes Single-Parent, Same-Sex Families', *Hindustan Times*, 29 July 2019, hindustantimes.com/india-news/maharashtra-sociology-textbook-includes-single-parent-same-sex-families/story-Thx65uxahpMTl4crKsJgKI.html.
37. Centre for Studies in Gender and Sexuality, csgs.ashoka.edu.in.
38. 'A Story Worth Telling', *Asain Age*, 17 April 2019, asianage.com/life/more-features/170419/a-story-worth-telling.html.
39. Ankit Bhuptani, phone conversation with the author, 12 November 2019.
40. Gopi Karelia, 'Thrown Out of Home At 11, This Dancer Is the First Transwoman to Receive Padma Shri', *Better India*, 28 November 2019, thebetterindia.com/204307/padma-shri-winners-narthaki-natraj-bharatnatyam-dance-first-transwomen-lgbtq-rights.

41. Megha Mandavia, 'Battleground India: TikTok Bests Facebook in Round 1', *Economic Times*, 14 May 2019, economictimes.indiatimes.com/tech/internet/battleground-india-tiktok-bests-facebook-in-round-1/articleshow/69316576.cms?from=mdr.
42. Snigdha Poonam, 'This Indian TikTok Star Wants You to Know His Name', *1843 Magazine*, 12 September 2019, 1843magazine.com/features/this-indian-tiktok-star-wants-you-to-know-his-name.
43. Shrabonti Bagchi, 'India Does Business on TikTok', *Mint*, 29 February 2020, livemint.com/mint-lounge/features/india-does-business-on-tiktok-1158289 1433146.html.
44. Alone Jigs (@jigarrathod169), TikTok, tiktok.com/@jigarrathod169.
45. 'Friendships in TikTok Part 12', Entertaining Video, video, youtube.com/watch?v=ceP9Ba7REr8.
46. Aniket (@aniketchitnawis), 'Creators on TikTok are …', Twitter, twitter.com/aniketchitnawis/status/1229118261037420544.
47. Homi K. Bhabha, 'Of Mimicry and Man: The Ambivalence of Colonial Discourse', in Bill Ashcroft, Gareth Griffins and Helen Tiffin, eds., *Key Concepts in Post-Colonial Studies* (London: Routledge, 1998); Bhabha, 'Signs Taken for Wonders: Questions of Ambivalence and Authority Under a Tree Outside Delhi, May 1817', in *Key Concepts in Post-Colonial Studies*.
48. Hansal Mehta, dir., *Aligarh* (Eros International and Karma Pictures, 2015).
49. Hitesh Kewalya, dir., *Shubh Mangal Zyada Saavdhan* (Colour Yellow Productions and T-Series Films, 2020).
50. Raghava Lawrence, dir., *Laxmmi Bomb* (Cape of Good Films and Fox Star Entertainment, 2020).
51. Thiagarajan Kumararaja, dir., *Super Deluxe* (Alchemy Vision Workz, East West Dream Works Entertainment and Kino Fist, 2019).
52. Ranjith Sarkar, dir., *Njan Marykutty* (Dreams N Beyond Production, 2018).
53. 'Moothan Review: Nivin Pauly Is Spot On, But Let Down By Inconsistent Writing', *HuffPost India*, 8 November 2019, huffingtonpost.in/entry/moothon-film-review-nivin-pauly-geetu-mohandas_in_5dc5430ce4b0fcfb7f647a40.
54. Chopra, dir., *Ek Ladki Ko Dekha Toh Aisa Laga*
55. Neeraj Ghaywan, Anurag Kashyap and Vikramaditya Motwane, dirs., *Sacred Games,* (Phantom Films and Reliance Entertainment, 2018).
56. Nupur Asthana, dir., *Romil and Jugal* (ALT Balaji, 2017).
57. Anu Menon, dir., *Four More Shots Please* (Pritish Nandy Communications, 2019).
58. Roopa Rao, dir., *The 'Other' Love Story* (Just Like That Films, 2016).
59. Amit Khanna, dir., *All About Section 377* and *Still About Section 377* (Creative Gypsy, 2016, 2018).
60. Zoya Akhtar, Nitya Mehra, Prashant Nair and Alankrita Shrivastava, dirs., *Made in Heaven* (Excel Entertainment and Tiger Baby, 2019).
61. Apurva Asrani, 'A Gay Man's Journey into Bollywood', *Rainbow Reflections: An Anthology of LGBTQ Narratives in Indian Cinema*, 2019. Released by Kashish Film Festival.
62. Deepti Naval, dir., *Do Paise Ki Dhoop, Chaar Aaney ki Baarish* (Kite Films and Fuse Media, 2009).
63. Sridhar Rangayan, dir., *Evening Shadows* (Solaris Pictures, 2018).
64. Tanuj Bhramar, dir., *Dear Dad* (Indian Film Studios and Peppermint Studios, 2016).

65. R. Raj Rao, *The Boyfriend* (New Delhi: Penguin Books, 2010).
66. Sachin Kundalkar, *Cobalt Blue* (New Delhi: Penguin Books, 2013).
67. Nishant Roy Bombarde, dir., *Daaravtha: The Threshold* (Pimpalpan Productions, 2015).
68. Rohan Parashuram Kanawade, dir., *U Ushacha* (Dark Stories and Lotus Visual, 2019).
69. Rohin Raveendran Nair, dir., *The Booth* (Ippirival Production, 2019).
70. Faraz Ansari, *Sisak* (Aparna Sud and Futterwacken Films, 2017).
71. Faraz Ansari, dir., *Sheer Qorma* (Futterwacken Films, forthcoming).
72. Priya Sen, dir., *Yeh Freedom Life* (2018).
73. Gagandeep Singh and Mitali Trivedi, dir., *Please Mind the Gap* (Public Service Broadcasting Trust, 2019).
74. Minal Hajratwala, *Out! Stories from the New Queer India* (Mumbai: Queer Ink, 2013).
75. Ashwini Sukthankar, ed., *Facing the Mirror: Lesbian Writing from India* (New Delhi: Penguin Random House, 2019).
76. Amruta Patil, *Kari* (New Delhi: HarperCollins India, 2008), 69.
77. Priya Babu, *Naan Saravanan Alla*, 2007.
78. Living Smile Vidya, *I Am Vidya: A Transgender's Journey* (New Delhi: Rupa and Co., 2008).
79. A. Revathi, *The Truth About Me: A Hijra Life Story* (New Delhi: Penguin Books, 2010).
80. A. Revathi (as told to Nandini Murali), *A Life in Trans Activism* (New Delhi: Zubaan, 2016), 234.
81. Arvind Narrain and Gautam Bhan, eds., *Because I Have a Voice: Queer Politics in India* (New Delhi: Yoda Press, 2005).
82. Sharma, *Loving Women*, 39.
83. Owais, *Gulabi Bagh* (Mumbai: Queer Ink, 2019).
84. Bindumadhav Khire, *Antarang: Samalingi Mula Mulincha Atmakatha* (Pune: Sampathik Trust, 2013).
85. Dhrubo Jyoti, 'A Letter to my Lover(s)', in *Eleven Ways to Love* (New Delhi: Penguin Viking, 2018), 10–11.
86. Khakhar, *Maganbhai's Glue.*
87. Sachin Kundalkar, *Cobalt Blue*, trans. Jerry Pinto (New Delhi: Hamish Hamilton, 2006), 64.
88. Vasudhendra, *Mohanaswamy*, trans. Rashmi Terdal (New Delhi: Harper Perennial, 2017).
89. Shekhar, *My Father's Garden.*
90. Dhall, *Out of Line and Offline.*
91. Pawan Dhall, *Queer Potli: Memories, Imaginations and Re-imaginations of Urban Queer Spaces in India* (Mumbai: Queer Ink, 2016).
92. Shahani, *Gay Bombay.*
93. Kareem Khubchandani, *Ishtyle: Accenting Gay Indian Nightlife* (The University of Michigan Press, forthcoming)
94. Horton, Skype conversation with the author.
95. Menaka Guruswamy, 'Section 377 Judgment Offers Lessons on How to Use Constitution to Build Coalitions, Bring Change', *Indian Express*, 6 September 2019, indianexpress.com/article/opinion/columns/section-377-judgment-supreme-court-indian-constitution-5970262.

96. The Queer Muslim Project (@thequeermuslimproject), Instagram, instagram.com/thequeermuslimproject.
97. Sandip Roy, 'Sandip Roy #315: Rainbow Lit Fest', radio show on *KALW*, 18 December 2019, kalw.org/post/sandip-roy-315-rainbow-lit-fest.
98. Pritam, music dir., 'Bhar Do Jholi Meri' (T-Series), in Kabir Khan, dir., *Bajrangi Bhaijaan* (2015).
99. TheChinkyHomoProject (@thechinkyhomoproject), Instagram, instagram.com/thechinkyhomoproject.
100. Pavel Sagolsem and Kumam Davidson, 'Do Queer Migrants from the Northeast Find Indian Cities Alienating or Empowering?', *In Plainspeak*, 19 March 2018, tarshi.net/inplainspeak/queer-migrants-northeast-find-indian-cities-alienating-empowering.
101. Dalit Queer Project (@dalitqueerproject), Instagram, instagram.com/dalitqueerproject.
102. Aroh Akunth, phone conversation with the author, 10 December 2019.
103. 'QUEERelief Active Fundraisers', Pink List India, pinklistindia.com/queerelief.
104. Mrinalini Bhat, 'Transwoman Sends Rations to the Poor', *Times of India*, 12 April 2020.
105. Kranti, facebook.com/kranti.india.
106. 'Support Starving Powerloom Workers in Bhiwandi!', Ketto, ketto.org/fundraiser/support-bhiwandi-powerloom-workers.
107. A COVID-19 Relief by Young India Fellows', Milaap, milaap.org/fundraisers/support-saloni-6.
108. Keshav Suri Foundation, Facebook, facebook.com/KeshavSuriFoundation.

20
Get Started Jaldi: Your Roadmap to Queeristan

1. 'Mental Health Professionals We Can Trust: A Crowdsourced List from iCall', Feminism in India, 16 January 2017, feminisminindia.com/2017/01/16/mental-health-professionals-crowdsourced-list.
2. 'The Crowdsourced List of Social Justice Collectives Across Indian Campuses', Feminism in India, feminisminindia.com/fii-feminist-resource-centre-india/crowdsourced-list-social-justice-collectives-indian-campuses.
3. 'The AOI List of Queer Support Resource of All Kinds', Agents of Ishq, agentsofishq.com/the-aoi-list-of-queer-support-resources-of-all-kinds.